Conciliation and Confession

Conciliation and Confession

THE STRUGGLE FOR UNITY IN THE AGE OF REFORM, 1415–1648

edited by

HOWARD P. LOUTHAN

and

RANDALL C. ZACHMAN

University of Notre Dame Press

Notre Dame, Indiana

Library of Congress Cataloging-in-Publication Data
Conciliation and confession : the struggle for unity in the Age of Reform,
1415–1648 / edited by Howard P. Louthan and Randall C. Zachman.
        p.   cm.
Includes index.
ISBN 0-268-03362-5 (hardcover : alk. paper)
ISBN 0-268-03363-3 (pbk. : alk. paper)
        1. Reformation.   2. Church—Unity.   3. Europe—Church history.
4. Church history—Middle Ages, 600–1500.   5. Church history—16th century.
6. Church history—17th century.   I. Louthan, Howard, 1963–   II. Zachman,
Randall C., 1953–
        BR305.2.C63   2004
        274'.05—dc22

                                                              2004016416

∞ *This book is printed on acid-free paper.*

CONTENTS

INTRODUCTION

IN 1573 GEORG EDER, A PROFESSOR OF LAW AT THE UNIVERSITY in Vienna and a zealous Catholic, wrote a vitriolic tract that attacked theological moderates who attempted to bridge the gap between Protestant and Catholic communities. These irenicists, claimed Eder, created "horrible confusion" within the church by attempting to mediate two theological systems irreconcilably opposed to each other.[1] Some twenty-five years later on the other side of the confessional divide, Theodore Beza, John Calvin's successor in Geneva, had equally strong words of criticism for the conciliatory work of the Huguenot pastor Jean de Serres, whom he described as "someone who by hopping from side to side wants to teach both parties to walk straight."[2] Rhetoric of more incendiary proportions was reserved for the seventeenth-century Capuchin missionary Valerian Magni, who endeavored to reunite Poland's Protestant and Orthodox communities with the Catholic Church. For these efforts his opponents reviled him as a "toad bloated with poison" and a "wolf in the sheepfold of the church."[3] By their very nature conciliators have always been vulnerable to resistance and critique as they mediate between groups devoted to ideological agendas that may allow little room for maneuver and negotiation. But in the age of Reform the normal challenges that peacemakers perennially faced were magnified. Tensions had heightened, dangers loomed larger, and the stakes had increased for those committed to conciliation. The church, the most important institution of European society, was divided, and as the crisis began in the late fourteenth century with the Great Western Schism (1378–1415) there did not appear to be any obvious solution to this grave situation that split the continent's Catholics into two rival "obediences." This volume will investigate the activities of those who worked for the restoration of ecclesial unity, first in the conciliar era, then in the early years of the Protestant Reformations, and finally during the "confessional age," when theological and cultural distinctions of competing religious groups began to emerge more clearly.

Lying in a murky terrain of imprecise contours and undefined parameters, conciliation has been a problematic area of research for a number of reasons. Its study has often been bound up with broader examinations of religious toleration. Though these phenomena are undeniably related, scholars have often conflated the two. Toleration was primarily a pragmatic and often less than satisfactory political solution to pressing problems of confessional coexistence. We distinguish conciliation as a more positive and constructive search for religious unity and theological rapprochement within the Christian community.[4] Our understanding of conciliation has also been affected by a significant historiographical shift with regard to the larger concept of toleration. The history of toleration in the late medieval and early modern periods was long the domain of theologians and intellectual historians. Arguably, the crowning work of this tradition was Joseph Lecler's encyclopedic synthesis, *Histoire de la tolérance au siècle de la Réforme* (1955).[5] Though Lecler rejected a Protestant triumphalism that had long dominated this discussion, ideas remained at the core of his analysis.[6] Since Lecler's day, the situation has changed considerably. Greater emphasis has been placed on social, political, and economic factors that contributed to the creation of a more tolerant society.[7] Though this new orientation has certainly broadened our understanding of toleration and has helped overturn a "whiggish" interpretation that quietly shaped the analysis of Lecler and others, it has not come without a cost.[8] The ideological currents of toleration are now often muted. For example, scholars of east central Europe today tend to view the development of toleration in this region as primarily a matter of political expediency.[9] Theological ideals that are at the core of conciliation are too frequently discounted in favor of more materialist concerns. Although it would be naïve to claim that those who sought confessional rapprochement were unaffected by the political and social context in which they worked—indeed this volume highlights these tensions in often dramatic fashion—conciliation remained an important dynamic in the late medieval and early modern world.

In theological circles, the neglect of conciliation has been compounded by the confessional outlook of scholars studying the Reformation. Scholars tend to project later confessional identities into the early sixteenth century, as though Luther and Melanchthon intended to form the "Lutheran tradition," while Zwingli, Bullinger, and Calvin intended to form the "Reformed" or "Calvinist" tradition. This isolation of Reformation theologians and teachers into their own anachronistically defined confessional camp leads to the marginalization of those who worked so hard to reconcile the emerging differences between religious parties, such as Melanchthon and Bucer among the evangelicals, and Contarini and later Cajetan in the Roman community. What is most often missed by the premature confessionalization of the early Reformation is that *all* the participants saw themselves as Catholic theologians working on behalf of the Catholic Church, including those who concluded that Rome had brought the church to captivity or ruin. Since there can be only one truly catholic church, the emergence of theological division had to be met with the desire to reconcile those differences as much as possible. Seeing all participants in the period of the Reformation as Catholics rather than "Lutheran" or "Reformed" highlights the theological and ecclesiological necessity of conciliation. A retrojected confessional perspective tends to make such conciliating efforts appear as the betrayal of confessional identity, a charge regularly leveled at an individual like Melanchthon.

Though our examination of concilation could well begin in the sixteenth century with the seminal figure of Erasmus, we start our investigation in the era of conciliarism, for the first two essays in this collection highlight many of the major themes that will be examined on a repeated basis throughout the volume. In forceful fashion, Karlfried Froehlich considers the efforts of the conciliarists during the early years of the Great Schism. His specific focus is Pierre d'Ailly and the neglected role of biblical exegesis in attempts to resolve the crisis. Froehlich immediately brings the central issue of authority to the fore. In an age of decentralized political power, to what source does one appeal in order to find common ground and repair the breach in western Christendom? At its most general level, this is a question that pertains to the entire period under consideration. The various protagonists of our narrative, Catholic theologians, Calvinist pastors, Orthodox emissaries, and Utraquist churchmen, all wrestled with this weighty issue. Turning to a broad array of sources, they appealed to patristic writers, a historic episcopate, a shared theological heritage, or Scripture itself as a common touchstone. Froehlich, who focuses on the conciliar solution, argues that the hermeneutical foundation upon which d'Ailly and his colleagues based their appeal for the authority of a general council "represents the mainstream of the medieval exegetical tradition."[10] As Zdeněk David and Howard Louthan later illustrate, the conciliar approach that Froehlich highlights resonated particularly well in Bohemia and the Polish-Lithuanian Commonwealth in the sixteenth and seventeenth centuries.

Nicholas Constas turns our attention to the Council of Florence and the struggle to find an understanding between Catholic and Orthodox. Constas addresses another set of issues that adds greater complexity to our investigation and understanding of conciliation. On the most basic level, he reminds us that the project of reunion extended beyond the traditional boundaries of western Christendom. One of the most important features of this volume as a whole is its scope. Constas's article is the first of a number that examine the interaction of the eastern and western Christian worlds. Constas also adds greater nuance to our discussion by considering religious dialogue within the larger cultural context of the day. As he astutely observes, the period we are examining is one in which Europe's horizons were expanding rapidly with discoveries of new lands and peoples. Thus, for Constas, cross-cultural communication is a critical component of this enterprise. He situates the conference at Florence within an environment of mutual misunderstanding and distrust. When the Byzantine Patriarch arrived in Venice at the height of carnival, the doge hosted a magnificent feast without realizing that Lent had already begun for the Greeks. The Byzantines for their part came to the West with their own misconceptions and prejudices. From "eating with dogs and tamed bears" to "mixing the wine of the Eucharist with cold water instead of warm" the emissaries of the East enumerated a host of cultural practices, both major and minor, that separated the two. As Tia Kolbaba has recently argued, it is often very difficult to disentangle the ethnic from the religious when considering the differences between Orthodox and Catholic.[11]

The articles of Froehlich and Constas present an intriguing tension that recurs throughout this volume in the activities of our conciliators. While Froehlich highlights the ideals of those who sought reunion, Constas reflects on how this process worked in the real world when mediators were forced to deal with the cultural, social, and political constraints of the setting in which they lived. Constas points to the *City of God*, where Augustine lays out the challenge as a fundamental problem of communication:

> After the city comes the world . . . which, being like a confluence of waters, is more full of danger by reason of its greater size. To begin with, on this level the diversity of human languages separates man from man. For if two men meet, and are forced by some compelling reason not to pass on but to stay in company, and if neither

knows the other's language, then it is easier for dumb animals, even of different kinds, to associate together than these men, although both are human beings.[12]

The problem of communication, central to Constas's more pragmatic discussion of the gap between the Greeks and Latins, stands in contrast to Froehlich's attention to the ideals undergirding conciliation. We do not attempt to resolve what we see as a healthy tension in this volume. Some of our contributors focus on the ideological underpinnings of conciliation while others more closely examine the social and political circumstances that influenced and gave rise to these efforts.

Our second group of essays explores the traditional heartland of Reformation history and theology. One of the common themes that quickly emerges is the great creativity and resourcefulness of those seeking reconciliation. Towards this end, Erika Rummel investigates Erasmus's 1533 treatise, *De sarcienda ecclesiae concordia* (On Mending the Peace of the Church). In a fashion reminiscent of Pierre d'Ailly's 1403 memorandum that Karlfried Froehlich examines, Erasmus laid out a broad series of strategies that could lead to the reunification of the church. From the calling of a general council to a policy of benign neglect, the text captures the mature reflections of a humanist who all too personally experienced the pain associated with the church's breakup. Among the options he outlined was the patristic concept of *sygkatabasis,* accommodation or leniency. The use of patristic sources to help reestablish confessional harmony is explored more fully by Irena Backus. Backus probes the work of two second-generation Erasmians, Georg Cassander (1513–1566) and Georg Witzel (1501–1573). She illustrates that Witzel combed patristic sources to develop a liturgical *via media* while Cassander sought theological solutions to the doctrinal disputes of his day by turning to the fifth-century theologian Vigilius of Thapsus.

This series of articles also poignantly illustrates the great difficulties confronting those who mediated between confessions. Rummel, in particular, emphasizes this point in the conclusion of her essay when she assays the reception of Erasmus's text. Though it went through ten editions and four translations between 1533 and 1535, and though it elicited a positive reaction from a number of quarters including the household of Cardinal Cajetan, the overwhelming response was negative. Luther deemed Erasmus's advice useless while the Catholic Paolo Vergerio wrote a bitter invective against the Dutch "heretic." Erasmus himself would reflect back on his mediating efforts, ruefully observing that he "was torn in pieces by both sides, while aiming zealously at what was best for both."[13] Even the humanist's friend, the sympathetic Jacopo Sadoleto, was muted in his praise. If those of a middle party faced significant resistance in the 1530s as Rummel illustrates, they fared no better at the end of the century as we see in the contribution of Karin Maag. Maag's article explores the French context in the second half of the sixteenth century culminating with the conversion of Henry IV. Her specific focus is the Huguenot pastor Jean de Serres, who in 1594 presented to the national synod a proposal for the reunification of the French church. The words of Beza noted above aptly capture both the Calvinist and Catholic critique of his efforts.

Though irenicism became increasingly marginalized as confessional traditions defined themselves more clearly, it would be a mistake to see this phenomenon as the theological or intellectual equivalent of tilting at windmills. Both Randall Zachman and Euan Cameron show us the unexpected strength of conciliation in surprising places. At first glance it may seem that Zachman is trying to square the circle as he explores the ecumenical theology of John Calvin. Calvin, after all, is better known for his intransigence in the Servetus affair. But though Zachman acknowledges that there were certain limits to theological compromise, he argues that Calvin was able to tolerate a surprisingly broad range of doctrinal difference. The key to this issue, Zachman contends, is the ability to distinguish the different modes of rhetoric Calvin employed. When core issues of the faith were at stake, the Genevan's rhetoric would be at its hottest and most polemical. When there was a basic understanding of Christian essentials, however, disagreements could be addressed by the milder means of *sermo* or conversation. Thus, as Zachman illustrates, it was quite natural for Calvin to be willing to publish the homilies of John Chrysostom even though there were significant theological differences between the two.

Euan Cameron turns our attention to the quintessential conciliator of the Reformation period, Philipp Melanchthon. Though Melanchthon's desire for rapprochement with the Catholic world and concord within the Protestant community is well known, Cameron presents a fundamentally new interpretation of the reformer. Melanchthon's Lutheran critics complained that the humanist theologian was an unreliable ally. His leadership was questioned during the affair of the Zwickau prophets in 1521–1522. Not a few believed that he was too eager to compromise with Catholics at Augsburg in 1530, and his behavior regarding the infamous Augsburg *Interim* of 1548 was excoriated by many. Cameron takes issue with this traditional critique of Melanchthon as the fickle reformer of inconstant theological conviction. Instead, a portrait emerges of a Protestant leader whose dogmatic stance was far more resolute than most have recognized. Cameron maintains that under closer examination Melanchthon's comportment at Augsburg in 1530, at the religious conferences of the early 1540s, and with the *Interim* of 1548 was far more principled in nature. This was a theologian who refused "to horse-trade over fundamental beliefs."[14] The picture of a weak-kneed Melanchthon wavering in the heat of battle needs to be reconsidered in light of these observations, for as both Zachman and Cameron have argued, conciliation was a stronger, heartier, and at times an even more polemic ideal than many have admitted.

Our third set of essays extends our understanding of conciliation both geographically and chronologically. Our view of confessional dialogue in the age of Reform has been shaped from a western perspective. Scholars have focused considerable attention on relations between Protestants and Catholics while too often ignoring the complex mosaic of religious communities to the east. The thriving trade entrepôt of L'viv (Lwów/Lemberg) now in the Ukraine boasted cathedrals of four Christian creeds. Religious change was both rapid and frequent in this region. The Transylvanian city of Kolozsvár (Cluj/Klausenberg) serves as a prime example. With the coming of the Reformation, the St. Michael's church in the city's central square passed from the hands of the Catholics to the Lutherans. By the end of the 1550s, however, the municipal council transferred control of the church to the Reformed. But change did not end there. Under the dynamic leadership of Ferenc Dávid, St. Michael's became an important Unitarian center a decade later.[15] It was also not uncommon for religious communities of the east to adopt cultural practices from their confessional neighbors. We have reports of the Reformed church in Poland following rituals that would have certainly raised the eyebrows of their confessional brethren in Geneva and Heidelberg.[16] In the seventeenth and early eighteenth century Hungarian Calvinists began building churches in a style that might best be described as "folk baroque."[17] When viewed from an eastern perspective then, conciliation appears as a more complex dynamic mirroring the great diversity and complicated religious landscape of the region.

Zdeněk David turns our attention to Bohemia with his consideration of Hus's successors, the Utraquists. This kingdom, of course, had long been a thorn in the side of the Roman church. By 1517 the Czech lands had a well-known reputation as a homeland of heresy. At Leipzig Eck hurled the epithet "Hussite" at Luther while in more popular circles similar stereotypes were very much in force. A proverb that widely circulated at the time proudly proclaimed that Germany was admirably self-sufficient in her vices. Swabia provided her prostitutes, Franconia her thieves and beggars, Frisia her perjurers, Saxony her drunkards, and *Bohemia her heretics*.[18] David tracks the relationship between the Utraquist and Roman church in the course of the sixteenth century. In doing so, he presents a surprising picture that challenges an older body of literature on the Czech lands. Though scholars have often assumed that after Luther the majority of Utraquists became fifth columnists of the Reformation, David argues that the Bohemian church retained its distinctive character and remained committed to the broad tenets of the Catholic communion.[19] In fact, up to the Council of Trent there was significant cooperation between Czech Utraquists and Catholics as relations between these two groups were generally positive. David examines the deterioration of this relationship in the post-Tridentine period as a remarkable era of confessional pluralism was reaching its height in the Bohemian kingdom. He concludes his overview by considering Utraquism as a non-Protestant reform movement. Erasmus and other like-minded thinkers of his day saw the Bohemian church as a potential model for confessional reunion on a broader scale.

Moving us farther to the east, Howard Louthan investigates the activities of the fascinating Capuchin missionary Valerian Magni, who was active both in Bohemia and the Polish-Lithuanian Commonwealth in the first half of the seventeenth century. The well-traveled Magni expands our understanding of conciliation in a number of critical ways. He introduces us to the Polish world, where since the reign of Sigismund II Augustus (1529–1572) there was a significant movement to reunite the kingdom's fractured religious community. In some respects Magni continues the story that was introduced in the essay of Nicholas Constas, for the Capuchin not only dialogued with the region's Protestants but also worked assiduously to reconcile the Commonwealth's Orthodox populace with Rome. His most important conversation partner among the Orthodox, Peter Mohyla, would look to the Council of Florence as a means to bridge confessional differences. Magni reminds us as well that conciliatory voices could still be heard from Catholics in early seventeenth-century central Europe despite an increasingly strident confessional culture that had arisen in the post-Tridentine era.

The case of Valerian Magni also clearly illustrates the historiographical challenges facing those who work in east central Europe. Magni was undeniably one of the most important Catholic churchmen of the early seventeenth century. A confidant of Pope Urban VIII (1623–1644), an advisor to Emperor Ferdinand II (1619–1637), and an intimate of the Polish king Władysław IV (1632–1648), Magni spent fifty years as a diplomat and missionary in central Europe. As a scientist, philosopher, and theologian, he produced a formidable body of work that earned him considerable notoriety in his day. Despite these significant contributions, he has languished in obscurity. This neglect is in large part due to the fact that his career does not fall into well-defined nationalist and confessional parameters that have all too frequently defined the research agendas of east central European scholarship. Magni was an irenicist in an area of militant Catholic revival, a displaced Italian in a region of emerging national identities.

Graeme Murdock and Howard Hotson expand the discussion with their considerations of the Hungarian and German worlds. Murdock surveys the complicated religious topography of the Hungarian lands in the late sixteenth and early seventeenth centuries. Murdock raises important questions concerning the limits of conciliation in central Europe. More specifically, he contrasts the situation in Royal Hungary where Lutherans and the Reformed were threatened by a resurgent Catholicism with the Transylvanian principality where religious toleration had a longer track record and the fear of Habsburg interference was much less. Though Murdock would not discount conciliation as an independent theological ideal, he is quick to point out that efforts for intra-Protestant union were greatly facilitated by the political pressures of the period. Continuing with this general theme, Howard Hotson concludes our volume with an extended article reviewing irenic activity in German territory from the end of Trent to the Peace of Westphalia. In this pathbreaking essay, Hotson argues that interconfessional dialogue undergoes a significant shift after 1563. Though attempts to reunite Protestant and Catholic become increasingly rare, Hotson has uncovered a tremendous body of conciliatory literature directed towards Calvinists and Lutherans. Charting the changing patterns of irenicism, he examines the long relationship between Germany's Lutheran and Reformed communities through the end of the Thirty Years' War.

A few remarks should be made regarding the chronological parameters of this volume. Our decision to begin with the Great Schism is at least from our perspective self-evident. The critical issue of conciliar authority, the establishment of a quasi-independent church in Bohemia, and the last great attempt at Florence and Ferrara to reunite east and west speak to the importance of the late fourteenth and early fifteenth century. Indeed, much of our subsequent discussion would make little sense without reference to this period. Erasmus, Melanchthon, and other sixteenth-century irenicists regarded the Utraquist settlement at Basel as a possible model for their time. The Orthodox communities of the sixteenth and seventeenth centuries reflected on the lessons of Florence, and issues of papal authority articulated in d'Ailly's day continued to shape the theological discourse of subsequent centuries. The decision of where to conclude our study was not as easy. In many respects, the Council of Trent (1545–1563) seems like a logical place to end. Trent was certainly a watershed terminating or at least seriously restricting possibilities of reconciliation with Rome. As Howard Hotson has argued concerning the German lands, conciliatory efforts after 1563 were primarily directed towards intra-Protestant union. Farther east, however, there was still a significant impulse to reunite Catholics and Protestants. Though Valerian Magni's irenic proposals found little support in Bohemia, his ideas were well received in the Polish-Lithuanian Commonwealth and culminated with the 1645 *Colloquium charitativum* of Toruń, the last great dialogue of the Reformation era between Catholics and Protestants. Ecumenical activity obviously did not stop in 1648 or with the death of Leibniz in 1716, but serious political support for broad-based reunion efforts was a scarce commodity after the reign of Władysław IV.

To conclude, we as editors are all too aware of important issues that have not been examined in this text. We never intended this volume to serve as a comprehensive study of conciliation in the late medieval and early modern periods. There has been no discussion of England. In the light of W. B. Patterson's scholarly contributions one thinks specifically of the Jacobean setting. Likewise, we devoted very little attention to Catholic moderates of the sixteenth century. The work of Reginald Pole, Gasparo Contarini, Girolamo Seripando, and Jacopo Sadoleto springs immediately to mind. The fascinating interchange of ideas in the Dutch lands has also received no significant notice.[20] From the beginning, however, we envisioned this volume as a type of blueprint or roadmap for future scholarship. Several factors, however, are distinctive about this volume. The essays of this collection are intended to provoke further debate, reflection, and research. As the reader will observe throughout the text, we believe that far more attention needs to be paid to Europe east of the Elbe. The confessional diversity of eastern and central Europe expands our understanding of a phenomenon that has often been reduced to a Protestant/Catholic dialogue. We also believe that our subject needs to be reconsidered chronologically. No one today would claim that the Reformation movement began abruptly in 1517 and ended promptly in 1563. In similar fashion, conciliation needs to be examined in a way that gives due justice to the earlier and later periods. Finally, Reformation scholarship in a theological context has tended to focus on the dynamics that led to the division of the Western Church into increasingly fragmented communities of faith. Such a perspective has been frequently reinforced by the work of scholars who study the major theologians of the Reformation primarily in terms of the way they shaped and defined the trajectory of specific confessional traditions. This volume challenges us to move beyond these parameters and explore the thought and theology of this period from a vantage point that does not presuppose permanent confessional division.

NOTES

1. Georg Eder, *Evangelische Inquisition: Wahrer und falscher Religion* (Dillingen, 1573), 72r–v.

2. Cited in Karin Maag, "Conciliation and the French Huguenots, 1561–1610," 145.

3. See Howard Louthan, "From Rudolfine Prague to Vasa Poland: Valerian Magni and the Twilight of Irenicism in Central Europe," 218.

4. Mario Turchetti is one scholar who does distinguish toleration from conciliation, although, as Karin Maag points out, his notion of "concord" does differ from our understanding of conciliation. For an overview of his thesis see "Religious Concord and Political Tolerance in Sixteenth- and Seventeenth-Century France," *Sixteenth Century Journal* 22 (1991): 15–25. Also useful is the essay of G. H. M. Posthumus Meyjes, "La tolérance et Irénisme," in C. Berkvens-Stevelinck, J. Israel, and G. H. M. Posthumus Meyjes, eds., *The Emergence of Tolerance in the Dutch Republic* (Leiden: Brill, 1997), 63–73.

5. Joseph Lecler, *Histoire de la tolérance au siècle de la Réforme,* 2 vols. (Paris: Aubier, 1955). For a more extensive bibliography on toleration see Hans Guggisberg, ed., *Religiöse Toleranz* (Stuttgart: Friedrich Frommann Verlag, 1984), 299–313.

6. Lecler was reacting at least in part to the Protestant orientation of historians like W. K. Jordan, whose *The Development of Religious Toleration in England* (4 vols., London, 1932–1940) was one of the foundational works in the field. Jordan in turn was drawing from nineteenth-century scholars such as W. E. H. Lecky, whose *History of the Rise and Influence of the Spirit of Rationalism in Europe* (London: Longman, 1865) highlighted the role of Protestantism in the creation of a more tolerant society.

7. For example see Henry Kamen's discussion of economic factors in *The Rise of Toleration* (New York: McGraw-Hill, 1967), 224–27.

8. An excellent example of the revisionist approach that has had a salutary effect on the field is Ole Peter Grell and Bob Scribner, eds., *Tolerance and Intolerance in the European Reformation* (Cambridge: Cambridge University Press, 1996).

9. See the essays by Jaroslav Pánek, Katalin Péter, and Michael Müller in *Tolerance and Intolerance in the European Reformation.*

10. Karlfried Froehlich, "New Testament Models of Conflict Resolution: Observations on the Biblical Argument of Paris Conciliarists during the Great Schism," 26.

11. Tia Kolbaba, *The Byzantine Lists: Errors of the Latins* (Urbana and Chicago: University of Illinois Press, 2000). See especially 163–72.

12. Cited in Nicholas Constas, "'Tongues of Fires Confounded': Greeks and Latins at the Council of Florence (1438–1439)," 51.

13. Erasmus, *Compendium vitae,* in Erika Rummel, ed., *The Erasmus Reader* (Toronto: University of Toronto Press, 1990), 20.

14. Euan Cameron, "The Possibilities and Limits of Conciliation: Philipp Melanchthon and Inter-confessional Dialogue in the Sixteenth Century," 82.

15. On Kolozsvár see Graeme Murdock, "The Boundaries of Reformed Irenicism: Royal Hungary and the Transylvanian Principality," 154.

16. In the seventeenth century there were accounts of Calvinists "ringing bells, observing fasts, striking their breast, covering the chalice with a cloth and the altar with a sheet, and separating it from the faithful with a railing—in short acting like Catholics." Janusz Tazbir, *A State without Stakes* (Warsaw: Państwowy Instytut Wydawniczy, 1973), 128.

17. George Starr, "Art and Architecture in the Hungarian Reformed Church," in P. Corby Finney, ed., *Seeing beyond the Word: Visual Arts and the Calvinist Tradition* (Grand Rapids: W. B. Eerdmans, 1999), 301–40.

18. Cited in Gerald Strauss, *Sixteenth-century Germany: Its Topography and Topographers* (Madison: University of Wisconsin Press, 1959), 11.

19. See for example David's earlier article, "The Strange Fate of Czech Utraquism: The Second Century, 1517–1621," *Journal of Ecclesiastical History* 46 (1995): 641–68. For a more traditional assessment of Utraquism see Winfried Eberhard's entry in Hans Hillerbrand, ed., *The Oxford Encyclopedia of the Reformation* (Oxford: Oxford University Press, 1996) 4:206–8. The older stereotypes of the weaknesses of Utraquism in the decades before White Mountain (1620) are still passed on uncritically even in the most recent scholarship. See for example the comments of Karl Vocelka in "Enlightenment in the Habsburg Monarchy: History of a Belated and Short-Lived Phenomenon," in Ole Peter Grell and Roy Porter, eds., *Toleration in Enlightenment Europe* (Cambridge: Cambridge University Press, 2000), 196.

20. On Jacobean England see W. B. Patterson, *King James VI and I and the Reunion of Christendom* (Cambridge: Cambridge University Press, 1997). For Catholic moderates one can begin with Elisabeth Gleason, *Gasparo Contarini: Venice, Rome, and Reform* (Berkeley: University of California Press, 1993), and Thomas Mayer, *Reginald Pole: Prince and Prophet* (Cambridge: Cambridge University Press, 2000). Concerning irenicism in the Dutch region the work of Posthumus Meyjes is best known. For a useful collection of essays see C. Berkvens-Stevelinck, J. Israel, and G. H. M. Posthumus Meyjes, eds., *The Emergence of Tolerance in the Dutch Republic* (Leiden: Brill, 1997).

I

New Testament Models of Conflict Resolution

*Observations on the Biblical Argument
of Paris Conciliarists during the Great Schism*

KARLFRIED FROEHLICH

THE ASSUMPTION OF A BASIC UNITY OF THE CHURCH IS THE presupposition of all ecumenism. "*Unitatis Redintegratio*" are the first words of the Decree on Ecumenism of the Second Vatican Council, and the second sentence states: "The Church, established by Christ the Lord, is indeed one and unique."[1] This assumption is securely anchored in the New Testament. Jesus prays "that all may be one" (Jn 17:21); Paul admonishes the Philippians to be "in full accord and of one mind" (Phil 2:2); the Pauline tradition behind Ephesians urges the recipients "to maintain the unity of the Spirit in the bond of peace" (4:3); and the author of the Acts of the Apostles is constantly at pains to demonstrate the unity of the earliest Christians: "*homothymadon*" (with one accord), a rare adverbial compound, is a favorite expression of his. "They were one heart and soul," he says (Acts 4:32).

Even in the New Testament, however, this emphasis on unity and harmony must be seen against the background of serious conflict and the evidence of disunity. The story in Acts does not pass over some unpleasant moments: complaints at Jerusalem over the discrimination of Greek-speaking widows (6:1); "no small dissension and debate" between Paul and certain Jerusalem emissaries (15:2); the angry breakup between Paul and Barnabas (15:36–40). Paul himself faced "schismata" at Corinth and in other mission churches, just as Matthew reports Jesus as saying, "Occasions for *skandala* are bound to come" (18:7) and, "I have not come to bring peace but a sword" (10:34). Later Christian generations shared the assumption of the church's basic unity and celebrated it as the true biblical vision, but in times of crisis, when division threatened, when much was at stake and hard decisions had to be made (*in rebus arduis,* as the conciliarists would say), they recalled the New Testament reality and sought help and guidance in the biblical texts.

The Great Western Schism of 1378–1415 was such a time of crisis. Psychologically, sociologically, and theologically it was different from the Schism between East and West which had culminated in the mutual excommunications of 1054 and had been exacerbated by the experience of the Crusades, but did not affect the lives of most people in the West. There had, of course, been many schisms even in the history of the Roman Church itself. Lists from the conciliar epoch count twenty-four, twenty-eight, or more of them.[2] But the impression almost from the beginning was that it was worse this time. We may speculate that the reason was what some scholars have called the "apocalyptic cloud" over the second half of the fourteenth century, but we may have to consider equally disturbing factors in other aspects of the historical situation and its impact on the actual life of people. Europe was divided in two rival "obediences," more or less along "national" lines, each with its own fiscal, administrative, and sacramental apparatus. There was no strong central political power to mediate in the conflict between two papal contenders, and it seemed impossible to find an easy way, any way, out of the impasse. If Ulrich von Hutten could exclaim in the early 1500s, "O saeculum! What a century! The humanities are thriving. It is a delight to be alive!", the cry in 1394 was, "O shameful and infamous century! Of all centuries you must bear never-ending reproach for all posterity!"[3]

The rhetoric of lament over the "abominable Schism" in sermons, treatises, and action memoranda was thoroughly biblical. It wallowed with gusto in the reproachful language of prophets and apostles. On the one hand, the ideal image of the church was painted in the most exquisite colors. She is all beautiful, majestic in her ordered structure like an army set in array (Cant 6:3).

She is the "one dove" (Cant 6:8), the chaste virgin (2 Cor 11:2) whom he, "the one man out of a thousand" (Eccl 7:29), wants to find presented to him gloriously, "without spot or wrinkle, holy and immaculate" (Eph 5:27). What a contrast to her sad appearance in the present situation! For his letter to the French king during the first year of the Schism, Conrad of Gelnhausen took as his biblical *thema* a verse from the Book of Tobit (4:3 f.): "Honor your mother! Remember the many hardships she endured in her womb for you!" The reality is that "Mother Church" is suffering violence from her own twin sons, split in her womb like Perez and Zerah, the twins of Tamar (Gen 38:29).[4] The Tamar story is used in an even more drastic form by an Urbanist who suggests that, like Judah, Robert of Geneva, the Avignon pope, figuratively raped his sister who bore "the twins of contention and discord." He adds the reference to Rebecca: her twins were fighting in the womb and greatly distressed their mother also (Gen 25:22).[5] Mother Church can only writhe in pain and shout, "O my bowels, my bowels!" (Jer 4:19 Vulg), or perhaps more to the point: "O my head! My head!", like the little son of the Shunamite woman in 2 Kgs 4:19.[6] One writer corrects Paul at this point: "If the foot hurts, not all the other members hurt, but when the head hurts they do" (1 Cor 12:26).[7] A few years later, the Schism still dragging on, Jean Gerson describes the violated mother as a "two-headed monster," or even worse, as a hellish Hydra which grows more prolific on every faltering cut.[8] The Schism breeds war, dissension, false dispensations, abuses of the sacraments, the promotion of unworthy persons, and the endangerment of souls.[9] It is an unspeakable calamity. The unthinkable has happened. Christ's seamless robe is torn.

How could it come to this? In our literature, not much blame is laid at the door of particular persons or groups of persons such as the cardinals. Rather, the accusing fingers point to the general moral corruption of the age, especially among clerics of all ranks. The needed "reformation in head and members" of which William Durandus spoke at the beginning of the century has not come about so far.[10] The first full-fledged conciliarist treatise, Henry of Langenstein's *Epistola Concilii Pacis* of May 1381, describes in five chapters the specifics of the rotten situation in the church and the necessary reforms.[11] These chapters soon were a classic and reappeared at the Council of Constance in the hands of Pierre d'Ailly, who incorporated them into his treatise *De reformatione ecclesiae*. There are also the apocalyptic voices. 2 Thess 2:3 announces that the end will not come "until a *discessio,* a separation, happens first and the man of sin is revealed." D'Ailly quotes the *Glossa Ordinaria,* which speaks of a "double *discessio,*" one from the Roman

Empire, the other from the Roman Church. He warns that many of the faithful now fear that both schisms have happened.[12] Langenstein reports that, if Jesus threatened with eternal fire anyone calling his brother or sister a fool, the name-calling between the two sides today is worse: it includes appellations such as wily serpent, Mohammed, and Antichrist.[13]

What could be done? Undoubtedly, the Schism with all its pains was a boom for canon lawyers, whose number had greatly increased since the times of Innocent III. They debated the question with professional zeal and delight. The volume of canonistic tracts and memoranda during the early years of the Schism is impressive. The reaction of theologians was slower in coming. An early letter from Langenstein to his younger colleague d'Ailly provides an indication of the despair and helplessness which they must have experienced in the face of this "monster of monsters." Henry speaks of penance and prayer as effective counteractions, quoting psalm verses in support. Perhaps the horrible event is God's will.[14] This idea is often accompanied by a reference to Israel and Judah: God decreed their division (1 Kgs 11:31 ff.) and did not want to see it healed (1 Kgs 12:21–24).[15] Henry mitigates the disturbing thought by quoting Paul: "To those who love God all things work together unto good" (Rom 8:28), that is, God allows evil for the sake of a greater good. Why should one not believe in the final good which may arise of a schism and other adversities? Perhaps this punishment for the sins of the time is God's way finally to reform the church.[16]

In the context of the need for moral reform, the call for a general council had been issued repeatedly throughout the fourteenth century. Langenstein mentions this possibility, and the canonists refer to it as well. Undoubtedly, the crisis of the Schism did find a conciliar solution, but the Constance Assembly defined its own purpose more broadly. It set out to address three *causae:* the *causa unionis,* the *causa fidei,* and the *causa reformationis,* only one of which concerned the Schism directly. It is this wider perspective which formed the matrix of the practical conciliarism that developed during the period from 1378 to 1415. I will not focus on questions of its definition, derivation, developmental stages, and political shifts, but on one element only: the role of biblical interpretation in the formation of its theory.

When a new interest in the history of conciliarism emerged at the end of the nineteenth century, attention was centered on the chronological unfolding of the Schism and the publication of relevant documents. The theory, scholars were convinced, followed the reality. At this stage, there was no interest in biblical exegesis. In his four-volume edition of the *Acta Concilii Constanciensis,* Heinrich Finke made it a frequent practice to insert a series of dots when he encountered biblical quotations in his sources, sometimes adding a note such as, "Here follows a string of scriptural prooftexts."[17] The historian saw them as nothing more than rhetorical embellishments. The second stage was marked by the discovery of Marsilius of Padua and William of Ockham as the presumed inventors of the "conciliar theory." Scholars did notice Marsilius's extensive use of biblical materials and suggested that most of the specific quotations in favor among conciliarists later on were owed to him.[18] To this day, however, no thorough study exists of his biblical argument in the context of medieval exegesis. The presumed parentage of Marsilius and Ockham immediately raised the question of a revolutionary ecclesiology as one of the hallmarks of the conciliar theory. Did the conciliarists not replace the traditional hierarchical vision of the church with a vision from below, an emphasis on the sovereignty of the entire body of the faithful and on delegated authority? A more detailed investigation after World War II of the leading conciliarists during the Constance era revealed that this was not the case.[19] Men like Pierre d'Ailly, Jean Gerson, Simon de Cramaud, and Francesco Zabarella were interested in restoring the existing constitutional order of the church, not in overthrowing it.

Progress came with the publication in 1955 of Brian Tierney's book on *The Foundations of the Conciliar Theory*, which, following the lead of the author's teacher, Walter Ullmann, concentrated on the demonstration that the details of concilarist thought were derived from specific controversies within the canonistic literature ever since Gratian.[20] Topics like the erring pope, representational government, the role of councils, and the rights of the laity had been extensively discussed there, and the results were now used in new combinations to lay the foundations for a conciliar solution to the problems created by the Schism and for the needed reform of the church. Tierney realized the important role of biblical interpretation in his sources. He devoted an entire chapter to the canonistic exegesis of Mt 16:18–19 and did the same for Lk 22:32 in a subsequent article.[21] The main result of his initiative, however, was a massive emphasis in subsequent years on the canonistic aspects of the phenomenon wherever the "conciliar theory" was thematized.

More recently, a fuller picture of the complicated situation has been slowly emerging. As more and more individual writers of the period are seriously researched, a bewildering diversity of "conciliarisms" has come into view, each with its own goals and idiosyncracies. During the 1960s, the Constance generation was at the center of intense study and debate triggered by the bold actions of Pope John XXIII and the events surrounding the council which he called. In the 1980s and 1990s, attention has shifted dramatically to the Council of Basel, its self-understanding, its main characters and adversaries. In the course of these studies, scholars have noted a phenomenon which they describe as a "theologizing tendency" in the development of the conciliar argument. Hermann Josef Sieben puts it this way: "From the canonistic treatise on the Council by Pierre Amcilh in 1379 to the *Concordantia Catholica* of Nicholas of Cusa a clear development can be observed: canon law is being replaced by a theology which argues biblically, patristically, and speculatively."[22] The theologians of the Basel generation, so it seems, tapped the biblical and patristic tradition directly with the result that new angles on the issues were discovered and old answers were enriched and deepened. The most significant publication of recent years, in my opinion, has been Rolf de Kegel's 1995 critical edition of John of Segovia's *Liber de magna auctoritate episcoporum in concilio generali,* a veritable compend of a mature Basel conciliarism, written by one of the main players at the council.[23] True, Segovia's intention is to plead his special case for a general council composed of bishops only, but he bases every step of his theological marathon on scriptural texts, exegetical considerations, and patristic confirmation. De Kegel has added a 10-page scriptural index to his 660-page book. I cannot consider the Basel materials in this essay, but the surprising turn of recent scholarship has been an encouragement to go back to the beginnings and inquire about the use of the biblical argument among the early Paris conciliarists.

When the English delegation of university masters passed through Paris on the way to the Council of Pisa in 1409, Jean Gerson, then chancellor of the university, drafted a speech in which he politely lauded the initiative which the University of Oxford had taken on behalf of a council in 1396 but pointed out that long before that date his own university had taken the lead in advocating a conciliar solution to the Schism.[24] He referred to the solemn assembly vote of May 20, 1381, the writings of "my venerable teacher," Pierre d'Ailly, "Master Henry of Hesse of most distinguished memory" (Henry of Langenstein), "the Lord Praepositus of Worms, a great, devout man" (Conrad of Gelnhausen), and "others" as can be seen from their extant treatises.[25] His list ends with the university's widely disseminated open letter to the French king issued in June of 1394.[26] Gerson does not mention his own interventions, the earliest of which occurred only shortly before in his academic "resumpta" on "spiritual jurisdiction," proposed in December 1392.[27] The primary sources for this essay are these early "classics," including Gerson's early writings.

The most urgent topic in all of them is, of course, the ending of the Schism, the resolution of a conflict within the church the magnitude of which still defied belief. All the treatises deal with *modi uniendi* or "*viae*" toward this end. Gerson mentioned that the University of Paris at first vigorously advocated the *via concilii generalis*. Shortly after 1381, under heavy pressure from the pro-Avignon king, the emphasis shifted to the *via cessionis*, resignation of one or both contenders, and after 1398 to the *via subtractionis*, the withdrawal of obedience and support for Benedict XIII which was in effect for five years. It was only after the failure of all these attempts that the *via concilii generalis* had a chance to become dominant at the university again.

At the end of 1403, shortly after the restoration of French obedience to Benedict XIII, Pierre d'Ailly wrote a memorandum, probably for the Avignon pope as well as the French crown, which lays out twenty *viae* that might lead to church unity at a time when everything seemed open again.[28] While the number twenty is somewhat misleading—many are subcategories of major *viae*—the list does present a comprehensive summary of the options under discussion, each of them coming with their own set of biblical-exegetical arguments along with appropriate canonistic considerations in our literature. The list provides a convenient framework to inquire about the biblical texts adduced.

D'Ailly's first two *viae* are variants of the *via cessionis*, which appears as number seven in the list. One party, he says, could confess to having been in error and then return to the obedience of the other, or it could take this step without such a confession simply *pro bono pacis*. The "peace of the church" was one of the highest goods violated by the Schism and therefore to be sought in any attempt at healing. In our treatises, the appeal to the popes to act in the interest of this peace was made by quoting the psalm verses on the peace of Jerusalem (Ps 121:7; 124:5; 127:6) and also the "peace" words of the Johannine Jesus (Jn 14:27; 20:19.21.26).

The third option is the *via facti*, the use of physical force and military action against one party or the other. This method was certainly contemplated at several points by both popes and their secular allies, but our theorists generally opposed it and gave biblical reasons. Henry of Langenstein quoted 2 Sam 7: David was prevented from building the Temple of the Lord because he was a man of blood.[29] D'Ailly in his memorandum judged that military action would "not be sufficient to calm the consciences." In an appendix to the document, dated January 1405, we learn that Pope Benedict at that time did scheme to make war on the other side with the help of French troops. D'Ailly again rejects the idea because the other means of fraternal correction according to Mt 18:15–17 were not yet exhausted.[30] The same point was made strongly by Gerson.[31] Violence against the rival popes already had occurred, however, and was to occur again. In 1398, the French king had laid siege to Avignon and held the pope his virtual prisoner there for several years. Later on, the Council of Constance imprisoned John XXIII after his deposition, relying on the biblical argument from the conclusion of the Matthew passage on fraternal correction, Mt 18:17: "If he refuses to listen to the church, let him be to you as a heathen and a tax collector." What exactly did that mean under the circumstances? Dietrich of Niem was crystal clear: "let him be punished as a schismatic and heretic, for someone who gives occasion for such great damage must be thrown out, imprisoned for life, or be killed." As biblical support he quoted the millstone around the neck of the one who causes scandal (Mt 18:6) and the punishment of the priests of Bel in Dan 14, who were thrown to the lions after their scam had been disclosed.[32] Not everyone would have gone so far, but most council fathers at Constance would have agreed that some form of violence might be part of the final step of Jesus' rule.

D'Ailly's fourth *via* is the *via revelationis*. In 1481, Henry of Langenstein had already entertained the notion that the Schism might be ended through some miracle or divine oracle indicative of the will of God.[33] In his memorandum, d'Ailly cautiously warns that to count on such a solution would be to tempt God. There certainly were prophetic and visionary voices during the Schism, such as that of Marie Robine and Constance de Rabastens, though none of them strong enough to bring about change of the order of Catherine of Siena's influence on Gregory XI.[34] In fact, motivated by the overwhelming biblical evidence, the church had always recognized special revelation from God as a means of guidance into new directions. Vincent Ferrer, originally an ardent defender of Benedict XIII, abandoned the cause of that pope after he had a vision in 1398 which sent him on a penitential preaching mission throughout Europe. He was convinced that the end was imminent after the fourth beast of Dan 7:7 was on the loose, a beast which he identified with the Schism.[35] Pierre d'Ailly himself had an interest in the application of biblical prophecies to his present; in later life, it seems, he trusted the scientific calculations of astrology more than visions and apocalyptic signs.[36] Even though it is only a variant of a solution by divine oracle, a decision between the two rival popes by lot is d'Ailly's fifth *via*. Casting lots in the church, he says, is problematic because it may give rise to abuse and illicit practices, but it has a clear New Testament warrant in Acts 1:26, the selection of Matthias as a replacement for Judas, and therefore it is a serious option. Augustine, he adds, recommended that the lot be used in certain extremely dangerous situations.[37]

Three of d'Ailly's following methods are different forms of a single one, the *via cessionis,* which was the major option pursued by France at the time the memorandum was written. D'Ailly knew that even a voluntary abdication of both popes by itself would not restore the unity of the church. For that, the *via concilii* was needed. But it would be a very useful first step since it would conclusively demonstrate the humility and peaceful intention of the pope. Could the present popes, each convinced of his divine calling and legitimate claim, afford such a self-humiliation without rendering their respective causes suspect? Obviously, this question was discussed in their circles and by their lawyers. Our theologians saw it as a moral issue and drew on many biblical texts to affirm the appropriateness of the act of ceding. In his earliest intervention of August 1379, Conrad of Gelnhausen pointed to an Old Testament example, the fight between the herdsmen of Abraham and Lot (Gen 13:7–8). Being the older and wiser of the two, Abraham settled the dispute by "ceding" to his brother.[38] Among the New Testament materials, Jesus' rule of fraternal correction in Mt 18:15–18 was obviously the most pertinent text, with its suggestion of specific measures and a clear procedure. The generality of that rule found special interest: "If your brother offends against you, you go and rebuke him." Conciliarists read here the right, even the duty of every Christian to correct an erring brother. This was the basis for their encouragement of secular rulers to intervene; rulers are members of the same church and are especially responsible for the honor of the oppressed mother.[39] For other New Testament texts, an important hermeneutical maxim came into play: "Every action of Christ must be our instruction."[40] This applies to Christ's childhood. "He was subject to them" (Lk 2:51), that is, to the maternal law which for the pope as for every Christian is the law of the church, his mother. Someone who would argue that she ceased to be mother after becoming bride was taking a stab at the pontiff's arrogance.[41] In this connection, Jn 10:11.15 was important: on the example of Christ, the pope as a good shepherd is not only obliged to cede but even to lay down his life as Christ did. Occasionally, Jn 10 was combined with the example of Solomon's judgment in 1 Kgs 3:16–27: a true mother gives up her right for the sake of her child's life rather than allowing the cruel division. Paul's advice on meat sacrificed to idols makes the same point (1 Cor 8:9.13): fraternal love obliges a person in a given case to refrain from doing what one has the right to do.[42] The moral case for the *via cessionis* was strong and led to definite promises from both sides. That these promises were never fulfilled was proof of these popes' immorality for many of their contemporaries.

The most extensive and most important section of d'Ailly's memorandum is devoted to the *via concilii generalis* as a potential solution of the conflict. The term *concilium generale* gained prominence in the canonistic discussions of "kinds of councils" commenting on dist. 15–17 of Gratian's Decretum, where the papal authority to call universal assemblies and confirm their decisions was defined on the basis of Pseudo-Isidorian texts.[43] William of Ockham's definition boldly challenged this tradition, brushing aside the link to papal authority and stressing instead the representational aspect: A general council is the assembly of as many leading representatives of the various parts of Christendom as possible for the purpose of deliberating about the common good in an orderly fashion.[44] D'Ailly and the other conciliarists of his generation clearly embraced this understanding. Quite apart from the question of who must call, preside over, and confirm the decisions of a general council, they saw the general council as a representative gathering of the entire church of the West, which, in the situation of the Schism, Pierre d'Ailly could envision as an assembly just of bishops, or of bishops, leading abbots, theologians, and jurists combined, or simply of an equal number of prelates from both obediences.

From the very beginning of the Schism, the proposals for a conciliar solution had been argued on biblical-exegetical grounds along with canonistic reasonings. Besides the example of the Maccabees (1 Macc 8:15), two Old Testament texts were regularly mentioned: Num 27:20 and Deut 17:8–13. The Vulgate text from Numbers speaks of a *"synagoga filiorum Israel"* and seemed to suggest that in order to conduct particularly difficult business, a full assembly was sometimes called in Israel.[45] The Deuteronomy text also concerns the procedure for handling major problems in the community, and the need to "remove an evil from your midst." H. J. Sieben has called the use of this passage by our writers "the main Old Testament contribution to conciliarism."[46] The exegetical tradition reflected in the *Glossa Ordinaria* already saw this text as an appeals procedure (*"nota: appellandi tribuit facultatem"*) and wanted to see it applied in the church (*"hoc quoque in ecclesia seruandum est"*).[47] At first glance, however, there seems to be nothing in the text to suggest a conciliar procedure. Innocent III, following older tradition, interpreted the "place which the Lord shall choose" (v.8.10) as the Apostolic See, the "priests of the Levitical tribe" (v.9) as the cardinals, and the "judge who shall be at that time" (v.9) as well as the "priest that ministers to the Lord your God at that time" (v.12) as the pope.[48] Yet there are exegetical difficulties with this interpretation. Are the "priest and the judge at that time" one and the same person? Verse 12 clearly distinguishes them. The conciliarists also pointed to the plural in verses 9–10: "the priests" which, in their reading, identified the "place which the Lord shall choose" as the meeting place of a general council. They even found support in the *Glossa Ordinaria*, which glossed "*locus*" as "*ecclesia*" and interpreted the "*sacerdos*" of verse 12 not as an ecclesiastical hierarch but as "Christ who replaced himself in this function by his vicars, the apostles."[49]

Of course, the New Testament evidence for the *via concilii* as a major model of conflict resolution in the church seemed even stronger. We mentioned the importance of Mt 18:15–19 as a model of the *via cessionis* with its clearly defined official steps. Conciliarists were especially interested in the last of these: *dic ecclesiae!* (Tell it to the church!). The Paris university letter of 1394 summarizes what has been done so far by the French king and the university, then paraphrases Mt 18:15–18, and concludes: "What else seems to be left, if we are to fulfill Christ's precepts, except to tell it to the church called together in a General Council."[50] The logic seems compelling: Christ's rule proceeds from the private, individual admonition by a brother, any brother, to an effort by a selected group and on to the representative assembly of the whole. Universal councils have been held to settle smaller matters than this Schism. How much more urgent is it then to pursue this *via* now!

The apostles took Jesus' precept seriously. Both Conrad of Gelnhausen and Henry of Langenstein argue that, numbers still being small and distances manageable in the early times, the apostles could have settled cases and conducted business without the convening of councils by letter or other direct means. If they did call "general councils," this was in order to present their successors with a "form and model" to imitate. The maxim about Jesus' actions bears expansion: "The actions of the Apostles are our instruction just as those of Christ."[51] The standard number of four "general councils" mentioned in the Acts of the Apostles, which both Conrad and Henry mention, goes back to the exegetical tradition, more precisely to the *Glossa Ordinaria*. The marginal gloss to Acts 21:22 states: "This fourth Synod was held in Jerusalem. The first dealt with the election of another apostle to replace Judas (Acts 1:15–26), the second with the election of the seven deacons (Acts 6:1–6), the third with the decision not to impose circumcision on those gentiles who had come to believe (Acts 15), the fourth with the decision not to disallow Jews at that time to practice the ceremonies of the law, where necessity demanded, on account of the offense taken by those who thought the apostles were condemning the law of Moses as idolatrous teaching."[52] The gloss itself already emphasizes the model character of the Apostles' conciliar action in each case. In Acts 1:6, the *Glossa interlinearis* notes with regard to the address, *viri fratres:* "whose common task it is to discuss the issues concerning individuals." To the phrase "the twelve calling together the multitude of the disciples," it adds, "through communal consent," and explains, "they seek the consent of the multitude, which must be taken as a model." A marginal gloss to Acts 15:6 even states: "Here an example is provided of arranging assemblies for the discernment of the things necessary for the faith."[53] Conciliarists were well aware of this tendency of the tradition and added their own observations.

Pierre d'Ailly, for example, pointed out that in two cases, Acts 6 and 15, the calling of a council was the swift answer (*statim!*) to crises with schismatic potential. He also noted like others that in the account of Acts 15, it was not Peter who called the council (v.6), that James pronounced the decision (v.19) with Peter being present, that not Peter but "the apostles and elders with the whole church" decided to elect ambassadors (v.22), that the letter of the council is written in the name of "the apostles and elder brothers" (v.23), not of Peter, and that the communication of the council's decision reads: "It has seemed good to the Holy Spirit and to us," not "It seemed good to Peter" (v.28).[54] Gerson explained that the convocation of a general council could happen *concordative* (by common agreement) or by authority. Obviously, the first mode was the practice of the early church, as the four councils of Acts demonstrate.[55]

The polemical thrust of all these observations is plain enough. They were important as arguments in the fight against the main obstacle the *via concilii generalis* was facing: the doctrine of the papal plenitude of power, as curialists and papal theorists had defined it in recent decades, with all its consequences for the convocation, the conduct, and the acceptance of a general council. The doctrine had grown slowly over the centuries as an application of the exegetical notion of a Petrine primacy in the New Testament. Innocent III, who provided the crucial ideological bridge between theology and canon law for the following centuries, had honed and refined the primatial interpretation of the Petrine texts to perfection.[56] His masterful synthesis of the three foundational passages which had been cited together since the time of Leo I—Mt 16:18–19; Lk 22:32; and Jn 21:15–17—was echoed time and again through the centuries. Three times the Lord committed the primacy over the entire church to the apostle Peter: before the passion, during the passion, and after the passion. He called Peter the rock and promised to build his church upon him, handing over to him the keys of the kingdom of heaven. He prayed for the indefectibility of Peter's faith right before Peter's deepest humiliation, and his prayer was always heard (Heb 5:7). He finally and irrevocably reinstated Peter and solemnly entrusted him with the care of the whole Christian flock for all times to come.

Our Paris conciliarists read these texts differently. Instead of paraphrasing their interpretation, I simply quote the words of Master Pierre Bohier, penned in 1379:[57]

> On Mt 16:18, You are Peter etc., it must be said that Peter acted there as a type of the Catholic Church. . . . And when the Lord said: Upon this rock I will build my church, he spoke of himself: Now the rock was Christ [1Cor 10:4]. . . . On the other verse: I will give you the keys of the kingdom of heaven [Mt 16:19], it must again be said (following Jerome, Ambrose, and Bede) that Christ spoke it to all apostles in the person of Peter. For Christ's question: Who do you say that I am? challenged all apostles, and Peter's confession: You are the Christ, the Son of the living God, was the confession and assertion of all apostles. That the promise which Christ made to Peter when he said: I will give you the keys of the kingdom of heaven, was made to the apostles in common is plain, since the fulfilment or transmission of the promise was a general one: common was the spiration, common the mission—"as my father sent me, so I send you"; common also was the transmission of the power: "Take the holy spirit; whose sins you forgive etc. [Jn 20:21–23].
>
> On [John 21:15–17] where Christ says to Peter three times: If you love me, feed my sheep, one can say that this is also meant to be addressed to all, because the other apostles were the same as Peter. They were endowed with the same participation, honor, and power, but [this] took its beginning from unity, so that Christ's church may be shown to be one, as the blessed Cyprian says. . . . [De unitate, cap. 4]
>
> In a different vein, some suggest that Christ says this to Peter individually so that Peter may not think himself excluded from the apostleship and the commissioning just mentioned, that is, from [Jesus' word:] As my father has sent me etc. Perhaps he believed himself excluded on the ground that he had thrice denied Christ publicly and had exposed him to a very serious temptation when he said: Be it far from you, Lord! [Mt 16:22] At that time Christ addressed him with a terrible word as if he was depriving him of the apostleship and even of his company: Get behind me, Satan, for you consider not the things of God [Mt 16:23]. In this way, he also

spoke of Peter individually through the mouth of the angel who said to the women: Tell this to his disciples and Peter [Mk 16:7]. This happened, as Gregory says, so that Peter should not think himself excluded because of his denial.

To complete the picture, here is Pierre d'Ailly on the third text, Lk 22:32: "This [i.e., Christ's prayer that Peter's faith may not fail] is not said of the personal faith of Peter, since Peter erred. Rather, it is said of the faith of the universal church (*ecclesia*) who is represented in a general council and about whom [Mt 16:18] says: 'The gates of hell will not prevail against her.' It does not say, 'against you,' that is, Peter. This makes clear that the judgment of the council is to be preferred over the judgment of the pope, since he can err in matters concerning the faith. It was the same with Peter about whom Paul says in Galatians, chapter 2, that he, Paul, opposed him in the face because he was blameworthy, not walking upright according to the truth of the Gospel."[58]

To ears attuned to hearing Innocent III's exegetical rhetoric and its echoes, this interpretation sounds shocking, revolutionary. I have argued elsewhere that, in reality, this understanding of the three primatial texts represents the mainstream of the medieval exegetical tradition, which was out of step with the primatial exegesis of papalist circles.[59] The reason lay in the methodological principle of explaining the Bible with the Bible. The power of cross connections, parallels, and verbal echoes from other pages of the Vulgate to shed light on individual verses and expressions was enormous. Matthew 16 presents a prime example. If Paul said, "The rock was Christ" (1 Cor 10:4), the conclusion seemed inevitable that, in Mt 16:18, Christ meant to say he would build his church upon himself. Few exegetes were able to escape this logic. A similar conclusion prevailed in the case of Christ's prayer in Lk 22:32: the prayer could not concern an unfailing, infallible faith of a Peter who would deny his Lord shortly thereafter. Exegetes tried to neutralize the threefold denial by interpreting the threefold command in Jn 21 to feed the sheep and tend the flock as a formal reinstatement of the fallen apostle. But there was evidence of an "erring Peter" even after Pentecost, as Pierre d'Ailly's text points out.

Here the power of cross-connections becomes evident. The confrontation between Peter and Paul at Antioch (Gal 2:11–14) played a major role in the medieval debates about an "erring Peter" and the canonical possibility of a heretical pope.[60] In a famous controversy with Jerome, Augustine had concluded that Peter *was* in error at Antioch and needed to be corrected. Placing the incident before the Jerusalem Council of Acts 15 allowed him, however, to assume that Peter humbly accepted the correction and the harmony between the two apostles was soon restored. His exegesis of the passage won the day. In his famous exception clause of c.6, dist. 40, Gratian conceded the point by allowing for the possibility that a pope may "err" in a matter of faith and become heretical: the pope cannot be judged by anyone "*nisi deprehendatur a fide devius.*"[61] In an unpublished *quaestio* from around 1380, Pierre d'Ailly discussed the details of Gal 2:11–14, reviewed the patristic controversy, sided with Augustine, and declared the incident to be an example for superiors not to resist being corrected by someone of lower status, especially if it concerns an error in matters of faith.[62] As theologians, our conciliarists carefully studied the exegetical tradition and followed it. Their interpretation of the Petrine key texts was no novelty but was fully in tune with the school tradition. Thus, they felt entirely justified in rejecting the notion of a papal plenitude of power which stood in the way of a general council as a solution to the problem of the Schism and of needed reforms.

More important than the no to the papal doctrine of the plenitude of power was the positive conviction of the superior promise which the *via concilii generalis* held for the attempt to reestablish the church's unity. It was not only the practice of the apostles that commended it, but even more the understanding that this unity also involved a plurality—not in the unsavory sense of rival factions, but in the sense of the coming together of different members of one body. For d'Ailly and most others, the central text at this point was Mt 18:20: "Where two or three are gathered together in my name, there I am in the midst of them." This saying comes on the heels of Jesus' rule of fraternal correction, and much could be said about its own context of consent and common prayer, a context on which our writers and the exegetical tradition did not draw. They read the verse predominantly as the assurance that there was a greater chance for the presence of truth in the judgment of a council than in the pronouncements of a single pope. Conrad of Gelnhausen adduced it against fears that the sheer numerical majority of one party at a council may be a danger for unity in truth. Not so, he argued. Even among as few as two or three, the Holy Spirit is present. And Henry of Langenstein explained that precisely because it is the Spirit, not numbers, who is the judge at the council, even a single believer could put his trust in the council against ten thousand.[63] The language of the verse certainly reflects the Deuteronomic wisdom that, in legal procedures, truth must rest on the mouth of two or three witnesses (Deut 19:15). But it is not the legal language of a requirement to be fulfilled in order for Christ's presence to be assured. Yves Congar[64] has pointed to early Christian texts which assume a fundamental trinitarian structure of the church: "Where there are three, the Father, the Son, and the Holy Spirit, there is the church which is the body of the three."[65] He concludes that Mt 18:20 encourages us to reckon with a "basic conciliarity" as belonging to the essence of the church.

The use of Mt 18:20 in the argument of our conciliarists for the *via concilii* was simple but made a strong point: "Christ himself, who is our peace and makes the two into one, teaches us [here] the shape of this way: Where two: namely, one from the one party and another from the other, or three: for the case that there is disagreement, are gathered in my name: the name of love, concord, and peace, there I am in the midst of them: recalling the quarrelling brothers to concord and reconciling in peace those who disagree with each other."[66] From the same presupposition, Langenstein simply cites the verse as evidence that "there is the greatest need for a General Council."[67] For the continuing presence of Christ in a gathering of Christians, Mt 28:20 is regularly quoted in this connection, "Lo, I am with you always, to the close of the age"—a verse which, it was thought, cannot just be addressed to the disciples because they died very soon. The unquestioned substitution of the presence of the Holy Spirit for Christ's presence goes back to patristic usage where conciliar decrees were declared to be divinely sanctioned by an appeal to Mt 18:20, and the formula of Acts 15:28 was used: "It seemed good to the Holy Spirit and to us." For our conciliarists, this formula expressed the biblical teaching that decisions made at a general council enjoy an authority not derived from the council's formal legitimacy only, but from an ultimate source, the guidance of the Holy Spirit. There was an almost mythical aura surrounding the vision of a general council in session, with the Holy Spirit as its main adviser. For d'Ailly, this thought assured the possibility that, even without the pope, the universal church could assemble a council on her own. Langenstein called the *via concilii generalis* the "way of the Holy Spirit" and gave a reason: "in a General Council where the Holy Spirit is judge, victory is not achieved by numbers but by truth."[68] To "lead into all the truth" is the work of the Holy Spirit according to Jn 16:13. Congar points out that Thomas Aquinas clearly saw the *ecclesia universalis* as the true recipient of the infallibility which this "final truth" of Jn 16:13 and Christ's prayer in Lk 22:32 imply. The conciliarists followed him and the tradition behind him: infallibility, the assurance of ultimate trustworthiness, if Christ promised it at all, can be ascribed only to the total church, the church universal which the general council represents.

As is well known, the doctrine of the infallibility of the representative body itself, the general council, became one of the pillars of Basel conciliarism because the superiority of the council over the pope was at stake. With all their awe and veneration for the council, our writers, facing the early stage of the Schism, could still hold different opinions at this point. Jean Courtecuisse could state, "If a council is assembled to treat serious matters of faith, one can boldly affirm that the General Council is led by the Holy Spirit in such a way that he will not permit it to err."[69] Pierre d'Ailly, on the other hand, remained doubtful precisely because the "general council" is a limited concept: It *is* not the universal church, it only represents it. "It is a special privilege of the universal church that it cannot err in faith. This may be piously believed of the General Council, namely, when it grounds itself on Holy Scripture and its authority which is inspired by the Holy Spirit. Otherwise it has often erred as we read."[70]

Here, conformity with Scripture is introduced as the touchstone for the ultimate authority of a conciliar decision under the Holy Spirit. This seems to be a dangerous move. Who decides what is conformable and what is not? Obviously not a pope issuing decrees studded with biblical "proofs" under the pretext of a papal plenitude of power. In his aggressive way, Dietrich of Niem specifies the problem: "How can a person bind and loose with the key of power who never was willing to attend to the study of sacred theology and of divine science nor ever knew how to preach the word of God? How can he discern leprosy from leprosy (Dt 17:8)? He certainly cannot. Therefore, let him first be strong in handling the key of knowledge and thereafter shine with the key of power."[71] The person he has in mind is Pope John XXIII. Almost all of our writers were masters of theology with a healthy sense of their professional role in church and world. In the discussions about Gal 2:11–14, the idea of a double magisterium, each with its own succession, one of Peter and one of Paul, had appeared. It found here the biblical basis for applying the distinction between a "key of power" and a "key of knowledge"—a distinction which Gratian's Decretum acknowledged—to pope, prelates, and masters. In his treatise, Jean Courtecuisse declared that doctors and teachers must be preferred to prelates and jurisdictional superiors when the interpretation of Scripture is at stake. He did so on the principle that "the one who enjoys greater authority in a particular field is not subject in it to one with lesser authority."[72] Both Conrad of Gelnhausen and Henry of Langenstein already introduced the Aristotelian principle of *epikeia*, the necessity of adjusting laws to unusual circumstances according to the intention of the lawgiver, into the discussion of the *viae* to end the Schism.[73] According to our conciliarist writers, this principle had clear and sufficient biblical warrant: David and his companions eating the sacred showbread at Nob (1 Sam 21); the Maccabees taking up arms on the sabbath day (1 Macc 2); and Jesus allowing his disciples to pluck grain on the sabbath (Mt 12). In pursuing the option of the *via concilii generalis* during the Schism, *epikeia* was needed to set aside the rule of "positive law" that only the pope can call a council. D'Ailly accused those who insisted on this rule under all circumstances of "clinging in a Jewish manner too tenaciously to the literal sense of the positive law, thus contradicting the word of the Apostle: 'The letter kills, but the Spirit makes alive,' that is: the spiritual sense."[74] Using *epikeia*, however, is not really a matter of spiritual sense versus literal in biblical interpretation, as d'Ailly seems to imply. At the end of the fourteenth century, everyone was interested in the literal sense. We have seen how much attention our scholars paid to the details of the texts they used. A remark by Langenstein moves us closer to the real issue. Justifying the need for *epikeia*, he says: "It is indeed permissible for theologians, who are the interpreters of the divine law, to interpret the mind of Christ and to declare, as is shown in the interpretation of the Great Commandment of the law, that it cannot be fulfilled literally by *viatores* (pilgrims), but according to the doctors' understanding of it."[75] To interpret the mind of Christ means reading the intention of the author, and this, ever since Thomas Aquinas, is a matter of expounding the *literal* sense, not the spiritual. Theologians cannot be dismissed by prelates and their lawyers as lofty dreamers removed from the realities of life, hunters after spiritual senses up in the clouds. Theologians are needed to discern the divine intention behind the words of the Bible for everyday living down here on earth. It is their responsibility to unmask the deceptive practices of schismatic popes who not only use canon law to block any *via unionis*, but also misread the intention of the divine author in the very Scriptures they quote. God's intention in this detestable Schism can only be reconciliation, peace, and unity, not discord, mutual accusation, and proud self-justification. Theologians have the right and even the duty to suggest the *viae*, the practical options, to the people, who can and must act, and they do this on the basis of the teachings of the Bible, looking at the models for action which are found in the biblical texts and pointing out where laws must be adjusted to the necessity of the hour. Gerson formulates it sharply: "The authority to use *epikeia* doctrinally resides in the first instance in the experts in theology, which is the architectural science with respect to others."[76] For him, to be a "theologian" means to be a biblical theologian who reads the mind of the divine author in order to discern what God's will and intention may be in a situation which, from the human vantage point, looks as hopeless as the Schism. The biblical argument of the early Paris conciliarists during one of the worst crises in Western Christendom is anything but mere embellishment of their political and personal ambitions. It is at the very heart of their calling.

NOTES

1. W. M. Abbott, S.J., ed., *The Documents of Vatican II* (New York: Guild Press, America Press, Association Press, 1966), 347.

2. See, e.g., H. Heimpel, ed., *Dietrich von Nieheim, Dialog über Union und Reform der Kirche 1410. De modis uniendi et reformandi ecclesiam in concilio universali* (Quellen zur Geistesgeschichte des Mittelalters und der Renaissance, 3; Leipzig: B. G. Teubner, 1933), 90 and note.

3. Epistle of the University of Paris to the King of France (1394): L. d'Achéry; E. Baluze et al., *Spicilegium sive Collectio veterum aliquot scriptorum qui in Galliae bibliothecis delituerant* (Paris: Montalant, 1723), 1:780b.

4. Conrad von Gelnhausen, Epistola Concordiae, in F. Bliemetzrieder, *Literarische Polemik zu Beginn des grossen abendländischen Schismas (Kardinal Petrus Flandrin, Kardinal Petrus Amelii, Konrad von Gelnhausen): Ungedruckte Texte und Untersuchungen* (Publikationen des österreichischen Historischen Instituts in Rom, 1; Wien and Leipzig: F. Tempsky, G. Freytag, 1910; reprint New York: Johnson Reprint Corp, 1967), 111–13.

5. See F. Bliemetzrieder, "Ein Traktat des Fr. Nikolaus Fakenham (1395) über das grosse abendländische Schisma," *Archivum Franciscanum Historicum* 1–2 (1908/09): 582.

6. Gelnhausen, in Bliemetzrieder, *Literarische Polemik*, 115.

7. Heimpel, ed., *Dietrich von Nieheim*, 17.

8. G. R. Dunstan, "Jean Gerson: Propositio facta coram Anglicis: A Translation," in C. M. Barron and C. Harper-Bill, eds., *The Church in Pre-Reformation Society: Essays in Honour of F. R. H. Du Boulay* (Dover, N.H.: Boydell Press, 1985), 73a.

9. William of Salvarvilla: F. Bliemetzrieder, "Conclusions de Guillaume de Salvarvilla, maître de théologie à Paris, sur la question du concile général pendant le grand schisme d'Occident (1381)," *Revue d'histoire ecclésiastique* 11 (1910): 47–55; here 53.

10. C. Fasolt, "William Durant the Younger and Conciliar Theory," *Journal of the History of Ideas* 59 (July 1997): 385–402.

11. These are chs. 16–20, printed separately in L. E. Du Pin's edition of Gerson's works, *Joannis Gersonii ... opera omnia* (Antwerp: Sumptibus Societatis, 1706), 2:314–18. Full text: ibid., 806–40. On the date and the manuscript tradition, see G. Kreuzer, *Heinrich von Langenstein: Studien zur Biographie und zu den Schismatraktaten unter besonderer Berücksichtigung der Epistola pacis und der Epistola concilii pacis* (Quellen und Forschungen aus dem Gebiet der Geschichte, N. F. Heft 6; Paderborn: F. Schöningh, 1987). Selections, including chs. 17–20, are translated by J. K. Cameron in M. Spinka, ed., *Advocates of Reform from Wyclif to Erasmus* (The Library of Christian Classics, 14; Philadelphia: Westminster Press, 1953), 106–39.

12. Tractatus de reformatione ecclesiae, in Du Pin, ed., *Joannis Gersonii ... opera omnia*, 2:906A; cf. 877B (Epist. "Dudum beatissime pater").

13. Epistola Concilii Pacis c. 2, trans. Cameron, 108.

14. The text of the letter has been published by Kreuzer, *Heinrich von Langenstein*, 250–53; Kreuzer dates it before 1395. Gerson quotes this kind of argument later indignantly as the opinion of the "animalis homo": Dunstan, "Jean Gerson," 75.

15. Epistola Concilii Pacis c. 12, in Du Pin, ed., *Joannis Gersonii ... opera omnia*, 2:820 f.

16. Kreuzer, *Heinrich von Langenstein*, 253.

17. *Acta Concilii Constanciensis*, 4 vols. (Münster i. W.: Regensbergsche Buchhandlung, 1896–1928; reprint Münster: Antiquariat Th. Stenderhoff, 1976–1982).

18. "Il apparaît assez net, que c'est Marsile de Padoue qui a mis sur la voie des textes généralement choisis": P. de Vooght, *Les pouvoirs du Concile et l'autorité du pape au Concile de Constance* (Unam Sanctam, 56; Paris: Cerf, 1965), 196.

19. See the survey by R. Bäumer, "Die Erforschung des Konziliarismus," in *Die Entwicklung des Konziliarismus: Werden und Nachwirken der konziliaren Idee* (Wege der Forschung, 279; Darmstadt: Wissenschaftliche Buchgesellschaft, 1976), 3–56; here 41.

20. B. Tierney, *Foundations of the Conciliar Theory: The Contribution of the Medieval Canonists from Gratian to the Great Schism* (Cambridge Studies in Medieval Life and Thought, 4; Cambridge: Cambridge University Press, 1955; "enlarged new ed.," Leiden: Brill, 1998).

21. B. Tierney, "A Scriptural Text in the Decretales and in St. Thomas: Canonistic Exegesis of Luke 22:32," *Studia Gratiana* 20 (1976): 363–77.

22. H. J. Sieben, *Traktate und Theorien zum Konzil vom Beginn des Grossen Schismas bis zum Vorabend der Reformation (1378–1521)* (Frankfurter theologische Studien, 30; Frankfurt a. M.: Knecht, 1984), 15; a similar observation is formulated by J. Helmrath, *Das Basler Konzil 1431–1449: Forschungsstand und Probleme* (Kölner historische Abhandlungen, 32; Cologne: Böhlau, 1987), 417–20 in a section entitled "'Theologisierung.' Bibel und Kanonistik."

23. R. de Kegel, ed., *Johannes von Segovia: Liber de magna auctoritate episcoporum in concilio generali* (Spicilegium Friburgense, 34; Fribourg: Universitätsverlag, 1995). See also H. J. Sieben's analysis of Segovia's treatise: *Vom Apostelkonzil zum Er-*

sten Vatikanum: Studien zur Geschichte der Konzilsidee (Konziliengeschichte; Paderborn: F. Schöningh, 1996), 157–73.

24. The Latin text of his "Propositio facta coram Anglicis" may be found in *Jean Gerson: Oeuvres complètes*, vol. VI: P. Glorieux, ed., *L'oeuvre ecclésiologique* (Paris, etc.: Desclée & Cie, 1962), 125–35; English translation: G. R. Dunstan, "Jean Gerson," 68–81.

25. Ibid., 130 and 76 respectively.

26. The full text is printed in the edition cited in note 3 above, 776–83.

27. Glorieux, ed., *Oeuvres complètes*, vol. III: *L'oeuvre magistrale*, 1–9.

28. The text is printed in an appendix (IV.6.e) entitled, "Peter d'Aillys Schrift über die Unionswege vom Ende 1403," in F. Ehrle, *Martin de Alpartils Chronica actitatorum temporibus Domini Benedicti XIII* (Quellen und Forschungen aus dem Gebiete der Geschichte, 12; Paderborn: Ferdinand Schöningh, 1906), 494–506.

29. Langenstein, Epistola concilii pacis c.14, trans. Cameron, 124.

30. See the texts in Ehrle, *Martin de Alpartils Chronica*, 504–6.

31. Glorieux, ed., *Oeuvres complètes*, 3:7.

32. Heimpel, ed., *Dietrich von Nieheim*, 70, 108.

33. Langenstein, Epistola concilii pacis, trans. Cameron, 124 f. and 130.

34. M. Tobin, "Les visions et révélations de Marie Robine d'Avignon, dans le contexte prophétique des années 1400," in M.-H. Vicaire, ed., *Fin du monde et signes des temps: Visionnaires et prophètes en France méridionale, fin XIIIe-début XVe siècle* (Cahiers de Fanjeaux, 27; Toulouse: Privat, 1992), 309–29; R. Blumenfeld-Kosinski, "Constance de Rabastens: Politics and Visionary Experience in the Time of the Great Schism," *Mystics Quarterly* 25 (Dec. 1999): 147–68.

35. B. Montagnes, "Saint Vincent Ferrier devant le schisme," in *Genèse et débuts du Grand Schisme d'Occident. Avignon 25–28 septembre 1978* (Colloques internationaux du CNRS, 586; Paris: Editions du CNRS, 1980), 607–13; here 611. The vision is described in a letter to Benedict XIII dated July 27, 1412: P.-H. Fages, *Notes et documents de l'histoire de saint Vincent Ferrier* (Louvain: A. Uystpruyst, 1905), 213–24.

36. This is the argument of Laura Ackerman Smoller, *History, Prophecy, and the Stars: The Christian Astrology of Pierre d'Ailly 1350–1420* (Princeton, N.J.: Princeton University Press, 1994).

37. The reference is to Epistle 228:12 (PL 33:1018).

38. Conrad of Gelnhausen, Epistola Brevis (1379), in H. Kaiser, "Der 'kurze Brief' des Konrad von Gelnhausen," *Historische Vierteljahrschrift* 3 (1900): 381–86; here 385.

39. Heimpel, ed., *Dietrich von Nieheim*, 22.

40. "omnis Christi actio nostra debet esse instructio": D'Ailly (= Niem!), in Du Pin, *Joannis Gersonii . . . opera omnia* (Den Haag: Petrus de Hondt, 1728), 2:902C.

41. Epistle of the University of Paris (1394), in d'Achéry, *Spicilegium*, 1:778a.

42. Gerson's "resumpta" exemplifies this combination: Glorieux, ed., *Oeuvres complètes*, vol. III: *L'oeuvre magistrale*, 1–2 and 8.

43. See H. J. Sieben, *Die Konzilsidee des lateinischen Mittelalters (847–1378)* (Konziliengeschichte; Paderborn: F. Schöningh, 1984), 224–31.

44. William of Ockham, Dialogus I.5.85: "Illa igitur congregatio est concilium generale reputanda, in qua diversae personae gerentes auctoritatem et vicem universarum partium totius christiantiatis ad tractandum de communi bono rite conveniunt, nisi aliqui noluerint vel [non] potuerint venire"; see H. J. Sieben, *Traktate*, 121 and note 40.

45. Gelnhausen, Epistola Concordiae, ed. Bliemetzrieder, 118; Langenstein, Epistola Concilii Pacis c. 13, trans. Cameron, 115.

46. See his section on "Dtn 17,8–13 im Zusammenhang des Konzils," in *Traktate*, 133–41.

47. Interlinear glosses to Dt 17:8: K. Froehlich and M. T. Gibson, eds., *Biblia Latina cum Glossa Ordinaria: Facsimile Reprint of the Editio Princeps, Adolf Rusch of Strassburg, 1480/81* (Turnhout, Belgium: Brepols, 1992), 1:996.

48. Sieben, "Dtn 17,8–13," in *Traktate*, 134 f.

49. *Biblia Latina cum Glossa Ordinaria*, 1:996 bottom.

50. d'Achéry, *Spicilegium*, 1:779a.

51. Conrad of Gelnhausen broadens the scope of the rule in this way and adds 1 Cor 11:1 to the quote of Mt 11:29 f, and Jn 11 (= 13:15): "non solum Christi accio nostra est instructio. . . , sed etiam accionem apostolorum imitari debemus": Epistola concordiae, ed. Bliemetzrieder, 118:30–32. Henry of Langenstein does the same: "Est enim Apostolorum actio nostra instructio sicut et Christi iuxta illud [1 Cor 4:16]": Du Pin, ed., *Joannis Gersonii . . . opera omnia*, 2:822D.

52. *Biblia Latina cum Glossa Ordinaria*, 4:499. On the various attempts in the history of the church to count apostolic "councils," see Sieben's section "Zur Tradition einer Vielzahl von Apostelkonzilien," in *Traktate*, 141–47.

53. *Biblia Latina cum Glossa Ordinaria*, 4:487.

54. Tractatus de materia, in Francis Oakley, *The Political Thought of Pierre d'Ailly: The Voluntarist Tradition* (New Haven, Conn.: Yale University Press, 1964) 306; in his later works: Tractatus de reformatione ecclesiae, in Du Pin, ed., *Joannis Gersonii . . . opera omnia* (Den Haag: Petrus de Hondt, 1728), 905; and sermon "Erunt signa in sole," ibid., 924BC.

55. Propositio coram Anglicis: trans. G. R. Dunstan, "Jean Gerson," 79.

56. See K. Froehlich, "Saint Peter, Papal Primacy, and the Exegetical Tradition, 1150–1300," in C. J. Ryan, ed., *The Religious Role of the Papacy, Ideals and Realities, 1150–1300* (Papers in Mediaeval Studies, 8; Toronto: Pontifical Institute of Mediaeval Studies, 1989), 3–44.

57. F. Bliemetzrieder, "Le traité de Pierre Bohier évêque d'Orvieto sur le projet du concile général," *Questions ecclésiastiques* (Lille) 47 (1909) [offprint, 1–14]; here 10–11.

58. Tractatus de materia, in Oakley, *The Political Thought of Pierre d'Ailly*, 307.

59. Froehlich, "Saint Peter, Papal Primacy, and the Exegetical Tradition, 1150–1300," 3–44.

60. On the history of interpretation for this passage, see K. Froehlich, "Fallibility Instead of Infallibility? A Brief History of the Interpretation of Gal. 2:11–14," in Paul Empie and Austin Murphy, eds., *Teaching Authority and Infallibility in the Church* (Lutherans and Catholics in Dialogue, VI; Minneapolis: Augsburg Publishing House, 1980), 259–69 and 351–57.

61. Decretum Gratiani, dis. 40, cap. 6, "Si papa," in E. Friedberg, ed., *Corpus Iuris Canonici* (Leipzig: B. Tauchnitz, 1879; reprint Graz: Akademische Druck- und Verlagsanstalt, 1959), 1:146b. On the history of this text: Tierney, *Foundations of the Conciliar Theory*, 57–67.

62. "Quaestio de reprehensione Petri apostoli a Paulo," MS Paris, Bibliothèque Nationale, 3122, ff. 64–66; cf. the excerpts in P. Tschackert, *Peter von Ailli (Petrus de Alliaco): Zur Geschichte des grossen abendländischen Schismas und der Reformconcilien von Pisa und Constanz* (Gotha: Perthes, 1877; reprint Amsterdam: Rodopi, 1968), Appendix, [28]-[29].

63. Gelnhausen, Epistola Concordiae, ed. Bliemetzrieder, 139; Langenstein, Epistola Concilii Pacis c. 15, trans. Cameron, 127.

64. Y. Congar, "Konzil als Versammlung und grundsätzliche Konziliarität der Kirche," in H. Vorgrimler, ed., *Gott in Welt: Festgabe für Karl Rahner* (Freiburg: Herder, 1964), 2:135–65. The article features a "collection of texts which have reference to Mt 18:20," illustrating the history of interpretation: 157–65.

65. "ubi tres, id est pater et filius et spiritus sanctus, ibi ecclesia quae trium corpus est," Tertullian, De baptismo 6:2, ed. Borleffs (*Corpus Christianorum*, 1; Turnhout: Brepols, 1954), 282, in an interpretation of 1 Jn 5:7f.

66. "Hujus viae nobis formam Christus, qui est pax nostra faciens utraque unum [Eph 2:14] nos docuit: Ubi inquit duo, unus scilicet ex una parte, et alius ex altera, vel tres, in casu scilicet discordiae, in nomine meo congregati, in nomine videlicet charitatis, concordiae, et pacis, illic ego in medio illorum sum, ad concordiam revocans altercantes fratres et inter se dissidentes in pace reconcilians": Epistle of the University of Paris (1394), in d'Achéry, *Spicilegium* I, col. 778a.

67. Epistola Concilii Pacis c. 15, trans. Cameron, 127.

68. Ibid., 128.

69. Johannes de Breviscoxa, Tractatus de Fide, Ecclesia, Romano Pontifice, et Concilio Generali, in Du Pin, ed., *Joannis Gersonii . . . opera omnia*, 1:899AB.

70. "Tamen secundum aliquos, hoc est speciale privilegium Universalis Ecclesiae quod non potest errare in fide, licet hoc idem pie credatur de concilio generali, videlicet quando innititur divinae scripturae, vel auctoritati, quae a Spiritu Sancto inspirata est. Alias saepe errasse legitur." This is a marginal note in one of the manuscripts at the end of the text from the Tractatus de materia cited in note 58 above: Oakley, *The Political Thought of Pierre d'Ailly*, 307, note 9.

71. Heimpel, ed., *Dietrich von Nieheim*, 116. On the necessary tie between the double keys of *"potentia"* and *"scientia"* (cf. Lk 11:52) or *"discretio"* in scholastic theology, see L. Hödl, *Die Geschichte der scholastischen Literatur und der Theologie der Schlüsselgewalt, 1. Teil* (Beiträge zur Geschichte der Philosophie und Theologie des Mittelalters, Texte und Untersuchungen, vol. 38:4; Münster: Aschendorff, 1960), 40–45.

72. Tractatus de Fide, in Du Pin, ed., *Joannis Gersonii . . . opera omnia*, 1:840AB.

73. Gelnhausen, Epistola Brevis (1379), ed. Kaiser (above note 38), 383 and 386; Epistola Concordiae (May 1380), ed. Bliemetzrieder, 137 f. These references were probably preceded by those in Langenstein's early "Epistola Pacis" of 1379: Kreuzer, *Heinrich von Langenstein*, 236. Thereafter: Langenstein's Epistola Concilii Pacis (1381) c. 15, trans. Cameron, 130 f. On the history of the concept, see F. D'Agostino, *La tradizione dell'epieikeia nel Medioevo latino un contributo alla storia dell'idea di equità* (Pubblicazioni dell'Istituto di filosofia del diritto dell'Università di Roma, ser. 3, 15; Milan: Giuffrè, 1976).

74. "Unde qui oppositum tenent, litterali sensui Juris positivi Judaico more nimis tenaciter adhaerent, contra quos ait Apostolus: 'Littera occidit, spiritus, id est spiritualis sensus, vivificat,'" sermon "Erunt signa in sole," in Du Pin, ed., *Joannis Gersonii . . . opera omnia*, 921D.

75. Langenstein, Epistola Concilii Pacis c. 15, trans. Cameron, 131.

76. Tractatus de unitate ecclesiae, in Glorieux, ed., *Jean Gerson: Oeuvres complètes*, vol. VI: *L'oeuvre ecclésiologique*, 138. On Gerson's theological use of *epikeia*, see the section on "The Concept of Epikie" in G. H. M. Posthumus Meyjes, *Jean Gerson, Apostle of Unity: His Church Politics and Ecclesiology* (Leiden: Brill, 1999), 242–46.

2

"Tongues of Fire Confounded"

Greeks and Latins at the Council of Florence (1438–1439)

NICHOLAS CONSTAS

As they moved from the East . . . they said, "Come, let us build to ourselves a city and a tower, whose top shall be to heaven" . . . but the Lord said "Let us confound their tongue, that they may not understand each the voice of his neighbor." And the Lord scattered them thence over the face of all the earth, and they left off building the city and the tower. On this account its name was called "Confusion," because there the Lord confounded the languages. (Gen. 10:2–9)

When the day of Pentecost had come, they were all together in one place. And suddenly a sound came from heaven like the rush of a mighty wind, and it filled all the house where they were sitting. And there appeared to them tongues as of fire, distributed and resting on each one of them. And they were all filled with the Holy Spirit and began to speak in other tongues, as the Spirit gave them utterance. (Acts 2:1–4)

When He descended and confounded the tongues, the Most High divided the nations (cf. Gen. 10:2−9); and when he divided the tongues of fire, He called all to unity (cf. Acts 2:1−4), and with one voice we glorify the Holy Spirit. (*Kontakion* from the Orthodox liturgy of Pentecost)

Introduction

The attempted unification of the Orthodox and Catholic churches at the Council of Ferrara-Florence in the mid-fifteenth century is perhaps one of the most fascinating chapters in the history of Christianity. One historian has called it "the greatest confrontation, ecclesiastically and intellectually speaking, between the medieval Byzantine and Latin worlds."[1] The dramatic encounter of East and West, when the twain met and mingled intimately, has been romanticized in the frescoes of the Florentine Chapel of the Magi, where the Orthodox delegates are depicted as exotically appareled wise men bearing costly gifts from the East. The splendid figures in Gozzoli's frescoes, however, are in marked contrast to the glass beads and moth-eaten grandeur of the Greeks themselves, whose penury was rendered particularly poignant during the patriarch's visit to Venice in order to inspect *spolia* taken from Hagia Sophia during the Fourth Crusade (1204).[2] These two moments exemplify the emerging western construction of "Byzantium," a dubious cultural project which took place at the expense of the so-called "Byzantines," who were reified beyond recognition in the religious art of the Italian Renaissance but whose own religious treasures had become the prized possessions of ascendant European powers.[3]

In retrospect, the gaps in painterly representation, along with those in the niches of Hagia Sophia, describe a series of vanishing points for the broken circuit of signs which distorted and foreshortened the work of the council. Greeks and Latins, like two mirrors reflecting each other's absence, were unable to communicate meaningfully, and the narrative of their prolonged interaction at the Council of Florence unfolds like the plot of a tragic play in which ill-fated actors suffer repeated failures of recognition and understanding. The confusion of tongues and the divergent habits of thought to which it gave utterance, the elisions and interpolations of translators and scribes, together with the pressure and confusion of convulsive political circumstances, ensured that the great encounter of East and West was ultimately a great failure. In terms of the theological dialogue, conflicting methodologies and narrow fixation on the microscopic particles of doctrinal statements prevented both parties from attending to larger contexts of meaning and interpretation. Arguments, for example, about how sins could be forgiven and salvation attained made little progress largely because neither side seemed to have realized that they did not agree on what sin and salvation were. The contested legacy of the Council of Florence has remained a critical point of reference for virtually all subsequent interactions between the Orthodox and Catholic churches, and may additionally serve to illuminate wider patterns in the cultural politics of religious dialogue.

The following historical and interpretive essay studies the encounter of Greeks and Latins at the Council of Florence both as a critical moment in the history of theology and the church, and as a larger social, cultural, and political phenomenon. The first part provides a brief historical narrative of the council, focusing on key themes, events, and personalities, along with a synopsis of the debates over matters of doctrine and belief. The second part offers a series of reflections on these themes and probes the various crosscurrents which frustrated the council's project. When and to the extent that it seems relevant to the data supplied by the sources, my analysis draws freely on anthropology and social history. I argue that the Council of Florence was a complex human transaction in which a range of cultural, political, and religious factors were misunderstood in a clash of largely incommensurable paradigms and values. The differentials of power; the intricate and seemingly inscrutable confusions of a divided Christian tradition; unavoidable lapses and irrepressible excesses of meaning; along with the contingent, the unforeseen, and the absurd, effectively obviated the council's attempt to overcome the multiple tongues of Christendom with the univocal fire of a Pentecost regained.

The Council of Florence

The Council of Florence was the culmination of more than four hundred years of effort aimed at reunifying the Greek and Latin churches, and proved by far to be more ambitious and grandly conceived than all such previous attempts.[4] This is especially true with respect to the council's extended duration and extraordinary number of Orthodox delegates. The Council of Lyons, by contrast, met for a mere two months (7 May–17 July 1274), and was attended by only three representatives of Emperor Michael VIII (1259–1282), who operated in utter disregard for the Orthodox Church, which subsequently repudiated the proceedings.[5] The Council of Florence, on the other hand, was attended by nearly seven hundred Byzantine ecclesiastical and secular elites with the emperor and patriarch at their head, a delegation which, from the spring of 1438 through the summer of 1439, dealt more or less exhaustively with matters of faith and doctrine.

Preparations for the council began in 1422 when envoys of Pope Martin V were sent to Constantinople in order to present the patriarch and his synod with a series of proposals for a union of the churches.[6] After some deliberation, plans were established for a general council, which was announced in 1430. At the same time, the emperor and the patriarch were receiving attractive counterproposals from the Council of Basel (1431–1439). The rival papal and conciliarist representatives competed aggressively for the favor of the Greeks, and, on one occasion, the supporters of the pope had to be restrained from launching a naval attack against the conciliarists moored in the harbor of Constantinople. In the end, the Greeks rejected the notion of a western council devoid of the pope's presence and its implicit denial of the principle of the pentarchy (i.e., the recognition of the pope as the patriarch of the West, in communion with the eastern patriarchs of Constantinople, Alexandria, Antioch, and Jerusalem).[7]

By 1436, Martin V had been succeeded by Eugenius IV, and the two churches agreed to gather in a general council to be held at Ferrara, Italy. However, the majority of the eastern patriarchs were living under Islamic rule far beyond the truncated borders of the late Byzantine Empire, and, being unable to travel, appointed various individuals to serve as their representatives. It was in this manner that Mark Eugenikos,[8] an educated layman who had recently become a monk, was ordained to the see of Ephesus, along with the humanist scholar (and later Catholic convert) Bessarion, who was elevated to the see of Nicaea. Both of these men assumed positions of leadership among the Orthodox delegates.[9] Eugenikos and Gennadios Scholarios (who later became the first patriarch of Constantinople under Turkish rule) had been further commissioned to collect manuscripts and other documents in preparation for the council,[10] partly in collaboration with the papal envoy Nicholas of Cusa.[11]

After a difficult two-month voyage across winter seas, followed by an overland trip from Venice to Ferrara, the council began in the spring of 1438. Preparatory conversations of an informal nature took place first, with Bessarion and Eugenikos speaking on behalf of the Orthodox Church. The first round dealt with the Latin doctrine of purgatory, about which Bessarion and Eugenikos differed and openly disagreed with each other. Bessarion dis-

missed the question as trivial, and the differences with the Latins as super-
ficial. Eugenikos, on the other hand, believed that the doctrine of purgatory
brought to light fundamental differences between the two churches. He argued that the punitive aspects of purgation compromised the gift of divine
forgiveness and devalued the body by implicitly reducing personhood to the
incorporeal soul (i.e., the object of punishment). Moreover, the notion that
the purgative fires of the afterlife would one day cease appeared to be nothing more than a vulgarized form of Origenism.[12] No agreement was reached,
and the proceedings were brought to an abrupt end (17 July) by an outbreak
of the plague, attacks on Ferrara by Milanese mercenaries, and by the un-
settling rumor that the Turks were about to launch a major offensive against
Constantinople.[13]

Discussions resumed some months later (6 October), this time focusing
on the addition of the *Filioque* (i.e., the doctrine that the Holy Spirit proceeds
from the Father and the Son) to the text of the Nicene-Constantinopolitan
Creed. Eugenikos stressed the illicit nature of the addition, arguing that
the unilateral insertion of the disputed clause into the text of the creed violated the tradition and canonical procedure of the ancient church.[14] At the
second session (13 October), Eugenikos, in keeping with eastern conciliar
protocol, insisted that the definitions (ὅροι) of the previous ecumenical
councils be read out publicly.[15] Despite Latin protests, they were read at
the third session (16 October), each one framed by Eugenikos's incessant
and pointed editorializing. At the reading of the definition of the Third
Council (Ephesus, 431), Eugenikos seized upon the so-called "Ephesine
decree," an ancient caveat prohibiting change or addition of any kind to the
creed, which became the centerpiece in his argument against the "legality"
of the *Filioque*.[16] At the reading of the definition of the Seventh Council
(Nicaea, 787), a Latin translation of the *acta* was brought forward with a
version of the creed containing the *Filioque*. The Greeks denied its authenticity, and codicological inquiries demonstrated that the Latin *acta*
had indeed been falsified.[17] Discussions on the legality of the addition continued until 14 December.

Owing to the reduced fortunes of papal finances, the fear of the plague's
return in the spring, and alarming reports of nearby political instability,
the council was relocated to Florence, where it reconvened in full session on
2 March 1439. Discussion now focused on the *Filioque* as a theological category and was sustained through several sessions. At the outset, however, the
delegates became embroiled in heated debates about the wording and interpretation of patristic texts, a question which occupied them for the first five

sessions (2, 5, 7, 10, and 14 March). Much of the discussion opened up around the writings of Basil of Caesarea (ca. 329–379) on the Holy Spirit. Contemporary with the Second Ecumenical Council (Constantinople, 381), where the creed was formalized, and produced at a time concurrent with the church's proclamation of the full divinity of the Holy Spirit, Basil's pneumatology became the focus of critical scrutiny and strong disagreement. Once again, the Latins produced manuscripts that had been poorly copied or, in one remarkable instance, directly contaminated. In a protracted discussion on a passage from Basil's *Against Eunomius* (III.1), the Latins championed a variant reading which the Greeks dismissed as a textual corruption and plainly heretical. Until recently, the Greek arguments on this point had been generally dismissed as wishful thinking. However, a study published in 1967 by Michel Van Parys has shown that the disputed passage is in fact derived from the writings of Eunomius and embodies the Arian principle that the Holy Spirit was *created* by the Son.[18]

At the sixth session (17 March), Eugenikos stated his case, discoursing at great length on the pneumatology of the Orthodox Church. Drawing on traditional patristic sources,[19] he deemed the procession of the Spirit "from the Son" to be heretical because it introduced two "causes" (αἰτίαι) and two "principles of origin" (ἀρχαί) into the nature of the Trinity, giving the Spirit a double origin both "from [ἐκ] the Father" and "from [ἐκ] the Son." Eugenikos argued that the *Filioque* confused the "mode of existence" (τρόπος ὑπάρξεως) and "personal attributes" (ἰδίωμα, ἰδιότης) of the Son with those of the Father, thereby compromising the personhood (or hypostasis) of the Father, who was no longer the sole source (μόνη πηγή) and cause of the other two persons. To the Latin suggestion that the preposition "from" (ἐκ) was interchangeable with "through" (διά), Eugenikos said that such an exchange of functions occurs in the temporal economy of creation but not within the eternal being of God, where it would reduce the Spirit to a creature.[20]

After much debate, promises of military aid from the pope, threats from the emperor, and the concoction of a somewhat specious Greco-Latin *consensus patrum*, the "Decree of Union" was signed on 6 July 1439.[21] In the end, the decree conceded nothing to the exotically appareled "wise men from the East," whose theological treasures, like the *spolia* embedded in the facade of San Marco in Venice, had become mere ornamental epithets within the imposing edifice of Latin doctrine.[22] The union was sealed with the celebration of the Latin Mass, at which the Greeks were present and vested, but in which they took no significant part. During the Mass, the union of the churches was proclaimed in both Latin and Greek, without, however, the mutual exchange of the liturgical embrace and greeting of peace. On the following day, the emperor invited the pope to participate in a celebration of the Divine Liturgy of Saint John Chrysostom. However, the cardinals averred that they were unfamiliar with the service, and requested that it first be performed in private so that it might be screened for approval, a response which caused the indignant emperor to withdraw the invitation.[23]

Eugenikos, who had absented himself from the final sessions of the council (21, 24 March), famously refused to sign his name to the Decree of Union.[24] Upon his return to Constantinople (February 1440), he was hailed by the populace as the pillar and champion of Orthodoxy,[25] the stage having been well set by his brother John, an official of the patriarchate who returned from Florence six months earlier and began agitating against the council. Yielding to the pressure of popular opinion, the other bishops quickly renounced the Decree of Union, some declaring that they had subscribed to it under duress, others confessing that they had done so for profit, having treacherously "sold the faith."[26] Upon returning to the palace, the emperor was informed that both his wife and daughter had died while he was in Italy, and, in the throes of mourning, he did nothing to implement the unionist agenda. The clergy of the capital, however, quickly divided into partisans and adversaries of the council, and each side refrained from concelebrating with the other, refusing even to set foot in each other's churches.[27] Their differences were resolved by the cannon fire of Mehmet II, whose troops took the city in the spring of 1453. After a period of adjustment to the new Islamic regime, the Greek Orthodox Church officially rescinded the Union of Florence in 1472.

If the Council of Florence was a failure, it was one of spectacular and far-reaching proportions. By dashing the hopes of both western and eastern conciliarists against the rock of papal primacy, the council, in the words of Joseph Gill, "made the Reformation inevitable."[28] Moreover, having failed to mend the schism between East and West, the council succeeded in introducing divisions not only within the fifteenth-century church of Constantinople, but also within the extended family of Orthodox churches. Moscow, for example, lost no time in denouncing the Greeks as "Latin-minded" apostates, and promptly exalted itself to the rank of "Third (and final) Rome," declaring its *de facto* autocephaly from Constantinople in 1448. For Georges Florovsky, the Muscovite rejection of Constantinople marked the beginning of a perpetual "crisis of Russian Byzantinism," a reaction which led to the demise of Russian theology as it distanced itself from its Greco-Byzantine

point of origin.[29] Even when making allowances for the tendentious character of Florovsky's reconstruction of Russian religious history, it is nevertheless
true that relations between the churches of Constantinople and Moscow are
to this day determined in no small measure by their respective postures vis-à-
vis the Roman Catholic Church (and toward the West in general) which resulted from the Council of Florence.[30]

Reflections on the Council of Florence

The encounter of Greeks and Latins at the Council of Florence was certainly a complex human transaction, a focused and frequently charged meeting of languages, cultures, and traditions of faith in which there were many
misperceptions and conflicts of value. Such negotiations are, of course, always fragile and precarious, even when dialogue takes place on balanced and
equal terms. But this was hardly the case at Florence, where the encounter
of the two parties was greatly impeded by the disproportion of power and
the asymmetry of place.

At the very moment when western Europe was embarking upon its cultural, political, and technological ascendancy, the beleaguered Byzantine
Empire was hurtling toward its violent denouement. In desperate circumstances since the thirteenth century, the Greek world never fully recovered
from the devastating blow inflicted upon it by the forces of western imperialism during the Fourth Crusade. During the ensuing western occupation of
Constantinople (1204–1261) and much of the Levant, the Orthodox Church
was aggressively subjugated to the Latin, an event which the Greeks experienced not only as a disavowal of their religious tradition, but as a threat to
their emerging national and cultural identity. Josef Macha has argued that
the "fear of the loss of their cultural identity made the Greek people violently
react to anything Latin." And that fear, Macha stresses, was "not unfounded."
Plans for the "Latinization" of the East called for the "dispersal of Greek
monks across the West, the forced education of Latin on one child in every
Greek household, and the education of Greek girls in Catholic convents."[31]
Recaptured by Michael VIII in 1261, the "restored empire" (limited to the
western coast of Asia Minor, northern Greece, and the southeastern Pelo-
ponnesos) was little more than a vassal to the surrounding Turkish emirates
and Latin principalities. A mere three years before the Council of Florence,
Constantinople was devastated by the plague, and on its Asiatic and European frontiers was under periodic siege by Turkish armies, against which it

would survive for only another fifteen years. The Greek delegation which made its way to Florence has thus been rather aptly, if somewhat romantically, described as "an embattled remnant of desperate men coming from a surrounded and dying city."[32]

Maculate Perceptions

In addition to the inequality of power, divergent and at times conflicting cultural and religious presuppositions created obstacles to the achievement of mutual recognition and acceptance. In considering this question, it will be instructive to examine a number of episodes that one of the Greek delegates, the patriarchal deacon Sylvester Syropoulos, deemed worthy of inclusion in his detailed written account of the council.[33] Upon his arrival in Venice at the height of Carnival, for instance, we are told that the Greek patriarch was greeted by the doge, who provided him with a lavish feast of "capons, partridges, hares, veal, and fish." However, Greek Lent had already begun, leaving the patriarch in a rather compromised position.[34] At the service of vespers, the Greek clerics, contrary to their liturgical practices, were made to remove their monastic hats, while at a later point the Greek deacons, who were candidates for rapid ordination to the episcopacy, were ushered to the back of the nave, contrary to the position they enjoyed in their own churches. Indeed, seating arrangements proved to be an especially sensitive and vexing matter.[35] Still worse were the plans for the papal reception of the patriarch upon the latter's arrival in Venice. For his part, the patriarch had anticipated a traditional liturgical embrace exchanged by prelates of equal rank, but was told that he was expected instead to prostrate himself before the pontiff and kiss his foot. The patriarch took great offense at this unprecedented and demeaning request and, with the support of the emperor, threatened to set sail immediately for Constantinople. The reception was called off, and a second, more informal meeting was arranged.[36]

The estrangement of the Greek East and the Latin West, to which these episodes (and many like them) bear witness, was expressed with particular finality by one of the Greek delegates, Gregory Melissenos, who would later become patriarch of Constantinople. Here is the text:

> When I enter a Latin church, I venerate none of the [images of] saints depicted there because I recognize none of them. Although I do recognize [the image of] Christ, I do not venerate him either because I do not know in what terms he is inscribed (ἐπιγράφεται).

Instead, I make the sign of the cross and prostrate myself, not to anything that I see in their churches, but only to the cross that I have made myself.[37]

These intriguing remarks critically assess Italian religious painting in terms of both its form and content. With respect to the latter, the Orthodox critic is unable to recognize the sacred figures (presumably western saints unknown in the East), and he therefore withholds his veneration, incapable of interacting with images that effectively elude or resist his gaze. In terms of form, the practice of depicting saints without their names or identifying inscriptions prevents the beholder from venerating even those figures whom he recognizes, including Christ himself, inasmuch as the name was seen as an irreducible aspect of the icon's ability to communicate the personal presence of the sacred figure.[38] Together, the unity (or absence) of form and content presents the eastern aesthete with the discomfiture of an impenetrable double barrier. Moreover, these reactionary perceptions additionally attest to the subject's reflexive production of sacred space. If the gaze corresponds to desire for self-completion through another, here it is decisively thwarted and thrown back upon itself. The aesthetic response consequently shifts from vision to gesture ("Instead, I make the sign of the cross"), as the relatively open and outward orientation of the gaze is contracted into the clenching of a fist. The act of repulsion constructs a *cordon sanitaire* coterminous with the limits of the body now contained within a locus described by the arc of a ritual gesture, the sign of the cross. Within such a limited set of possibilities, the subject ends by becoming the object ("I . . . prostrate myself, not to anything that I see in their churches, but only to the cross that I have made myself").

As Hans Belting has argued, concern for the "correct" and "incorrect" presentation of religious images corresponds closely with concern for precision in doctrine. Belting suggests that the central reservation has to do with notions of purity, in this case associated with the fear of contamination through the images of a religious sect other than one's own. As we shall see, the problems detailed by Melissenos's complaint are virtually identical with those encountered in the theological exchanges at the council, which were similarly thwarted by differences of form (i.e., theological method) and content (i.e., doctrine). In both cases, the symbolic representations of the respective parties proved to be mutually unrecognizable (if not completely invisible), and whereas the shared source of those representations (i.e., the common figure of Christ) could be clearly discerned, it nevertheless remained unavailable to religious experience. It is worth noting, finally, that in 1054, when Cardinal Humbert pronounced the Greeks to be in a state of schism with Rome, he sealed his anathematism by objecting to Byzantine icons of the crucifixion. "How can you nail the image of a dying man to the cross of Christ," the papal legate asked, "in such a way that any anti-Christ may take the place of Jesus on the cross, and seek to be worshipped, as though he were God?"[39]

It might be tempting to dismiss these various anecdotes as the insignificant marginalia in an already crowded and confused historical palimpsest, but the true spirit of an age, or even a moment, is often most tellingly captured through its banalities and absurdities. During their prolonged sojourn in the centers of the early Italian Renaissance, the Greeks found themselves in unfamiliar surroundings, and they became increasingly sensitive to those breaches of protocol and hospitality which seemed to efface their cultural identity and imperial status. Over time, the cumulative effect of these various estrangements and humiliations drained them of that by which they were recognizable and identified both to themselves and to the world around them. Seeing and being seen, recognizing and being recognized, are activities that are essential for mutuality, dialogue, and the restoration of order—a form of communion, and even redemption, one might say, through intersubjective knowledge and understanding.

Because the Council of Florence has been studied almost exclusively from the perspectives of theology and ecclesiastical history, I would like to conclude this section by turning toward a different method of approach. With no great leap of the historical imagination, one may readily observe a number of suggestive parallels between the interaction of East and West at the Council of Florence and that which obtained between western voyagers and native populations during the colonialist expansion of Europe. One thinks especially of the work of Gananath Obeyesekere, who challengingly revisits the voyages of Captain Cook (d. 1779), an English explorer who reached Hawaii during the festival of Makahiki and was mistaken for the returning god Lono. Even though Obeyesekere rejects the traditional (i.e., European) interpretation of that event, he nevertheless underscores the extent to which Cook's encounter with the Hawaiians was marked by a series of mutual and ultimately tragic misrecognitions. As was the case in Florence, the barriers of language and culture effectively nullified attempts at meaningful communication, and even the most basic signs and gestures were at critical moments understood in terms contrary to their intention.[40]

During the two hundred years following the Council of Florence, western Europe would be increasingly drawn out of itself, coming into contact with new cultures and religions.[41] There was consequently tremendous excitement (over the discovery, for instance, of an Aztec neo-paradise and its frenzied spoliation), but also tremendous incomprehension and confusion in the face of such radical otherness. Similar incomprehension prevailed with respect to the Christian East, at least until the great Orientalist recoveries of the eighteenth and nineteenth centuries. However, one suspects that western Christians continue to have difficulties believing that for more than a millennium the Roman Empire had its capital in Istanbul; or that the Greco-Roman Christian culture of late antiquity survived through the fifteenth century and indeed to this very day; or that a figure such as Haile Selassie could be anything more than a pitiful curiosity and not himself a rightful descendent of the myth of Rome (and Jerusalem as well). Thus it may not be far off the mark to suggest that the "age of exploration," or at least a kind of drawing-room dress rehearsal of it, began with the massive and sustained "voyage of discovery" of the East by the West at the Council of Florence, or even perhaps with the Latin colonialist occupation of Constantinople in 1204.

Theology East and West

By the fifteenth century, the Christian traditions of East and West had developed rather different and somewhat exclusive models of theology. It would indeed be difficult to compare meaningfully the scholastic theology of the High Middle Ages with the patristic and Hesychastic paradigm operating contemporaneously in the East. Like the differing architectural systems to which they have often been compared, the theologies and theological methods of East and West bodied forth alternative visions of the world.[42] At the council, a rather naïve attempt was made to transliterate the language of the patristic period into the categories and concepts of scholastic theology. In the ensuing alchemy of language, the base metal of the early church fathers was heated and transformed, although not into anything resembling the substance of theological gold. Similarly, the Jesuits in China transposed Confucianist beliefs into scholastic categories with equally questionable results.[43] At the Council of Florence, such linguistic and conceptual sleights of hand encouraged the Greeks to conclude that the Latin doctrine of purgatory was merely warmed-over Origenism, and the double procession of the Spirit flagrant Arianism. These permutations aside, the Greeks in general had no taste for what they saw as rationalistic and sophistical methods of argumentation, and found the western fixation on Aristotle to be rather ludicrous.[44] On the other hand, Byzantine intellectual polyphony, with its paradoxical chorus of radical antinomies, was equally bewildering to the Latins, who had no idea what all the shouting was about. When asked, for example, about the fate of the soul after death, the Orthodox maintained that "souls *both do and do not* attain the bliss of paradise." To the frustrated Latins, however, this was but surplus evidence of the notorious *inscientia Graecorum*.[45]

As one might expect, the massive social, economic, and political crises of the late Byzantine world had taken their toll on education and culture, and many Greek intellectuals had long since fled to the relative safety of western Europe. As a result, the Orthodox Church had almost no competent theologians among its bishops, most of whom remained inarticulate throughout the duration of the council. Those who did find the courage to speak were understandably on the defensive.[46]

One wonders, too, if the very activity of theological dialogue did not itself unwittingly serve to deepen the breach between the two churches. If theological dialogue is defined as a situation in which everyone wants to and is able to talk, and where all the voices are rational and coherent, the Council of Florence exposes the blind spots in such a vision. As the record of the council demonstrates, the dream of a reasoned and dispassionate consensus-building conversation becomes problematic when it fails to attend to differentials of power and the historical realities of oppression, marginalization, and violence. Eugenikos, however, seems to have been acutely aware of these imbalances, and brazenly declared that the Latins were not only schismatics but heretics, although the Orthodox Church dared not call them such due to the superior economic and military power of the Latin West.[47]

In retrospect, the Orthodox-Catholic dialogue at Florence can be seen as a process not of mutual understanding and convergence but of intensified separation and alienation. The prolonged encounter made both parties vividly conscious of their differences, and resulted in the systematic mapping of their mutually alien coastlines, whereby the treacherous rocks of disagreement were reified and made to stand out in exaggerated relief. The Florentine theological cartography, with its sharply drawn lines and static magnitudes, has continued to define the theological boundaries between the Orthodox and Catholic churches to this very day, and always with the same results.[48] At the council, divergent theological paradigms hardened into confessional and, to a certain extent, nationalistic identities, especially for the Christians of the East, who came more and more to see themselves as "Greeks" and fundamentally different from their Christian counterparts in the West.[49] And if the majority of Greek delegates at the Council of Florence, far from home for a prolonged period of time, were able to undergo a change of attitude and subscribe to the Decree of Union, the effect was only temporary, and did not survive their return to their native culture and environment.

Perhaps most striking of all is the fact that the Florentine delegates took absolutely no account of the fourteenth-century Hesychastic (or "Palamite") controversy, which had significantly influenced the shape of Orthodox Trinitarian theology. Hesychasm was a major religious movement which arose in the thirteenth century, reached its peak in the fourteenth, and thereafter remained a powerful force throughout the Orthodox world. For its principal architect, Gregory Palamas (d. 1357), the nature of the Holy Spirit's procession "through" the Son—a question which had so vexed the council—was understood as pertaining to the relationship of the Son and the Spirit on the level of the uncreated divine energies, and not in terms of ontological derivation or hypostatic origin from the divine essence.[50] Rooted in the theology of the early church fathers, Palamas's notion of uncreated energies as a reality within the divinity distinct from the divine essence was canonized by the Orthodox Church at a series of councils held in the mid-fourteenth century. In addition to its impact on soteriology and the theology of the Trinity, the victory of Palamas over his western-oriented, scholastic opponents signaled the definitive triumph of (largely monastic) religious experience over Aristotelian philosophy in the theory and practice of theology.

Despite the obvious importance of these developments for the debates at Florence, the Greek delegates were not permitted to make mention of them. In the midst of a pointed exchange with Mark Eugenikos (14 March), John of Montenero breathtakingly declared that "the Holy Spirit is the creator, but the energies of the Holy Spirit are created things." To the Orthodox, such a remark was blatantly heretical. However, the emperor had ordered the Greek delegates to avoid any mention of the distinction of essence and energies, and in response to Montenero's assertion, Eugenikos "said nothing, and was silent for a long time." Montenero continued to push his line of argument, at which point the emperor intervened and ordered the conversation to cease.[51] What had become central to the theological conscience of the Orthodox Church was the very thing which could not be uttered at Florence.

At the signing of the Decree of Union, the Greeks chanted a hymn celebrating the unity of the church under the grace of the Holy Spirit. The hymn in many ways epitomizes the dubious work of the council, and raises some critical questions.[52] Was the Council of Florence an attempt to overcome the confusion of Babel by seeking to regain the lost unity of Pentecost? Did it seek to impose a single theological language on the Christian world? Was it an attempt to build the city of God on earth? A "city with a tower whose top shall be to heaven"? If it was the latter, the tongues of fire were quickly confounded and the entire project quenched, "for desiring to build a tower, they did not sit down and count the cost" (Lk. 14:28).

Beginning in the thirteenth century, and increasingly in the fourteenth and fifteenth centuries, a select number of Augustine's works were translated into Greek and circulated among Orthodox thinkers. It is to be regretted that the *City of God,* perhaps owing to its length, was not among them, for there Greeks and Latins could both have learned that:

> After the city comes the world . . . which, being like a confluence of waters, is more full of danger by reason of its greater size. To begin with, on this level the diversity of human languages separates man from man. For if two men meet, and are forced by some compelling reason not to pass on but to stay in company, and if neither knows the other's language, then it is easier for dumb animals, even of different kinds, to associate together than these men, although both are human beings. For when men cannot communicate their thoughts to each other, simply because of difference of language, all the similarity of their common human nature is of no avail to unite them in fellowship. So true is this that a man would be more cheerful with his dog for company than with a foreigner. I shall be told that the Imperial City has been at pains to impose on conquered peoples not only her yoke but her language also . . . but think of the cost of this achievement! Consider the scale of those wars, with all the slaughter of human beings, and all the human blood that was shed![53]

As a postscript, I conclude with an excerpt from an article which appeared in the *Ecumenical International Daily News Service* (28 July 2000):

> High-level talks between the Roman Catholic and Orthodox Churches which ended in the United States last week were marred by "methodological deficiencies" and a "polemical atmosphere," leaving the relations between the two communities at a dead-end, according to an expert on ecumenism who took part. Professor Waclaw Hryniewicz, a Catholic theologian and director of the Ecumenical Institute at Poland's Catholic University of Lublin, said that the leaders of Catholic and Orthodox churches now appeared "unwilling or hesitant" to recognize their churches as "sister churches."[54]

NOTES

1. Deno Geanakoplos, *Interaction of the "Sibling" Byzantine and Western Cultures in the Middle Ages and Italian Renaissance* (New Haven: Yale University Press, 1976), 213. The same author has elsewhere described the Council of Florence as "the most brilliant convocation of Greeks and Latins in the entire Middle Ages," *Byzantine East and Latin West* (Oxford: Basil Blackwell, 1966), 84; cf. John Meyendorff, "Was There an Encounter Between East and West at Florence?" in *Christian Unity: The Council of Ferrara-Florence,* ed. Giuseppe Albergio (Leuven: Leuven University Press, 1991), 152, who states that "doubtlessly, the council of Ferrara-Florence was the most significant attempt, made in the late Middle Ages, to reverse the course of history and to restore a unity of faith and communion."

2. On the frescoes, see Christina Luchinat, *The Chapel of the Magi: Benozzo Gozzoli's Frescoes in the Palazzo Medici-Riccardi Florence* (London: Thames and Hudson, 1994); cf. Anthony Cutler, "The Pathos of Distance: Byzantium in the Gaze of Renaissance Europe and Modern Scholarship," in *Reframing the Renaissance: Visual Culture in Europe and Latin America 1450–1650,* ed. Claire Farago (New Haven: Yale University Press, 1995), 23–45; for an opposing view, see Lisa Jardine and Jerry Brotton, *Global Interests: Renaissance Art between East and West* (Ithaca: Cornell University Press, 2001). On the tour of the treasury of San Marco, Venice, see Vitalien Laurent, *Les "Mémoires" de Grand Ecclésiarque de l'Église de Constantinople, Sylvestre Syropoulos sur le concile de Florence,* CFDS, Series B, vol. IX (Rome, 1971), IV, 25, pp. 222–24; cf. Appendix IV, no. 25, p. 628, lins. 16–36. (Hereafter: Syropoulos, *Mémoires.*) For a study of Venetian imperialism within the late Byzantine Empire, see Donald M. Nicol, *Byzantium and Venice: A Study in Diplomatic and Cultural Relations* (Cambridge: Cambridge University Press, 1988), 283–422.

3. Note that the "Byzantines" never called themselves by that name, which was coined by western scholars in the sixteenth century. Neither did they use the word "Byzantine" to describe their empire, church, or theology. Instead, they understood their government to be a continuation of the Roman Empire, and their church to be the "one holy, catholic, and apostolic church."

4. Which were thirty in number, as calculated by Louis Bréhier, "Attempts at Reunion of the Greek and Latin Churches," *Cambridge Medieval History* IV (1936): 594, cited in Geanakoplos, *Byzantine East and Latin West,* 84, n. 2.

5. The "Union" of Lyons, along with the *Filioque,* was officially condemned by the Orthodox Church at the Council of Blachernae in 1285, on which see Aristeides Papadakis, *Crisis in Byzantium: The* Filioque *Controversy in the Patriarchate of Gregory II of Cyprus (1283–1289)* (Crestwood, N.Y.: St. Vladimir's Seminary Press, 1996). Papadakis provides an English translation of the council's *Tome* (212–26), which he characterizes as "possibly the single most important conciliar decision of the entire thirteenth century."

6. Vitalien Laurent, "Les préliminaires du concile de Florence: les neuf articles du pape Martin V et la réponse inédite du patriarche de Constantinople Joseph II," *Revue des études byzantines* 20 (1962): 5–60; see also Joseph Gill, *The Council of Florence* (Cambridge: Cambridge University Press, 1959), 16–45.

7. On the rival delegations, see Syropoulos, *Mémoires* III, 15, pp. 176–78; on the decision of the Greeks, see ibid., III, 11–20, pp. 172–82; and Gill, *Council of Florence*, 46–84, who is particularly helpful in setting the council within the context of western church history and politics; cf. Joachim W. Stieber, *Pope Eugenius IV, the Council of Basel, and the Secular and Ecclesiastical Authorities in the Empire* (Leiden: Brill, 1978), esp. 35–44; Johannes Helmrath, *Das Basler Konzil 1431–1439* (Cologne: Bohlau, 1987); and Damaskinos Papandreou, *Die Konzilien von Basel und Ferrara-Florenz* (Basel: Helbing & Lichtenhan, 1992). Geanakoplos, *Byzantine East and Latin West*, 95–96, adduces the following additional factors: both the emperor and the patriarch had insisted on the presence of the pope at the council (which could not be guaranteed at Basel); the Greeks were less inclined to travel to distant Basel (or Avignon, or Savoy); the allure of papal prestige in contrast to the relatively recent emergence of western conciliarism; and the emperor's desire to negotiate with a single absolute authority instead of a pluralistic assembly.

8. On whom see Nicholas Constas, "Mark Eugenikos," in *La théologie byzantine et sa tradition*, ed. Carmelo G. Conticello and Vassa Conticello (Turnhout: Brepols, 2002), 411–75.

9. Syropoulos, *Mémoires* III, 3, pp. 162–64. In the spring of 1437, Ioasaph, the metropolitan of Ephesus, died and the emperor appointed Eugenikos to the vacant see (ibid., III, 11, p. 172, lin. 5). Ephesus was third in rank after Constantinople and Caesarea, and since the metropolitan of Caesarea was not at the council, Eugenikos was the senior ranking prelate after the patriarch. Eugenikos resisted the appointment, and when he refused to sign the Decree of Union, he reminded the emperor that "I never wished to become a bishop, nor to come to this Council. Instead, I preferred to live in the monastic life. . . . Nonetheless, your majesty insisted on both, and I obeyed" (ibid., X, 9, pp. 482–84; cf. Mark's *Apologia* 1, *Patrologia Orientalis* 17, pp. 305–6). Further changes led to Eugenikos's temporary appointment as the delegate of the see of Jerusalem and then Antioch (Syropoulos, *Mémoires* IV, 44, p. 248, lins. 19–21; cf. IV, 43, p. 246, lins. 26–27, and IV, 47, p. 252, lins. 18–26). Eugenikos, Bessarion, and Dionysios of Sardis were the spokesmen (πρόκριτοι) for the Orthodox Church, although many regarded Eugenikos as the chief delegate due to his "erudition and holiness" (ibid., III, 23, p. 184, and V, 31, p. 286, lins. 6–7, 16).

10. Syropoulos, *Mémoires* III, 8–10, pp. 168–70. On Scholarios, see Franz Tinnefeld, "Georgios Gennadios Scholarios," in *La théologie byzantine*, 477–549. Eugenikos and Scholarios were particularly concerned with the anti-Thomistic essay of Neilos Kabasilas, *On the Holy Spirit*, which Eugenikos pronounced Orthodox, despite the protestations of Isidore of Kiev (Syropoulos, IX, 13, pp. 446–48);

cf. Emmanuel Candal, *Nilus Cabasilas et theologia S. Thomae de Processione Spiritus Sancti*, Studi e Testi, 116 (Rome, 1945), 187–384; and Athanasios Jevtic, "Recontre de la scolastique et de l'hésychasme dans l'oeuvre de Nilus Cabasilus," in *L'art de Thessalonique et des pays balkaniques et les courants spirituels au XIVe siècle* (Belgrade, 1987), 149–57. Neilos's work has been recently edited by Théophile Kislas, *Nil Cabasilas: Sur le Saint-Esprit. Introduction, texte critique, traduction et notes* (Paris: Cerf, 2001).

11. *Acta Graeca* IV (VI), p. 91, lins. 20–21; cf. B. L. Fonkic and F. B. Poljakov, "Markos Eugenikos als Kopist. Zur Tätigkeit eines Gelehrtenkreises an den Konstantinopolitaner Skriptorium im ersten Drittel des 15. Jahrhunderts," *Byzantinische Zeitschrift* 84–85 (1991–1992): 17–23. On Cusa's activity in Constantinople, see J.-L. Van Dieten, "Nikolaus von Kues, Markos Eugenikos und die Nicht-Koinzidenz von Gegensätzen," in *Studien zum 15. Jahrhundert. Festschrift E. Meuthen* (Munich, 1994), I, 355–79; H. Lawrence Bond, "Nicholas of Cusa from Constantinople to 'Learned Ignorance': The Historical Matrix for the Formation of the *De Docta Ignorantia*," in *Nicholas of Cusa on Christ and the Church*, ed., Gerald Christianson and Thomas M. Izbicki (Leiden: Brill, 1996), 135–64.

12. Syropoulos, *Mémoires* V, 17–18, p. 272, and V, 26–39, pp. 280–92; cf. the *Acta Graeca* IV (VI), pp. 19–25; Kallistos Ware, "'One Body in Christ': Death and the Communion of the Saints," *Sobornost* 3.2 (1981): 179–91; and Robert Ombres, "Latins and Greeks in Debate over Purgatory, 1230–1439," *Journal of Ecclesiastical History* 35.1 (1984): 1–14. For a discussion of Eugenikos's eschatology, see Nicholas Constas, "'To Sleep Perchance to Dream': The Middle State of Souls in Patristic and Byzantine Literature," *Dumbarton Oaks Papers* 55 (2001): 113–19.

13. Syropoulos, *Mémoires* VI, 7, pp. 298–300, describes the chaos caused by the plague, with bishops and cardinals fleeing the city in droves. He notes that while many of the Russians died, not a single Greek was lost or even became ill, which was seen as something of a miracle. Syropoulos mentions the attacks (led by Niccolo Piccinino) in V, 24, p. 278, and the rumors about the Turks in V, 19, p. 272. When the terrified Byzantines had apprised the cardinals of the imminent threat to their capital, they initially received no response whatsoever (V, 19, p. 274, lin. 12), but were then told by Ambrogio Traversari to "make union quickly, and then we shall send ships to Constantinople . . . and, if need be, recover your wives and children" (V, 20, p. 274, lins. 18–27).

14. *Acta Graeca* I, p. 47, lins. 11–20, and I (III), pp. 49–58; cf. Mark Eugenikos, *Dialogue against the Addition to the Creed* (*Patrologia Orientalis* 17, pp. 277–83). It is worth mentioning that Eugenikos attributed the text of the creed of 381 to Gregory Nazianzus, known in the East as "the Theologian": "The great Gregory was the champion of that Synod, and the author of its Symbol of Faith, as a result of which, they say, he was given the surname of 'Theologian' (*Acta Graeca* VII [XXIII], p. 377, lins. 19–23); Xanthopoulos attributes the final draft to Gregory of Nyssa (*Hier. eccl.* 12.13 [PG 146:784B]), an attribution supported by Michael Haykin, *The Spirit of God: The Exegesis of 1 and 2 Corinthians in the Pneumatomachian Controversy of the Fourth Century* (Leiden: Brill, 1994), 199–201.

15. *Acta Graeca* II (IV), pp. 59–66; cf. Syropoulos, *Mémoires* VI, 31, p. 330, lins. 7–10, who notes that the Latins expressed their annoyance with this procedure by "excluding the attendance of visitors, keeping the Holy Gospel closed on the altar table, removing the statues of the Apostles from view, and by leaving the candles unlit."

16. *Acta Graeca* III (V), pp. 68–74. The force of the "decree" itself was bolstered by Eugenikos's reading of Cyril of Alexandria's letter to John of Antioch (ACO, I, 1, 4, p. 19, lins. 20–26) barring the change even of a "single word or syllable"; cf. Hans Jürgen Marx, *Filioque und Verbot eines anderen Glaubens auf dem Florentinum* (Bonn: Steyler Verlag, 1977), 183–228; H. J. Vogt, "Das Verbot einer 'hetera pistis' auf dem Konzil von Ephesus 431," *Annuarium Historiae Conciliorum* 22 (1990): 234–41.

17. *Acta Graeca* III (V), p. 85, lins. 14–26; cf. Syropoulos, *Mémoires* VI, 31, pp. 330–32 (who mistakenly notes that the Latins produced a *Greek* manuscript, and not a Latin translation; cf. ibid., p. 330, n. 5); cf. Mark Eugenikos, *Confession of the Orthodox Faith* 2 (*Patrologia Orientalis* 17, p. 300, lins. 18–29).

18. *Acta Graeca* II (XVIII), pp. 262–98; Michel Van Parys, "Quelques remarques à propos d'un texte controversè de Saint Basile au concile de Florence," *Irenikon* 40 (1967): 6–14; Guy M. De Durand, "Un passage du 3e livre *Contre Eunome* de S. Basile dans la tradition manuscrite," *Irenikon* 54 (1981): 36–52; Ernst Gammilscheg, "Das Konzil von Ferrara-Florenz und die Handschriftenüberlieferung," *Annuarium Historiae Conciliorum* 21 (1989): 297–316; C. Sabbatou, "The Use and Abuse of Basil at Florence," *Theologia* 67 (1996): 157–74; and Milton Anastos, "Basil's Κατὰ Εὐνομίου, A Critical Analysis," in *Basil of Caesarea: Christian, Humanist, Ascetic,* ed. Paul Fedwick (Toronto: PIMS, 1981), 112–13, n. 153, who notes that "it can no longer be doubted that the text championed by the Latins represents some kind of interpolation . . . it is therefore somewhat ironic that the Latins should unwittingly have relied upon this heretical doctrine." For a critical edition with apparatus and commentary, see Bernard Sesboüé, *Basil de Césarée, Contre Eunome,* SC 305 (Paris: Cerf, 1983), 146–47, n. 1. See also the text edited and translated by George Dennis, "An Anti-Latin Essay Attributed to Psellos," *Orientalia Christiana Periodica* 64 (1998): 404–5: "[T]he manner in which the Spirit [is] from the Father, they [i.e., the Latins] somehow substitute from the Son. But this is the impiety which Arius invented and kept hidden, whereas Eunomius formulated it more precisely." Dennis dates the text to the "first half of the eleventh century, or earlier."

19. On which see V. Lur'e, "L'attitude de S. Marc d'Ephèse aux débats sur la procession du Saint-Espirt à Florence," *Annuarium Historiae Conciliorum* 21 (1989): 317–33.

20. For overviews, see Constas, "Mark Eugenikos," 441–52; Dietrich Ritschl, "The History of the Filioque Controversy," in *Conflicts about the Holy Spirit,* ed. Hans Küng and Jürgen Moltmann (New York: Seabury Press, 1979), 3–30; and Markos Orphanos, "The Procession of the Holy Spirit according to Certain Later Greek Fathers," in *Spirit of God, Spirit of Christ: Ecumenical Reflections on the* Filioque *Controversy* (London: SPCK/Geneva: WCC, 1981), 22–45.

21. Syropoulos, *Mémoires* X, 13, pp. 490–92.

22. The Latin text of the "Decree of Union" can be found in Gill, *Council of Florence*, 412–15, along with a plate reproducing the Greek signatures and a printed transcription (p. 295). Laurent, *Mémoires,* provides a reproduction of the entire document (plate 1, figure 1 = *Parisinus Graecus* 430). It should be noted that the decree acknowledged a measure of liturgical pluralism by recognizing the validity of both leavened and unleavened bread for the Eucharist, a traditional point of contention since at least the eleventh century, on which see Mahlon Smith, *And Taking Bread: Cerularius and the Azyme Controversy of 1054* (Paris: Beauchesne, 1978).

23. Syropoulos, *Mémoires* X, 16–17, pp. 497–503. At the "International Symposium on Christian Unity 550 years after the Council of Ferrara-Florence" (23–29 September, 1989, Florence), two separate liturgies were celebrated: a Roman Catholic Mass, presided over by Cardinal Piovanelli, and the Liturgy of Saint John Chrysostom, under the presidency of Metropolitan Damaskinos, cited in Albergio, *Christian Unity,* who points out that the "two Holy Liturgies" were celebrated "in the margin of the Conference" (p. xi).

24. When the pope's signature was affixed to the document, he asked if Eugenikos had signed, and upon receiving a negative reply is said to have remarked: "Then we have accomplished nothing." Syropoulos, *Mémoires* X, 15, p. 496, lins. 19–20.

25. A hostile source, Joseph of Methone, notes that as the metropolitan of Ephesus disembarked from his ship, he "saw the crowds glorifying him for not signing, and they venerated him as if he were Moses or Aaron, and they praised him and called him a saint," *Dialogue on the Council of Florence* (PG 159:992C).

26. Recounted by the Byzantine historian Doukas, *Historia Byzantina* 32 (Bonn, 1834), 215–16; trans. Harry Magoulias, *Decline and Fall of Byzantium* (Detroit: Wayne State University Press, 1975), 181–82. Doukas, a western-oriented aristocrat, accuses the bishops of hypocrisy, insisting that they were under no compulsion to sign, but rather subscribed to the Decree of Union in exchange for a specified sum of money, which, he insisted, they were now obligated to return for having rescinded their signatures. For a recent study of this episode, see George Demacopoulos, "The Popular Reception of the Council of Florence in Constantinople, 1439–1453," *St. Vladimir's Theological Quarterly* 43 (1999): 37–53.

27. Syropoulos, *Mémoires* XII, 1–3, pp. 546–48. Doukas would later excoriate the anti-unionists as they sought refuge in Hagia Sophia from the Turkish onslaught: "O miserable Romans (i.e., Byzantines)! O wretches! The church which only yesterday you called a 'cave and altar of heretics,' and refused to enter because the liturgy was offered by clerics who embraced the Union, now, because of the impending wrath, you push your way inside, seeking to be saved!" (Doukas, *Historia Byzantina,* 37.5; trans. Magoulias, *Decline and Fall,* 207–8).

28. Gill, *Council of Florence,* vii, who adds that "a dictum like that is a challenge to discussion rather than a statement of fact."

29. Georges Florovsky, *Ways of Russian Theology*, vol. 1 (Belmont, Mass.: Nordland, 1979), 1–32; cf. John Meyendorff, *Rome, Constantinople, Moscow: Historical and Theological Studies* (Crestwood, N.Y.: St. Vladimir's Seminary Press, 1996), 113–47.

30. On which see Meyendorff, "Was There an Encounter between East and West?" 169–74; and Thomas Ferguson, "The Council of Ferrara-Florence and Its Continued Historical Significance," *St. Vladimir's Theological Quarterly* 43 (1999): 55–77, who argues persuasively that responses to the Council of Florence are "indispensable in understanding the relationship between the Russian and Greek churches to this day." See also I. Pavlov, "The Ferrara-Florentine Union: A View from Moscow," in Albergio, *Christian Unity*, 493–507; and Borys Gudziak, *Crisis and Reform: The Kyivan Metropolitanate, the Patriarchate of Constantinople, and the Genesis of the Union of Brest* (Cambridge, Mass.: Harvard University Press, 1998).

31. Josef Macha, *Ecclesiastical Unification: A Theoretical Framework Together with Case Studies from the History of Latin-Byzantine Relations*, OCA 198 (Rome, 1974), 92–96. See also Athanasios Angelou, "'Who am I?' Scholarios' Answer and Hellenic Identity," in *Philhellen: Studies in Honour of Robert Browning*, ed. C. Constantinides, et al. (Venice: Instituto Ellenico, 1996), 1–19.

32. Meyendorff, "Was There an Encounter between East and West?" 164.

33. Syropoulos was born in Constantinople before 1400 and survived the city's fall in 1453. The *Oxford Dictionary of Byzantium* notes that "although his account is far from impartial, it is neither worthless nor an intentional falsification of the facts. Even though it contains little on the public debates themselves, its information about the council's private intrigues and discussions (otherwise unavailable), is invaluable. Moreover, its bias or partisanship, for which it is frequently criticized, is also characteristic of the acts of the council" (ed. Alexander Kazhdan and Alice-Mary Talbot; Oxford and New York: Oxford University Press, 1991), 3:2001.

34. Syropoulos, *Mémoires* IV, 19, pp. 214–16, who notes that it was the "8th of February, the Saturday of the Prodigal Son" (p. 216, lin. 2); cf. Gill, *Council of Florence*, 98–99, 184. Tia Kolbaba, *The Byzantine Lists: Errors of the Latins* (Urbana and Chicago: University of Illinois Press, 2000), 127, draws attention to the problematic dating of this episode, suggesting that Syropoulos may have deliberately confused the date.

35. Syropoulos, *Mémoires* IV, 27, p. 226, lins. 15–18; cf. Gill, *Council of Florence*, 103, n. 1 (on the hats). Syropoulos, *Mémoires* IV, 39–40, pp. 240–44; cf. Gill, *Council of Florence*, 107, n. 1 (on the seating arrangements).

36. Syropoulos, *Mémoires* IV, 29–33, pp. 230–34. In describing the patriarch's negative response to the papal reception, Syropoulos reports that earlier the patriarch had said the following: "If the pope is older than I am, I shall embrace him as a father. If he is close to my age, I shall embrace him like a brother. If he is younger, then as a son. And if there is a dwelling next to his . . . I hope that he shall give it to me, so that I might come to him . . . and provide him with advice, for I know that he does not have good advisors." To this Syropoulos adds that the patriarch was

himself hoping for a bit of good advice from the pope, namely, on how to free the Orthodox church from its "slavery" (*douleia*) to the Byzantine emperor, p. 230, lins. 16–23; cf. below, at n. 47.

37. Syropoulos, *Mémoires* IV, 46, pp. 250, lins. 24–28. It should be noted that Gregory, who at the time was the emperor's confessor, is the villain of Syropoulos's narrative. Melissenos's critique was part of his objection to the patriarch's desire to celebrate Easter in a Latin church. Note that when the patriarch had earlier venerated a Venetian reliquary said to contain the hand of St. George, he was informed by one of his clerics that it was actually a fake, inasmuch as the martyr's body had been destroyed by fire; cf. Syropoulos, *Mémoires* IV, 27, p. 226, lins. 7–11.

38. On the relationship of the name to the figure, see the acta of the Council of Nicaea 787 (Mansi XIII, 252D; 257D; 261D; 269E; 301C; 340E; 344B; 416D). In the ninth-century *Life of St. Stephen the Younger,* the icon of Christ is said to be the "tabernacle of the divine name" (PG 100:1164D).

39. Hans Belting, *Likeness and Presence,* trans. Edmund Jephcott (Chicago: University of Chicago Press, 1994), 1, 270. Humbert's remarks are usually taken as a polemic against the Byzantine image of a dead Christ in favor of a western *Christus Victor* type. Others have suggested that the cardinal was objecting to the lack of differentiation between Christ and the two thieves; cf. Mitchell B. Merback, *The Thief, the Cross, and the Wheel: Pain and the Spectacle of Punishment in Medieval and Renaissance Europe* (Chicago: University of Chicago Press, 1999), 82; and John R. Martin, "The Dead Christ on the Cross in Byzantine Art," in *Late Classical and Medieval Studies in Honor of Albert Mathias Friend, Jr.,* ed. K. Weitzmann (Princeton: Princeton University Press, 1955), 196.

40. Gananath Obeyesekere, *The Apotheosis of Captain Cook: European Mythmaking in the Pacific* (Princeton: Princeton University Press, 1992). Obeyesekere finds similar models of misrecognition between Cortés and the Aztecs and in the actions of Columbus and Pizarro in the Americas. With respect to England and Hawaii, Obeyesekere notes that "both were hierarchical societies, but the English were as incapable of critical reflection about their own hierarchies as the Polynesians were regarding theirs. Both, however, could be critical of each other, in their own different ways" (29). Within these interactions, Obeyesekere further posits two "myth models," i.e., the "Prospero syndrome" and the "Kurtz syndrome." The former "remains immune to savage ways, maintaining his integrity and identity," while the latter "loses his identity and becomes native." Eugenikos, who refused to capitulate to the Latins, corresponds to the "Prospero syndrome"; Bessarion, who after the council converted to Catholicism moved to Rome and was made a cardinal, corresponds to the "Kurtz syndrome." See also Inga Clendenin, *Ambivalent Conquests: Maya and Spaniard in Yucutan, 1517–1570* (Cambridge: Cambridge University Press, 1988); Nicholas Thomas, *Double Vision: Art Histories and Colonial Histories in the Pacific* (Cambridge: Cambridge University Press, 1999); and Terry Ellingson, *The Myth of the Noble Savage* (Berkeley: University of California Press, 2001).

41. For two recent studies, see David Abernathy, *The Dynamics of Global Dominance: European Overseas Empires, 1415–1980* (New Haven: Yale University Press, 2000); and Philip D. Curtin, *The World and the West: The European Challenge and the Overseas Response in the Age of Empire* (Cambridge: Cambridge University Press, 2000).

42. The question of hermeneutics at the Council of Florence, and of theological methodology in East and West in general, has been dealt with in a number of studies; cf. André de Halleux, "Palamisme et scolastique: exclusivisme dogmatique ou pluriformité théologique?" *Revue théologique de Louvain* 4 (1973): 409–42; id., "Problémes de méthode dans les discussions sur l'eschatologie au Concile de Ferrare et Florence," in Albergio, *Christian Unity,* 251–302; V. Phidas, "Herméneutique et patristique au Concile de Florence," ibid., 303–24; James Jorgenson, "The Debate over the Patristic Texts on Purgatory at the Council of Ferrara-Florence in 1438," *St. Vladimir's Theological Quarterly* 30 (1986): 309–34; Bernard Meunier, "Cyrille d'Alexandrie au Concile de Florence," *Annuarium Historiae Conciliorum* 21 (1989): 147–74; and, more generally, Kallistos Ware, "Scholasticism and Orthodoxy: Theological Method as a Factor in the Schism," *Eastern Churches Review* 5 (1973): 16–27; Andrew Sopko, "Patristic Methodology in Late Byzantium," in *The Making of Byzantine History: Studies Dedicated to Donald M. Nicol,* ed. Roderick Beaton and Charolotte Roueché (Aldershot: Variorum, 1993), 158–68; and Gerhard Podskalsky, *Theologie und Philosophie in Byzanz* (Munich: C. H. Beck, 1977), esp. 124–73. On theology and architecture, see Christos Yannaras, "The Ethos of Liturgical Art," in his *The Freedom of Morality,* trans. Elizabeth Briere (Crestwood, N.Y.: St. Vladimir's Seminary Press, 1984), 231–64.

43. See Qiong Zhang, "Translation as Cultural Reform: Jesuit Scholastic Psychology in Transformation of the Confucian Discourse on Human Nature," in *The Jesuits: Cultures, Sciences, and the Arts,* ed. John O'Malley (Toronto: University of Toronto Press, 1999), 364–79; cf. Robert Wardy, *Aristotle in China: Language, Categories, and Translation* (Cambridge: Cambridge University Press, 2000). I am thankful to John O'Malley for these references.

44. Cf. Eugenikos, *Relatio 2* (*Patrologia Orientalis* 17, p. 308, lin. 16); Syropoulos, *Mémoires* VIII, 5, p. 394, lins. 5–7; and the anti-Aristotelian sentiments of the Georgian bishop (ibid., IX, 28, p. 464, lins. 11–22): "'You and your Aristotle! A fig for your fine Aristotle!'; and when asked: 'What then is fine?', the Georgian replied: 'St. Peter, St. Paul, St. Basil, Gregory the Theologian, Chrysostom; but a fig for your "Aristotle, Aristotle"!'" (trans. Gill, *Council of Florence,* 227). See also Eustratius Argentis (b. ca. 1690): "One thousand years after the birth of Christ, there appeared the heresy of the Latin scholastic theologians who wished to unite the philosophy of Aristotle with Christian theology. The scholastics were not like the ancient holy teachers of the church, who subjected philosophy to theology, but they did just the opposite, and subjected the Gospel, and the holy faith of Christians, to the doctrines of that sophist Aristotle," *Treatise against Unleavened Bread,* ed. G. Hagiotaphites (Leipzig, 1760), 171, cited in Podskalsky (above, n. 42).

45. Ombres, "Latins and Greeks in Debate over Purgatory," 2, n. 6, citing Hubert of Roman, *Opus Triparatitum* 2.11.216; cf. Illtyd Trethowan, "Irrationality in Theology and the Palamite Distinction," *Eastern Churches Review* 9 (1977): 19–26; and Katerina Ierodiakonou, "The Anti-Logical Movement in the Fourteenth Century," in ead., *Byzantine Philosophy and its Ancient Sources* (Oxford: Oxford Univeristy Press, 2002), 219–36. Here, too, Obeyesekere's model (above, n. 40) seems relevant in highlighting the fact that the European notion of the "savage mind as given to prelogical or mystical thought and fundamentally opposed to the logical and rational ways of modern man . . . or given to unreflective traditional thought, or governed by a rigid cosmic or mythic world picture, is the social scientists' myth of the Other" (15–16). Paraphrasing the work of Tzvetan Todorov, *The Conquest of America: The Question of the Other* (New York: Harper, 1987), Obeyesekere notes that according to European stereotypes, "Aztec culture [like Byzantine culture?] was overdetermined by signs . . . Indians are bound by signs; consequently they can easily be subjugated by the Spanish who have mastery over signs . . . preliterates cannot manipulate signs to their advantage; their thought processes are inflexible; they cannot rationally weigh alternative or multiple courses of action" (17–18).

46. With the exception of Eugenikos and Bessarion, the Greeks were no match for the likes of Cardinal Giuliano Cesarini and the Dominican theologians Andrew Chrysoberges, the Latin archbishop of Rhodes; John of Montenero, the Dominican provincial of Lombardy; and John of Torquemada, to mention only a few; cf. G. Meersseman, "Les dominicains présents au Councile de Ferrara-Florence jusqu'au décret d'union pour les Grecs," *Archivum Fratrum Praedicatorum* 9 (1939): 62–75; and Claudine Delacroix-Besnier, *Les Dominicains et la chrétienité grecque* (Rome: École Française de Rome, 1997), 335–405.

47. CFDS V/1, 400–401; Syropoulos notes that several of the Orthodox bishops were outraged at this and heaped much abuse on him (*Mémoires* IX, 10, p. 444); cf. Eugenikos, *Encyclical Letter* 4 (*Patrologia Orientalis* 17, p. 314).

48. See the postscript to this essay.

49. Cf. Macha, *Ecclesiastical Unification,* 79–100 ("Florence: A Process of De-Unification").

50. Amphilochios Radovitch, "'Le Filioque' et l'énergie incrée de la Sainte Trinité selon la doctrine de Saint Grégoire Palamas," *Messager de l'Exarchat du Patriarche Russe en Europe Occidentale* 23 (1975): 11–44; cf. Duncan Reid, *Energies of the Spirit: Trinitarian Models in Eastern Orthodox and Western Theology* (Atlanta: Scholars Press, 1997). Note that Mark Eugenikos wrote a series of hymns in praise of Palamas (cf. Constas, "Mark Eugenikos," 438, no. 103). In popular devotion, Palamas and Eugenikos became closely intertwined, a testimony to Eugenikos's standing as a Palamite theologian. In a diatribe against the opponents of union with Rome, Joseph of Methone remarked that "you [i.e., the anti-unionists] glorify and praise Palamas and Mark of Ephesus, painting icons of them, and, venerating their memories, you revere them as saints," *Apodeixis on the Council of Florence* 5, 12 (PG 159:1357B, lins. 7–8;

11–14). An article by Michael Kunzler (cited below, n. 51) studies Eugenikos's *Syllogistic Chapters against the Heresy of the Akindynites on the Distinction of the Divine Essence and Energy,* a little-known work edited and appended to *Die Mystik des Nikolaos Kabasilas vom Leben in Christo,* ed. W. Gass (Greifswald, 1849; repr. Leipzig, 1899), 217–32.

51. *Acta Graeca,* CFDS V/2, pp. 345–46; cf. Michael Kunzler, "Die Florentiner Diskussion über das Filioque vom. 14. März 1439 im Licht des Palamismus," *Annuarium Historiae Conciliorum* 21 (1989): 334–52; Nicholas Lossky, "Climat théologique au Concile de Florence," in Albergio, *Christian Unity,* 249.

52. Syropoulos, *Mémoires* X, 16, p. 498, lin. 15. The hymn, of which Syropoulos gives only the opening line, runs as follows: "Today the grace of the Holy Spirit has gathered us together, and we all take up Thy cross and say: Blessed is He that comes in the Name of the Lord; Hosanna in the highest," trans. Mother Mary and Kallistos Ware, *The Lenten Triodion* (London: Faber & Faber, 1984), 489. One senses a degree of irony in the choice of this particular hymn, which is chanted during the Orthodox liturgy of Palm Sunday. Stressing, as it does, the Pentecostal unity of the church and the triumphal arrival of the Savior, it is nevertheless tinged by the shadow of the cross and death. Similarly, in the Byzantine iconography of the fifteenth century, the Entry into Jerusalem was depicted as proceeding down a precipitous incline, foreshadowing Christ's descent into the inferno.

53. Augustine, *City of God* XIX, 7, trans. Henry Bettenson (London: Penguin, 1984), 861; cf. Alfons Fürst, "Augustinus im Orient," *Zeitschrift für Kirchengeschichte* 110 (1999): 293–314.

54. For some of the background to this statement, see John Borelli and John H. Erickson, eds., *The Quest for Unity: Orthodox and Catholics in Dialogue. Documents of the Joint International Commission and Official Dialogues in the United States, 1965–1995* (Crestwood, N.Y.: St. Vladimir's Seminary Press, 1996).

3

Erasmus and the Restoration of Unity in the Church

ERIKA RUMMEL

IN 1533 ERASMUS PUBLISHED A PSALM COMMENTARY TO WHICH HE appended suggestions on how to restore unity in the church. His purpose is reflected in the title of the commentary: *De sarcienda ecclesiae concordia* (On Mending the Peace of the Church).[1] Before discussing reactions to Erasmus's proposals, it is important to provide the context in which the proposals emerged and to discuss the events leading up to the publication of the work.

In 1530 there was a general expectation that Erasmus would be present at the Diet of Augsburg and lend at least moral support to the negotiations for religious peace. Erasmus, however, was in poor health at the time and unable to travel to Augsburg in person. He was, moreover, reluctant to get involved in negotiations which he apparently regarded as hopeless and which he feared would bring him a great deal of unpopularity. These, at any rate, were the explanations he offered in contemporary letters. For example, in July of 1530 he wrote to Simon Pistorius, chancellor of Duke George of Saxony, if Charles were to command him to travel to Augsburg, he would first have to command his health to improve.[2] In the same letter he called the religious question "inextricable," and in a contemporary letter to the Cologne jurist

Johann Rinck he declared that not even an ecumenical council could solve the problem if it were to sit for three years running.[3] He added that any call for an equitable settlement was bound to expose him to hostility: "If anyone as much as mentions equity, he is immediately told that that amounts to Lutheranism."[4]

There are indications, however, that Erasmus was not completely inactive in 1530. A letter from the imperial councilor Cornelis de Schepper mentions that Erasmus had been in touch with Mercurio Gattinara before the chancellor's untimely death in June 1530, and that Gattinara had solicited his advice and had promised to keep it confidential.[5] It is possible therefore that Erasmus was in the early summer of 1530 engaged in writing the counsel, which he published three years later under the title *De sarcienda concordia*. This conjecture is supported by the fact that he used the title phrase "consilium sarciendae concordiae" in a letter to Christoph of Carlowitz, dated 7 July 1530.[6]

Although the Diet of Augsburg did not bring about the desired settlement, the reformers continued to negotiate with representatives of the imperial court, and attempts to involve Erasmus continued as well. For example, Julius Pflug, councilor to Duke George of Saxony, told him in 1531 that "all those who seek peace are looking to you." Pflug explicitly compared Erasmus's role with Melanchthon's, saying that Catholics, too, needed "a good man standing up for Christian concord, just as Melanchthon did [on behalf of the reformers]."[7] Indeed, Melanchthon himself pleaded with Erasmus in 1532: "Bring your authority to bear on the peace-making process, whenever an opportunity presents itself."[8] Georg Witzel, a Lutheran who had returned to the Catholic faith and was active in negotiations between the parties, similarly urged Erasmus to come forward. The emperor, he said in a letter of 1532, should not take a no from Erasmus: "If I were the emperor, I would not listen to [the excuse] 'I am ill with the stone.' . . . It is not Luther's voice we need to hear . . . but the voice of Erasmus."[9] It may be that these exhortations prompted Erasmus to resurrect the counsel he had intended for Gattinara's ears and to add it to the psalm commentary he was about to publish. He had set a precedent for combining such counsel with a biblical commentary earlier on, when he embedded his advice *De bello Turcico* (On War Against the Turks) in his commentary on Psalm 28, published in 1530.

By appending his counsel to a psalm commentary, Erasmus gave notice to readers that he was offering spiritual rather than political advice. As in *De bello Turcico,* he made the success of any plan of action contingent on the spiritual state of the parties, their willingness to acknowledge and correct their vices, and to put their trust in God.[10] I am not sure, however, that this message was absorbed by readers or at any rate that it was what they wanted to hear from Erasmus. At that time, I believe, readers, Catholic readers especially, were looking for a method or principle to guide the negotiators.

Is there a discernible principle behind Erasmus's advice in *De sarcienda concordia?* There is, in fact, more than one principle, and that is what makes his advice problematic. Erasmus suggests a number of approaches without discussing their respective merit or assigning priorities. His methodological remarks are, moreover, buried in the discussion of specifics. It is left to the reader, therefore, to unearth his principles. Indeed, a close analytical reading reveals no fewer than five approaches.

Approach number 1 consists of devising a wording vague enough to satisfy all parties. Thus Erasmus says on the subject of justification by faith: "Let us agree that we must attribute a great deal to faith, *as long as* we say that it is the peculiar gift of the Holy Spirit and more wide-spread than most people believe. . . . Let us grant justification by faith, that is, that the hearts of the believers are purified, *as long as* we say that works of charity are necessary to obtain salvation."[11] In each of these sentences Erasmus gives with one hand and takes away with the other by introducing a qualifying *modo,* "as long as." Erasmus's remarks on the nature of the Eucharist are another example of carefully qualified wording: "If Christ is present in the Eucharist in his entirety, why not worship him? . . . But since no one, except the priest himself, can be certain that he has truly consecrated [the bread and wine], no one worships Christ in the Eucharist except with this qualification in mind."[12] Here Erasmus suggests achieving consensus by allowing a mental reservation. In view of such efforts to equivocate, it is ludicrous to read a few lines further on: "Let us not fight about words, as long as we agree on the substance."[13] Erasmus's tactics suggest in fact the opposite approach: Let us not fight about the substance as long as we can agree on a suitable wording.

Approach number 2 consists of waiting for a general council to provide definitive answers. For example, Erasmus suggests that the finer points of the Eucharistic controversy could be settled at a later time. Once there was agreement on whether or not Christ is present in the Eucharist, questions such as "what happens to the body when it has been consumed, and other similar matters could be defined by a synod." In a summary statement, moreover, Erasmus stressed that he did not mean to impose his views on others. "I do not want my words to be taken as definitive statements or as anticipating the church's decision, but only as an interim solution until arrangements can be made for a synod."[14]

Approach number 3 suggests that there is no need to settle all outstanding issues. Some may be left to the individual's discretion. For example, "questions concerning principal and secondary merit or *opus operans* and *opus operatum,*" Erasmus says, "could be placed in the category of human opinions until a synod pronounces on them or leaves it up to each individual's judgment." Another example of approach number 3 concerns the rather important question whether or not confession was instituted by Christ. On that point too people might be allowed to follow their own interpretation, according to Erasmus. "As for those who believe that confession, as it is practiced today, has been instituted by Christ: let them observe it all the more piously and leave others to the quiet enjoyment of their own interpretation until a synod makes a clearer pronouncement on this matter."[15]

Approach number 4 suggests that it is better to maintain the status quo. One must remember that "it is neither safe nor useful in fostering concord rashly to depart from what has been handed down by the authority of our forefathers and confirmed by century-long usage and consensus." Change invariably brought upheaval. "There should be no innovation whatsoever, unless there is a compelling necessity or a significant benefit," Erasmus writes.[16]

Approach number 5 suggests a compromise. In this context Erasmus uses the patristic term *sygkatabasis,* accommodation or leniency, and suggests that "each party making some concessions to the other" was the sine qua non of a religious settlement. Further on in the text, he describes *sygkatabasis* as a preliminary step to achieving concord, comparable to a doctor's prescription of syrup to prepare the patient for more potent medicine. "My admonition is addressed to both parties. If a moderate *sygkatabasis* softens the paroxysm of discord, the medicine of the synod will be more effective in producing concord."[17]

Offering multiple approaches without ranking them is always problematic, but especially when they are difficult to combine or mutually exclusive, as is the case with several of the approaches mentioned here. For example, making concessions goes against preserving the status quo. Of course Erasmus tries to gloss over the incompatibility of the two approaches by hedging behind modifiers. He does not say, "you must make concessions and preserve the status quo," which would be an open contradiction, but "you must make small concessions" and not break with tradition "rashly." However, such equivocations cannot have impressed readers. In other cases, the difficulties remain unresolved. For example, allowing people to follow their own judgment for the time being militates against asking them to submit to a council later; similarly, working on an acceptable wording only to reopen discussion when an ecumenical council finally can be assembled does not make sense. Erasmus's failure to provide clear direction accounts for the lukewarm reception of his proposals.

Initial interest in Erasmus's suggestions was surprisingly high, considering that they amounted to only a dozen pages in print and were placed inconspicuously at the end of a psalm commentary. This shows that Erasmus was still a power to be reckoned with and could have rallied public opinion if he had advanced a compelling plan. The strong interest taken in his proposals meant that Froben's edition of 1533 was immediately reprinted by five other publishers (in Antwerp, Cologne, Leipzig, and Paris). Altogether, the work saw ten editions and four translations between 1533 and 1535.[18] The fact that the tract was a publishing success did not mean, however, that the proposals were a success with readers. Erasmus, who was an expert in public relations, would have reported all positive reactions, but we find only two favorable testimonies in his published correspondence. One comes from Etienne Desprez, rector of a school in Besançon, who says that "all the canons are in the habit of clasping your book *De concordia* to their bosoms and are reading it over and over again"; the other response comes from Giovanni Danieli, a member of Caietanus's household, who reports on the positive reception of the book in the cardinal's household and at the papal court.[19] In addition, there is a friendly letter from Jacobo Sadoleto thanking Erasmus for the book, but keeping silent on its merits.[20] There is, then, a certain paucity of positive reactions in the correspondence published by Erasmus. From other sources we know that the tract was not well received in Scotland and, notwithstanding Danieli's letter, did not please everyone in Rome.[21] Indeed, several theologians immediately composed hostile responses to Erasmus's tract. The critics came from both the Catholic and the reformed camps.

On the reformers' side we have two published responses: one from the Lutheran Antonius Corvinus, the other from Bucer's colleague, Wolfgang Capito. Corvinus, who later played a significant role as reformer in Hesse and Brunswig-Lüneburg, took the position that Erasmus was out of his depth when he spoke on religious questions. Erasmus's "judgment in religious matters was not sound," he said, but he could be trusted in his own area of expertise, namely, humanistic studies. [22] In 1534 Corvinus published a dialogue, entitled *Quatenus expediat . . . Erasmi de sarcienda ecclesiae concordia rationem sequi* (To What Extent It Is Useful to Follow Erasmus's Method of Mending the Peace of the Church). There he expressed admiration for Erasmus's scholarly attainments, but firmly rejected his demands for accommodation in religious matters. "We share with Erasmus the desire for concord," he said, "but only as far as the authority of Scripture permits it." In other words, if peace was to be made it must rest on the Protestant principle of *sola scriptura.* Corvinus rejected the idea of temporizing and deferring the final decisions to a council because such a council would be controlled by Rome: "I regard myself a member of the catholic, not the papal, church," he said. "Thus I shall listen only to Christ, the bridegroom of the church."[23]

Corvinus's dialogue was published with a preface by Luther, who endorsed his views, adding that Erasmus's counsel was useless. Corvinus's own stand hardened over the next decade. Commenting on the Diet of Regensburg (1541), he declared that reconciliation was impossible in his opinion. In 1547, he was among those who rejected the Interim and expressed contempt for Melanchthon's diplomacy. His increasing reservations about the negotiations are reflected in a revised edition of *Quatenus expediat* (1544), in which he replaced some of the diplomatic phrases in the original text with more radical language. The party in favor of accommodation was wrong, he said: "They hunt only after what is useful and good for themselves, and not what promotes the glory of Christ and spreads the gospel message. They err and spin out senseless dreams. Among them Erasmus easily holds first place." It was foolish to think that the schism could be reversed through negotiations: "What hope was there of concord between Abel and Cain? How could the true church be reconciled with the hypocritical church?"[24]

A second response from the reformed party came in the form of a German translation of Erasmus's tract by the Strasbourg reformer Wolfgang Capito. He dedicated his work to Albert of Brandenburg, archbishop of Mainz, his former employer. Capito had, until his defection to the reformed camp, been on intimate terms with both the archbishop and Erasmus, who repeatedly called him his alter ego and regarded him as his spiritual heir.[25] Their friendship came to an end when Capito broke with the Catholic Church. Erasmus complained bitterly of Capito's duplicity, and in 1532 lashed out against his former protégé, declaring that there was plenty he could say against him, if he were a man to engage in mudslinging.[26] A year earlier he had told Bucer point-blank: "I don't have a high opinion of your and Capito's integrity."[27] The translation was no doubt an effort on Capito's part to mend bridges, but Erasmus remained unforgiving and did not respond to Capito's overture, if that is what it was. For, although Capito had taken the trouble of translating Erasmus's tract, which would suggest a certain degree of approval of its contents, he used it primarily as a foil, to advertise the position of the Strasbourg reformers. In his preface Capito disagreed with Erasmus's statements on free will, on the importance of works, and on the nature of the Eucharist, yet insisted that there was common ground between them and that he meant to recommend Erasmus's work to readers. Indeed, his stated purpose was to further the peace process and to make Erasmus's views accessible to a larger readership that did not have a ready command of Latin.[28]

The reaction in the Catholic camp was similarly critical, but the two men who composed replies, the Louvain theologian Jacques Masson and the papal legate Paolo Vergerio, both left their responses unfinished and un-published. Jacques Masson had earlier on engaged in controversy with Eras-mus over the merit of language studies and over the origin of confession. In both cases, he was discreet, however, and refrained from mentioning Eras-mus's name. Although he cited Erasmus's words, he formally directed his at-tacks against Petrus Mosellanus and Johannes Oecolampadius, men who were at the time associated with Erasmus.[29] In his rebuttal of Erasmus's *De sarcienda concordia,* by contrast, he left no doubt about his target. He named Erasmus in the title, but then left the work unpublished. This was a matter of prudence since Erasmus had complained about the hostility of the Lou-vain theologians and succeeded in obtaining imperial and papal decrees im-posing silence on them. It was presumably in compliance with these decrees that Masson suppressed his sharply worded reply, entitled *Adversus Erasmi librum de sarcienda ecclesiae concordia* (Against Erasmus's Book on the Mend-ing of the Church). The manuscript was found among his papers at the time of his death in 1544 and was published by his nephew in 1550. We find that the Catholic Masson was as uncompromising as the Lutheran Corvinus in his insistence that there was no need to wait for a council to clarify doctrine. While Corvinus claimed that all answers could be found in Scripture, Mas-son asserted that they could be found in the papal decrees and were there-fore not subject to bargaining. Erasmus, he said disapprovingly, spoke of the religious question as if it were a quarrel over a piece of real estate, in which each party was expected to give a little ground to arrive at an equitable settle-ment. Such an attitude was wrong: Catholics must defend their position tooth and claw, and, if necessary, die for it.[30]

Paolo Vergerio's response likewise remained unpublished during his life-time.[31] His diplomatic posting to Vienna in 1533 had been a patronage ap-pointment. He was catapulted into the position at Ferdinand's court without any preparation. As he himself admitted, he was a complete novice as far as the religious debate in Germany was concerned. However, his inexperience did not keep him from writing an invective against Erasmus when asked to give his opinion on *De sarcienda ecclesiae concordia.* Seemingly unaware of

Erasmus's prestige in Vienna and the support he enjoyed at Ferdinand's court, Vergerio began composing a response, or rather a tirade, against the "heretic" Erasmus, whose name he repeatedly coupled with Luther's. The piece trails off into disjointed notes. It seems that Vergerio abandoned the draft when he became more familiar with the mood at Ferdinand's court.

Finally, Georg Witzel published a German translation of Erasmus's work in 1534. Witzel, who was for a while an ardent Lutheran, returned to the Catholic faith in 1531 and eventually came to serve as imperial councilor to Ferdinand I. Nicolaus Amsdorf, for one, sized him up as a follower of Erasmus. Witzel, he said in a letter to Luther, had "stolen all his ideas from Erasmus."[32] Witzel had expressed admiration for Erasmus in his works, but indignantly denied that he had committed intellectual theft, and indeed his own approach to the religious question differs significantly from Erasmus's. It is a historical approach, that is, a plea for a return to the doctrine and ceremonies of the early church (which Witzel mistakenly assumed was uniform), and it shows no tolerance for any deviation from what he termed the *via regia*, the Royal Road of the Catholic Church. Witzel's translation of the Erasmian tract has no preface or other commentary, but we may assume that it was meant as a tribute to Erasmus. However, his German version offers an odd translation for the term *sygkatabasis*, rendering it as "*semptliche verzichtung*," a complete relinquishing, which does not convey Erasmus's meaning, accommodation or making concessions, and suggests self-denial or deference rather than flexibility.[33] Thus Witzel subtly changed Erasmus's meaning, imposing his own interpretation on Erasmus's words, namely the notion that reunification meant bringing the evangelicals back to the Catholic *via regia*. Erasmus never replied to Witzel's fawning letters. He told his friends that Witzel was too impetuous for his taste and that he disapproved of his militant rhetoric. In later years Witzel acknowledged that he had used radical language but defended his style, arguing that it had been appropriate to those militant times. Although he adopted a less categorical tone in his later writings, he cannot be regarded as an Erasmian in the full sense of the word and never espoused the idea of accommodation.

The five responses to Erasmus's work described here reflect the range of positions taken on the question of reunification in the 1530s. They furthermore show the difficult position of the peacemakers, the so-called "middle party" which was often identified in the sixteenth century as the party of Erasmus. As a group, those who advocated concessions as a means of achieving religious peace were unpopular in both camps and were often disparaged as unprincipled or irreligious. This was, after all, the age of confessionalization, and the trend was toward doctrinal precision rather than the latitudinarianism that is characteristic of Erasmus's thought. In 1573 Georg Eder, the rector of the University of Vienna, bitterly inveighed against peacemakers as "men half Lutheran and half popish, yet not completely of either party. They turn their coats to the wind, choosing their position according to the weather vane."[34] Georg Cassander, Witzel's colleague on a committee to advise Ferdinand on the religious question, therefore complained that the task of the peacemaker was fraught with danger. "In places where party stalwarts govern, advocates of neutrality and moderation are barely tolerated; indeed, they are often regarded as enemies by both parties," Cassander wrote in 1562. It appears that the climate for peace through accommodation had not improved since the 1530s, when Erasmus expressed reluctance to accept the role of the peacemaker, declaring: "Far be it from me to play the arbiter in this inextricable tragedy, for I will get no thanks from either party."[35]

NOTES

1. First published by the Froben Press, Basel, 1533. The work is an exposition of Psalm 83 (84). A critical edition of the text can be found in A. Stupperich, ed., *Opera Omnia Desiderii Erasmi Roterodami* (Amsterdam, 1986), V-3, 258–313 (in the following cited as "ASD"). Erasmus's proposals appear at the end of the commentary, on pp. 303–13. See the prefatory letter to Julius Pflug in P. S. Allen, *Opus Epistolarum Des. Erasmi Roterodami* (Oxford, 1906–1958), Ep. 2852:5–8, referring to "the great number of your letters . . . making pressing demands on me, asking that I offer my services as a peacemaker in this tempest. You might just as boldly command a Pygmy to take Atlas' place in holding up the heavens, yet you accept no excuse from me."

I would like to express my gratitude to the Getty Research Institute for the History of Art and the Humanities, Los Angeles. I wrote this paper while I was a resident scholar at the Institute.

2. Allen, Ep. 2344:19–20.
3. Allen, Ep. 2355:24.
4. Allen, Ep. 2343:3–4; similarly Ep. 2347:8, 2342:8–9.
5. "There was no need to make it known that you are the author" (Allen, Ep. 2336:25).
6. Allen, Ep. 2342:7–8.
7. Allen, Ep. 2492:37–40.
8. Allen, Ep. 2732:13–16.
9. Allen, Ep. 2786:5–6.

10. Cf. ASD V-3, 303:589–90: "The principal source of this tumult are people's impious minds."

11. ASD V-3, 304: "Conveniat inter nos fidei plurimum esse tribuendum, modo fateamur et hoc esse peculiare Spiritus Sancti donum, idque multo latius patere quam vulgus hominum credit. . . . Concedamus fide iustificari, hoc est, purificari corda credentium, modo fateamur ad consequendam salutem necessaria charitatis opera."

12. ASD V-3, 309–10: "Si in Eucharistia totus est Christus, quur non est adorandus? . . . Quoniam autem nemo certus est, an sacerdos vere consecraverit, praeter ipsum unum, nullus adorat ibi Christum, nisi sub tacita conditione."

13. ASD 304:643.

14. ASD 310:845–48: "quomodo sit ibi corpus et sanguis Domini . . . poterant in synodo definiri"; 311:876–78: "non ut quae dicimus pro certis haberi velimus aut praeeamus ecclesiae quid sit statuendum, sed ut interim, dum apparatur synodus."

15. Ibid., 309:794: "suo quenque arbitrio relinqueret"; 307:743: "sinantque alios in suo sensu acquiescere."

16. ASD V-3, 304:621–23.

17. Ibid., 304: 617: "Accedat illa sygkatabasis, ut utraque pars alteri sese nonnihil accommodet," 309:884–85.

18. Cf. the editor's preface to the text in ASD V-3, 254–55.

19. Allen, Ep. 2895: 83–84, 2935:3–10.

20. Allen, Ep. 2973.

21. Cf. Allen, Ep. 2906:5–6, to John Choler: "quod scribis meam Concordiam Romae Cardinalibus quibusdam displicuisse, demiror sinistra quorundam hominum iudicia." Needless to say, Erasmus did not publish this letter in his correspondence.

22. P. Tschackert, *Briefwechsel des Antonius Corvinus* (Hannover, 1900), 1.

23. Antonio Corvinus, *Quatenus expediat aeditam recens Erasmi de sarcienda ecclesiae concordia rationem sequi* (Wittenberg, 1534), D3 recto–verso.

24. Cf. E. Rummel, *The Confessionalization of Humanism in Reformation Germany* (New York, 2000), 132–34.

25. On Capito's relationship with Erasmus, see J. Kittelson, *Wolfgang Capito: From Humanist to Reformer* (Leiden, 1975), especially chapter II: "The Humanist at Basel."

26. ". . . quasi mihi deessent quae dicerem, si mihi permitterem agere scurram" (Allen, Ep. 2486:29–31).

27. "Nec de tua nec de Capitonis integritate tam magnifice sentio ut hanc animulam sim in fidem vestram commissurus" (lines 518–20 in Allen, Ep. 2615).

28. For a summary of the contents of the preface, see O. Millet, *Correspondance de Wolfgang Capiton (1478–1541)* (Strasbourg, 1982), 173–74.

29. On these controversies, see E. Rummel, *Erasmus and His Catholic Critics* (Nieuwkoop, 1989), I:67–92 and II:10–11.

30. Cf. ibid., II:12–15.

31. For the text, see L. Hunt and E. Rummel, "Vergerio's Invective Against Erasmus and the Lutherans: An Autograph in the Biblioteca Marciana," *Netherlands Archive for Church History* 80 (2000): 1–19.

32. WA Briefe VII: 16–17. On Witzel's reform plans see B. Henze, *Aus Liebe zur Kirche Reform: Die Bemühungen Georg Witzels (1501–1573) um die Kircheneinheit* (Münster, 1995).

33. Georg Witzel, *Von der einigkeyt der kyrchen. Durch Erasmus von Roterodam ytzt new ausgangen* (Erfurt, 1534), Bi recto.

34. Cited by H. Louthan, *The Quest for Compromise: Peacemakers in Counter-Reformation Vienna* (Cambridge, 1997), 128, n. 24.

35. Cassander in *De officio pii ac publicae tranquillitatis vere amantis vir in hoc religionis dissidio* (On the Duty of a Pious and Peace-loving Man in This Religious Strife), p. 30 (without place of publication, 1562); Erasmus in Allen, Ep. 2344:16–17.

4

The Possibilities and Limits of Conciliation

Philipp Melanchthon and Inter-confessional Dialogue in the Sixteenth Century

EUAN CAMERON

Melanchthon, the Unreliable Reformer

Of all the leading sixteenth-century Protestant reformers, Philipp Melanchthon seems to offer the most attractive possibilities for exploring the theme of conciliation. With Martin Bucer, whom he initially distrusted but with whom he later collaborated quite extensively, Melanchthon was involved in nearly every major effort towards mediation between Protestants and Catholics up to the definitive Peace of Augsburg in 1555.

Yet this "conciliating" quality has done more harm than good to Melanchthon's esteem from his own times up to the recent past. He has gained some notoriety for being unstable and unreliable, all the more so when contrasted to the colossal personality of his greater colleague Martin Luther. Melanchthon's confidence wobbled badly when confronted with the Zwickau prophets at

Wittenberg in 1521–1552, until his resolve was stiffened by letters from Luther.[1] At Augsburg in 1530 he seemed ready to barter away nearly the whole Reformation for the sake of peace, and was prompted by colleagues to be more steadfast.[2] He was party to the discussions at Regensburg in 1541, which produced a mediating book speedily disowned by both Wittenberg and Rome.[3] In the negotiations after the defeat of the Schmalkaldic League in 1546–1547, Melanchthon temporized with the notorious Leipzig *Interim* settlement during 1548, sparking off the fratricidal "adiaphorist controversy" within the Lutheran camp. At various times he was suspected or even accused outright of having been corrupted, suborned, or bribed by the Catholic side, even of seeking a cardinal's hat for his pains.[4] Forged drafts of compromise theologies were circulated under Melanchthon's name, either to blacken his name with other Lutherans, or to borrow his prestige to assist in some ulterior project.[5]

Melanchthon was deemed unstable in temperament as well as tactics. At Augsburg both Veit Dietrich and Johannes Brenz compared his depressive and worried state to Luther's serene confidence, while Osiander puzzled over his melancholy. Those were just the opinions of his friends.[6] As for his critics, at a critical point Hieronymus Baumgartner of Nuremberg called him "more childish than a child" for his negotiating posture.[7] Melanchthon was not only irresolutely Lutheran: he seemed at times to be resolutely unLutheran. His insistence on the role of repentance and "good works" in the life of the redeemed Christian distanced him first from minor figures like Agricola and Cordatus,[8] and much more seriously from the Gnesiolutherans of the Ernestine university at Jena after the Schmalkaldic war.[9] His Eucharistic theology was deemed insufficiently aggressive in its defense of the bodily presence of Christ. His hostility to preaching the doctrine of predestination to ordinary people appeared a curious foible.[10] Recent analysis of Melanchthon's theology has tended, in contrast to the writers of the early twentieth-century "Luther-Renaissance," to stress his "through and through Lutheran character."[11] However, the worries remain.

Melanchthon was always ready to defend himself, as he often needed to do. His watchwords were moderation, reasonableness (*epieikeia*),[12] the search for clarity and consistency in theological formulae, and absolute frankness in discussion.[13] Yet his experiences in the inter-confessional dialogues suggest that it was an uphill struggle both to keep to those principles, and to avoid being blackened by the accusation of temporizing and appeasement. This essay will try to see the dialogues of the period 1530–1548 through Melanchthon's eyes and through his words. It will suggest that Melanchthon's attitude to conciliation was colored by a stronger dogmatic cast than many of his hostile critics could ever acknowledge. Clarity and frankness, however laced with moderation and reasonableness, made the process of conciliation more difficult rather than easier. Disagreements could not be covered over with a haze of words.

Melanchthon at Augsburg, 1530

Because of Luther's outlawry under the Ban of the Empire after the Diet of Worms in 1521, it fell to Melanchthon to lead the delegation of Saxon theologians at the crucial meeting of the Diet at Augsburg in 1530. From Melanchthon's correspondence at the time, it is clear that he attended the meeting under a shadow of impending religious war. The Peasant War of 1525, with its tens of thousands of casualties, had been bad enough; what would follow if peace talks failed would, it was expected, be far worse.[14] He believed that some of the other side were absolutely resolved on fighting.[15] He affirmed that he "would accept peace even on harsher conditions" than those on offer when the diet was meeting.[16]

In these circumstances Melanchthon adopted an interesting strategy, which can be viewed as either brilliant or naïve, depending on one's perspective. In the first place, his negotiations with the emperor's secretary Alfonso Valdes and later with Cardinal Lorenzo Campeggio focused most upon the second main division of the Confession of Augsburg, which was entitled, in irenic mode, "articles in which there are listed abuses which have been changed."[17] The rhetoric of this section ran something as follows. Everyone acknowledged that there were errors and "abuses" in the medieval church. All that the Lutherans had done was to anticipate the work of a future General Council by reforming some of them on their own account. The re-ordering of affairs to eliminate these "abuses" therefore constituted the absolute minimum that the Protestant states and cities would accept as terms for a compromise. The "wish list" which Melanchthon then presented followed the order in which these so-called "changed abuses" were listed in the Augsburg Confession. First and foremost came the right of the laity to receive both kinds in the Eucharist, and that of priests to marry. At various times in the negotiations Melanchthon and his colleagues also stipulated the abolition of private masses, and the continued dissolution of most monasteries.[18] Melanchthon's view was that it had always been planned to make some compromises with the Catholics;[19] however, these demands were *faits accomplis* from which the Lutherans could not be asked to slide back.[20]

The main carrot to be dangled before the Catholic and imperial representatives was that, subject to certain conditions, the Protestants might be willing to acknowledge and restore obedience to the bishops of the church in their regions, whose authority had *de facto* lapsed.[21] Given that Melanchthon was ready to acquiesce in princely power over the churches, calling the princes *praecipua membra ecclesiae*,[22] it is most intriguing that in the context of the negotiations he viewed the restoration of *episcopal* authority with something approaching enthusiasm. The church, Melanchthon felt, needed a structure, a polity (*politeia*), within which it would be governed by those who cared about religion.[23] Doubtless the near chaos which had been revealed in the visitations of the Saxon Church in the late 1520s may have influenced him here.[24] Needless to say, the bishops who were to be restored to some sort of supervision over the Lutheran churches would have had to act towards them in a quite different manner from previously. They would also have had to respect some of the reservations on church power as set out in the Augsburg Confession.[25] Most importantly, they would have to connive at the distinctive practices and preferences of their Protestant subjects over the Eucharist, married priests, and so forth. Melanchthon seems, in effect, to have envisaged a solution not entirely dissimilar to that arrived at by the Council of Basel in the *Compactata* with the Hussite churches in 1433–1436. The Protestant churches would have become a privileged and peculiar section within the western Latin communion.[26]

Of course, Melanchthon's vision of a return to the Catholic communion on certain terms raised a huge number of intractable practical problems, which were immediately seized upon by objectors. As Geryon reported to Spalatin around 20 August 1530, did this mean that only those priests already married could remain married, while others would be punished if they married subsequently? Were the Lutherans to be forced to agree (as the Hussites had been required to) that receiving the Eucharist in one kind was not unlawful? In that case, what was the point of their insisting on receiving both elements themselves? If the canon of the Mass were to be restored, how could a Lutheran interpretation of the Eucharist be sustained?[27] Similar problems would have arisen with the bishops. Could Protestants accept as their bishop someone who connived at Protestantism where it was already established, but continued to persecute it elsewhere?[28] The bitterest criticisms, however, came quite predictably from the representatives of the free cities, led by Nuremberg and its delegate Hieronymus Baumgartner. Had they fought for centuries to exclude episcopal authority from their cities and ultimately from their churches, only for Melanchthon to bring it

back again?[29] Confronted with such furious reactions, Melanchthon, anticipating many a later Reformation historian, remarked to Luther:

> The common people who have become used to freedom, having
> once shaken off the yoke of the bishops, takes it badly to have those
> old burdens laid on them again; the imperial cities especially detest
> that overlordship. They are nothing bothered about the teachings
> of religion: they are only concerned with power and freedom.[30]

At this point Melanchthon may seem to have falsified the claim made by
many Reformation historians: that the core, the beating heart as it were, of
the Reformation was the doctrine of justification, and that everything, including liturgical and ecclesiological changes, flowed by logical progression
from that doctrine. Can Melanchthon possibly have failed to appreciate the
point which his own works, such as the *Loci communes,* had so clearly eluci-
dated? Here the brilliance—or the naïvety—of Melanchthon's tactics becomes especially clear. At least in the early stages of the Diet of Augsburg of
1530, he took the doctrines of the first part of the Confession of Augsburg
entirely for granted. Of course this was the correct interpretation of the doctrine of the one Catholic Church! The Protestants and the followers of the
Roman Church taught the same doctrines (against others, such as the Zwinglians, who dissented from them); therefore, he reasoned, there was no need
for savage repression, since only details of ritual divided them.[31] It might be
the case that a few "illiterate and disgraceful theologians" disagreed with this,
but they were just wrong. Melanchthon could exploit the doctrinal confusion
and disagreement over the theology of the Reformation, which suffused the
Roman Church from the 1520s until Trent, to claim that his theology was
the true Catholic teaching. Melanchthon made it clear that he despised his
Catholic opponents as incompetents, and expected their limitations to be
clear to all.[32] Eck, he believed, had been unable to raise cogent arguments
against *sola fide;* by late August 1530 he believed that Eck had been forced to
yield the point.[33] This was, as it were, the Trojan horse in Melanchthon's
strategy. As Brenz pointed out to Isenmann on 11 September, if the Catholic
bishops allowed Protestant doctrine to be preached freely, then they would
have sold the pass entirely. In their bargaining position, the Lutheran theologians had not really given anything away that mattered.[34]

At the Diet of Augsburg Melanchthon, whether through guile or simplicity, distracted attention from the crucial doctrinal issues by making the
negotiations revolve around relatively peripheral ceremonial and disciplinary

matters. Had the negotiations succeeded, the doctrinal sections of the *Augsburg Confession* might have been enshrined, even if only by default, in a formal agreement. It would then have been difficult for the Council of Trent, seventeen years later, to have resolved its decree on justification as it did. The whole ceremonial machinery of Catholicism might even have gradually unravelled. On the other hand, given that negotiations failed, Melanchthon appeared to have made far more significant concessions than he had actually done, as Brenz, for one, realized. The screams of protest from sections of Lutheran opinion may have helped to convince the emperor and leading Catholics that Melanchthon, and the Wittenberg faculty as a whole, had been more conciliatory than they were. On 30 August, according to Melanchthon, Eck had jested that since the emperor had put off suppressing Lutheranism long enough for Melanchthon, Bruck, and the others to make their case, his mind had calmed and he lacked the necessary zeal. "So you see," Melanchthon wrote with gentle irony to his friend Joachim Camerarius, "there is not a total lack of judgment or prudence in our enemies."[35]

Melanchthon and the Religious Conferences of c. 1540

Melanchthon's attitudes to religious conciliation changed in various subtle ways as both his theology and his perception of the ecclesio-political realities altered during the late 1530s. The threat of religious war, once so fearsome, receded somewhat.[36] The confusion and disarray among Roman Catholic theologians increased, to the point where Philipp Melanchthon could be seriously hopeful of winning over significant numbers of them.[37] Against this background two apparently contrary tendencies manifested themselves in Melanchthon's theology. On one hand, in the revisions of the *Loci communes* leading up to the 1535 edition, Melanchthon placed ever greater emphasis on the role of "good works" and "new obedience" in the life of the Christian believer. He even found a formulation, to which he held firm subsequently, by which good works done after justification could be said to be "rewarded" in this life and in the life to come, even though they did not as such contribute to justification.[38]

On the other hand, Melanchthon became increasingly aware that as a statement of definitive Protestant theology, the original Augsburg Confession was inadequate.[39] During the period leading up to the religious conferences of 1540 Melanchthon produced the *Confessio Augustana Variata*, which then formed the basis for the discussions.[40] Subsequent history has made the *Variata* notorious for the leeway which it later offered German Calvinists to accept it, and not the 1530 *Invariata*, and thereby to claim civil rights under the 1555 Peace of Augsburg.[41] However, at the time, most of the changes made in the *Variata* actually made it less, not more conciliatory to the Catholic side: it was toughened up, not watered down.[42] In keeping with this tendency, Philipp Melanchthon acquired something of a reputation at the conferences for becoming a much tougher cookie either than Bucer or his own earlier self.[43] At the Worms conference, Charles V's representative Nicholas Perrenot de Granvelle cut short a speech proposing Melanchthon as one who would make a temperate response to the papal nuncio by growling, "I know he is temperate—when he wants to be."[44]

During the negotiations leading up to the Hagenau, Worms, and Regensburg conferences, the moderate Catholic theologians, led by Julius Pflug of Meissen, Johannes Gropper of Cologne, and (slightly more surprisingly) Johannes Eck, adopted a common tactic, albeit in slightly different ways. Pflug, in the Meissen draft for reforming Albertine Saxony, Gropper in his *Enchiridion,* and Eck in his draft articles for the Worms conference of 1540, all concocted theologies which based themselves loosely on Melanchthon's moderate Protestantism, but tried to draw the sting of the Lutheran *sola fide* with a host of qualifications and ambiguities designed to save as much of the old Catholic ways as possible.[45] Bizarrely to modern ears, Johannes Eck, before the Worms conference, had boasted that he had composed so "Lutheran" a set of articles that they would be unacceptable to his own side. To his chagrin, however, when the majority of the Catholics accepted them for discussion, the Brandenburg, Palatinate, and Jülich delegates wished for a draft even closer to Lutheranism.[46] The outcome was a constant frenzy of drafting and re-drafting in the Catholic camp: one observer remarked that articles were drawn up and then dismantled like Penelope's web.[47]

One might have expected, given the apparently ambivalent theology of Melanchthon's *Loci* in the mid-1530s, that he would have regarded such compromise articles as an opportunity. In fact, his response to this verbal and theological juggling was quite the opposite. He detested it. Having worked so hard to achieve balance and clarity in his own writing, he saw nothing but treachery and obscurity in this game. Of Gropper's *Enchiridion* he wrote to Archbishop Hermann von Wied of Cologne: "I wish for such a concord as does not pour a fog over the truth, and does not establish old errors with a cunningly devised excuse . . . deceptive things are not durable."[48] In his will, written late in 1539 when his astrological readings made him fear an early death, he wrote: "there will be, perhaps, new sophistical conciliations of doctrines after this age, in which old errors will be restored, covered up a bit, and these conciliations will corrupt the purity of doctrine which is now handed on. About these also I warn my [successors], lest they approve sophistical conciliations."[49] Melanchthon's vehemence on this point surprised his contemporaries. At Worms it was even suggested that he should be excluded from the discussions because of his displays of anger. He wrote to Luther: "it is just a childish game to throw up clouds in front of the simple by means of unlearned and ambiguous phrases."[50] Part of this anger seems to have been provoked by the Catholic tactic of claiming that the key issues dividing the parties, especially on justification, were strife over words, "*Wortgezänk.*" To Melanchthon, someone who could say such a thing was either so ignorant or so cynical as not to think that Christian doctrine mattered.[51]

Nevertheless, Melanchthon held a consistent and firm view of how the process of conciliation *ought* to work, which once again suggests either brilliance or naïvety, or even a little of both. He believed that the purpose of the conferences was to discuss the articles of the *Confessio Augustana Variata,* and to adjudicate on them, with absolute freedom and without preconceptions, in accordance with Scripture and the testimony of the early church. He wished for a genuinely free disputation, which he then expected to win, because he was so unshakably sure of his theological ground. At Worms, he complained to Granvelle that the Catholic negotiators "call nothing a conciliation unless it is a defection from the truth"; rather than genuinely negotiating, they sought to find a form of words which would, in effect, trick the Protestants into recantation. As Melanchthon's colleague Caspar Cruciger complained to Bugenhagen on 14 December 1540, "they call a conciliation not a true consensus on doctrine, nor any change of the status of popery, but simply a defection to their side."[52]

As at Augsburg ten years earlier, Melanchthon perceived the importance of getting the key doctrines right. His negotiating strategy was to divide the contested issues into (1) essential doctrines, (2) essential external things, and (3) externals which might be things indifferent (*adiaphora*) including jurisdiction, ordination, church property, and suchlike.[53] The problem was, however, that there could be no meaningful coming together over *adiaphora* while there remained fundamental division over the essentials of faith.[54]

It must now now be clear that the failed strategy of the Regensburg book of 1541 belonged more properly to the tactics of Bucer on one side and the Catholic moderates on the other, than to Philipp Melanchthon. It embodied precisely that search for ambiguous mediating phrases which Melanchthon so disliked.[55] The main legacy of the Regensburg book lay in its influence on the *Interim* imposed on the defeated Lutheran states in 1548, to which I now turn briefly.

Philipp Melanchthon and the *Interim*, 1548

The aftermath of the war of the League of Schmalkalden gave Melanchthon an opportunity to display his commitment to the key doctrines of the Reformation in the most pressing and dangerous of circumstances. After the Diet of Augsburg of 1548, the victorious Charles V sought to impose a moderate, mediating Catholic settlement of doctrine and worship on the empire. Melanchthon had chosen, despite many hostile comments, to return to Wittenberg when the war ended rather than joining others in the Ernestine university at Jena. He thus fell under the jurisdiction of the new elector, Duke Moritz of the Albertine Saxon Wettin dynasty. Moritz, detested as a traitor by many Lutherans, might easily have handed Melanchthon over to Charles V, and was indeed asked to do so at one point.[56] Moritz instead asked for Melanchthon's and his colleagues' opinions on the *Interim*, in ways which eerily echoed the problems and dilemmas of 1530.

Melanchthon and his allies, including Cruciger, Pfeffinger, and Maior, subjected the *Interim* to a detailed and exhaustive theological review, which went through no less than five drafts of increasing sophistication and detail.[57] One need not linger over the details. Melanchthon's suspicion of such cunning formulae remained unallayed. At one point he called the *Interim* "the Sphinx of Augsburg."[58] He reacted strongly to the wording which described faith as merely a "preparation for righteousness" which was to be amplified with love and other virtues. In contrast, he defended the Augsburg Confession's statement on justification as containing "the unalterable truth of the Gospel."[59] While the *Interim*'s carefully worded section on the Mass explicitly denied that the Mass was a "thank-offering" rather than a work earning merit for the soul, Melanchthon's keen senses detected enough potential ambiguities, especially in the wording of the canon, to cause trouble unless they changed. As in 1530, he was willing to consider the restoration of episcopal authority (by now a real possibility as Julius Pflug took up his see of Naumburg), but warned that unless the bishops changed their treatment of the Protestants, it would be like making peace between wolves and sheep.[60] For the *adiaphora* which would cause such trouble thereafter, Melanchthon actually left very little room, assigning to this category only the trivial visual appurtenances of worship. That did not, of course, prevent some of his ultra-Lutheran colleagues from thundering that wearing a surplice for worship (the only significant change introduced by the Leipzig *Interim*) was an act of idolatry.[61]

Conclusions

It seems that the cost of doing justice to Melanchthon as a theologian is to damage his reputation as a religious conciliator! Yet when Melanchthon's approach is considered in its own context and within his own world of ideas, there is something surprisingly cogent about it. He felt hemmed in by the zealous partisan fundamentalism of some of his Lutheran colleagues on one side, and the fluid, slippery verbiage and negotiating tactics of the Catholic liberals on the other. If one accepts that credal formulae can capture divine truths—and this assumption went largely unchallenged in the sixteenth century—then Melanchthon's refusal to horse-trade over fundamental beliefs appears honest and sincere, while his readiness to negotiate on peripheral issues of ritual and organization was both realistic and responsible.

Melanchthon was indeed a conciliator, in that he saw a clear need to protect and establish the nascent Protestant churches as far as was practicable in the real world. Here lies one of many differences which separate Melanchthon from Luther. Luther, especially in his more apocalyptic moods, could send his enemies to the devil, in the expectation that whatever cosmic or earthly chaos ensued, Christ would soon come again to sort things out. Melanchthon could never overlook the fact that tomorrow, almost certainly, one would have to live with the consequences of today's decisions.[62]

Melanchthon's remarks about Luther got him into trouble on several occasions. An interesting example is afforded by the letter which he wrote to Moritz's counsellor Christoph von Carlowitz when the latter pressed him to agree to the *Interim* on 28 April 1548. Melanchthon took the opportunity to defend himself from the charge of obstinacy by setting out his record as a moderate. He described his earlier career as a "servitude," because "often Luther paid more heed to his temperament, in which there was no little love of controversy, than either to his own good or to the public welfare." Melanchthon found himself embroiled in controversies not of his making, selected the teachings which were true and necessary, and "removed or polished up certain absurd opinions." The people and unlearned preachers "poured oil on the flames," and Melanchthon's temperate attitude even brought his life into danger.[63] Despite these caustic remarks, there is no doubt whatsoever that Melanchthon viewed Luther's key insight on justification as the voice of God revealing the truth to humanity: he said so in so many words.[64] However, Melanchthon was a moderate, and a conciliator, because he saw that a stable church could not be established in the midst of the pyrotechnics of adversarial confessional rhetoric such as Luther so readily allowed himself. His desire to calm tempers and to balance theological language arose not from uncertainty or weakness, but from a passionate faith which passionately required clarity, balance, stability, and order. So great was his commitment to honesty and integrity in theological questions, that he could bear neither to see positions exaggerated from hostility, nor to participate in attenuating truths by specious word games. If conciliation was to achieve anything, it had to be based on genuine agreement rather than spurious ambiguities. To reason in this way was to take the business of conciliation with the seriousness it deserved.

NOTES

1. For Melanchthon's responses to the "Wittenberg movement," see *Melanchthons Briefwechsel: Kritische und kommentierte Gesamtausgabe*, ed. H. Scheible (Stuttgart-Bad Cannstatt, 1977–) (hereafter *MBW*), T1, 416–18, 444, 492. A recent discussion of this crisis in Melanchthon's career is provided in S. Kusukawa, *The Transformation of Natural Philosophy: The Case of Philip Melanchthon* (Cambridge, Cambridge University Press, Ideas in Context, 1995), 51–58; on the Wittenberg movement itself, see R. W. Scribner, *Popular Culture and Popular Movements in Reformation Germany*, (London, 1987), 145–49.

2. See below; also the letters of Lucius Paulus Rosellius in *Philippi Melanchthonis Opera quae supersunt Omnia*, ed. C. G. Bretschneider and others (*Corpus Reformatorum*, vols. 1–28, Halle, 1834–1860), (hereafter *CR*), vol. 2, cols. 227–28, 243–44.

3. On these negotations see esp. Peter Matheson, *Cardinal Contarini at Regensburg* (Oxford, 1972).

4. For occasions when Melanchthon was accused of being bribed or corrupted by the Catholic side, see *CR*, vol. 2, cols. 332–33, 336; vol. 3, col. 827; vol. 6, col. 881; vol. 7, col. 352. On the adiaphorist controversy, see R. Kolb, *Nikolaus von Amsdorf (1483–1565): Popular Polemics in the Preservation of Luther's Legacy* (Nieuwkoop, 1978), 69–112; R. Kolb, "Dynamics of Party Conflict in the Saxon Late Reformation: Gnesio Lutherans vs. Philippists," *Journal of Modern History* 49 (1977): D1289–1305; R. Stupperich, *Melanchthon* (London, 1977), 122 ff; C. L. Manschreck (ed. and trans.), *Melanchthon on Christian Doctrine: Loci Communes 1555* (New York, 1965), 280–302.

5. *CR*, vol. 3, cols. 830–37.

6. *CR*, vol. 2, cols. 158–60, 163–64, 186.

7. *CR*, vol. 2, col. 363: "Philippus ist kindischer denn ein Kind worden."

8. On the controversy with Agricola see Timothy J. Wengert, *Law and Gospel: Philip Melanchthon's Debate with John Agricola of Eisleben over Poenitentia*, Texts and Studies in Reformation and Post-Reformation Thought (Grand Rapids, 1997), *passim;* on the controversy between Cruciger and Cordatus, in which Melanchthon became embroiled, see Wengert, *Law and Gospel*, 154, 206 ff, and *CR*, vol. 3, cols. 159–61, 181–82, 184–86, 202–4, 206–8, 341–49.

9. Kolb, *Nikolaus von Amsdorf*, 123–224; E. Muehlenberg, "Synergia and Justification by Faith," in L. W. Spitz and W. Lohff (eds.), *Discord, Dialogue and Concord: Studies in the Formula of Concord* (Philadelphia, 1977), 15 ff.

10. For Melanchthon's later attitudes to the Eucharist, see *MBW*, vol. 8, 72–73, 179–81; *CR*, vol. 9, cols. 156, 157, 409, 431. On Melanchthon and predestination, compare the 1521 *Loci*, in *Melanchthons Werke in Auswahl: Studienausgabe*, ed. R. Stupperich and others (7 vols. in 8, Gütersloh, 1951–1971) (hereafter *MWA*), vol. II/i 10–12; the 1533 and 1535 *Loci* in *CR*, vol. 21, cols. 330 ff, 450 ff; the 1555 *Loci* in Manschreck (ed. and trans.), *Melanchthon on Christian Doctrine*, 187 ff; and the final version in *CR*, vol. 21, cols. 912 ff, and *MWA*, vol. II/ii 592–602. He began to show active hostility to teaching the doctrine during the 1540s especially.

11. H. Scheible, "Melanchthon, Philipp (1497–1560)," in *Theologische Realenzyklopaedie* vol. XXII, 395, quoting Oswald Bayer, " 'Die Kirche braucht liberale Erudition': Das Theologieverständnis Melanchthons," in *Kerygma und Dogma* 36 (1990): 243.

12. See e.g. *CR*, vol. 2, col. 358: "Pacem videremur consecuturi, si paulo essent aequiores et tractabiliores isti, qui meam ἐπιείκειαν reprehendunt."

13. See e.g. *CR*, vol. 3, cols. 343–45, 1144, 1244.

14. See the anonymous letter to Melanchthon in *CR*, vol. 2, cols. 342–43: "persuadeas tibi velim, me omnia sincera et recta mente tentasse, ne novus tumultus praetextu Evangelii in Germania oriretur, forte et maiori clade quam prior ille fatalis rusticorum tumultus." C. G. Bretschneider observed, ibid., col. 168, that Melanchthon was so terrified by the prospect of war that he would make peace at more or less any price.

15. *CR*, vol. 2, cols. 146, 197, 383.

16. *CR*, vol. 2, cols. 119, 328.

17. Part II of the *Augustana* was entitled "Articuli in quibus recensentur abusus mutati": see e.g. B. J. Kidd, *Documents Illustrative of the Continental Reformation* (Oxford, 1911), 270–89.

18. *CR*, vol. 2, cols. 122–23, 168–74, 246–49, 280–85.

19. *CR*, vol. 2, cols. 140–41, 145–46, and esp. 334: "nihil adhuc concessimus adversariis, praeter ea, quae Lutherus censuit esse reddenda, re bene ac diligenter deliberata ante conventum."

20. *CR*, vol. 2, cols. 249, 347–48, and, for the reasons for the rejection of private masses, cols. 353–55.

21. *CR*, vol. 2, cols. 173–74, 247, 283–84: "mag man die Bischöffen ihre Obrigkeit über die Pfarrer im Kirchenregiment zustellen, als mit ordiniren, so sie unsre Lehre nicht verfolgen, und die Priester nicht mit ungöttlichen Eiden und Bürden verfolgen."

22. For Melanchthon's view of the princes as "praecipua membra ecclesiae," see e.g. W. D. J. Cargill Thompson, *The Political Thought of Martin Luther*, ed. P. Broadhead (Brighton, 1984), 147, 151; H. Strohl, *La Pensée de la réforme* (Neuchâtel and Paris, 1951), 183–88, 245–46. Given Melanchthon's caustic comments about lay magistrates' conduct towards the church in the correspondence reviewed here, emphasis on this aspect of Melanchthon's thought should be tempered somewhat.

23. *CR*, vol. 2, cols. 233, 303, 334, 341: "Quo iure enim licebit nobis dissolvere πολιτειαν ecclesiasticam, si Episcopi nobis concedunt illa, quae aequum est eos concedere."

24. The classic text on this point is Luther's preface to the Shorter Catechism of 1529: see e.g. [Evangelisch-lutherische Kirche], *Die Bekenntnisschriften der Evangelisch-lutherischen Kirche, herausgegeben im Gedankjahr der Augsburgischen Konfession 1930* (Berlin-Charlottenburg, 1930, and subsequent edns.), 501–7.

25. The issue of prelatical power is addressed explicitly in Article VII of the Confession of Augsburg: see Kidd, *Documents*, 283–88; see also Brenz's comments to Isenmann, 11 September 1530, in *CR*, vol. 2, cols. 361–62: "De dominatione autem episcoporum in ministros ecclesiae eadem nobiscum sentiunt boni quique. Sed, inquis, pseudoprophetae sunt et homicidae. At, si nostra media et conditiones acceptarent, desinerunt esse pseudoprophetae et homicidae."

26. *CR*, vol. 2, cols. 169–71, 173–74, and esp. col. 327, where Melanchthon explicitly compared his negotiating position to that of the Bohemians at the Council of Basel, though his stand on both kinds was firmer than theirs.

27. Geryon to Spalatin, in *CR*, vol. 2, cols. 295–97; but cf. cols. 317–18, where Brenz made it clear that the Protestants would not give the asked-for endorsement for communion in one kind.

28. See Eberhard Schnepf's critique of Melanchthon's proposals on episcopal authority, in *CR*, vol. 2, cols. 329–31: "Ob einer mir nit verbeut die Lehre des Glaubens, verbeut sie aber meinem Bruder, ist er gleichwohl ein Antichrist." The same problem was recognized by the other Protestants by 17 September, as in *CR*, vol. 2, cols. 375–76.

29. For the Nuremberg representatives' reports of Melanchthon's negotiating posture, see *CR*, vol. 2, cols. 121–24, 312–14; and Melanchthon's comments, cols. 328–29, 333–36.

30. *CR*, vol. 2, col. 328: "nam vulgus assuefactum libertati, et semel excusso iugo Episcoporum, aegre patitur sibi rursus imponi illa vetera onera; et maxime oderunt

illam dominationem civitates imperii. De doctrina religionis nihil laborant; tantum de regno et libertate sunt solliciti."

31. *CR,* vol. 2, col. 170: "Ecclesiae Romanae dogmata summa constantia defendimus"; but cf. col. 172, and for clearer listing of areas of disagreement, cols. 297–99, 377–78.

32. For Melanchthon's contempt for the opposing side's theologians, see e.g. *CR,* vol. 2, col. 173 ("tantum vociferantur adversus me theologi quidam illiterati et improbi"), also cols. 252–53.

33. *CR,* vol. 2, cols. 299–300, 316–17, 335.

34. *CR,* vol. 2, col. 362: "Si enim quis diligenter rem consideret, ita proposuimus, ut videamur aliquid concessisse, cum re ipsa nihil plane concesserimus; idque ipsi plane intelligunt."

35. *CR,* vol. 2, col. 335.

36. Melanchthon reported to Camerarius, 5 April 1540, that the ancient German manliness had all but died out, and there was "great laziness on both sides" so war was less likely: *CR,* vol. 3, col. 987.

37. Athina Lexutt: *Rechtfertigung im Gespräch: Das Rechtfertigungsverständnis in den Religionsgesprächen von Hagenau, Worms und Regensburg 1540/41* (Forschungen zur Kirchen- und Dogmengeschichte, Bd. 64, Göttingen: Vandenhoeck and Ruprecht, 1996), 28–30; see also *CR,* vol. 3, cols. 1159, 1209–10, 1226.

38. For "good works" and "new obedience" in the 1533 and 1535 revisions of the *Loci communes,* see *CR,* vol. 21, cols. 308–19, 428–38; for similar themes in the *Confessio Augustana Variata,* see *MWA,* vol. VI, 17–18, 30–35; for Melanchthon's discussion of this theme during the Cordatus affair, see *CR,* vol. 3, cols. 180, 185, 356, 385–86.

39. See e.g. Melanchthon's letter to the Nuremberg clergy of 17 February 1540, *CR,* vol. 3, col. 961, in which he wrote, presumably of the *Variata,* "De doctrina plane sic decrevimus, nos prorsus nullam mutationem ullius articuli Confessionis et Apologiae admissuros esse . . . Sunt autem res nostrae aliquanto pluribus lucubrationibus ita iam patefactae atque illustratae, ut quid vere sentiamus satis liqueat." The implication is that the *Variata* was intended specifically to avoid ambiguity.

40. The complete text of the *Variata* is in *MWA,* vol. VI, 12–79; for discussion see Lexutt, *Rechtfertigung,* 113–25.

41. On the use made of the *Variata* in Germany's "Second Reformation," see e.g. Henry J. Cohn, "The Territorial Princes in Germany's Second Reformation, 1559–1622," in Menna Prestwich (ed.), *International Calvinism 1541–1715* (Oxford, 1985), 142–45.

42. For the "toughened" passages in the *Variata,* see *MWA,* vol. VI, 16–17, 19–21, 38–45; see also E. Cameron, "Philipp Melanchthon: Image and Substance," *Journal of Ecclesiastical History* 48, no. 4 (1997): 716–19.

43. Lexutt, *Rechtfertigung,* 45, 231; see C. G. Bretschneider's comment, in *CR,* vol. 3, col. 1143, that "the manner of writing which Melanchthon used seemed too

bitter . . . to the delegates." On 14 December 1540 Cruciger reported that Melanchthon had been excluded from certain discussions "quem accusant, quod nunc sit factus asperior": *CR,* vol. 3, col. 1213.

44. *CR,* vol. 3, col. 1230: "Granvellus, cui cum diceret Franciscus, me modeste
responsurum esse, respondit ille: Scio modestum esse, cum vult."

45. For the Lutheran theologians' reaction to Pflug's "Meissen book" see *CR,*
vol. 3, cols. 728–38; for Gropper's *Enchiridion* see R. Braunisch, *Die Theologie der
Rechtfertigung im "Enchiridion" (1538) des Johannes Gropper: sein kritischer Dialog mit
Philipp Melanchthon* (Münster, 1974), which makes detailed comparisons with
Melanchthon's *Loci;* for an example of Eck's technique at the conferences see his ar-
ticles in *CR,* vol. 3, cols. 1054–59.

46. *CR,* vol. 3, cols. 1225–28; Lexutt, *Rechtfertigung,* 158–73.

47. *CR,* vol. 3, cols. 1209–10.

48. *CR,* vol. 3, col. 652.

49. *CR,* vol. 3, col. 826.

50. Melanchthon to Luther, 17 December 1540, in *CR,* vol. 3, col. 1229: "Est
omnino puerilis ludus ineruditis amphibologiis offundere nebulas rudibus."

51. *CR,* vol. 3, col. 932: "die Weltweisen halten allen Streit in der Religion für
Wortgezänk"; see also cols. 1158, 1229–30.

52. *CR,* vol. 3, col. 1213: "Sed illi conciliationem vocant non verum consensum
de doctrina, nec ullam mutationem papistici status, sed simpliciter defectionem ad
ipsos." Compare cols. 998, 1243.

53. *CR,* vol. 3, cols. 926–45, 961–65.

54. *CR,* vol. 3, cols. 999–1000: "Quorsum enim prodesset, aliquid pacisci de
ritibus aut de iurisdictione cum iis, qui adhuc revera in articulis principalibus doctrinae dissiderent?"

55. Lexutt, *Rechtfertigung,* 236–70; Melanchthon expressed his ultimate hostility to the final document in *CR,* vol. 4, cols. 413 ff; ironically, Eck said that it abandoned the manner of speaking of the church and the fathers and "Melanchthonized"
instead.

56. On 17 March 1548 Charles V asked Elector Moritz of Saxony to hand Melanchthon over to him for writing seditiously against him; on 31 August he demanded that Moritz exile him from his territories: see *CR,* vol. 6, xvii, and vol. 7, vii;
on 6 December Melanchthon complained that his correspondence was being inter-
cepted: see *CR,* vol. 7, cols. 230–31.

57. For these intricate theological pieces, written in German for Moritz's benefit,
see *CR,* vol. 6, cols. 839–42, 853–57, 865–74, 924–42, and *CR,* vol. 7, cols. 12–45.

58. *CR,* vol. 7, col. 73.

59. *CR,* vol. 6, col. 911: "Diese Lehre ist die unwandelbare Wahrheit des
Evangelii."

60. *CR,* vol. 6, col. 889.

61. *CR*, vol. 7, ix, and col. 404.

62. For the contrast between Luther and Melanchthon, see Heiko A. Oberman, *The Reformation: Roots and Ramifications,* trans. Andrew C. Gow (Edinburgh,
1994), 23–52.

63. *CR*, vol. 6, cols. 879–85.

64. See Melanchthon's will, in *CR*, vol. 3, col. 827; and his oration to the students of Wittenberg on Luther's death, in *CR*, vol. 6, cols. 58–59.

5

The Conciliating Theology
of John Calvin

Dialogue among Friends

RANDALL C. ZACHMAN

JOHN CALVIN IS NOT WIDELY REPUTED TO HAVE BEEN A CONCILIATING theologian. Instead, Calvin is most often portrayed in light of his controversy with Bolsec over the doctrine of double predestination, and his contribution to the condemnation and execution of Servetus, leaving one with the clear impression that Calvin was incapable of tolerating the slightest degree of doctrinal diversity or disagreement. In his first lectures on Calvin in 1922, Karl Barth described Calvin in theological controversy in this way: "How cutting he is, how self-conscious, how sharply prepared to be in the right at any price, how ready not only to smash his foe intellectually but also to destroy him morally."[1] The recent study by Philip Holtrop of the Bolsec controversy has confirmed this impression of Calvin. "He was capable of conniving, contriving, distorting, and even wanting his enemies to be put to death."[2] As Francis Higman has noted, the style Calvin developed in refuting his opponents reinforces this sense of his intolerance, for he would usually describe his opponents as insane or as various animals, especially pigs and dogs, and would reduce their positions to the ravings of lunatics or the barking of dogs.[3]

There is, of course, more than a little truth to this portrait of Calvin. However, this picture of Calvin has tended to eclipse another aspect of Calvin's work as a teacher that led him to tolerate a remarkable degree of doctrinal diversity so that apparent doctrinal opponents might be reconciled through an open and mutual dialogue in pursuit of the truth. Although Calvin had concluded early on that reconciliation with Rome was neither possible nor desirable, he was profoundly distressed by the tendency among evangelical teachers to condemn and separate from one another over every difference of opinion, most strikingly in the rupture between Luther and Zwingli concerning the holy Supper of the Lord. "It does not follow that every difference of opinion should immediately break out into an open rupture. . . . For it behooves us not rashly to break up our connection with those whom the Lord has joined with us in the fellowship of his work."[4] Those working to restore the Gospel should be viewed as members of one body, so that separation from them should be avoided with the same aversion with which one would view dismemberment. "Good God, to what a point we have come. We ought to consider a separation from the ministers of Christ, with the same disposition as if our own bowels were torn out. Now it is almost a sort of sport not only to cut off certain members, but to retrench the most vital parts from their connection with us."[5] Calvin was well aware that serious differences existed between himself, Luther, Melanchthon, Bucer, and Bullinger on this question, but he was concerned lest any teacher insist on the correctness of his own position over against those with whom he disagreed. "For this is my purpose, that banishing all suspicions which are an obstacle to us, we should confidingly on the one side and the other listen to each other's reasons, reserving for our own judgment the question itself intact until the truth be discovered."[6] The same Calvin who sought to destroy some opponents intellectually and smash them morally also had within himself the heartfelt desire to tolerate doctrinal diversity in an effort to seek confessional unity through a dialogical inquiry into the truth.

How are we to account for this underappreciated willingness of Calvin to live in unity with those with whom he disagreed doctrinally? I shall argue that Calvin adopts a distinction from Cicero and Erasmus regarding two distinct forms of discourse or rhetoric, *contentio* and *sermo*.[7] One engages in contention when the essentials of the Christian faith are at stake, in an effort to destroy both the opponent and his argument. This is the genre for which Calvin is especially well known. However, where there is agreement about the essentials of Christian teaching, then one addresses disagreement not in the mode of contention, but by conversation (*sermo*), in an attempt to discern the truth through a mutual, dialogical inquiry. "The orator's purpose in *contentio* is to beat the opponent; the speaker's purpose in *sermo* is to seek the truth, collectively, with the other interlocutors."[8] According to Cicero, conversation assumes friendship, which is based on the recognition of the virtues of the other participants in the conversation, and their willingness to listen to one another until the truth be discovered. This means that conversation must follow a certain *decorum* that is not found in contention, most notably the lack of any appeal to emotions, and the exercise of moderation and self-restraint. "The *decorum* of conversation, which does not permit emotional manipulation, impels speakers, instead, to seek an emotional equilibrium in the conversation, that is, to produce a condition of tranquility that would permit reason to come to the fore. . . . 'Conversations' [*sermones*], Cicero writes, 'flourish best in friendships' (*De officiis* 1.17.58)."[9] Gary Remer argues that Erasmus applied Cicero's rhetoric of conversation to the discussion of non-essential articles of faith. Where there is agreement about the essential doctrines of faith, one may accept diversity and even disagreement with regard to non-essential doctrines. Such differences should not be argued contentiously and publicly in sermons and published treatises, but should rather be discussed dispassionately and in private, by sober, learned, and godly people, in a collective effort to discern the truth. "The effect of Erasmus's *decorum*, governed by the search for truth, is to foster controlled debate in the interest of truth. Because Erasmus sees conversation as the means to reveal greater truth, he supports discussion of nonessential doctrines. Yet he also regulates the discussion to ensure the proper rhetorical environment. For Erasmus, discussion must be free of both verbal and physical abuse, lest the discovery of truth be obstructed."[10]

Calvin is able to seek the reconciliation of certain doctrinal disputes because he, like Erasmus, operates with a distinction between the essential elements of Christian teaching and the non-essentials about which there can be legitimate disagreement. "For not all the articles of true doctrine are of the same sort. Some are so necessary to know that they should be certain and unquestioned by all men as the proper principles of religion. . . . Among the churches there are other articles of doctrine disputed which still do not break the unity of faith."[11] Like Cicero and Erasmus, Calvin insists that learned and godly men discuss such disagreements in private, in an open attempt to discern the truth through dialogue. The basis for such conversation is the trust that is created between friends, who are drawn to the virtues that they discern in one another, following Cicero's understanding of friendship. "But of all the bonds of fellowship, there is none more noble, none more powerful than when good men of congenial character are joined in intimate friendship; for really, if we discover in another that moral goodness on which I dwell so much, it attracts us and makes us friends to the one in whose character it seems to dwell."[12] The best way to understand Calvin's method of attempting to conciliate doctrinal disputes is to begin by examining those virtues that attracted him to other teachers of doctrine, and led him to see them as his friends, thereby creating the conditions in which *sermo,* and not *contentio,* could take place.

The Essential Virtues of the Godly Teacher

According to Calvin, the office of teacher involves two essential tasks: seeking the genuine meaning of Scripture, and teaching in a clear and simple way the doctrine drawn from the genuine meaning of Scripture. Since Calvin was convinced that the Roman Church had come to ruin by distorting the meaning of Scripture, the work of teachers is the primary means by which the church may be both restored and preserved. "We have many disputes on a variety of matters with the realm of the Roman Antichrist, but almost all of them derive from the fact that we want a hearing to be given to Christ, the prophets, and the apostles, while our adversaries, not daring openly to impose silence on them, require them to take second place to their own imaginings."[13] Hence Calvin encouraged rulers such as Edward VI to support the work of godly interpreters in his land. "As interpreters of Scripture according to their ability supply weapons to fight against Antichrist, so you also must bear in mind that it is a duty which belongs to your Majesty, to vindicate from unworthy calumnies the true and genuine interpretation of Scripture, so that religion may flourish."[14] The presence of godly teachers in the church is as necessary as Scripture itself, for without them the genuine meaning of Scripture cannot be brought to light. "God does not wish the aids, which he appoints for us, to be despised, and does not allow contempt of them to go unpunished. And we must keep in mind here, that not only is Scripture given to us, but interpreters and teachers are also added to help us."[15] Not even the illumination of the Holy Spirit makes such teachers and their gifts irrelevant or unnecessary, for "the Lord, with the same consideration by which he illumines us through his Spirit, has, in addition, granted us aids, which he intends to be of assistance in our labor of investigating his truth."[16]

What, then, are the gifts that the godly teacher needs, both to seek the genuine meaning of Scripture, and to teach the doctrine drawn from that meaning with simplicity and clarity to the Church? Calvin seems to have a hierarchy of gifts that he admires in others, and that draw him into various forms of fellowship with them. Some gifts are seen in pagan teachers; others are found both in Jews and in members of the Church of Rome; and some are unique to the community of orthodox evangelicals. Although Calvin would only view orthodox evangelicals as his friends, this should not lead us to slight his association with others outside this group in whom he discerns the virtues and gifts of a teacher.

To begin with, the teacher and interpreter must be a person of sound judgment. This means that he must agree on the principles that form the basis of all sound judgments in theology, namely, that there is a sense of divinity in all people teaching them that there is some god whom all must worship, obey, and adore; that the soul is an immortal essence distinct from the body; that there is a natural sense of equity in the reason and conscience of every person; and that purity of conscience is more important than external sacrifices. Since such sound judgment is found in Cicero and Plato (whom Calvin calls "the most religious of all and also the most sober"), they are viewed by Calvin as fellow teachers of those doctrines that God teaches all people, over against those whom Calvin calls the Epicureans, who deny such principles.

The next level of gifts has to do specifically with the interpretation of Scripture itself. Since Scripture is written in both Hebrew and Greek, and is interpreted in Latin, a godly teacher needs to be learned, i.e., skilled in Hebrew, Greek, and Latin literature. "The sacred oracles of God were delivered by Moses and the Prophets in Hebrew, and by the Apostles in Greek. That no corner of the world might be left destitute of so great a treasure, the gift of interpretation was added."[17] Skill in Hebrew literature is found among Jews as well as Christians, especially in Rabbi Kimchi, whom Calvin respected as "the most faithful among the Rabbis."[18] Skill in Greek and Latin is found among interpreters who remained members of the Roman Church, such as Lorenzo Valla, Desiderius Erasmus, Guillaume Budé, and Faber Stapulensis. Even though they were not members of the evangelical movement, Calvin makes common cause with them to refute the claim of the Council of Trent that the Old Vulgate should be normative. "What! Are they not ashamed to make the Vulgate version of the New Testament authoritative, while the writings of Valla, Faber, and Erasmus, which are in everybody's hands, demonstrate with the finger, even to children, that it is vitiated in innumerable places?"[19] Even Jacopo Sadoleto is respected by Calvin as a learned man skilled in literature, in spite of the fact that he wrote the Genevans to win them back to Rome. "In the great abundance of learned men whom our age has produced, your excellent learning and distinguished eloquence hav[e] deservedly procured you a place among the few whom all, who would be thought studious of liberal arts, look up to and revere."[20] Calvin could genuinely respect the gift of learning even in those who were otherwise his doctrinal opponents.

The third level of virtues—piety and teachableness—distinguished the evangelical and orthodox teachers from Jews and members of the Roman Church. Piety is the practical knowledge that God offers himself as the fountain of every good thing in Jesus Christ through the Holy Spirit and the Gospel, so that one seeks access to God only through Christ in the Holy Spirit. This knowledge is central to what all Christians should seek in their reading of Scripture. "This is what we should in short seek in the whole of Scripture: truly to know Jesus Christ and the infinite riches that are comprised in him and are offered to us by him from God the Father. . . . [O]ur minds ought to come to a halt at the point where we learn in Scripture to know Jesus Christ and him alone, so that we may be directed by him to the Father, who contains in himself all perfection."[21] Knowledge of the free self-giving love of God in Christ therefore forms the core of the essential doctrines that all orthodox Christians must believe and confess. "Such [necessary doctrines] are: God is one; Christ is God and the Son of God; our salvation rests in God's mercy; and the like."[22] These essential doctrines of piety lie at the foundation of the Church, for they direct us to the fountain of every good thing that the Father offers to us in Christ. "For since Christ is the foundation of the Church, because he is the one and only source of salvation and eternal life, because in him we know God the Father, because the fountain of all blessings is in him, then if He is not acknowledged as such, He immediately ceases to be her foundation."[23]

Directly related to piety for Calvin is teachableness, which leads one to be taught by God through Christ by the Holy Spirit in sacred Scripture. "For our wisdom ought to be nothing else than to embrace with humble teachableness, and at least without finding fault, whatever is taught in Sacred Scripture."[24] The godly teacher will always seek to be a student of sacred Scripture, making sure that what he teaches to others he has first drawn from the genuine meaning of Scripture itself. "Therefore let this first axiom stand, that no doctrine is worth believing except such as we perceive to be based on the Scriptures."[25] However, since the godly teacher always has other interpreters to guide him, he must be willing to listen to them and learn from their instruction. "For no one will ever be a good teacher, if he does not show that he himself is teachable, and always ready to learn; and the man will never be met who is so self-sufficient in the fullness and completeness of his knowledge that he would gain nothing by listening to other people. All, therefore, should carry out their duties as teachers in such a way as not to decline their turn as learners, or to be annoyed at having to do so, whenever others are given the opportunity of giving instruction to the Church."[26] Teachers should therefore make every effort to maintain unity and consensus with one another, and should only disagree with the interpretation of others out of the necessity of maintaining the genuine meaning of Scripture, and not out of a desire to set themselves apart from them. "When, therefore, we depart from the views of our predecessors, we are not to be stimulated by any passion for innovation, impelled by any desire to slander others, aroused by any hatred, or prompted by any ambition. Necessity alone is to compel us, and we are to have no other object than that of doing good."[27]

Even when endowed with all the gifts and virtues of a godly teacher, a given teacher may be more skilled as an interpreter of Scripture than as a teacher of doctrine, for "there is a peculiar gift of interpreting Scripture, so that sound doctrine may be kept."[28] Calvin tended to think that the most skilled and reliable interpreter of Scripture of his day was Martin Bucer. "In addition to his profound learning, abundant knowledge, keenness of intellect, wide reading, and many other varied excellencies, in which he is surpassed by hardly anyone at the present day, this scholar, as we know, is equaled by few and is superior to very many. It is to his special credit that no one in our time has been more precise or diligent in interpreting Scripture than he."[29] Such skills clearly make Bucer a reliable teacher for Calvin, and he cites them as evidence that Heinrich Bullinger can trust Bucer as much as Calvin does, in spite of their different understandings of the Lord's Supper. "Endowed, as indeed he is, with a singularly acute and remarkably clear judgment, there is, at the same time, no one who is more religiously desirous of keeping within the simplicity of the word of God, and is less given to hunt after niceties of interpretation that are quite foreign to it, but who actually holds them in more abhorrence, than himself."[30] After Bucer, Calvin also acknowledged the considerable gifts of Philipp Melanchthon as an interpreter of Scripture, especially in light of the impressive breadth of his learning. "Philip Melanchthon has given us a great deal of light by reason of the outstanding character both of his learning, industry, and the skill in all kinds of knowledge in which he excels, in comparison with those who had published commentaries before him."[31] Calvin was especially impressed by Melanchthon's knowledge of history: "Master Philip . . . excels in genius and learning, and is happily versed in the studies of history."[32] After Melanchthon, Calvin was most impressed by the interpretive work of Oecolampadius, Bullinger, Musculus, Zwingli, and Luther, although Calvin made note of Luther's comparative lack of learning.[33] "Luther is not so particular as to propriety of expression or the historical accuracy; he is satisfied when he can draw from it fruitful doctrine."[34]

Just as the highest virtue of the interpreter is seeking above all else the natural and genuine meaning of Scripture, so the chief virtue of the teacher of godly doctrine is the ability to teach clearly, simply, and straightforwardly, in a manner accommodated to the capacities of the audience; for "the task of teachers consists in preserving and propagating sound doctrines (*sana dogmata*) so that purity of religion may remain in the Church."[35] If Bucer took pride of place for his skill as an interpreter of Scripture, then Melanchthon excelled all others as a teacher of godly doctrine. Calvin called Melanchthon "the greatest of theologians," a person "of the most penetrating judgment, and profoundly learned in heavenly doctrine."[36] Calvin was especially impressed by the clarity and simplicity of Melanchthon's style of teaching, telling him: "you are pleased by an unembellished and frank clarity which, without any concealment, sets a subject before the eyes and explains it. This quality of yours has often stirred in me great admiration, for, although you are outstanding for your amazing insight, you still rank nothing above straightforwardness."[37] Calvin had the highest praise for Melanchthon as a teacher, calling him the "most illustrious light and most distinguished teacher of the church," who "had discharged with the highest fidelity and diligence the office of a teacher, and also deserved the highest honors from the whole church."[38] After Melanchthon, Calvin praised his colleague Martin Luther, noting "the excellent endowments with which he is gifted," especially his "strength of mind and resolute constancy," and his "efficacy and power of doctrinal statement," which he used "to diffuse far and near the doctrine of salvation."[39] Calvin also admired Martin Bucer, calling him "that most faithful teacher of the Church of God," and Heinrich Bullinger, whom he praised for his ease of doctrinal expression.[40]

From Disagreement to Conversation (*Sermo*)

We now can see all the virtues that Calvin considered to be essential in the godly teacher in the church. Such a person must be of sound judgment; learned in Hebrew, Greek, and Latin; pious; teachable; skilled in seeking the genuine meaning of Scripture; and able to teach doctrine drawn from Scripture clearly, simply, and forcefully. When Calvin detected all these virtues in another teacher, he was drawn into friendship with him, and saw himself as one in Christ with that person, even when Calvin did not agree with him on all matters of Scriptural interpretation or doctrine. Indeed, Calvin thought that such differences of opinion are inevitable even among the most gifted teachers. "We have continually found, however, that there is by no means universal agreement even among those who have not been found wanting in zeal for godliness, or piety and moderation in discussing the mysteries of God." The reason for this is that God wants us to be teachable, so that we are willing to learn from those with whom we disagree, and humble, so that we do not prematurely separate from those with whom we differ. "God has never so blessed his servants that they possessed full and perfect knowledge of every part of their subject. It is clear that his purpose in so limiting our knowledge was first that we should be kept humble, and also that we should continue to have dealings with our fellows. Even though it were otherwise highly desirable, we are not to look in the present life for lasting agreement among us on the exposition of Scripture."[41]

So long as the essential doctrines, virtues, and skills are in evidence among teachers who disagree, the proper way to conciliate differences of opinion between them is through conversation (*sermo*), and not through contention (*contentio*). "For this is my purpose, that banishing all suspicions which are an obstacle to us, we should confidingly on the one side and the other listen to each other's reasons, reserving for our own judgment the question itself intact until the truth be discovered."[42] Such conversation is made possible above all else by the virtue of teachableness, which includes both the willingness continually to learn from Scripture and the humility to learn from other teachers. Calvin thought that the dispute that erupted between Zwingli and Luther over the holy Supper of the Lord had been so damaging because both sides resorted to contention, when they should have followed the decorum of conversation. They should have recognized each other as one in Christ and as teachers of the church, and should therefore have reconciled their differences of opinion in a dialogical inquiry into the truth, following the proper decorum of moderation, openness, mutual trust, and respect. "And this alone I ask of you, that you constantly retain that faith in which you have hitherto stood, but in such a manner as that you may not appear of your own free will to seek for a rupture with those to whom you cannot refuse the right of being esteemed both by you and all pious men as among the leading servants of God."[43] Instead, both sides resorted to the rhetoric of *contentio,* creating discord and inflaming passions, thereby obstructing almost completely a dialogical inquiry into the truth. "Both parties failed altogether to have patience to listen to each other, in order to follow the truth without passion, wherever it might be found."[44] In particular, both sides went astray by placing one of their teachers—either Luther or Zwingli—above the other. "Howbeit, in the Church, we must always be on our guard, lest we pay too great a deference to men. For it is all over with her, when a single individual, be he whoever you please, has more authority than all the rest, especially where this very person does not scruple to try how far he may go."[45] Calvin's concern for open participation in the conversation clearly echoes Cicero's description of the decorum governing *sermo:* "And the one who engages in conversation should not debar others from participating in it, as if he were entering upon a private monopoly; but, as in other things, so in a general conversation (*sermone*) he should think it not unfair for each to have his turn."[46]

The attempt to reconcile differences of opinion by conversation can take place only if those who disagree see themselves as one with those with whom they are conversing. Only on the basis of this prior unity, based on the discernment in the other of the essential virtues of the teacher, is it possible to work for further unity by seeking a consensus on the matters about which there is still disagreement. Because Calvin admires and is drawn to the virtues he sees in Luther, Zwingli, Oecolampadius, Melanchthon, Bucer, and Bullinger, he assumes that he is one with them in Christ, in spite of their differences with regard to the interpretation of the verse of Scripture, "This is my body." Thus, ten years before he and Bullinger arrived at the Zurich Consensus regarding the Supper, Calvin reminded Bullinger that they were already one in Christ, and therefore had an obligation to come to an agreement on the matters about which they still disagreed. "We see indeed of how much importance it is, not only on our own account, but for the sake of the whole body of professing Christians everywhere, that all those on whom the Lord has laid any personal charge in the ordering of his Church, should agree together in a sincere and cordial understanding." However, such agreement is only possible if those who disagree refuse to resort to contention, and instead follow the decorum of conversation among friends. "I require of you, dear Bullinger, or rather, again and again I entreat you, that we may not only be as far removed as possible from all hatred and contention, but even from all appearance of offence."[47] Calvin also repeatedly professed his unity in Christ with Philipp Melanchthon, in spite of his failure ever to come to public agreement with Melanchthon concerning the matters about which they disagreed, especially the Lord's Supper, free will, and election. "Whatever happens, let us cultivate with sincerity a fraternal affection towards each other, of which no wiles of Satan shall ever burst asunder the ties."[48] So long as Melanchthon remained alive, Calvin had hope that a public agreement could be reached between Geneva and Wittenberg about these matters.

Unity amid Diversity: Calvin, Chrysostom, and Melanchthon

As we have seen thus far, when Calvin discerned in other teachers sound judgment, learning, piety, skill in Scripture, and skill in doctrine, he saw himself as one with them, even in light of clear differences of interpretation or doctrine. Calvin's sense of unity with those with whom he differed doctrinally is further revealed by two translation and publication projects that he planned to undertake between 1540 and 1546. These translation projects show that Calvin was not only willing to seek the conciliation of differences of opinion among godly teachers, but was also willing to publish interpretations of Scripture and summaries of doctrine that clearly differed from his own. Calvin was willing to do this because he was convinced they were teaching the essential doctrines of the Christian faith, and because he discerned in them the essential gifts needed for sound interpretation and teaching. He therefore wanted the French people to benefit from their teaching, even though they often differed in significant ways from his own teaching.

By 1540, even after he had begun work on his own biblical commentaries, Calvin devised a plan, never to be executed, of translating and publishing the homilies of John Chrysostom in French.[49] Calvin chose Chrysostom above all other patristic authors because he was learned and skilled in Greek, and sought to use his gifts in order to set forth the plain and genuine sense of Scripture. "The chief merit of our Chrysostom is this: he took great pains everywhere not to deviate in the slightest from the genuine plain meaning of Scripture, and not to indulge in any license of twisting the straightforward sense of the words."[50] This is the same virtue that Calvin praised in his contemporaries, especially Bucer, indicating Calvin's unity with Chrysostom on the essential skills of the interpreter of Scripture. Moreover, Chrysostom, like Calvin, sought to make this genuine sense available to all the people of God. "That I share a common concern with Chrysostom is unquestionably more than adequate justification for me, because I am just imparting to ordinary people what he wrote specifically for ordinary people."[51]

Calvin sought to translate Chrysostom into French in order to put into the hands of his unlearned countrymen a faithful guide to the interpretation of Scripture, which is the same task that Calvin had set for himself as a godly teacher. "The point is, if it is right that ordinary Christians be not deprived of the Word of their God, neither should they be denied prospective resources, which may be of use for its true understanding."[52]

The decision to translate and publish Chrysostom in French reveals just how tolerant Calvin was of doctrinal differences in those whom he viewed as godly and skilled teachers, for Chrysostom and Calvin differed rather markedly in their doctrines of free will, justification, and election. The extent of their differences is revealed in Calvin's comments about Chrysostom in the 1539 *Institutes:* "the Greeks above the rest—and Chrysostom especially among them—extol the ability of the human will."[53] Calvin also published his own commentary on Romans in 1540, which contained extensive discussions of the doctrines of free will, justification, and election. If doctrinal unity per se were more important to Calvin than setting forth the plain and genuine sense of Scripture, there is no question that Calvin would have translated Augustine into French, and not Chrysostom. By choosing Chrysostom, Calvin sought to make available as widely as possible an interpreter of Scripture who both sought the true meaning of Scripture and who needed to be assessed by the very Scripture whose meaning he was so adept at uncovering. "I am saying: let us make a frank assessment of everything which has been written, but respectfully and impartially [i.e., following the decorum of *sermo*], and let us not accept anything unless it has been subjected to scrutiny."[54] Calvin indicates to the reader those places where he finds Chrysostom to be wanting—i.e., in the not negligible doctrines of free will, grace, merit, vocation, and election. These criticisms or corrections have the effect of placing the authority of Chrysostom under the authority of Scripture, which the teachable teacher should be willing to do. However, by seeking to publish these homilies, Calvin also shows himself to be teachable, making it clear that his own work as an interpreter of Scripture is done in unity with the efforts of Chrysostom, in spite of the doctrinal differences lying between them.

In 1543, Calvin published the third edition of his *Institutes,* and as was his custom, it appeared both in Latin and in a French translation. In the same year, Melanchthon came out with another edition of his *Loci communes.* Calvin and Melanchthon had met at the Diets of Frankfort, Worms, and Ratisbon, and based on Calvin's recognition of Melanchthon's superlative skills as a teacher of godly doctrine, Calvin considered Melanchthon to be his friend until the latter's death in 1560.[55] In 1543, as a token of his friendship, Calvin dedicated his reply to Pighius to Melanchthon. In his letter of dedication, Calvin depicts Melanchthon as a defender of the same doctrine of the bound and liberated will as Calvin—something that would be true of the 1521 *Loci,* but not of editions after 1535. In his letter to Calvin thanking him for his dedication, Melanchthon makes clear his disagreement with Calvin's doctrine of free will and election, which Melanchthon thinks borders on Stoic necessity, making God the author of sin. "I maintain the proposition that God is not the author of sin, and therefore cannot will it. David was by his own will carried into transgression. He might have retained the Holy Spirit. In this conflict there is some margin for free will. . . . Let us accuse our own will if we fall, and not find the cause in God. . . . So says the Word of God, and in this let us abide."[56]

In spite of their clear differences on free will and election, about which Calvin could have no doubt, in 1546 Calvin published a French translation of the 1543 edition of Melanchthon's *Loci communes.* In his preface to the translation, Calvin indicates that he and Melanchthon agree on the essential and necessary doctrines of piety, for he says that the godly will find in the *Loci* a brief summary of all the things a Christian must know in order to be guided on the road to salvation, which is the same goal Calvin set for himself in his *Institutes.* Calvin also praises Melanchthon for using his learning in the service of building up piety by means of the simplicity and clarity of his teaching, which Calvin viewed as the essential task of the teacher of godly doctrine. As in his Chrysostom preface, Calvin sets forth for the godly reader those places where Melanchthon is found to be in need of correction, namely in his teaching about free will, election, and absolution. Again, this indicates the necessity of judging all teachers by the teaching of Scripture, something that Calvin encouraged the readers of his French *Institutes* to do.[57] However, Calvin concludes his preface by exhorting the reader to approach the *Loci* in a teachable way (*se render docile*), in order to be conducted by the hand to the pure truth of God.[58]

Just as Calvin intended to set forth Chrysostom in French as a genuine interpreter of Scripture, in spite of the different ways they interpreted significant passages of Scripture, so also Calvin sought to make Melanchthon known to French readers as a true teacher of pious doctrine, in spite of their clear doctrinal differences. As Philip Schaff has rightly pointed out, such an event is unique in the Reformation period; yet it is significant for our purposes to show how Calvin could accept doctrinal differences if the other teacher taught the essential doctrines of piety, and manifested the essential skills of a teacher of doctrine.[59] It is true that Calvin privately became increasingly exasperated with Melanchthon because of his teaching on free will and election, which was turned against Calvin in the Bolsec controversy, and also due to Melanchthon's silence when some of Melanchthon's students attacked the Zurich Consensus. However, in spite of these differences, Calvin always considered himself to be one in Christ with Philipp, because of his love of piety, his great learning, and his clear and superlative gifts as a teacher of sound and edifying doctrine.

Conclusion

Both the planned Chrysostom translation project, and the actual publication of Melanchthon in French, clearly reveal how Calvin was able to see himself as one in essentials with teachers who disagreed with him in rather significant ways. Given how well known Calvin was in his own day for his doctrines of free will and election, his ability to publish interpretations of Scripture and summaries of godly doctrine which contained positions on those topics contrary to his own reveals that unity in the essential skills and virtues of the godly interpreter and teacher was more important to Calvin than unity in all interpretations of Scripture, or consensus in all doctrinal loci. Calvin was willing to live in unity with those with whom he disagreed doctrinally if he sensed that they were committed to seeking the natural meaning of Scripture, and if they wished to set forth clearly and accurately the doctrine they drew from Scripture. Moreover, such a commitment to inquire into the meaning and doctrine of Scripture was the only basis Calvin saw for establishing doctrinal unity in the future. Calvin was convinced that the prior unity of godly teachers made possible a way of seeking consensus that avoided the animosity and inflamed passions of the rhetoric of contention, namely, by following the decorum of conversation (*sermo*), in which differences between friends are worked out in an open-ended dialogue, in an attempt to come to a greater discernment of the truth of Scripture. "Now, seeing that a serious and properly adjusted agreement between men of learning upon the rule of Scripture is still a desideratum, by means of which Churches, though divided on other questions, might be made to unite; I think it right for me, at whatever cost of toil and trouble, to seek to obtain this object."[60]

NOTES

1. Karl Barth, *The Theology of John Calvin*, trans. by Geoffrey Bromiley (Grand Rapids: Wm. Eerdmans, 1995), 321.

2. Philip C. Holtrop, *The Bolsec Controversy on Predestination from 1551 to 1555*, vol. 1 (Lewiston, Penn.: Edwin Mellen Press, 1993), 3.

3. Francis Higman, *The Style of John Calvin in His French Polemical Treatises* (London: Oxford University Press, 1967).

4. John Calvin to Zebedee, 19 May 1539, *Ioannis Calvini opera quae supersunt omnia*, ed. Wilhelm Baum, Edward Cunitz, and Eduard Reuss (Brunswick: A. Schwetschke and Son [M. Bruhn], 1863–1900), vol. 10, p. 346C; henceforth CO 10:346C, *John Calvin: Selections from His Writings*, ed. John Dillenberger (New York: Anchor Books, 1971), 51.

5. Ibid.

6. Ibid.

7. I will be drawing from the work of Gary Remer on this distinction, in his book *Humanism and the Rhetoric of Toleration* (University Park, Penn.: The Pennsylvania State University Press, 1996), 1–101.

8. Ibid., 37.

9. Ibid., 36–37.

10. Ibid., 100.

11. Inst. IV.i.12, *Institutio Christianae religionis, 1559, Ioannis Calvini opera selecta*, ed. Peter Barth, Wilhelm Niesel, and Dora Scheuner (Munich: Chr. Kaiser, 1926–1952), vol. V, p. 17, lines 4–12; henceforth OS V.17.4–12; *Calvin: Institutes of the Christian Religion*, ed. John T. McNeill, trans. Ford Lewis Battles (Philadelphia: Westminster, 1960), vol. 2, pp.1025–26; henceforth *Inst.* IV.i.12, OS V.17.4–12; (2:1025–26).

12. Cicero, *De officiis* I.xvii.55, trans. Walter Miller (Cambridge, Mass.: Harvard University Press, 1990), 59.

13. John Calvin, *The Bondage and Liberation of the Will: A Defense of the Orthodox Doctrine of Human Choice against Pighius*, ed. A. N. S. Lane, trans. G. I. Davies (Grand Rapids: Baker Books, 1996), 13; CO 6:238.

14. Calvin to Edward VI, *Calvin's New Testament Commentaries*, ed. David W. Torrance and Thomas F. Torrance (Grand Rapids: Eerdmans, 1959–1972), vol. 12, p. 226, henceforth CNTC 12:226.

15. Comm. Acts 8:31, CO 48:192B; CNTC 6:247.

16. "Calvin's Preface to Chrysostom's Homilies," trans. W. Ian P. Hazlett, in *Humanism and Reform: The Church in Europe, England, and Scotland, 1400–1643* (Oxford: Blackwell Publishers, 1991), 141; CO 9:832C.

17. John Calvin, "The Acts of the Council of Trent with the Antidote," in *Tracts and Treatises*, vol. 3, trans. Henry Beveridge (Edinburgh: Calvin Translation Society, 1936), 71; CO 7:414A.

18. Comm. Psalm 112:5, CO 32:174C; CTS 21:252.

19. "Trent with the Antidote," op. cit., 74; CO 7:416A.

20. *Responsio ad Sadoleti Epistolam,* CO 5:385B; *A Reformation Debate,* ed. John C. Olin (Grand Rapids: Baker Book House, 1976), 49.

21. *Praefatio in N.T. cuius haec summa est: Christum esse Legis finem,* CO 9:815B; *Calvin: Commentaries,* ed. Joseph Hartounian (Philadelphia: Westminster, 1958), 70.

22. *Inst.* IV.i.12, OS V.17.10–11; (2:1026).

23. Comm. 1 Corinthians 3:11, CO 49:354B; CNTC 9:74.

24. *Inst.* I.xviii.4, OS III.227–8; (1:237).

25. Comm. Acts 17:7, CO 48:398.

26. Comm. 1 Corinthians 14:31, CO 49:530B.

27. Calvin to Grynaeus, *Ioannis Calvini Commentarius in Epistolam Pauli ad Romanos,* ed. T. H. L. Parker (Leiden: E. J. Brill, 1981), 3–4; henceforth *Romans* 3–4; CNTC 8:4.

28. Comm. Ephesians 4:11, *Ioannis Calvini Opera Exegetica,* vol. XVI, *Commentarii in Pauli Epistolas,* ed. Helmut Feld (Geneva: Librarie Droz, 1992), 230.16–17; CNTC 11:179.

29. Ibid., 2.52–59; CNTC 8:2.

30. Calvin to Bullinger, 12 March 1539, *The Letters of John Calvin,* trans. Jules Bonnet, IV vols. (New York: Burt Franklin, 1972), vol. I, p. 114; henceforth *Letters* I:114.

31. Calvin to Grynaeus, *Romans* 2.45–47; CNTC 8:2.

32. Comm. Daniel 9:25, CO 41:176B; CTS 25:209.

33. "Zwingli, although he is not wanting in a fit and ready exposition, yet, because he takes too much liberty, often wanders far from the meaning of the prophet.... No one, I think, has more diligently applied himself to this pursuit than Oecolampadius, who has not always, however, reached the full scope of meaning" (Calvin to Viret, 19 May 1540, CO 11:36B; *Letters* I:188). "Bullinger has expounded doctrine with an ease of expression, and for this he has been widely commended" (Calvin to Grynaeus, *Romans* 2.51–52; CNTC 8:2). "And had the commentaries of Wolfgangus Musculus at that time been published, I would not have omitted to do them justice, by mentioning them in the same way, since he too, in the judgment of good men, has earned no small praise by his diligence and industry in his walk" (Preface to the Psalms, CO 31:13; CTS 8:xxv).

34. Calvin to Viret, 19 May 1540, *Letters* I:188.

35. Comm. 1 Corinthians 12:28, CO 49:506C; CNTC 9:271.

36. Calvin to Melanchthon, 27 August 1554, *Calvin: Selections,* 54.

37. Preface, *The Bondage and Liberation of the Will,* 3–4; CO 6:230.

38. Calvin to Melanchthon, 13 December 1558, CO 17:386; *Letters* III:484.

39. Calvin to Bullinger, 25 November 1544, CO 11:774B; *Letters* I:433.

40. John Calvin, "Preface to the Psalm Commentary," CO 31:13; CTS 8:xxv; "Calvin to Grynaeus," *Romans* 2:47–50; CNTC 8:2.

41. Calvin to Grynaeus, *Romans* 3; CNTC 6:4.

42. Calvin to Zebedee, CO 10:346; *Calvin: Selections,* 49.

43. Ibid., 51.

44. John Calvin, "Short Treatise on the Holy Supper of Our Lord and Only Savior Jesus Christ," CO 5:460A; *Calvin: Theological Treatises,* trans. J. K. S. Reid (Philadelphia: Westminster, 1954), 166.

45. Calvin to Melanchthon, 18 June 1545, CO 12:99; *Letters* I:467.

46. *De officiis* I.xxxvii.134.

47. Calvin to Bullinger, 12 March 1539, *Letters* I:115.

48. Calvin to Melanchthon, 13 December 1558, CO 17:386; *Letters* III:484.

49. "Following his admiration of Chrysostom's exegesis and preaching, it is no wonder that Calvin would have the idea of translating him into French in the period 1538–1540" (Hazlett, op. cit., 133. See also Irena Backus, "Calvin and the Greek Fathers," in *Continuity and Change: The Harvest of Late Medieval and Reformation History* (Leiden: E. J. Brill, 2000), 253–76; and A. N. S. Lane, *John Calvin: Student of the Church Fathers* (Grand Rapids: Baker Books, 1999).

50. Ibid., 145–46; CO 9:835A.

51. Ibid., 142–43; CO 9:833B.

52. Ibid., 141; CO 9:832C.

53. *Inst.* II.ii.4, OS III.245.18–19; (1:259).

54. "Preface to Chrysostom," 146; CO 9:835B.

55. See Randall C. Zachman, "Restoring Access to the Fountain: Melanchthon and Calvin on the Task of Evangelical Theology," in *Calvin and His Contemporaries: Calvin Studies Society Papers 1995, 1997* (Grand Rapids: CRC Product Services, 1998), 205–28; and Timothy Wengert, "'We Will Feast Together in Heaven Forever': The Epistolary Friendship of John Calvin and Philip Melanchthon," in *Melanchthon in Europe,* ed. Karin Maag (Grand Rapids: Baker Books, 1999), 19–44.

56. Melanchthon to Calvin, 11 May 1544, quoted in Philip Schaff, *History of the Christian Church* (Grand Rapids: Eerdmans, 1995), vol. 8, 392.

57. "Above all, I must urge him to have recourse to Scripture in order to weigh the testimonies that I adduce from it" ("Subject Matter of the Present Work," OS III.8.25–27; (1:8).

58. "Preface de la Somme de Melanchthon, 1546," CO 9:850.

59. "This is the only example of a Reformer republishing and recommending the work of another Reformer, which was the only formidable rival of his own chief work on the subject (the *Institutes*), and differed from it in several points" (Philip Schaff, op. cit., 393).

60. Calvin to Cranmer, April 1552, *Letters* II:348.

6

The Early Church as a Model of Religious Unity in the Sixteenth Century

Georg Cassander and Georg Witzel

IRENA BACKUS

ALTHOUGH AN INCREASING AMOUNT OF ATTENTION HAS BEEN devoted in recent years to studying how the early church was claimed by the main protagonists in the confessional struggles of the sixteenth century, scholars have tended to concentrate on thinkers with a clearly defined theological stance, paying little or no attention to the so-called middlemen of the period and the particular nature of their appeals to the early church in support of their positions. Georg Witzel and Georg Cassander, although very well known, have not been studied at all from that angle. This essay will throw a light on their projects of religious unity by examining the nature of their appeal to the early church. I thus hope to revise the received view of the two as pacific middlemen with no particular convictions.

Georg Cassander

In 1555 a curious volume came out from the presses of the heirs of Arnold Birckmann in Cologne. It contained "the works of blessed Vigilius, martyr and bishop of Trent, some of them never published previously in their entirety and now finally attributed to their author," together with a "commentary on two natures and one single person in Christ against the main heresies of this age. "[1]

The edition and the treatise were by Georg Cassander (1513–1566), an irenic Catholic theologian who sought to mediate between Catholics and Protestants, advocating, among other things, concessions by Catholics in the issues of communion in both kinds and clerical celibacy. He is mainly known for his work *De officio pii ac publicae tranquillitatis vere amantis viri in hoc religionis dissidio* (1561), where he sets out to show that abuses do not constitute a sufficient reason for leaving the Roman Catholic Church while openly airing his dislike of papal abuse of power. The work managed to offend both sides at the colloquy of Poissy in 1561.[2]

My intention here is not to discuss Cassander's peacemaking efforts but to examine his view of the early church as a model of unity, concentrating on his introduction to the works by Vigilius and his treatise *De duabus in Christo naturis*. According to Pontien Polman, Cassander in *De officio pii viri* argues that a religion acceptable to both Catholics and Protestants can be found in the faith of the early Christians as expressed by the Apostles' Creed. Cassander thus reduces the role of the Bible to that of a text already interpreted by tradition. On the other hand, concludes Polman, given that Cassander sees tradition simply as a means of putting biblical precepts into practice, it is plain that his position cannot really be assimilated to that held by orthodox Roman Catholic theologians.[3]

The relationship between the Bible and tradition figures very largely in Cassander's edition of Vigilius and in his treatise on the two natures of Christ. Is it really true to say that he sees tradition simply as a means of putting biblical precepts into practice? I argue that to Cassander the church of the first five centuries provides the universal standard of orthodoxy, regardless of how it interpreted the Bible. He thus takes it for granted that the early church was not free from heresies. Although he does not establish a correlation between the early church and either Catholics or Protestants, in *De duabus in Christo naturis* he does establish an exact correlation between the ancient heretics Eutyches and Nestorius on the one hand, and the sixteenth-century Anabaptists Menno Simmons and Adam Pastor on the other. However, to Cassander, their identification with fifth-century heretics is not an ultimate condemnation, as we shall see.

Who Was Vigilius?

His vision of the early church means that Cassander inevitably commits some historical blunders. Thus he works under the assumption that he is publishing the works of Vigilius, third bishop of Trent. In fact, the author is none other than Vigilius of Thapsus, who took part in the dramatic talks between Catholics and Arians called by the Vandal king, Huneric, in February 484. Nowadays he is presumed to have been the author of the pseudo-Augustinian *Contra Felicianum,* a brief work that presents in dialogue form the themes of the Trinitarian controversy on a purely rational basis without any recourse to scriptural quotations. This work was not among those published by Cassander. The two works that were published by him are now attributed to Vigilius of Thapsus without any doubt. One of them is the *Dialogus contra Arrianos, Sabellianos et Photinianos* in three books, where the dialogue between a Catholic and three heretical spokesmen aims to refute one heresy by another. The main thrust of the work, however, is anti-Arian, and it also survives in a recension with only three speakers, one Catholic, one Arian, and Probus, the pagan judge. This short recension was not published by Cassander. Also in the *Dialogus,* Vigilius mentions two more of his anti-Arian works, against Maribadus and against Palladius of Ratiaria. The other work published by Cassander, *Contra Eutycheten* in five books, presents the orthodox doctrine of Christology as intermediate between the errors of Nestorius and Eutyches and defends the Chalcedonian doctrine of Christ's two natures, divine and human, as coexistent without confusion and without separation in a single person.[4]

The *Vita* of Vigilius of Trent that Cassander published together with the works would have been at least partly responsible for his confusing the two Vigiliuses. It is a mysterious document which bears very little relation to the standard sixth-century *Life*[5] of Vigilius of Trent, which Cassander obviously did not know. According to the latter document, the bishop of Trent was famous for his missionary activities and for the building of numerous churches. During his episcopate in 397, Sisinnius, Martyrius, and Alexander, his co-workers, were killed. Vigilius is supposed to have sent an account of their martyrdom to Bishop Simplicianus of Milan and, later, another of John

Chrysostom accompanied by relics. He himself was stoned by pagans and after his death became the patron saint of his diocese. The *Life* omits to say that at the beginning of his ministry Vigilius received a letter from Ambrose accompanied by pastoral instructions.[6]

According to the *Vita* published by Cassander, Vigilius was made bishop of Trent at the age of twenty. He performed miracles and combated heresies in his work against Eutyches, still extant, in five books. In it he mentions other books, since lost, against Sabellius, Photinus, and Arius. He died a martyr at the age of forty when, after smashing the statue of Saturn, he stood on its plinth and preached that salvation came only from Jesus Christ. This was construed by pagans as profanation of their relics and Vigilius was stoned to death. He lived in the reign of the Emperor Anastasius at the same time as Pope Gelasius, around the year 500.[7]

In a short commentary that he appends to the *Vita* Cassander says that he did not look for any other sources of the life of "Vigilius of Trent." He also supplements the account with a mixture of fact and fiction. He claims (rightly) that the work mentioned in book five of *Aduersus Eutycheten* is in fact the *Dialogus* and that Vigilius mentions (in the *Dialogus*) that he also wrote a treatise against the Arian Palladius. At this point Cassander narrowly misses correctly identifying the author whose works he has edited. He notes that "Gennadius [of Marseille] mentions a certain Vigilius who lived around the time of Augustine and who wrote a work in praise of martyrs as well as a letter containing an account of the martyrs of his time in barbaric lands. I suspect—he concludes—that this is a different Vigilius, perhaps it is the same one to whom Ambrose wrote a letter."[8] He then concludes, again rightly, that the Vigilius whom he is editing could hardly have been a contemporary of Ambrose's seeing as Ambrose died in the reign of Arcadius and Honorius when Vigilius would have just been born. Cassander then speculates on the other discrepancies of date and concludes wrongly that the author whose works he edited is none other than Vigilius of Trent, who he thinks lived around 500. Although admitting the existence of two Vigiliuses, he cannot identify Vigilius of Thapsus and so attributes his dates and works to Vigilius of Trent.

Cassander's Understanding of the History of the Early Church

However, Cassander was not ignorant in matters of church history. Indeed, as is suggested by his introduction to the volume,[9] he showed considerable acumen in attributing the *Dialogus* (which had hitherto been attributed to Athanasius) to the misidentified Vigilius.[10] Before we go on to examine his conception of unity in the introduction,[11] and in the treatise on the two natures, some remarks about Cassander's historical methods are in order.

He first became acquainted with Vigilius's work on his sickbed nearly two years previously around 1553, when a friend read out to him *Aduersus Eutycheten.* On having the unnamed friend read in the fifth book of *Adu Eut.* that Vigilius had written books against Sabellius, Photinus, and Arius under the name of Athanasius, he immediately identified the *Dialogus* and reattributed it to its rightful author. Indeed, he adds, he never thought that the work was by Athanasius but could not reattribute it. Whether Cassander is simply claiming twenty-twenty hindsight or whether he really doubted the *Dialogus*'s Athanasian authorship is immaterial. What matters is that the arguments he adduces in the introduction as to why the work could not have been written by Athanasius are solidly based. He adduces grounds of style and of chronology. It is well known, he notes, that Arius died before the accession of Constantius II, in whose reign the *Dialogus* is set. The author of the *Dialogus,* however, seems to be someone living in the fifth century, as he follows the error of Rufinus in extending Arius's life up to the reign of Constantius.[12] Cassander is then led to explain why no one prior to him had correctly identified the author of the *Dialogus.* It was most likely due to the fact that hitherto no manuscripts and no printed books were available that contained *Contra Eutycheten* as well as the *Dialogus.* The sole cause for doubting his identification is Vigilius's statement that he wrote books and not a book against Arius, Sabellius, and Photinus. Casssander explains the discrepancy by suggesting that the *Dialogus* could have been divided into two books, with the second day's discussion constituting book two. This explanation calls for some comment, and we shall return to it.

Apart from extending the lives of Arius and Athanasius into the reign of Constantius II, Vigilius does not seem to have committed many anachronisms and he is judged by Cassander to have been a fairly accurate historian. His sole other blunders are to situate Sabellius in the reign of Constantius (whereas according to Eusebius he was a third-century theologian) and to attribute some chronologically incorrect statements to Athanasius:

> He has Athanasius mention the blessed Ambrose and Palladius, condemned for Arianism by the synod of Aquileia [381]. Athanasius mentions that Palladius wrote against Ambrose although this happened after his, Athanasius's, death, and he also says that he him-

self replied to Palladius in a treatise. These facts do not fit Athanasius, who died before Ambrose was made bishop.[13]

Indeed, Athanasius died in 373, whereas Ambrose (339–397) was made bishop in 374. Palladius of Ratiaria wrote against Ambrose's *De fide* in 379, six years after the death of Athanasius.[14] Cassander is once again historically accurate, which makes his confusion between Vigilius of Thapsus and Vigilius of Trent all the more incongruous. Indeed, if one excepts this basic error, it can be said that Cassander was doing his contemporaries a great favor by making available to them the works of the bishop of Thapsus, with their accurate account of the major Trinitarian controversies of the third through fifth centuries. Vigilius of Thapsus has certainly received very little attention since Cassander's pioneering effort.[15]

A few chronological discrepancies notwithstanding, Cassander found Vigilius to be a very sound author. True, like most writers who devoted most of their time to denouncing heresy, he spent all his time collecting arguments and testimonies instead of selecting the most apt. The drawback of this method, according to Cassander, is that adversaries tended to highlight the less pertinent arguments against them and were confirmed in their mistaken opinions. The advantage, however, is that over one thousand years later, one can pick out the most convincing arguments and use them against similar adversaries.[16] It is thus that Cassander was led to publish the hitherto unknown *Dialogus* and the five books against Eutyches as most appropriate against the heresies of his own age. He thought the church should be thankful that, although heresies had invaded parts of it, ancient remedies against them were being brought to light.

The Early Church as Source of All Theology

Despite his efforts to set the Trinitarian controversies in their own age by correcting Vigilius's anachronisms (which were probably deliberate anyway), Cassander saw no fundamental distinction between the church of his own day and that of the fifth century. Fifth-century remedies were, in his view, applicable to sixteenth-century schisms. It is no doubt because of this feeling of unity with the ancient church and its heretics that Cassander did something that no modern editor would do, and indeed no other sixteenth-century editor did, which is to publish his own treatise on the two natures of Christ together with the two works of Vigilius.

His own treatise is not introduced separately. The comments Cassander makes about it are in the introduction to the works of Vigilius—another indication that our theologian did not distinguish between late Antiquity and the concerns of his own day. The part of the introduction that deals with the treatise on the two natures is particularly interesting as it shows that Cassander not only sees heresy as an intrinsic part of Christian religion from time immemorial, he also sees the Bible as the source of the orthodox doctrine of the Trinity.

He claims that nearly all heresies are to do with misunderstanding of Scripture, especially of passages to do with the Trinity and the Incarnation.[17] Contrary to what some have claimed, these attacks should be countered, thus inciting many pious men to look to the Scripture for elucidation. It is thus, according to Cassander, that divine providence has transformed the devil's plot into something of use for the church.[18] Again so as not to mislead his readers into thinking that this state of affairs is particular to his century, he takes up Martin Bucer's interpretation of John the Evangelist's motives for writing his Gospel: John wanted to demonstrate Jesus' divinity because it had already came under attack from Cerinthus and the Ebionites.[19] This for Cassander is a perfect example of the workings of divine providence and the way it turns evil into good.

Conversely, however, the devil's malice turns good things into bad, and it is thus that errors have arisen about the Incarnation. To Cassander, however, this is not an occasion for anger and despair. He admits that Scripture is not clear and that when it comes to the doctrine of the Incarnation some statements in it concern only Christ's human, others only his divine, nature. Those who concentrate on the latter recognize only Christ's divine nature, the best examples being Menander, Basilides, Valentinus, Manes, Marcion, and Cerdon. Those who concentrate on passages which privilege Christ's human nature recognize only that, as did Sabellius, Paul of Samosata, Marcellus, Photinus, and Mahomet—"that most detestable of all heretics."[20] Even the scriptural statement of John 1:1—"the word became flesh"—has been variously interpreted, some seeing in it a conversion of divine nature into flesh, others an assumption of humanity. The former confused the two natures, the latter separated them completely.

Still adhering to examples from Antiquity, Cassander notes that frequently exaggerated persecutions and refutations of one heresy give rise to another. Thus Arius's doctrine was due to his exaggerated reaction to Sabellius, the doctrine of Eutyches, to his reaction to Nestorius. These heresies, while harmful in themselves, can be highly beneficial if they are carefully compared, in that each contains some truth.

Without making any transition, Cassander then cites at some length an example from his own era, which is simply to be placed alongside the examples from the past. Thus two Anabaptists, Menno Simmons and Adam Pastor, give conflicting interpretations of "word became flesh" but neither is completely wrong. Menno takes *logos* to be a person (which is right), but does not understand "became flesh" as a taking on of humanity. Pastor, on the other hand, rejects *Verbum* as hypostasis (i.e. denies Christ's pre-existence as Son of God), but interprets "became flesh" correctly. Thus, concludes Cassander, if we follow Menno's definition of *logos* and Pastor's definition of *egeneto* we arrive at the correct interpretation.[21]

It is obvious, although Cassander does not say so in so many words, that the same method can be applied to any pair of heresies, ancient or modern: Arius understood correctly Christ's human nature, Sabellius his divine nature; Nestorius is to be followed on Christ's humanity, Eutyches on his divinity, etc. Historically, Cassander cannot be faulted here as Eutyches notably was driven into his own heterodox thinking because of his vigorous opposition to Nestorius. What is interesting is that he sees in the heresies of the early church a model of unity as viable as that of the orthodox fathers. Working on the assumption that every heterodox doctrine has something orthodox about it and carefully comparing heresies ancient and modern, so as to identify the orthodox and heterodox aspect of each of them, enables us to reconstruct the unified orthodox teaching as much as study of the most respectable authors. This does not mean, however, that heresies should be given free rein, and here again the orthodox early church provides (in Cassander's view) a model of how they should be dealt with. Cassander refers particularly to the second book of Eranistes by Theodoret of Cyrrhus, where Orthodoxus convinces Eranistes that heresies, just like physical illnesses, can be cured by application of contraries.[22]

Cassander's recourse to Theodoret is interesting, as he seems not to know or care that Theodoret's own Christology was not above suspicion.[23] Cassander finally insists that heresies need to be cured, as they come to resemble public contagion if they are allowed to spread. A heretic who has been allowed to gain any kind of public status is compared to a madman, thought by many to be sane, who tries to throw himself over the edge of a cliff and take several people with him. Such a person should not be killed but is to be treated with pity.[24] However, at no stage does the reader get the impression that any heresy whatsoever was or is likely to fracture either the continuity between the ancient and the later church or the basic harmony of the Christian society, even though, like any society, it is sometimes attacked by the contagion. Several examples of bishops in the early church who treated heretics with gentleness are cited at the end of the preface.

Contrary to reformers and other Roman Catholic theologians of the period, Cassander does not identify the early church with his own. While no less selective in his use of sources and no less dogmatically oriented than, for example, Calvin,[25] he sees the fathers and heretics of the first five centuries as incarnating a model of a unified Christian community ultimately proof against all attacks. This model could not be viable in the sixteenth century, with its determination not to relativize anything in matters of Christian religion.

The Text of Vigilius as Published by Cassander

We have seen that Cassander could make well-informed statements about dates, times, and places. However, when it came to textual criticism, his acumen seemed to desert him. Although troubled by Vigilius's mention of his treatise against Arius, Sabellius, and Photinus in three books, he took the matter no further. In fact, what he published was a truncated and corrupt text of that treatise, along with the opening of Vigilius's treatise against the Arians substituted for the missing opening. The error was corrected for the first time in 1664, by Father Chifflet, who found it quite inadmissible.[26] According to Chifflet, Vigilius wrote his treatise against the Arians when he was still worried about the Vandals and so did not want to reveal his identity. The treatise against Arius, Sabellius, and Photinus dates from a later period when he could allow himself some autobiographical remarks without exposing himself to danger. Moreover, Chifflet notes that the treatise against the Arians, most of which was incorporated by the author into the work against Arius, Sabellius and Photinus, deliberately imitated the style of Athanasius, which explains why both the works lack the sparkle of *Contra Eutycheten*.

In 1897, Gerhard Ficker sharply contradicted Chifflet[27] and put forward the hypothesis that the *Treatise against the Arians* was simply a shortened version of the *Treatise against Sabellius, Arius, etc.*, put together most likely by a clumsy copyist. Ficker based his conclusion on the number of non sequiturs in the treatise against the Arians, which could be explained only by its being a poor abridgement of a longer work.

Do these parts of the work which were imported from the treatise against the Arians into Cassander's manuscript of the longer treatise have any distinct features which should have made it possible for him to tell that he was putting a rather poor compilation at the disposal of his readers? To answer this question, a summary comparison of the structure and the contents of the two treatises is necessary. The *Treatise against the Arians*[28] is composed of two books. The introductory paragraph to book one outlines the "historical" circumstances of the disputation, which involve having Arius outlive Constantine, as Cassander quite rightly noted. According to the introduction, the dispute was ordered by Constantine's son, Constantius, who, after his father's death, fell into the snares of Arianism and thought the dispute would be a useful preliminary to a general synod. There were only two protagonists, Arius and Athanasius, with a pious pagan called Probus acting as judge. There is a brief but graphic description of the public setting for the disputation at Laodicea in Syria, with crowds pressing from every side.[29] Then Constantius's order to hold the disputation is read out by Probus.[30] The disputation proper begins with Arius and Athanasius each stating their creed and Probus expressing surprise at the fact that both seem to worship three Gods (Father, Son, and Holy Spirit) and not one. The protagonists then explain their faith in greater detail. In the course of book one the discussion is narrowed down to the issue of consubstantiality of the three persons (which Arius denies), which is then developed in the second book. Naturally, Athanasius wins the disputation by successfully proving consubstantiality against Arius. In a brief summing up, Probus judges his faith to be orthodox.

The *Dialogus* against Arius, Sabellius, etc. is in three books, the third book being composed of a lengthy summing up by Probus. There is no "historical" introduction and no indication of any emperor ordering the disputation. The *Praefatio incerti autoris*,[31] which figures in most manuscripts, is obviously of a later date than the treatise itself. All it does is attempt to find an explanation as to why Athanasius is disputing with Arius when according to Theodoret's *Ecclesiastical History* 1.5, the latter is supposed to have died a particularly gruesome death. The author of the preface reminds the reader that according to Sulpicius Severus there were two Ariuses. Thus it is probably the other Arius who disputes against Athanasius, or else simply a disciple.[32] This preface is followed by one, equally brief, written by Vigilius himself,[33] where he explains that he found the dialogue form convenient to express concisely the doctrines of the main Trinitarian heresies. Although he does not say so directly, it is obvious that the four protagonists are symbolic and that he never intended to make them correspond, in anything other than their doctrines, to the historical characters of Photinus, Sabellius, Arius, and Athanasius.[34] Book one then begins *in medias res* with Probus expressing an interest in the Christian faith because it worships only one God. He shortly finds out that all the protagonists, judging by their confessions of the faith, seem to worship three Gods and asks for further explanation. Book one ends with neither side having argued successfully for either one substance or three substances in the Godhead. In book two, however, Athanasius manages to out-argue all his opponents. Book three is a lengthy summing up by Probus of the Trinitarian theology of all four protagonists, prior to declaring Athanasius the sole upholder of the true faith.[35]

Although all protagonists take an active part from the beginning, Arius and Athanasius are the ones with the most to say. Cassander's text is composed of the *Prefatio incerti autoris* (1r–v) to the *Dialogus*, the "historical" introduction (1v–3v) to the *Treatise against the Arians*, and Constantius's decree ordering the disputation between Arius and Athanasius from the same treatise (3v–4r). The first three and a half pages of the disputation proper are taken from the *Treatise against the Arians*, with only Arius and Athanasius arguing, so that Sabellius's assertion of monotheism seems to come in out of the blue. The rest of the text, however, is taken from the *Treatise against Arius, Sabellius, etc.*, although there is no division into three books.

Had Cassander's manuscript included Vigilius's preface, he would have seen that the characters were intended to be symbolic and he probably would not have raised all the points to do with the discrepancies of place and date. What is astonishing, however, is that at no stage did he see fit to comment on the historical inaccuracy of Vigilius's portrayal of Constantius's religious open-mindedness, which apparently caused him to order a disputation between Arius and Athanasius in order to be able to make a decision himself about which was the true faith! In fact, Cassander either did not know or did not want to know that by his refusal to compromise with Arianism, Athanasius incurred the enmity of the powerful Arianizing party in the reigns of Constantine and Constantius. He was deposed at the Council of Tyre in 335 and exiled to Trier in 336. He returned on the death of Constantine in 337 but in 339 was forced to flee to Rome. He was restored in 346 by the influence of Constans, the western emperor, against the will of Constantius, who drove him from his see again in 356. Had the disputation that Vigilius describes actually taken place by the order of Constantius, it would have certainly ended with the victory of Arius. It would appear that the historical introduction to the *Treatise against the Arians* was pure fabrication either by Vigilius or, more

likely, by a later author in order to make Constantius a champion of orthodoxy and so a model to any civil ruler. Cassander could have easily expressed
surprise at this, but did not. Nor did he make any particular comment about
the structure of the work, yet it must have seemed strange to him that Constantius, who orders the disputation, is not mentioned in Probus's summing
up. In the *Treatise against the Arians* on the other hand, where the "historical" introduction belongs, the question of imperial authority is raised at the
end when Arius is told expressly not to seek the emperor's protection, as this
will not make his doctrine any more orthodox.

It may well be that the amalgam of the *Treatise against the Arians* and
the *Treatise against Arius, Sabellius, etc.* suited our author, as it portrayed civil
authorities playing a crucial role in organizing peaceful and objectively judged
disputations, the purpose of which was to determine which doctrines were
heterodox. Six years after the appearance of his edition of Vigilius, Cassander tried to take over the part of the *"Probus iudex"* at the colloquy of
Poissy. It could well be that the disputation depicted by Vigilius served as an
inspiration for this aborted attempt.

De duabus in Christo naturis

Given this very strong emphasis on the continuity between the early church
and the church of his own time, it is not surprising that Cassander sees the
Christological pronouncements of Adam Pastor and Menno Simmons as a
continuation of the ancient Trinitarian heresies. We shall now examine his
treatise on the two natures of Christ, and ask the question: How does Cassander use patristic testimonies in order to combat the heresies of Pastor
and Simmons?

Adam Pastor (Roelof Martens, ca. 1510–1552) was active in the Mennonite Church in the Netherlands. His views could be called "adoptionist trithe-
ism." God the Father acts through his miraculously born son, who shares his
power, wisdom, and will, but Christ is later in time than the Father and less
than the Father while the Holy Spirit is merely divine breath that inspires us
to a good life. Pastor's doctrine was condemned in 1574, and he was excom-
municated and dismissed from his position as Mennonite minister.[36]

Menno Simmons (ca. 1496–1561), leader of the nonviolent wing of the
Dutch Anabaptists, adopted Melchior Hoffman's doctrine of the "heavenly
flesh of Christ." Hoffman had asserted in 1533 that in the Incarnation the
external word did not assume flesh from the Virgin Mary but became flesh

in a new act of creation *in* and not *from* Mary, so that "there exists only one nature and a heavenly flesh." Menno also insisted that Christ was not born of Mary but became human in her (*factus in Maria virgine*), as he thought that it was not permissible for the redeemer to have any part in the sinful substance of creature.[37]

Indeed, there was a definite resemblance between Pastor's Christology and Nestorianism on the one hand and Menno's views and those of Eutyches on the other. However, while pointing out the similarity, Cassander does not find that Pastor and Menno are respectively Nestorius and Eutyches or that their heresies are merely an empty repetition of heresies already condemned. Seeing continuity between ancient heresies and those of his own time, Cassander tries to teach Pastor and Menno the error of their ways by situating them in the context of former Christological struggles. This has the predictable consequence that both Pastor and Menno are barely referred to after the first few pages while the accumulation of patristic evidence becomes more and more dense.

Rather than refuting his adversaries, Cassander simply submerges their statements in a wealth of evidence disproving their doctrine. In order to become one with the church of all times, the two Anabaptists have only to abandon their heretical positions. The tone of the treatise, however, is neither haranguing nor admonitory. Cassander is not a polemicist. Rather he seeks to show his adversaries the points that their doctrines already have in common with the orthodox teaching and so minimizes the differences.

He begins by attributing all Christological heresies to the work of the devil. The devil's work, or so he implies, is made all the easier by the problem of two natures—one person in Christ. Temptation is either to do what Eutyches and Menno did, that is, postulate one divine nature that somehow took on flesh which was not human, or to do what Nestorius and Pastor did as a reaction to monophysitism and postulate an immortal person in the Godhead, the Son, who joins up with Christ's mortal person not by nature but by spiritual grace.

The best way to eradicate Christological heresies, according to Cassander, is to very clearly define the term *nature,* which causes all the difficulties. In philosophy, he claims, *natura* is *arché,* that is, a beginning or a cause of movement. It is used of substances that have a body and applies to both matter and form. However, he notes, seeing as it is form rather than matter which determines that things are, most often *nature* is used to designate the form or species of a substance rather than its matter.[38] Drawing on Boethius's *De duabus naturis* Cassander then affirms that *natura* can designate the form or species of both a material substance (e.g., man) and an immaterial substance (e.g., God). According to this definition, when we say that the word of God took on human nature, we do not mean that he just took on the appearance of man but that he took on something concrete composed of matter and form. However, when we say that Christ has two natures, divine and human, we do not mean to say that divine nature is embodied.

After carefully taking his reader through Greek and Latin terminology and particularly drawing attention to the fact that the distinction between *ousía* and *hupostásis* (*natura* or *substantia* or *essentia* and *persona*) only arose in the context of Christological controversies, Cassander briefly mentions Menno again. His error is to think that if two natures can be distinguished in one person, then that person must divide into two. Yet, says Cassander, every man consists of a spiritual and physical nature or substance. Adam Pastor figures in the body of the treatise only as Nestorius, whose error it was to think that a person was made by divine power in the Virgin's womb and that the word then linked itself to that person, so that Christ was two persons. However, a person cannot take on a person any more than nature can take on a nature, or indeed a person. A person, however, can take on one or more natures.

The rather disorderly treatise ends with an affirmation by Cassander that he holds to the orthodox Christological doctrine as decreed at the Council of Ephesus against Nestorius and Eutyches. Whatever one may think of Cassander's arguments and of his chaotic citing of extracts from Athanasius, Augustine, John of Damascus, Peter Lombard, Cyril of Alexandria, and many others, it cannot be denied that he manages to blend the heresy of Menno and Pastor into the background of the Christological controversies of the fourth and fifth centuries without any respect for differing historical circumstances but without ever saying explicitly that Menno and Pastor were putting forward doctrines that had already been condemned.

Is it then true that when it came to reconciling Catholics and Protestants, Cassander postulated that tradition was merely a putting into practice of biblical precepts? It would appear that for Cassander the church of the first five or six centuries provides the sole standard of orthodoxy to the extent of enabling Christians to take the Bible for granted. Indeed, the study of the historical background of the Bible or historico-critical exegesis was of no interest to him. Following Vincent of Lérins, he argues in *De officio pii viri* that two things are essential if we want to be protected against all heresies: the authority of the canon and Catholic tradition, seeing as works of the Scripture tend to get twisted without tradition to interpret them. He then gives the example of *John* 1:1, *In principio erat Verbum.* No one doubts the apostolic authorship of the sentence, but there have already been count-less disputes about its meaning, which can only be settled if we turn to the writings of the fathers.[39] The canonicity of the Scripture was no longer an issue in the mid-sixteenth century when Cassander was writing. However, there was much disagreement not only about the exact meaning of *John* 1:1 but about various other biblical statements. Those disagreements, according to Cassander, could only be settled by looking not to the Bible but to the de-cisions made by the early church at a time when it faced similar disagree-ments. The church's decree could then be taken as the sole standard of or-thodoxy so that heretics like Menno and Pastor did not need to be refuted in their own context. It was enough to confront them with the writings of Vigilius, Augustine, Athanasius, or Cyril. The same applied to the differ-ences between Catholics and Protestants. Tradition for Cassander was all-important and the sole guarantor of unity to the extent of pushing biblical precepts into the background.

Georg Witzel

Witzel and Cassander are usually mentioned in one breath as representing a similar unionist tendency in the second stage of the Reformation.[40] In fact, as we shall have occasion to see, although both saw the early church as pro-viding the sole model of unity and universality, Witzel's concept of unity was vastly different from Cassander's.

A pupil of Martin Luther and an early convert to Lutheranism, Georg Witzel (1501–1573) was also one of the first to reject Luther. Returning to the Church of Rome, he devoted himself to the defense of the Catholic faith, while admitting papal abuses and denying the supremacy of the bishop of Rome. Upon appointment as consultant in religious matters to the Court of Duke George of Saxony in 1538, Witzel assisted in the formation of a reform program that would follow a middle path between papal and Lutheran ex-tremes. In 1539, in collaboration with Martin Bucer at the religious colloquy of Leipzig, he worked out a reform program based on the principle of the return to the church of apostolic times. The program emphasized simplicity and the communal nature of the divine services. It set out to abolish private Mass, place Latin and German on an equal footing, revise the canon of the Mass, and reduce the number of feast days. These ideas were subsequently developed by Witzel and published in a work entitled *Typus ecclesiae prioris* in

1540. Together with *Typus ecclesiae* we shall look at his *De moribus veterum haereticorum et quibus cum illi hac aetate affinitatem habeant*[41] as being most revealing of his concept of the early church as model of unity.

Although Witzel was the author of some 130 theological writings of uneven importance, unlike Cassander he did not edit any patristic writings. He does, however, quote extensively from the fathers in both his Latin and his German writings. How does he see ancient heresies in relation to the heresies of his own era? First, in contrast to Cassander, he considers Lutheranism as a heresy. Second, he sees it as embodying all the ancient heresies. Thirdly, he bases his conviction that heresies are necessary on St. Paul's *oportet haereses esse,* and in general distinguishes sharply between human tradition and the Bible instead of considering the former as a full expression of the latter. In a sense, he had a more difficult task than Cassander, who criticized Menno and Pastor, neither of whom were considered respectable. Witzel was an ex-Lutheran who was replying to the Lutherans' refusal to be associated with any ancient heresy whatsoever at a time when Lutheranism was considered highly respectable in many circles. He therefore cannot argue, as Cassander did, that the heresies of his own day are absorbed into the heresies of the early church and are thus contained in an eternal body of doctrine. He has to show his opponents that Lutherans are heretics, in spite of their protestations to the contrary.

Indeed, as Witzel admits himself in his preface to *De moribus,* the Lutherans are well aware that they cannot be identified with Arius, as they do not deny the Trinity. Neither can they be called Manichaeans, as they do not deny the Old Testament, and as they do not deny the title *theotokos* to Mary they cannot be called Nestorians.[42] He has therefore no choice but to redefine ancient heresies and their relationship to contemporary heresy, that is, Lutheranism. He does so in two ways. First, he sets out to show that heresy such as Arianism was not limited to denial of the Trinity but that Arius's teaching and indeed behavior corresponded to Luther's in other respects. Second, using Celsus as an example, he attempts to show that one of the essential features of heresy, be it ancient or modern, is its tampering with the biblical canon and its selective use of the Bible.

After all, notes Witzel, Pelagius could also flatter himself that he did not deny the Trinity, and could, along with the Ebionites, Sabellius, and Macedonius consider himself a good Catholic just because he upheld the Trinitarian dogma.[43]

According to Witzel, the chief point of similarity between Luther and the Arians is their attitude to the Catholic Church. Just as Arians in their resentment at being called Arians refused to call the ancient orthodox Christians Catholics, calling them instead Eustathians, Chrysostomians, Athanasiacs, etc., so Luther and his party refuse to talk about the Catholic Church and refer to their adversaries as papists as if the Catholic faith were the invention of the popes of Rome. On the contrary, notes Witzel, Catholics not having a human founder cannot be legitimately called anything other than Christians. Lutherans, on the other hand, have to be called Lutherans, as they take their origin from Martin Luther.[44]

Another parallel between Arians and Lutherans is their insistence on basing their disputations on Scripture alone. It is true, adds Witzel, that Maximinus (Augustine's opponent) declared that he would accept no arguments except scriptural ones, yet Maximinus was an Arian. The Lutherans' resort to Scripture is simply due to their dislike of the church fathers, whom they know to disagree with them and whose writings they cannot twist whichever way it suits them, as they can the Scripture.[45] It is important to note here that Witzel is keen to stress the gulf that separates the Lutherans from tradition rather than stressing, as Cassander does, the capacity of tradition to absorb and neutralize any heresy from any period. Lutherans to Witzel are heretics precisely because they constitute (together with Arians and other heretical groups) a discordant voice in the chorus of the church fathers.

Although summoning the Roman Catholic clergy to acquire a better knowledge of Scripture so they can face their opponents on their own ground,[46] Witzel finds the Lutherans' appeal to the Scripture to constitute a link not only with Arius and his followers but also with other heretical sects. Like the heretics condemned by Origen, and like the Jews, they want to pervert the meaning of the entire Scripture on the basis of one or two sentences in the Epistle to the Romans.[47] Like Maximinus and Nestorius they want to talk Scripture but do not want to listen to their opponents' replies.[48]

Although Luther and his followers have something of all the ancient heresies, it is their similarity to Arius and Celsus that most detains Witzel. His intention is thus to separate the Lutherans from the church and to show that historically they rank with two major outcasts, Arius, considered as the worst of all heretics, and Celsus, a pagan.

Having shown in a more or less contrived manner that the Lutheran appeal to the Scripture assimilates them to Arians, Jews, Nestorians, and other heretics, Witzel then sets out to show that Luther's criticism of certain biblical books which are a part of the canon corresponds to Celsus's striking of Moses from the catalog of wise men and to his omitting to refer to those biblical books and passages which support the truth but which do not suit his position or argument. According to Witzel, Christians accept the whole of Scripture and not selected passages or books.[49]

Witzel in contrast to Cassander has established two distinct camps, the orthodox and the heterodox. By careful use of sophistry he has redefined ancient heresies so that they all substantiate at least one aspect of Lutheranism. What he wants above all is to show that Lutheranism is a heresy notably in its appeal to the Bible and its relative neglect of the orthodox fathers, who are the real guarantors of Christian unity and universality.

Our next step is to see how Witzel views the orthodox fathers in his *Typus ecclesiae prioris.* The work, despite its title, is in German with only some of the quotations from the fathers in Latin.[50] It was dedicated by Witzel to Johann, count of Henneberg, "erwelten und bestettigten Antisten des Stiftes Fuld."[51] In the preface, he notes that after he was asked by the Duke of Saxony to survey the ancient authors of the church for the Leipzig colloquy, God granted that he write what became the *Typus ecclesiae* "in a short space of time but with much toil and labor."[52] His objective was to write a book that would be useful to the whole of Christendom. Indeed, he notes that it was used to some effect at the Leipzig colloquy although a change of political climate in the land postponed its going to press until 1540, when Witzel found Johann to be as interested in the cause of unity as the greatest princes. He therefore decided to dedicate the work to him not only to encourage him in his work for unity but also thank him for financial assistance and give Johann an occasion to look through the library at Fulda to see if ancient works not mentioned in the *Typus* could be found there.[53]

Despite his fulsome praise of the library at Fulda, Witzel does not say whether any of the numerous patristic works cited in the *Typus* actually came from there. However, he does give a full account of the genesis of the book and of how he set about compiling patristic evidence. Following the Duke of Saxony's orders, he visited libraries notably in Berlin and Leipzig and went through the writings of the fathers without any partisan intentions, simply wishing to set down the origin of the church and the organization of worship in its early days so that the unlearned could see how many ceremonies that were being discarded by the reformers as popish invention did in fact go back to apostolic or ante-Nicene fathers. Although he admits that practices which conform to the Scripture but not to the practices of the early church should not be abolished,[54] he does see a return to the ancient rituals as the only means not only of improving or reforming the church but also of restoring its universality.[55] The church's condition is best, he claims, when it most resembles that of the very early church. His purpose therefore is to wipe off the dust from the latter and bring it to life again so that the children (the faithful) can recognize their mother again.

Unlike Cassander, Witzel is not at all interested in the dogma of the early church. His sole preoccupation is with practices and rituals. The second edition of the *Typus ecclesiae* is divided into fifteen chapters of unequal length which deal with apostolic preaching, holy baptism, synaxis or the sacrament of the altar, holy penance, holy marriage, holy ordination, holy unction, other things (notably prayer) that take place in Christian assemblies, ceremonies of the ancient church, fasting, prayer and alms, the life of the early church, miracles in the early church, persecutions of the apostolic church, church councils, monasticism, heresy, and last rites.

It is interesting to note that in his brief chapter on heresy (barely a side and a half) Witzel presents a more dramatic picture of heresy than in *De moribus*. Far from pleading for the necessity of heresies or for their usefulness, as Cassander did, he notes that the true Catholic Church has withstood three hundred heresies and could withstand more *if* it were reformed. "Otherwise there will be sorrow!"[56]

The long extracts from patristic texts cited by Witzel and the numerous references to works by ancient authors or by authors he supposed to be ancient show how thoroughly he collected his evidence from printed books and manuscripts in Berlin, Leipzig, and perhaps Fulda. The chapter on baptism, which is some ten pages long, provides a very good illustration of Witzel's method. Before analyzing it in detail and drawing conclusions about Witzel's aims, a brief reminder of sixteenth-century baptismal reforms is in order. As Mark Tranvik and others have pointed out, there was no uniform baptismal rite in the late medieval period and the liturgy was permeated by local customs.[57] However, it can reasonably be stated that infant baptism was the norm and that the service itself consisted of three parts: the making of a catechumen, the blessing of the font, and the orders for baptism. At the church door several prayers and exorcisms were performed over the infant. Often, salt would be used to symbolize the candidate's preservation in the faith. The account of Jesus blessing the children was read, and the priest would spit into his hands and touch the ears and nose of the infant to make him or her receptive to the word of God. The blessing of the font took place in the church and involved lengthy prayers, frequent invocations of the Trinity, and the mixing of oil with the water. In the baptism itself the godparents renounced Satan, the assembled party affirmed the creed, and the priest dipped the child three times into the water. The infant was then dressed in a white robe, anointed with chrism, and presented with a candle.

Martin Luther's first order for baptism (1523) proposed relatively few changes. It eliminated several of the exorcisms and the blessing of the font but included instead the Flood Prayer on God's saving use of water in the Bible. The service was to take place in the vernacular. Luther's rite of 1526 was much shorter: it retained only one exorcism. It also kept the Flood Prayer, the Gospel account of Jesus blessing the children, the creedal affirmation, and the renunciation of the devil. Faced with a Lutheran rite that was structurally similar to the Roman rite although far shorter, Witzel appealed to the early church in the widest sense possible so as to portray an enormously long and complex rite that, according to him, should serve as a universal model.

After describing in great detail the baptismal ceremony after Pseudo-Dionysius's *Ecclesiastical Hierarchy* 2.2[58] (whose authenticity he does not doubt for one moment), Witzel settles the issue of child baptism in one sentence, referring only to Augustine:

> Although at the beginning it was mostly adults or young people who had come to their senses who were submitted to the Christian baptism as we described it, children of Christians too were baptized because of the original sin and because the holy assembly wanted to receive them. And this was possible because of the faith of the church, as Augustine often says.[59]

It is obvious that sixteenth-century discussions on child baptism and indeed baptismal theology are of no interest at all to Witzel. What is essential is the liturgy. The account by Pseudo-Dionysius does indeed provide extensive information on a liturgy which resembles closely the Roman Catholic rite and explains why Witzel had no interest whatsoever in doubting the authenticity of Dionysius. According to the latter, the baptizand asked the bishop to be baptized and promised to change his life accordingly. The bishop would then put his hands on his head, make the sign of the cross over him, and order that the baptizand and his godfather be registered. The baptizand would be undressed by the priests, placed facing towards the west, and asked to deny the devil three times. He would then be placed towards the east and asked to raise his hands and eyes to heaven and to submit himself totally to Christ. He would confess Christ three times. The bishop would then pray and lay hands on him, and he would be anointed with holy oil after the bishop made the sign of the cross over him three times. The bishop then went over to the baptismal font and consecrated the water. Once the baptizand's name was pronounced, he was led to the baptismal font and immersed three times with the bishop invoking the Holy Trinity. The priests then led him to the godparent and put a clean garment on him. The bishop would then make a sign of the cross on the newly baptized Christian's forehead and allow him to participate in the Holy Communion.[60]

Taking this (relatively late) account of baptismal practices as his basis, Witzel then cites other patristic testimonies to both supplement it and to bear out some of the practices it attests to, which happen to be the very practices that were abolished by Luther. He then notes that some fathers attest that the newly baptized were given a symbolic meal of milk and honey as proof of their newly acquired youth and gives Tertullian, *De corona militis* 3, as his source. As continuation of this ancient practice in his own times Witzel cites the Thüringen custom of maintaining the Sunday after Easter as the *Dominica in albis* when milk was drunk and the newly baptized set aside their white robes, a custom known as *depositio albarum* according to the medieval *Vitaspatrum*. It is important to note that Tertullian in *De corona* says that milk and honey were given to the newly baptized after the sacrament and that they then had to fast for a week. In *De baptismo* 19 Tertullian, although he states that Easter, or Whitsun, are particularly appropriate times to be baptized, emphasizes that any day and any time is suitable. Moreover, he does not mention the white robes, a custom that only came into general use in both East and West in the fourth century (cf. Cyril, *Catechetical Lectures* 22.8). It is obvious that the Thüringen custom had very little to do with the early church and was simply an accumulation of medieval practices. Its connection with Tertullian was minimal. However, having Tertullian as guarantor of a similar, albeit a great deal more minimalist, custom sufficed to validate the Thüringen tradition and make it universally applicable.

Witzel is on safer ground with the other features of baptismal ceremonies, but even there one can see how inclusive his notion of the early church is. Thus Tertullian, Chrysostom, Augustine, and Salvian of Marseille are all cited as attesting the renunciation of the devil, without Witzel so much as adverting to the number of years that separates them. He adopts the same method in defending chrisms and fasting before baptism. His intention is to show the universal nature and duration of certain rites and ceremonies.

Whereas Cassander thought that sixteenth-century schisms could be settled through careful investigation of ancient conflicts and decisions, Witzel was of the opinion that heresy was an ever-present agglomeration of wicked opinions that threatened the orthodox church. Lutheranism represented the high point of heresy and Witzel thought that the church would be unable to withstand it unless it reformed itself. Whilst Cassander thought that both ancient orthodoxy and ancient heresy guaranteed the universality and the unity of the church, Witzel sought the universal model of unity in the perpetuity of liturgical rites and ceremonies. If the Roman Catholic Church reformed itself by abolishing papacy and applying the ancient liturgy *ad litteram*, it would withstand the onslaught of heretics. The model of liturgy and church government that Witzel proposed contained enough elements of the heretical (i.e., Lutheran) system for the Lutherans not to feel completely excluded.

It is significant that whereas Cassander was particularly interested in the doctrine of the early church, Witzel concentrated on its rites and institutions. Neither made the Bible the foundation of their reform program, although Witzel made very sure that he cited biblical passages that justified the different rites and ceremonies of the early church. Both programs were doomed to failure, not so much because, as Polman would have it, "there is usually no place for middlemen in a conflict of religious convictions,"[61] but because their models of Antiquity, unity, and universality were found to be inapplicable. Cassander's was doomed because of its easy assimilation of heresy, which neither Catholics nor Protestants were prepared to view constructively; Witzel's was doomed because its insistence on rites and ceremonies made it a model appropriate for the conciliar period but not for the sixteenth century.[62] In other words, both men's appeal to the early church was founded on the mistaken perception of the church of their own era as being still the one holy catholic church and on their consequent underestimation of the depth of confessional divisions.

NOTES

1. *B. Vigilii martyris et episcopi Tridentini Opera, quorum aliqua nunquam antehac integre edita et nunc demum suo auctori vendicata, horum titulos versa pagina demonstrabit. Adhaec. Commentarius De duabus in Christo naturis et vnica hypostasi adversus praecipuas huius aetatis haereses.* Georgii Cassandri, Coloniae, apud haeredes Arnoldi Birckmanni. Anno 1555.

2. For Cassander cf. J. P. Dolan, *The Influence of Erasmus, Witzel and Cassander in the Church Ordinances and Reform Proposals of the United Duchees of Cleve during the Middle Decades of the 16th Century,* Reformationsgeschichtliche Studien und Texte, 83 (Münster: Aschendorff, 1957); M. Erbe, "François Baudouin und Georg Cassander. Dokumente einer Humanisten—Freundschaft, " *Bibliothèque d'Humanisme et*

Renaissance 40 (1978): 537–60; Erika Rummel, *The Confessionalization of Humanism in Reformation Germany* (New York: Oxford University Press, 2000), 144–49.

3. Pontien Polman, *L'élément historique dans la controverse religieuse du 16ème siècle* (Gembloux: J. Duculot, 1932), 383–88.

4. Vigilius's works, cf. PL 42:1157–1172, and PL 62:5–238.

5. *Bibliotheca Hagiographica Latina Antiquae et Mediae Aetatis.* Ediderunt Socii Bollandiani. Subsidia Hagiographica, VI. 2 vols. (Brussels: Société bollandiste, 1898–1901) 2: 8602.

6. *Ep.* 17, PL 16:1024–1036.

7. *Vigilii Opera,* †*5v–†*6v.

8. *Vigilii Opera,* †*7v: "Commemoratur a Gennadio Vigilius quidam episcopus sub Augustini tempora qui libellum in laudem martyrum conscripsit et epistolam continentem gesta sui temporis apud barbaros martyrum, quem alium ab hoc fuisse suspicor et forte eundem, ad quem B. Ambrosii extat epistola."

9. *Vigilii Opera,* †2r–†*4v.

10. *Vigilii Opera,* +2v: "Cum itaque legendo ad quintum librum (Aduersus Eutycheten) in quo sub initium haec verba continentur: et quanquam de conciliorum diuersis sanctionibus et nominum religiose additis nouitatibus plenissime in iis libris, quos aduersus Sabellium, Fotinum et Arrium sub nomine Athanasii tanquam si praesentes cum praesentibus agerent, vbi etiam cognitoris persona videtur inducta, conscripsimus—his auditis ut subsisteret amicus monui eamque orationem bis terue legendo repeteret. Quod cum fieret, statim mihi visus est auctor eum librum quasi digito demonstrare qui sub Athanasii nomine operibus Athanasii hactenus quamquam mutilus et imperfectus atque adeo deprauatus insertus legitur. . . ."

11. Addressed to Henry Barsius Oliverius, chancellor to William, the duke of Jülich-Cleve.

12. *Vigilii Opera,* +3r: "Eum sane cum aliquando legissem, facile quidem fuit animaduertere, non esse illum magni et incomparabilis Athanasii cum nec stylus congrueret nec temporum ratio vllo modo conueniret. Nam constat Arrii mortem Constantii imperium antecessisse, sub quo haec disputatio facta inducitur. Magis autem posterioris aetatis Latini alicuius hominis Ruffinum secuti qui Arrii vitam vsque ad Constantii imperium falso produxit, esse videbatur."

13. *Vigilii Opera,* +4r: ". . . Cum videlicet ex persona Athanasii B. Ambrosii meminerit ac Palladii in Aquilegiensi synodo Arianismi damnati, quem Palladium aduersus Ambrosium post eius mortem scripsisse, seque Palladio eidem libello vno respondise commemorat, quae sane Athanasio minime conueniunt cum is vita prius excesserit quam Ambrosius episcopatum inierit."

14. On Palladius see esp. Claudio Moreschini and Enrico Norelli, *Storia della letteratura cristiana antica greca e latina,* (Brescia: Morcelliana, 1996), 2, 1: 381–83.

15. Editio princeps of his works appeared in Dijon in 1664 (ed. P. F. Chifflet, sj). See also G. Ficker, *Studien zu Vigilius von Thapsus* (Leipzig: A. J. Barth, 1897) and M. Simonetti, "Letteratura antimonofisita d'Occidente," *Augustinianum* 18 (1978): 505–22.

16. *Vigilii Opera,* +4v: ". . . quamuis id (Vigilius) cum reliquis quoque ecclesiasticis scriptoribus (quo sane honori illorum nihil detractum velim) commune habeat, quod in disputatione aduersus haereticos magis laborarint et multa testimonia congererent, quam vt aptissima quaeque deligerent . . . qua in re id incommodi accidit quod aduersarii neglectis firmioribus et solidioribus testimoniis et argumentis ex iis quae leuiora et nonnunquam ad rem ineptiora erant, reliqua omnia aestimauerint et caussae suae fiduciam tanquam quae firmis rationibus conuelli non possit, maiorem conceperint. . . . Illud tamen commodi nos in horum auctorum lectione consequimur, quod ex magno argumentorum et testimoniorum aceruo quem nobis illorum scripta subministrant, aptissima quaeque et firmissima nobis deligere et aduersus similes hostes quales illi experti sunt, proferre et torquere liceat."

17. *Vigilii Opera,* †5v: "Quum igitur haeresis pleraque omnis falso Scripturae intellectu nitatur, tam id maxime in iis diuinae Scripturae testimoniis, quibus vel inexplicabilis sacrosanctae Triados vel Christi incarnationis sacramentum exponitur vsu venit."

18. *Vigilii Opera,* +6r: ". . . ita haereticorum commenta quibus abditissima quaeque diuinarum rerum mysteria eruere seu potius subruere et euertere conantur, sanctorum et eruditorum virorum meditationem exacuerunt et ad Scripturarum sacrarum diligentiorem et accuratiorem explicationem et illustrationem impulerunt; itaque diuina prouidentia diaboli conatum ad ecclesiae vtilitatem conuertit."

19. *Vigilii Opera,* †6r: "Quid an non Ioannem Euangellistam ad diuinam illam quae ex omni aeternitate fuit Verbi naturam et vt ita loquar, consistentiam et cohaerentiam initio Euangelii sui ab aliis praetermissam exponendam Ebionis et Cerinthi improbitas induxit?" Cf. *Martini Buceri Enarratio in Euangelion Iohannis,* ed. Irena Backus (Leiden: Brill, 1988), 17–18.

20. *Vigilii Opera,* †7r.

21. *Vigilii Opera,* †7r–v.

22. *Vigilii Opera,* †*1r–†*v: "ERANISTES: Est inhumanum eos qui laborant despicere. ORTHODOXUS: Conuenit ergo eorum misereri et pro viribus mederi. ERA.: Maxime. ORTHO. : Si corporibus ergo mederi scires, multi autem circumsistentes rogarent vt medereris et diuersas affectiones ostenderent . . . dic mihi quid faceres, vnumne omnibus medicamentum componeres, an vnicuique morbo id quod conuenit? ERA: Id scilicet quod vnicuique morbo conuenit et ad morbum propulsandum est appositum." The editio princeps of *Eranistes* appeared in 1547, in Rome (Stefano Sabbio). Cassander is quoting the Latin translation of Gentien Hervet, which appeared in Venice in 1548 (per Ioannem Farreum et fratres): *Theodoreti episcopi Cyri Eranistes seu Polymorphus . . .*, 44v–45r.

23. By insisting excessively on Christ's two natures, the one, divine, prior to the Incarnation, the other, human, which was assumed by the divine nature on Incarnation, Theodoret was accused of creating two Christs by Cyril of Alexandria. Cf. Moreschini and Norelli, *Storia* 2, 1: 231–47 and literature cited ibid.

24. *Vigilii Opera,* +*2v: "Quid si in phreneticum et mente captum hominem, qui tamen a multis sanus putetur, quis incidat, qui et se praecipitare et alios in idem praecipitium inducere tentet, non puto iratus illum interimendum sed comiseratus cohibendum et curandum censebit."

25. On Calvin's use of sources see A. N. S. Lane, *John Calvin: A Student of the Fathers* (Edinburgh: T&T Clark, 1999), and Irena Backus, "John Calvin and the Greek Fathers," in *Continuity and Change: The Harvest of Late-Medieval and Reformation History. Essays Presented to Heiko A. Oberman on His 70th Birthday,* ed. R. J. Bast and A. C. Gow (Leiden: E. J. Brill, 2000), 253–76.

26. Cf. Chifflet's preface in PL 62:475: "Altercationis Athanasii atque Arii coram Probo iudice editiones duas codices antiqui repraesentant. Prior tres tantum, nempe Athanasium, Arium et Probum interlocutores habet; posterior Sabellium insuper et Photinum loquentes indicit. Prioris praefatio incipit *Cum apud Niceam,* quam excipit fictitia Constantii sacra; posterioris praefationem quae incipit *Dum mecum de fidei veritate* antehac non editam vnus dedit codex Thuanus, post quam omissa praefatione Cum apud Niceam et epistola Constantii imperatoris initium fit in codice Thuano ab his verbis: *Probus iudex dixit prospiciens in idolorum cultura.* Prior duabus constat actionibus seu libris totidem et concluditur appellatione Arii ad tribunal principis: posterior praeter duas actiones habet ad finem, libri tertii instar, sententiam Probi iudicis quae ab Athanasio, Sabellio, Ario et Photino dicta summatim colligit. Prior longe est breuior posteriore, in qua magnam partem continetur, non tamen plane tota. Priorem scripsit Vigilius cum adhuc Vandalorum iugo premeretur adeoque eius auctor agnosci nollet; posteriorem, cum extra eorum potestatem esset, quippe in qua se et Athanasii personam ementitum esse et Maribadum et Palladium Arianos, scriptis libris confutasse palam profitetur. Cum igitur editio prior ad stylum velut Athanasii studiose temperata sit ac deinde post annos aliquot paucis exceptis in posteriorem inculcata, nihil mirum si posterior editio, quamlibet eo tempore instructa quo alienum stylum fingere nihil necesse esset, librorum tamen aduersus Eutycheten genium non redoleat. Caeterum has duas editiones reddere integras operae precium duxi. Quamuis enim priorem magna ex parte coplexa sit posterior, non tamen totam. Adde quod et principio et fine et methodo diuersae sunt, nec in vnam compilari absque autoris iniuria potuerunt, vti eas compegit Casander. Nos vtramque e quatuor praesertim mss. codicibus recensuimus, vno Iurensi, altero et tertio Thuanis, quarto S. Mariae Remensis. Et posteriori praefationem vulgatam praefiximus quae incipit: *Cum in manus strenui lectoris beatissime papa Materne* etc. quod et in antiquis mss. exemplaribus reperiatur, nec a Vigilii scopo ingenioque aliena sit. Nunc ad alia eius opera inuestiganda vlterius progrediamur."

27. Cf. Gerhard Ficker, *Studien zu Vigilius von Thapsus* (Leipzig: J. A. Barth, 1897), 25–41.

28. PL 62:155–180.

29. *Inc.* Cum apud Niceam vrbem Bithyniae *des.* astantibus, Arium atque Athanastium his alloquitur verbis.

30. *Inc.* Constantinus Constantius pius *des.* Data Constantinopoli XII. calendas Ianuarias.

31. *Inc.* Cum in manus strenui lectoris, beatissime papa Materne *des.* haesitatione, Deo auxiliante, valeant custodire.

32. PL 62:179–180.

33. *Inc.* Dum mecum de fidei veritate *des.* Fastidium legentibus amputaret.

34. PL 62:180: "Sabellium ergo, Photinum, Arium atque ad nostras partes Athanasium introduxi, vt veritas, summo confligentium certamine eliquata, ad omnium notitiam peueniret et diversitate personarum vel responsionum ac interlocutionum huius operis variata digestio fastidium legentibus amputaret."

35. PL 62:179–238.

36. Cf. George H. Williams, *The Radical Reformation,* 3rd ed. (Kirksville, Mo.: The Sixteenth Century Journal Publishers, 1992), 739–42.

37. On Menno's Christology, see Egil Grislis, "The Doctrine of the Incarnation according to Menno Simmons," *Journal of Mennonite Studies* 8 (1990): 16–33.

38. *Vigilii Opera: De duabus,* 3v–4r: "Notum itaque est naturam a philosophis dici *archèn,* id est principium seu caussam motus eamque in substantiis tantum corporatis intelligi eaque notione materiam et formam comprehendi. Cum autem ex his duobus forma magis sit natura quam materia (propter formam enim res esse dicitur) fit vt naturae vocabulo forma seu species in vnaquaque substantia potissimum designetur. Apud Boetium De duabus naturis, tres seu verius quatuor huius nominis rationes explicantur. . . . Natura est quod facere vel quod pati possit: facere quidem ac pati, vt omnia corporea ac corporeorum anima, facere vero tantum vt Deus. . . ."

39. *G. Cassandri Opera omnia,* apud Abrahamum Pacard, Parisiis, 1616: *De officio pii viri,* 783: "Non inepte igitur Vincentius Lyrinensis qui sub aetatem Augustini vixit, cum iam multae et variae haereses ecclesiam vexarant et exercuerant, eum qui se aduersus haereses omnes munitum et tutum esse velit, haec duo sibi proponere debere confirmat: canonicam authoritatem et catholicam traditionem. Non quin canonica auctoritas sufficiat sed quod Scripturae verba in varias sententias ab impiis et imperitis hominibus distrahantur. Quare certam aliquam sententiam constituendam quae a catholica traditione petatur. Quae quidem catholica traditio tribus notis deprehenditur: antiquitate, vniuersitate et consensione. Huius intelligentiae ex catholica traditione, id est antiqua, perpetua et vniuersali consensione, necessitatem hodie quoque deprehendimus. Nam exempli causa, haec verba: *In principio erat Verbum* quin ab Apostolis scripta sint nemo inficiatur. De intellectu autem huius vocis Verbum ingens certamen est et qui diuersam ab ecclesia sententiam sequuntur non minus probabilibus rationibus nituntur. Nos autem ex perpetua hac traditione et antiquissimorum patrum concordissimis scriptis et veterum conciliorum grauissimis decretis, ad nos vsque propagata, per *logon* non propositum aut *diathesin,* non ideam quandam et formam in mente diuina, sed personam et *hupostasin* significari credimus."

40. Cf. Dolan, *The Influence of Erasmus, Witzel and Cassander;* Barbara Henze, *Aus Liebe zur Kirchen-Reform. Die Bemühungen Georg Witzels (1501–1573) um die*

Kircheneinheit (Münster: Aschendorff, 1995); Rummel, *Confessionalization*, 138–47, and literature cited ibid. For a bibliography of Witzel's writings see Gregor Richter, *Die Schriften Georg Witzels bearbeitet bibliographisch nebst einigen bisher ungedrückten Reformationsgutachten und Briefen Witzels*, reprint of 1913 edition (Nieuwkoop: de Graaf, 1963). Hereafter cited as Richter.

41. *De moribus veterum haereticorum et quibus cum illi hac aetate affinitatem habeant. Authore Georgio Wicelio. Paulus ait: oportet haereses esse inter vos vt qui probati sunt manifesti fiant inter vos.* Anno 1537. Cf. Richter, 30, nos. 2–3. The work went through two editions in 1537. The third expanded edition appeared in 1564 in Paris (G. Chaudière).

42. *De moribus*, A5v: "Arius, inquiunt, fuit haereticus. Nam ille reiecit Trinitatem quod nos non facimus. Ergo. Nec repudiamus Vetus Testamentum instar Manichaeorum. Ergo. Nec negamus Mariam Theotocon sicut Nestoriani. Ergo non sumus schismatici."

43. *De moribus*, A5v: "Sic poterat sibi Pelagius adblandiri; 'non doceo contra Trinitatem sicut Ebion, Sabellius et Macedonius. Igitur non sum haereticus. Contra vero, quia doceo pro Trinitate, Catholicus sum'. "

44. *De moribus*, A6v: "Olim solebant Ariani Catholicos nominare ab Epistolis suis idque in vltionem quod ipsi dicerentur Ariani. Atque inde erant Eustathiani, Chrysostomiani, Athanasiaci, Pauliani, Macariani. . . . Sic fere nostrates dedignantur nos vocare catholicos aut ecclesiasticos. Papistas vocant quasi papae Romani sint nostrae fidei ac doctrinae autores, quemadmodum Luterus ipsis est suae princeps doctrinae et persuasionis nouae autor, vnde non possunt Luteritae non vocari."

45. *De moribus*, G5r–v: ". . . Maximinus testificabitur initio disputationis se praeter Scripturas nihil audire aut recipere velle. En speciem recti. Attamen erat Ariani dogmatis defensor. Vix vnquam dolo caruit in haereticis ista protestatio: praeter Scripturas nihil audiemus. Nam oderunt sanctos ecclesiae patres et ab horum scriptis abhorrent quod sciant sua noua scita ab his improbari. Auget doli suspitionem quod soleant Scripturas propria interpretatione quo volunt torquere."

46. *De moribus*, G5v: "Optandum sit hac tempestate vt ecclesiastici in Scripturis sanctis ita essent exercitati vt huiusmodi protestationem haudquaquam fugerent."

47. *De moribus*, G6v, G7r: "Tale sic effert Origenes: haeretici ex paucis verbis Epistolae ad Romanos totius Scripturae sensum conantur euertere. Attigit scopum Origenes. Videmus enim in Lutheranis perque verissimum esse. . . . Hoc habent cum Iudaeis commune Euangeliomachi Germaniae qui adeo bello callent verbum Dei scriptum a genuino sensu in nothum ac alienum deflectere."

48. *De moribus*, G6v, G7r: "Idem Maximinus sermonen suum longissimum pertraxerat vsque in noctem. Mane vero facto ex Hippone discesserat ne Augustino respondendi tempus esset . . . Nestorius legitur fuisse naturaliter eloquens atque ea naturae dote emicuisse."

49. *De moribus*, H4r–H5r.

50. I shall be referring to the (second) 1541 edition: *Typus ecclesiae prioris. Anzeigung, wie die heilige Kyrche Gottes, inwendig siben und mehr hundert. jaren, nach unsers herrn Auffart, gestalt gewesen sey. Reichlich gemehret und von newem gedrückt. Cum gratia et priuilegio caesareo.* 1541. Cf. Richter, 52, no. 1–52, editions 1–8. The work was vastly expanded during the author's lifetime, up until 1566. I will not deal with Witzel's additions to it here.

51. *Typus ecclesiae prioris,* 2r.

52. *Typus,* 2r: ". . . hat Gott reich von gnaden, dis büchlin über mein hoffnung geben, und in dis nicht langer weil, aber mit viler mühe und wache."

53. *Typus,* 2r–3v.

54. *Typus,* 4v: "Ist etwas in gemeinem brauch zu disen zeiten, das sich mit der heiligen Schrift vertregt, und doch bey den alten nit gewesen, bevor, wenn wenig daran gelegen, so kan man dasselbig gleich wol im schwang bleiben lassen, bis jm on tumult und ergernis füglich zu helffen."

55. *Typus,* 4v: "Were besser die zeit kome bald wieder, das man nicht mehr weder von einerley Glauben und Euangelio wisset durch die gantze Cristenheit."

56. *Typus,* 68v: "Die Römisch Kyrch hat bey drey hundert häresey ausgewartet und möcht jr mehr auswarten, wenn sie reformirt were. Sonst hats kummer."

57. See Mark Tranvik, "Baptism: Popular Practices," in *The Oxford Encyclopedia of the Reformation,* ed. Hans J. Hillerbrand (New York: Oxford University Press, 1996), 1: 114–17 and bibliography.

58. Pseudo-Dionysius, *Hier. eccl.* 2.2, PG 3:391–404.

59. *Typus,* 8v: "Wiewol aber zur ersten zeit der Kyrchen das mehrer teil betagte leute, oder auch jungen so zu jrer vernunfft kommen, auff gesagte weise Christlich getaufft, sind doch auch daneben der Christen kinder getaufft worden, von wegen der erbsünde vnd auch vmb der heiligen gemeinschafft willen, dieselbigen zu bekommen. Vnd das geschah auff der Kyrchenglauben, wie offt in Augustino."

60. *Typus.* 7v–8v. For a modern account of the earliest baptismal practices see *Le baptême d'après les Pères de l'Église,* ed. A. G. Hammann and others, 2d ed. (Paris: Brepols, 1995).

61. Polman, 490: "Dans un conflit entre des convictions religieuses, il n'y a généralement pas de place pour les hommes de 'juste milieu'. "

62. On conciliarism generally the best study is that of Giuseppe Alberigo, *Chiesa conciliare: Identita e significato del conciliarismo* (Brescia: Padeia, 1981).

7

Conciliation and the French Huguenots, 1561–1610

KARIN MAAG

Ainsi tous deux unis en leur capitaine
Ferez sourdre (o miracle) un amour de la haine.
Et chacun demeurant devot envers son Roy
Sera dans sa maison desormais en requoy,
Vivant selon sa foi, content en sa patrie
Avec ses chers enfants et sa douce partie
Jusques à ce que Dieu, regardant d'un oeil doux
Son peuple my-partie, estanche son courroux,
Et que las de nous voir flotter en telle guise
Nous réunisse enfin tous sous une mesme eglise.

As two groups united in their king most great
Love springs as a miracle from this realm of hate.
And each man remaining faithful to the king
Will dwell at home from now on without suffering.
He will follow his faith, live at peace in his land
With his dear children and gentle wife close at hand.
Until viewed with mercy by the God of each age
His divided people will cease to feel His rage,
He will no longer let us from war to war lurch
But bring us together again into one church.[1]

This poem was composed by the Catholic lawyer and writer Etienne Pasquier in France in 1570 to mark the occasion of the Peace of St. Germain, one of the many treaties that sought to put an end to France's civil wars in the sixteenth century. Like the treaties before it and subsequent ones, the Peace of St. Germain failed, and war began again in 1572 following the St. Bartholomew's Day massacre.[2] The roots of the conflict were political but also religious. France was divided between Catholics and Protestants, and apart from short intervals of peace, coexistence on a national scale seemed a distant hope and conciliation an impossible dream.[3]

Before analyzing the French situation in greater detail, we should clarify our understanding of conciliation. As the editors of this volume have argued, there is a distinction to be made between conciliation and toleration. Though these two phenomena were related and at times even intertwined, toleration was often a more pragmatic solution of managing conflict in religiously diverse communities. Conciliation, on the other hand, represented a more constructive quest for theological unity. It was an active dynamic. Seeking to do more than simply permit a variety of churches and confessions, conciliation sought for common ground.[4]

This essay seeks to look in more detail at the issue of conciliation between Catholics and Huguenots in France during the sixteenth and early seventeenth century, particularly from 1561, the date of the Colloquy of Poissy, to 1598, the proclamation of the Edict of Nantes.[5] This time period has been selected for a number of reasons. Firstly, I would argue that interest in conciliation grew as the exhaustion of war took hold. The wars began in 1562, and thus by the 1590s, the country had suffered through nearly thirty years of intermittent conflict. Secondly, the death of Henry III in 1589 left his cousin, the Protestant Henry of Navarre, later Henry IV, as the closest male heir to the throne. Although this situation exacerbated tensions among ultra-Catholics and Protestants, it also presented one of the best opportunities for moderates on both sides to consider laying aside their religious antagonisms to preserve France from external enemies at a dangerous time of transition. Thus, the quest for confessional reunion became a more likely option once the last Catholic Valois king died. Finally, Henry IV's conversion to Catholicism in 1593 and his aim to restore peace to France also put this issue at the forefront of both Catholics' and Huguenots' thoughts. Evidence for support of conciliation on both sides of the confessional divide comes primarily from pamphlets and other works published in France during this period.

Yet the rise of interest in conciliation among some Huguenots and Catholics in France did not represent a generalized trend. Indeed, this essay

seeks to highlight how difficult this task was, particularly as those supporting such an approach were easily and often attacked by both camps as traitors to their own side. In fact, a measure of cementing of confessional borders, rather than conciliation, emerged as the chosen option by 1598 with the
Edict of Nantes.[6] In the end, early modern France offers a fascinating religious landscape, in which conciliation was only one possible route in the quest
to resolve the country's enduring religious and political conflict.

Like many of the European monarchies of the sixteenth century, the
unity of France lay not only in its ruler but also in his faithfulness to Catholicism. *"Un roi, une foi, une loi"* and the king's title as "the most Christian
king" illustrate how important a role religion played in bringing the country together. Until the early sixteenth century, this religion was Catholicism.
Yet by the 1550s, the message of Reformation had spread into France and
began to become established in its Calvinist form. As the Calvinists grew in
number, they made their presence felt, especially in the early 1560s, by establishing congregations, bringing in ministers, especially from Geneva, and
setting up national church structures.[7] Even more threatening to the Catholic faithful were the Huguenot attacks on Catholic worship and images, on
the Mass and Corpus Christi processions, and the Protestant takeover of
Catholic churches.[8] At the same time, the French political situation began
to deteriorate. After the death of Henry II in a jousting accident in 1559, his
successors were his sons, two of whom, Francis II and Charles IX, came to
the throne as youths or children rather than adults, thus ushering in periods of regency and power-grabbing among the leading noble families. This
combination of political instability and religious tension opened the way for
France's extended period of civil wars.

By the time of the Colloquy of Poissy in 1561, the last official attempt
at conciliation through a council, France was already polarized between two
opposing groups and on the brink of open conflict. On one side stood the
newly established Calvinist churches, led by their Genevan-trained pastors.
Indeed, the main spokesman for the Huguenots at the Colloquy of Poissy
was Theodore Beza, Calvin's right-hand man. On the other was the Catholic hierarchy, led by the Cardinal of Lorraine, a member of the powerful
Catholic Guise family. The colloquy had been called together by Catherine
de Medici, the regent and queen mother, in an attempt to lessen the religious
tensions that were already threatening to spill over into religious war.[9] Yet
the Colloquy of Poissy foundered because there was little common theological ground, especially due to the differing understandings of the sacrament of the Eucharist and Lord's Supper. This was the same issue that had

scuttled the Colloquy of Regensburg between Lutherans and Catholics in 1541.[10] The theological disagreement in France was exacerbated by the rising tensions among the nobility. Without a strong monarch to exercise control, noble families divided into factions, each trying to gain power over both the rest of the nobility and the king. The two main factions were led by the Guise family, which was strongly Catholic and had its stronghold in northern France, and by the Condé-Chatillon and Montmorency families, whose lands lay farther south and who supported the nascent Protestant churches. The pattern of allegiances among other nobles varied depending on the period, but each side commanded sufficient support both within and outside France to sustain the conflict for many years.[11] Hence in the 1560s, confessional rapprochement was defeated both by conflicting theological positions and by the potent alliance between religious and political aims among the leaders of each faction. Theological discussions did not operate in a vacuum. Seeking a theological compromise not only had religious repercussions, but would also threaten political positions that had already been drawn up.

During the civil wars that followed the massacre of Protestants at Vassy by the forces of the Duke of Guise in March 1562, compromise was a scarce commodity, only occurring occasionally during the establishment of the edicts of pacification that ended each phase of the wars. The specific terms of each edict were shaped by the balance of powers at the close of each conflict. Indeed the Peace of Monsieur in 1576, negotiated by Henry III's younger brother François, duke of Anjou, was the most favorable to the Huguenots, granting them extensive rights of worship across all of France.[12] Yet these edicts provided for limited toleration, rather than conciliation, as there was no attempt to bring the opposing theological positions closer together. Instead, these declarations sought to ensure a measure of coexistence, always understood as a temporary expedient until everyone returned to Catholicism.[13] However, the edicts at times had the opposite effect of what was intended. The liberal terms of the Peace of Monsieur led to the creation of the Holy League, a group of ultra-Catholics whose purpose was to defend Catholicism against the "heretics" and ultimately defeat them. The League intended to bring both the kingdom and the court back to true devotion and faithfulness to the Catholic church, its doctrines, and teachings. Thus the members of the League became some of the foremost opponents to any form of toleration, let alone conciliation vis-à-vis the Huguenots.[14]

However, the destructiveness of the wars and the dangers for France if the conflict were to continue did serve to concentrate the minds of some of the members of each faction. These men gradually came to believe that the threats to France's stability outweighed any benefits that could be gained by continuing the struggle until one side or the other was vanquished. Centered around the chancellor, Michel de L'Hôpital, these men shared a common outlook, putting compromise and negotiation above a more hard-line stance. Pragmatism was their main feature. Those who sought a middle ground did not choose conciliation over conflict because they necessarily favored theological moderation per se, but in their search to preserve the French monarchy and the country as a whole from utter collapse, they were willing to entertain notions of theological rapprochement.[15]

The moderates' support for conciliation became even more important during the reign of Henry III, especially after 1584, following the death of his younger brother François, duke of Anjou. The duke of Anjou's death meant that Henry III was the last of the male Valois, as he himself had no sons. The nearest male relative, were Henry III to die without sons, was Henry of Navarre, whose territory lay in the strongly Protestant southwest of France. Henry of Navarre himself had emerged as the leading Protestant nobleman following the death of his kinsman Condé. Although he had abjured Protestantism following the St. Bartholomew's Day massacre in 1572, Henry of Navarre repudiated this conversion in 1576, returning to the Huguenot church.[16] By the mid-1580s, the thought that this "relapsed" Protestant was next in line to the throne was too much for some Catholics. The Holy League gained in strength and numbers and gradually gained control of the city of Paris. By controlling the capital, even in an age of peripatetic royal courts, it made ruling more difficult for the king and his counselors, and weakened his authority. The League also began to consider seriously other possible candidates for the French throne, including Henry of Navarre's uncle, the Cardinal of Bourbon. After the aged Cardinal's death in 1591, yielding to the pressure of its Spanish allies, the League considered placing Charles de Guise on the throne after a marriage to the Spanish infanta Isabella.[17] Spain and France had long been enemies, but the League needed Spanish troops and money to support its struggle against the forces of Henry of Navarre. Isabella also had the advantage of being unquestionably Catholic.

Thus by the end of Henry III's reign, any attempts at conciliation faced an uphill struggle in a divided France. The Huguenots had seen attempts at conciliation fail to succeed at the Colloquy of Poissy and had largely moved to securing a place for themselves through armed conflict rather than through negotiation. In general, up to 1589, the Protestant call was for toleration rather than conciliation. Too much was at stake as a confessional group to be willing to jeopardize their identity through attempts at theological compromise. One should also be clear that the Huguenot calls for toleration applied only to themselves as a persecuted minority group. Evidence from areas in France controlled by the Huguenots suggests that they were no more willing than the Catholics to accept confessional diversity when they were in power.[18]

On the Catholic side, most of the works dealing with the issue of two confessional groups in one country tended to agree that the best way to resolve the conflict between Catholics and Huguenots in France was to force the latter into submission through execution, war, and exile. For instance, Jean de la Vacquerie's 1560 tract entitled *Catholique remonstrance aux roys et princes chrestiens* suggested that the best remedy for heresy is the extermination of the Huguenots.[19] De la Vacquerie and the anonymous author of the tract *Discours du vray moyen*, published in 1570, both also attributed the strength of the Huguenots' position to the sinfulness of Catholics and the failure of the church to redress these abuses. In doing so, the authors made no attempt to acknowledge any merit in the Huguenot criticism. If anything, the Calvinists were seen as the instruments of God's wrath, but that did not make the authors any more conciliatory in their approach to Protestantism.[20]

Voices of conciliation were thus heard infrequently on the Catholic side prior to 1589. The *Exhortation aux princes et seigneurs du Conseil Privé*, written by the Parisian lawyer Etienne Pasquier in 1561, was one of the few tracts that stressed the common features of the two confessions rather than their differences. Pasquier stated that the solution to the current conflict was to have two churches, so that the Protestants in France could be allowed freedom of worship and the right to celebrate the sacraments. Pasquier's strategy was to remind his readers of what the Catholics and Protestants held in common. Addressing the king's council, he wrote, "in God's name, gentlemen, do not force our consciences with your swords. All of us (Catholics and Protestants) are Christians, united together through the holy sacrament of Baptism, all revering and adoring the same God, not necessarily in the same way, but just as fervently. We all love and assist our neighbor according to the same command, and we all gladly obey the human edicts of our prince."[21] Thus for Pasquier, Catholics and Protestants shared the same baptism and followed the same commandments to love God and their neighbors. He also rejected the idea that the Huguenots' religious difference made them more likely to be traitors, since he insisted that both Catholics and Protestants were loyal to the king.[22] This last statement is crucial, as Huguenots in France were condemned not only for their religious choice but also because by breaking with one faith, they would necessarily also reject the authority of one king.

Pasquier's views were echoed in an anonymous tract published in Lyon by Benoit Rigaud in 1568 entitled *Les Louanges et recommandations de la paix*. Published during the second civil war that had begun the previous year, the tract insisted that war was not the solution to the problem of two confessional groups in one country. The author argued that Christianity was a religion of peace, and that to engage in armed conflict was contrary to the faith. Like Pasquier, the author of this tract focused on what Calvinists and Catholics held in common, in order to show how evil the war was.

> It is both absurd and dishonest that those who are continually at war with each other are people who belong to the same house (which is the church), who are members of the same body, who rejoice in the same leader, namely Jesus Christ. They have the same father in heaven, they are brought to life and sustained by the same spirit, they profess the same faith as they were bought by the same blood. They are regenerated by the same baptism and are nourished and sustained by the same sacraments and fight under the leadership of the same captain and king. Their life comes from the same celestial bread and they share in the same chalice. They have a common enemy, namely the devil, and finally they are all called to the same inheritance.[23]

This tract goes beyond Pasquier in terms of listing what the two confessions shared. Few other members of either party would have agreed that both the Huguenots and Catholics shared the same sacraments. Indeed, the controversy over the different theologies of the Eucharist and the Lord's Supper was precisely one of the main divisive issues of the Reformation.

Although this tract is exceptional in its willingness to see much common ground between Catholics and Protestants in France, its approach was not unique. By the time of Henry III's death, attempts to reconcile the two sides continued apace. Events from 1589 to 1610, the year of the assassination of Henry IV, helped to make conciliation a more pressing concern and hotly debated matter, especially among the Huguenots. As the wars following the last Valois king's death dragged on, and particularly as the city of Paris, the heart of the country, refused to recognize Henry of Navarre as legitimate because he was a Huguenot, Henry increasingly realized that peace would not be restored to France until he took on the religious confession of the majority. Thus, in 1593, Henry IV converted to Catholicism, this time not officially under duress, but of his own volition.[24] Interestingly, the flurry of works that were written and published on conciliation from the Huguenot side date primarily from the period 1594 to 1598. The correlation between the king's conversion and writings on conciliation from both sides of the confessional divide needs to be investigated further.

On the one hand, one could argue that among those who accepted the king's conversion as genuine, his action was more likely to harden positions than to push confessional adversaries towards conciliation. The Catholics who embraced Henry IV's conversion (and there were many who did) could see the king's conversion from heresy and error as the sign that the heretics were definitively beaten, since even their leader had embraced Catholicism.[25] Thus, such Catholics would not seek reunion as there was little point in making the first step towards those whom the king had abandoned. On the Huguenot side, following the king's conversion, to seek conciliation was tantamount to admitting that there might be some truth in the Catholic doctrines that the Calvinists had opposed for so long. To seek conciliation might even be to legitimate the king's actions and could be seen as the first step for others to convert. If both confessions had so much in common, there were few reasons not to make the switch to the church of the majority.[26]

On the other hand, among those (both Catholic and Protestants) who were suspicious of the king's motives for conversion (and there were many who were), confessional compromise was also not likely to be the path these skeptics took. From the Catholic side, if the king had changed confessions for personal gain, it was better to keep a close eye on his piety and his faithfulness to his new church rather than get involved in the risky activity of attempting to find common ground with the Huguenots.[27] From the Calvinists' standpoint, even if one were skeptical about the king's true motivations, such an attitude would not lead to attempts at conciliation but rather to retrenchment and consolidation of one's own position.[28]

Thus even after the king's conversion there were many reasons for the two confessional groups to keep at a distance from each other, and to reject any attempts at reunion. Yet those who did advocate conciliation seized on the fact that at least through the king's conversion his authority was gradually being reasserted over the whole of France, and the prospects for a lasting peace seemed vastly improved. These individuals felt that their hour had finally come. With warfare subsiding and everyone adjusting to the new situation, perhaps their fellow citizens would be more ready to listen to the possibility of a rapprochement. The conciliators in essence felt that mere toleration was not sufficient. Toleration only entrenched, pacified, and regulated relations between the two communities. It did not strive to clear any common ground and bring the two back into one whole.[29] However, the conciliators failed to take sufficient account of the strength of opposition to their plans. By examining in some detail the case of Jean de Serres, we can begin to understand both the parameters of conciliation as understood by a late sixteenth-century Huguenot and the depth of hostility from his fellow believers regarding his project.

Jean de Serres was a Huguenot pastor, professor, and scholar. Born in France around 1540, he had studied in Geneva and worked in its rural territories as a pastor before teaching in Lausanne's Latin school. He returned to France to take up a position of pastor in the city of Nîmes in 1579 and then taught in the local academy before being dismissed ten years later due to conflicts with the city consistory. De Serres then worked as a pastor in the principality of Orange, in southern France. He died, still a Calvinist, in 1598.[30] He was primarily a historian, who published works on the history of France and who had studied extensively the writings of the church fathers. De Serres was also active politically, as he served Henry of Navarre on several missions beginning in 1579.[31] Once Henry became king, and particularly after his conversion to Catholicism, de Serres's interest in conciliation between the two confessional groups increased. In part, his concern was to help maintain the delicate balance that Henry IV was striving to build after decades of war and conflict. Moves towards confessional rapprochement, if successful, would have rendered Henry's work to establish a settled peace more straightforward.[32] In 1594, de Serres presented to the French National Synod of Montauban an account of a project to reconcile the two confessions, entitled *Harmonie*.[33]

In the French manuscript summary of the work, de Serres, like the anonymous author of the *Louanges et recommandations de la paix,* sought to bring to light all the points of agreement between the two groups. He began by giving an overview of the last decades on the religious and political situation of France. "Experience has shown us in this kingdom that neither weapons nor bitter disputations are helpful in resolving the differences between the two religions. . . . Weapons have not won souls for God but instead have led to an infinite flood of impiety everywhere. Our debates have not been any wiser or more successful. Not only have they caused a great uproar, but they have increased dissension because of mutual animosity."[34] Thus, de Serres argued that it was useless to begin discussions on the points of doctrine that divided the two sides, since such a strategy was unlikely to do anything except cause further contention. Instead, he searched for a consensus on doctrinal matters that the two sides could agree upon. If the two sides could uphold common beliefs, then agreement on controversial matters would be, according to de Serres, much less difficult to achieve. To bolster his position, de Serres looked to two sources of authority: the Scriptures and the church fathers. He also took great care to define the characteristics of true doctrines. They had to be ancient, self-explanatory, and credible without further proofs, and catholic in the sense of universally accepted among Christians.[35] His summary of Christian doctrine is as follows:

> There is one God, Father, Son, and Holy Spirit, born of the Virgin Mary who was a virgin before, during, and after Christ's birth. Christ is Redeemer, Mediator, Chief, and sovereign pastor in His church. He shed his precious blood for the remission of our sins and offered a perfect sacrifice through his death and passion. His blood is the purgatory of our souls. [Christ] instituted two sacraments: Baptism and the Eucharist, or the sacrament of Communion, which St. Paul calls the Lord's Supper. His flesh is truly meat, and his blood is truly drink. We truly eat this flesh and drink this blood, and thus we receive his body in the Lord's Supper or the Eucharist in reality, and not figuratively, through our imagination, or in fantasy. We are justified and saved by the grace and mercy of God, which we enjoy through faith. This true faith which justifies us is manifested in charity and is accompanied necessarily by good works. Eternal life is a gift of God. We must honor the memory of the saints, their holy doctrine, and good life. We must pray to God with intelligence and the true affection of our hearts. Fasting is necessary to make us ready to pray to God. We must eat with restraint, dress modestly, mark the day of rest, honor marriages and funerals, and overall behave in an orderly way in God's church. To this faith we join the doctrine of the law of God, the rule to live well, which teaches us to flee from evil and seek to do good, that is to live religiously [and] honestly. . . . We must believe that our soul is immortal and that truth is the path to our happiness.[36]

As Thierry Wanegffelen points out, by seeking out the points of agreement between Protestants and Catholics, de Serres was likely to end up with the doctrines of the "lowest common denominator."[37] In doing so, de Serres risked antagonizing those who felt that he was misrepresenting their doctrines in an effort to achieve consensus.

De Serres's work shows how some members of the Reformed church in France were willing to seek out common ground with their Catholic brethren.

Yet this attempt at conciliation was not successful, largely because of the sharply negative reaction of his fellow believers to his project. In examining how various bodies of the Calvinist church responded to de Serres's efforts, we can begin to see why conciliation was not an option in sixteenth-century France. One of the copies of his French summary of his conciliation proposal ends with the following statement: "I submit this document to the judgement of the Reformed church, which I believe to be the true church of God. I believe that the doctrine in its Confession is ancient, Catholic, and true. I am resolved to obey its discipline, as I have done since my youth."[38] It is hard to discern how genuine de Serres's statement was. Certainly his opponents within the Reformed church, both in Geneva and in France, accused him of going ahead with his project and publishing the Latin text, *De fide catholica*, in 1597 in spite of the repeated condemnations of his fellow Calvinists.[39]

Already in 1594, when his conciliatory writings were first brought to the attention of the National Synod of Montauban, reactions were guarded. The synod asked for two copies of the work to be circulated among the French churches for their opinion, and for one copy to be sent to Geneva, so that a decision could be reached as to whether the work was to be printed or not. The minutes on this matter ended with the synod assembly warning de Serres not to publish any part of the work until a decision had been rendered on its suitability for printing.[40] By the fourteenth national synod, held in Saumur in 1596, the synod's attitude towards any attempt to bring the churches closer together had hardened. The first article under general matters reads, "The delegate from Champagne will alert the church of Paris to be on the alert regarding a minister who wants to mix the two religions."[41] At the same meeting, when de Serres complained that he could not manage to make three copies of his *Harmonie*, the synod assembly still insisted that he had to get the approval of the pastors and delegates of the area where the book would be printed, whether it was Geneva, or La Rochelle, or some other location.[42] In other words, the synod still wanted to have the book evaluated before it was brought to print.

By 5 February 1598, in the last months of de Serres's life, he received a letter from Theodore Beza, Geneva's most senior pastor, which clearly stated that his project had no support from the Calvinist establishment. Beza condemned his endeavors on several grounds. Firstly, he had never been commissioned by any church authority to investigate the question of conciliation, and secondly, he was trying to find common ground where there was none. Beza made liberal use of references to the church of Rome as the whore of Babylon and the Antichrist. Clearly, from his perspective there was no possibility of achieving consensus with those who had spilled the blood of the martyrs and who were still persecuting the true church. Beza also objected to de Serres's overall strategy, as the Genevan pastor argued that de Serres was not evenhanded and was much too favorable to the Catholic side, so much so that rumors were flying that de Serres would renounce his Calvinist faith and adopt Catholicism. Thus, according to Beza, de Serres had little credibility on his side as an advocate of a just conciliation. In a phrase that is both telling and picturesque, Beza described his correspondent "as someone who by hopping from side to side wants to teach both parties to walk straight."[43]

Beza's critique was taken up and amplified by the National Synod of Montpellier that met in 1598, shortly after de Serres's death. The synod delegates echoed the protests of a number of Reformed churches across Europe, namely from Geneva, Berne, Basel, and the Palatinate among others, regarding a number of works written by de Serres to bring Catholics and the Reformed closer together. The synod minutes provide a summary of condemned statements taken from these writings. "True doctrine has always remained complete among those who call themselves Christians, those of the Roman church have the same articles of faith, the same commandments from God, the same prayers, the same baptism, and the same means as we do to reach salvation. Therefore they are the true church and the controversy is only one of words, and not of substance, and the ancient councils and writings of the Fathers should be our judges."[44] Here too, the synod delegates objected strongly to what they saw as a falsifying of the Reformed position, and once again, all the Huguenot churches in France were warned to be on their guard against such writings.

The synods' less than enthusiastic approach to de Serres's project was not merely a witch hunt against him. Other suggestions from Reformed members for conciliation or rapprochement between the two confessional groups were greeted equally coldly, or were openly condemned by the national synod delegates. The 1598 synod, for instance, expressed itself in the following way:

> Although all the faithful should wholeheartedly desire the reunification of all the kingdom's subjects in one religion, for the glory of God and the peace of this land, this is a matter of desire rather than of hope, because of our sins. Some persons of evil intent have taken advantage of these desires and have pretended to unify and mix the two religions. Pastors must carefully warn their flocks not to pay attention to this, as there can be no communion between God's temple and that of idols. Furthermore, such people try to

seduce the credulous, so as to get them later on to abandon their allegiance to the true Gospel. Therefore, all those who try to reach such a reconciliation, either through speeches or through written works, will be severely condemned.[45]

Thus the national synod's concern in this instance was not only the danger of mixing Catholic and Reformed doctrine, but also that such endeavors were the first step on the road to the abjuration of the Reformed faith.[46]

The strongly negative reaction of the Huguenot church authorities to the entire issue of conciliation as advocated by their members may have helped limit the impact of such works. Indeed, after 1598, the issue of such conciliatory treatises disappears almost entirely from the synodal records.[47] Yet I would suggest that the reason for the decrease in the number of texts (both Catholic and Protestant) advocating conciliation was that the political and religious situation changed again in France with the Edict of Nantes. The Edict of Nantes was not an edict of conciliation. But it did serve to regulate relations between the two communities of faith in France and ushered in a period of national peace well into the seventeenth century. Paradoxically, the edict, which finally recognized that the Huguenots in France had certain rights (albeit limited ones), ended up reinforcing confessional boundaries rather than knocking them down. In an ironic fashion the conciliators actually contributed to this process. Although they sought a core set of beliefs all Christians shared to mitigate the damage that religious conflict was causing in their homeland, the proponents of conciliation unintentionally may have strengthened the growth of the confessional churches, in that their enthusiasm for finding common ground was rebutted by those of their own church, who countered by emphasizing again what made their beliefs both true and unique.

NOTES

1. Etienne Pasquier, *Oeuvres* II, cols. 919 and 920, quoted in D. Thickett, ed., *Lettres Historiques pour les années 1556–1594* (Geneva: Droz, 1966), 17–18. The English translation is mine.

2. For a survey of the French wars of religion and their impact on France, see Mack Holt, *The French Wars of Religion, 1562–1629* (Cambridge: Cambridge University Press, 1995).

3. For an in-depth study of the violence affecting relations between Catholics and Protestants in France, see Denis Crouzet, *Les Guerriers de Dieu: la violence au temps des troubles de religion (vers 1525–vers 1610)* (Seyssel: Champ Vallon, 1990), 2 volumes.

4. A helpful analysis of toleration and its various forms can be found in Mario Turchetti, "Religious Concord and Political Tolerance in Sixteenth- and Seventeenth-Century France," *Sixteenth Century Journal* 22, no. 1 (1991): 15–25. For a fuller treatment see his *Concordia o tolleranza?: François Bauduin (1520–1573) e i "moyenneurs"* (Milan: F. Angeli, 1984). I am less convinced by his analysis of the term "concord," as he seems to include both conciliation and compulsory enforcement of Catholicism under the same term.

5. In this respect my essay differs from Philip Benedict's consideration of toleration in the French context. See his *"Un roi, une loi, deux fois:* Parameters for the History of Catholic-Reformed Co-existence in France, 1555–1685," in Ole Peter Grell and Robert Scribner, eds., *Tolerance and Intolerance in the European Reformation* (Cambridge: Cambridge University Press, 1996), 65–93.

6. Interpretations of the Edict of Nantes are varied. Recent historiography has interpreted the edict as providing for confessional coexistence, rather than toleration in the modern understanding of the term. See Olivier Christin, *La Paix de Religion: l'autonomisation de la raison politique au XVIe siècle* (Paris: Seuil, 1997), 207–12; Michael Wolfe, *The Conversion of Henri IV: Politics, Power and Religious Belief in Early Modern France* (Cambridge: Harvard University Press, 1993), 182–83; Bernard Cottret, *1598: L'Edit de Nantes: pour en finir avec les guerres de religion* (Paris: Perrin, 1997). The temporary character of the edict, underlining the majority's desire to see the Huguenots rejoin the Catholic fold, is highlighted in Holt, *The French Wars of Religion,* 3–4, and in Turchetti, "Religious Concord," 24.

7. See Robert Kingdon, *Geneva and the Coming of the Wars of Religion in France* (Geneva: Droz, 1956), and his *Geneva and the Consolidation of the French Protestant Movement 1564–1572* (Madison: University of Wisconsin Press, 1967).

8. See Natalie Zemon Davis, "The Rites of Violence: Religious Riot in Sixteenth Century France," *Past and Present* 59 (1973): 51–91.

9. See W. B. Patterson's analysis of the colloquy and its aims, "Henry IV and the Huguenot Appeal for a Return to Poissy," in Derek Baker, ed., *Schism, Heresy and Religious Protest* (Cambridge: Cambridge University Press, 1972), 247–48. For a fuller account see Donald Nugent, *Ecumenism in the Age of the Reformation: The Colloquy of Poissy* (Cambridge, Mass.: Harvard University Press, 1974).

10. On the Colloquy of Poissy and its connections with German attempts at conciliation, see Alain Dufour, "Le Colloque de Poissy," in *Mélanges d'histoire du XVIe siècle offerts à Henri Meylan* (Geneva: Droz, 1970), 127–37.

11. For a detailed analysis of the role of the nobility in France's civil wars (especially the role of the Guise family) see Stuart Carroll, *Noble Power during the French Wars of Religion: the Guise Affinity and the Catholic Cause in Normandy* (Cambridge: Cambridge University Press, 1998), especially the introduction and 89–95.

12. Mack Holt, *The Duke of Anjou and the Politique Struggle during the Wars of Religion* (Cambridge: Cambridge University Press, 1986), 63–69.

13. Turchetti, "Religious Concord," 21–22.

14. On the League see J. H. M. Salmon, "The Paris Sixteen, 1584–1594: The Social Analysis of a Revolutionary Movement," in J. H. M. Salmon, ed., *Renaissance and Revolt: Essays in the Intellectual and Social History of Early Modern France* (Cambridge: Cambridge University Press, 1987), 235–66. For a study of the mind-set of the League, see also Crouzet, *Les Guerriers de Dieu*, 2:210–514.

15. Following the analysis of Edmond Beame, "The Politiques and the Historians," *Journal of the History of Ideas* 54, no. 3 (1993): 357–79, I will not use the term "Politiques" in this context. The Politique label carried pejorative connotations from the start, and cannot adequately encompass the wide range of motivations and actions of those who displayed "a readiness to sacrifice religious unity for peace" (Beame, 379). On de L'Hôpital see Thierry Wanegffelen, *Ni Rome ni Genève: des fidèles entre deux chaires en France au XVIe siècle* (Paris: Honoré Champion, 1997), 210–20.

16. See Wolfe, *The Conversion of Henri IV*, 22–29.

17. Mark Greengrass, *France in the Age of Henri IV: The Struggle for Stability* (London: Longman, 1984), 56–58.

18. See Joseph Lecler's analysis in his *Histoire de la tolérance au siècle de la Réforme* (Paris: Aubier, 1955), 2:89.

19. Jean de la Vacquerie, *Catholique remonstrance aux roys et princes chrestiens, a tous magistrats & gouuerneurs de repub. Touchant l'abolition des heresies, troubles & scismes qui regnent aujourd'huy en la Chrestienté* (Paris: C. Fremy, 1560), D3v–G3v.

20. De la Vacquerie, *Catholique remonstrance* G5v–G8v; *Discours du vray moyen pour parvenir a la paix entiere, & se maintenir en icelle* (Paris: T. Belot, 1570), C1r–C4r.

21. Etienne Pasquier, *Exhortation aux princes et seigneurs du Conseil Privé du roy, pour obvier aux seditions qui occultement semblent nous menacer pour le faict de la religion* (s.n., n.p., 1561), F2r.

22. Ibid., F3r–v.

23. *Les Louanges et recommandations de la paix, extraictes de l'Escriture Saincte. Remonstrant que c'est chose fort deshonneste que les Chrestiens ayent guerre ensemble* (Lyon: Benoit Rigaud, 1568), A3v–A4r.

24. Wolfe, *The Conversion of Henri IV*, 115–58.

25. Ibid., 175–76.

26. Ibid. Indeed, the prominent Protestants who did convert to Catholicism in the later 1590s underlined the influence of the king's conversion on their own decision.

27. Ibid., 159–63.

28. See Bernard Cottret's analysis in *1598: L'Edit de Nantes*, 156–66.

29. For an analysis of the characteristics of toleration in late sixteenth-century France, see Christin, *La Paix de Religion*, 207–8.

30. For information on de Serres's life, the most comprehensive work is Charles Dardier, "Jean de Serres, historiographe du roi. Sa vie et ses écrits d'après des documents inédits 1540–1598," *Revue Historique* 22 (1883): 291–328; 23 (1883): 28–76.

31. See W. B. Patterson, "Jean de Serres and the Politics of Religious Pacification," in Derek Baker, ed., *Church, Society and Politics* (Oxford: Blackwell, 1975), 223–28.

32. Wanegffelen, *Ni Rome ni Genève*, 452–53.

33. The Latin title of the work, published in 1597, was *Apparatus ad fide catholicam*, also known as *De fide catholica*.

34. Geneva, Bibliothèque publique et universitaire (BPU), Archives Tronchin 5, fol. 32r.

35. Ibid., fol. 32v.

36. Ibid., fol. 32v–33r.

37. Wanegffelen, *Ni Rome ni Genève*, 456.

38. Geneva BPU, Manuscrits français 412, fol. 29v.

39. For an in-depth look at the controversy, see Dardier, "Jean de Serres," 29–69.

40. Jean Aymon, *Tous les synodes nationaux des églises réformées de France* (The Hague: Delo, 1710), 1:186–87.

41. Ibid., 200.

42. Ibid., 206.

43. Geneva BPU Arch. Tronchin 5, fols. 24–27, esp. fol. 27v.

44. Aymon, *Tous les synodes nationaux*, 1:222. See also Dardier, "Jean de Serres," 73–74; and Patterson, "The Politics of Religious Pacification," 241–42.

45. Aymon, *Tous les synodes nationaux*, 1:219.

46. Indeed, persistent rumors circulated among both Huguenots and Catholics regarding de Serres's supposed conversion to Catholicism, either during his lifetime or on his deathbed. See Dardier, "Jean de Serres," 70–73.

47. Some projects for unification did surface in the synod minutes, but these focused on reaching common confessional standards among Protestants, rather than between Protestants and Catholics. See W. B. Patterson, "Pierre Du Moulin's Quest for Protestant Unity, 1613–1618," in R. N. Swanson, ed., *Unity and Diversity in the Church* (Oxford: Blackwell, 1996), 240–50.

8

The Boundaries of Reformed Irenicism

Royal Hungary and the Transylvanian Principality

GRAEME MURDOCK

THE REFORMATION FRACTURED RELIGIOUS UNIFORMITY IN HUNGARY but resulted in almost no violent conflict between a range of different confessional communities. Though ideas about religious reform first arrived in Hungary in the 1520s, they began to spread rapidly in the 1540s, and within a few decades Protestantism had come to dominate Hungarian society. By the late sixteenth century perhaps as many as three-quarters of the people living across the territories of the former Hungarian kingdom were attending Lutheran, Reformed, or anti-Trinitarian church services.[1] Sixteenth-century Hungarian society faced not only the breakdown of confessional uniformity but also the collapse of the state after the catastrophic defeat of Louis II by the Ottoman sultan Suleiman "the Magnificent" at the battle of Mohács in 1526. Under the impact of Ottoman invasion, Hungary was divided into three parts. To the north and west, Habsburg Royal Hungary stretched from the Adriatic coast to the mountains of Upper Hungary. Southern and central Hungarian counties fell under the control of the Ottomans. To the east, a Hungarian kingdom was established in Transylvania

and the counties of the *Partium* beyond the river Tisza. This territory became known as the Transylvanian principality, ruled over by a series of native nobles elected as princes by the diet.[2]

Towards the end of the sixteenth century the Habsburg court and
episcopal hierarchy began to revive the Catholic Church in Royal Hungary.
Faced with this wave of Catholic Reform, some Hungarian Calvinists began
to suggest that Lutherans should recognize them as true Christian brethren
and form a united front against their common Catholic opponents. This
essay will examine the emergence of this Protestant unionism in Hungary
and consider why its impact was largely confined to parts of Royal Hungary
and made little headway within the Transylvanian principality. This study will
raise a number of questions about the significance of irenicism in early modern confessional relations in Hungary and across the Continent. Was support
for a unified Protestant Church among Calvinists entirely dependent upon
the existence of a political, legal, and social environment which made compromise with Lutherans seem necessary? Should irenicism primarily be understood as a rhetoric of confessional peace taken up by Reformed communities under threat as a means of defending their own interests against
the Catholic Reformation? To what extent did irenic projects prove abortive
largely because of the shallow roots of any commitment by Reformed churchmen to make the necessary concessions on key issues dividing the two Protestant traditions? How important were popular attitudes in preventing Protestant union, and were Lutherans rightly suspicious of Reformed motivations
and entirely justified in rejecting Reformed irenic advances outright? This
study will first chart the developing relationship between the churches of
Transylvania and consider why irenicism was not pursued by Reformed clergy
there. It will then examine the support expressed by some Reformed ministers in Royal Hungary for Protestant union, looking in particular at the
career of Péter Alvinczi, his attitude to confessional identity, and his attempts to achieve Protestant unity over the contentious issue of communion theology.

The Lutheran Reformation spread first to the German-speaking community of Hungary. The German towns of Upper Hungary and Transylvania accepted Lutheran preaching in the 1540s. The five royal free towns of
Upper Hungary, Kassa (Košice/Kaschau), Eperjes (Prešov/Preschau), Bártfa
(Bardejov/Bartfeld), Lőcse (Levoča/Leutschau), and Kisszeben (Sabinov/
Zeben), declared their support for reform. In 1549 Leonhard Stöckel, the
minister at Bártfa, completed a version of the Augsburg Confession for these
towns as a *Confessio Pentapolitana*. This confession acknowledged the real

presence of Christ in the Eucharist and was designed to protect the towns' churches from the 1548 diet's decision to outlaw "sacramentarians" and Anabaptists. Although Protestant churches were not granted legal status in Royal Hungary, given widespread noble support for reform and the continued threat posed by the Ottomans, the court could do little to prevent the spread of Protestantism in the mid-sixteenth century.[3]

Meanwhile in 1557 the Transylvanian diet granted legal freedom to Lutherans in the German or Saxon towns of the principality. Lutheran preaching also made some progress among Hungarian speakers as well, but from the late 1550s Reformed, or Calvinist, ideas were accepted by many Hungarian nobles and in market towns, especially in the *Partium*.[4] Hungarian and German clergy in Transylvania debated different ideas about the Eucharist from the late 1550s. Hungarian clergy were at first labelled as "sacramentarians" because of their view that communion must be seen as merely a commemoration of the Last Supper and their rejection of any notion that Christ's body was really present in the elements of the sacrament. By 1564 it had become clear that no consensus would be possible between Transylvanian clergy on sacramental theology, and the diet granted freedom of worship to two Protestant churches, one for Germans and the other for Hungarians. The doctrine of the Hungarian Reformed Church became clearly established around a Calvinist confession drawn up at Debrecen in 1562 by Péter Méliusz Juhász, and in 1567 Reformed clergy also accepted the Second Helvetic Confession.[5]

Protestantism in Transylvania fractured once more during the 1560s when a group of Hungarian clergy, led by Ferenc Dávid, challenged a Trinitarian understanding of Christ's nature. A number of debates were held in the 1560s about the scriptural basis for the doctrine of the Trinity. The position taken by anti-Trinitarians received some approval from prince János Zsigmond Szapolyai and support in a number of Hungarian towns in the principality.[6] In 1568 the Transylvanian diet again considered how to deal with the impact of different ideas about religious reform and reached the remarkable conclusion that ministers should be permitted to preach the Gospel according to their understanding of it. If a local community did not accept their minister's preaching, then they could find another minister, but no one was to be subjected to abuse or violence on account of their beliefs. The diet declared that as "faith is a gift from God," it could not be compelled against conscience. The diet then granted legal freedoms to three religions in the principality: the Lutheran, Reformed, and anti-Trinitarian churches.[7]

The decisions reached by the Transylvanian diet on religious freedom up to 1568 reflected the weakness of princely power in the fledgling state and the need to reach some accommodation between the three estates represented in the diet of Hungarian nobles, Saxon towns, and Szeklers. The magnates, gentry, and urban magistrates played a decisive role in the developing patterns of religious loyalty across the principality. The prince remained at least nominally Catholic, and some Hungarian nobles and Szekler lords were Catholic, but the Saxon towns solidly adhered to Lutheranism, while most Hungarian nobles and Szeklers supported either the Reformed or anti-Trinitarian churches. The legal acceptance of religious diversity in Transylvania was a political necessity, but at the same time it reflected peaceful social interaction between the principality's different confessional groups. Transylvanian society had long since adapted to coexistence between a range of linguistic, ethnic, and religious communities, and although not represented in the diet, Transylvania's Romanian peasantry also continued to be granted rights of free practice of their Eastern Orthodox religion by princes.[8]

From 1564 Transylvanian law required that the religion of each parish was to be decided by the local majority. In cases where this meant that a church building changed hands, the minority religious community that had lost its place of worship was supposed to be provided with a new building constructed at the expense of the majority community. While the diet continued their attempts to order local relations between the received religions through such laws, it also acted to prevent any further religious change. Under the Catholic prince István Báthori, a 1572 law was passed by the diet which demanded that the churches make no further alterations to their doctrinal statements.[9] When anti-Trinitarian clergy split over the issue of the adoration of Christ in the mid-1570s, the non-adorantists were therefore outlawed. Most anti-Trinitarians argued that Christ, although not equal to God the Father, ought to be adored in worship, and they continued to hold services of communion. However, radicals rejected this adorantist position and moved towards a form of Judaistic faith that rejected the worship of Christ as God altogether. Despite occasional persecution of these radicals, the support of some nobles for this so-called Sabbatarian strain of anti-Trinitarianism allowed this community to survive into the seventeenth century.[10] The range of religions in Transylvania extended still further in the early seventeenth century when small settlements of Anabaptists and Jews received legal protection in the principality.[11]

Support within Transylvanian society for a range of churches was reflected in the principality's laws that gave the four major churches equal legal status by 1600. The Lutheran Church was largely self-contained within the German-speaking community, the Catholic Church was mostly restricted to the lands of a few sympathetic nobles, and confessional rivalry was most strident between the predominantly Hungarian-speaking Reformed Church and the anti-Trinitarian, or Unitarian Church. All four received religions worked to strengthen their respective positions by cooperating with princes, powerful noble patrons, and urban magistrates. Confessional relations in Transylvania during the late sixteenth and early seventeenth centuries saw a balance emerge between the power of loyalty to a particular church and set of ideas, legal protection of a range of religions, and widespread social acceptance of confessional difference in regions, towns, and even within families.[12]

Some sense of the degree of confessional diversity in Transylvania and of the fluctuating fortunes of different churches can be gauged from the history of Kolozsvár (Cluj/Klausenburg), one of the principality's largest towns. Kolozsvár was divided between German and Hungarian residents, and the two communities shared control of the town's offices. The state appropriation of Catholic property in 1556 and collapse of Catholic institutional structures left Kolozsvár's magistrates to control the direction of religious life in the town. The council had already decided in the mid-1540s to give control of the church of St. Michael in Kolozsvár's central square to Lutheran preachers. In 1556 the Dominicans and Franciscans were ordered to leave the town, and the altars and images in their chapels were destroyed. In 1558 the council decided to transfer control of St. Michael's to clergy from the emerging Reformed Church. At the end of the 1560s the German and Hungarian residents of Kolozsvár embraced anti-Trinitarianism under the charismatic influence of Ferenc Dávid. From 1570 St. Michael's became a center of anti-Trinitarian preaching, and Kolozsvár emerged as the main base of the Unitarian Church.[13]

In 1579 prince István Báthori tried to reverse Catholic fortunes by inviting Jesuits to set up a teaching station near Kolozsvár. Although Báthori also gave the Jesuits possession of the Farkas street church in 1581 and supported a Jesuit school, anti-Trinitarians continued to dominate the town. Pressure from the diet forced the temporary exclusion of the Jesuits from Transylvania in 1588. The halting progress of Catholic recovery was disrupted again when Kolozsvár's citizens took advantage of the confusion of the Fifteen Years' War against the Ottomans to force the Jesuits out of town once more in 1603, destroying the monastery and church that they had occupied in the process. Kolozsvár's reception of different waves of Reformation ideas and resistance to attempts to enforce Counter-Reform demonstrates the ability of urban magistrates and the estates to establish and defend local religious change in sixteenth-century Transylvania.[14]

At the beginning of the seventeenth century Rudolf II tried to take advantage of renewed war with the Ottomans to establish control over the Transylvanian principality and to impose Catholicism on the region. In 1603 Protestants were expelled from towns in Royal Hungary, officials confiscated some Protestant property, and the leading Lutheran magnate, István Illésházy, was brought to trial and found guilty of sedition. Complaints brought to the 1604 Hungarian diet were ignored since archduke Matthias, acting for Rudolf, introduced a law that prevented any religious grievances from being raised. In response a Reformed noble, István Bocskai, led a coalition of landless Heyduck mercenaries, Reformed and Lutheran nobles, gentry, and towns to defend Protestant liberties and the traditional privileges of the estates. Bocskai's army defeated Habsburg forces in 1604 and 1605, and in February 1605 Bocskai became the first Reformed noble to be elected as prince of Transylvania.[15]

Under Bocskai and a succession of Calvinist princes in the seventeenth century the Reformed Church came to dominate the Transylvanian principality. The Reformed Church received princely backing in disputes with rival confessions and support to develop its centers of education and printing. Through preaching, catechising, and printed literature, Reformed clergy spread understanding of key points of Calvinist doctrine across Transylvanian society. The Reformed Church also developed a broader and deeper relationship with the rest of the Calvinist world during the early decades of the seventeenth century.[16] Reformed student ministers were sponsored to attend universities and colleges in Germany until the outbreak of the Thirty Years' War. Reformed students at first had followed Lutheran colleagues to Wittenberg in the sixteenth century, but when formulas of Lutheran orthodoxy were imposed on Wittenberg students from 1592, they travelled instead to Heidelberg. After Heidelberg was taken by Catholic forces in 1621, Reformed students turned to the universities of the Dutch Republic and to a lesser extent also studied in England. Reformed orthodoxy among Hungarian clergy was bolstered through university training in dogmatic and polemic theology, and as students translated and published a series of catechisms, creeds, sermons, polemic tracts, and works on piety and morality upon their return home.[17]

Closer connections with western Europe raised awareness among Hungarian Reformed clergy of their place within the international Calvinist community. This growing sense of Reformed identity often resulted in ever more strident confrontations with domestic confessional rivals. The increasing range of Reformed religious literature published in Hungarian assisted ministers both in instructing their congregations about the fundamentals of their faith and also clarified points of difference with the doctrine of other churches.[18] Leading clergy also produced polemical writings directed against the beliefs of other religions, including a 1617 work by István Melotai Nyilas which claimed to clear away "evil thorn bushes" of dangerous errors and false opinions.[19] Melotai, who had been a student at Heidelberg in 1601, became superintendent of the eastern Tisza Reformed Church province in the *Partium* in 1614. He resigned his post in 1618 and moved to become a court preacher at the Transylvanian capital Gyulafehérvár (Alba Iulia/Weissenburg), where in 1621 he published a service order-book dedicated to prince Gábor Bethlen.[20] When Melotai discussed communion services in this book, he emphasized that the sacrament should be held as a spiritual memorial of Christ's death. Melotai concentrated on the importance of striving for accuracy in copying the exact details of the original Last Supper. He then went on to argue that "the wafer is the bread of the Antichrist in communion" which "infects Christian knowledge." He accused Lutherans of being indistinguishable from Catholics in their style of worship, in the way their churches were decorated, in their ministers' vestments, and above all in their conduct of the sacraments. Melotai illustrated his point by referring to a story which he had heard when a student in Germany on the dangers of using wafers rather than bread in communion services. According to Melotai, a minister in a town near Heidelberg had wanted to use wafers in communion but was unable to do so when the wafers flew out of the plate as he prepared for the service.[21]

Similar attitudes were taken towards the Lutheran Church by other leading Reformed clergy. István Geleji Katona, who studied in Heidelberg from 1615 to 1617 and again in 1619, became superintendent of the Transylvanian Reformed Church province in 1633. In a vast collection of published sermons, Geleji expressed hostility towards all the other received religions of the principality, most especially the Unitarians or Binarists as he preferred to call them, but also against Lutherans. Geleji claimed that their doctrine of Christ's ubiquity and real presence in the Eucharist denied the humanity of Christ as intercessor between God and man. In a long cycle of sermons on the conduct of communion services, Geleji charged both Catholics and Lutherans with causing the "hideous corruption of the holy sacrament." Geleji attempted to demonstrate that the Lutheran interpretation of Christ's words at the Last Supper was false and attacked Lutheran and Catholic communion ceremonies, including their use of altars and wafers and the delivery of the elements by priests into the mouths of communicants.[22]

Protestants within the Transylvanian principality remained largely insulated from the icy blasts of the Catholic Reformation during the early seventeenth century. Their position was protected by law, and the law was defended by the diet and by Reformed princes. The clerical elite of the Reformed Church in Transylvania directed polemical attacks against their rivals, but the force of their increasingly strident confessionalism met the immovable object of the laws on religious freedom, which were maintained in the principality throughout the early modern period. Each of Transylvania's churches looked to their own patrons for support, and Reformed clergy put their trust above all in co-religionist princes to promote their church's interests and to protect the Transylvanian Reformed community against the Habsburgs and the Catholic hierarchy of Royal Hungary.

In the wake of István Bocskai's 1604 revolt, Protestant nobles in Royal Hungary had been able to win freedom of religious practice for nobles, towns, and military garrisons through the 1606 Peace of Vienna. The terms of this treaty were confirmed by the diet in 1608, which reflected the strong bargaining position of Lutheran and Reformed nobles during the struggle between Matthias and Rudolf for control of Royal Hungary.[23] However, Protestant domination of Hungarian noble and urban society came under increasing pressure during the early decades of the seventeenth century from Habsburg efforts to galvanize the Catholic hierarchy and gain prominent converts among the nobility. By 1619 Catholics held a majority in the Upper Chamber of the diet. This provided an entirely different political context for confessional relations in Royal Hungary as compared with the Transylvanian principality. To the east, Reformed dominance of the principality, but political and social acceptance of laws permitting confessional diversity. In Royal Hungary, a Catholic dynasty anxious to recover ground lost to Protestants and undermine concessions that had been granted to both Lutherans and Calvinists after Bocskai's revolt.

In Royal Hungary some Reformed ministers began to consider the possibility of combining with local Lutherans to combat the Catholic Church more effectively. The Lutheran and Reformed churches only gained rights freely to regulate their own affairs in Royal Hungary in 1608, and separate church structures had been slow to emerge. In western and northwestern Hungary debates over communion theology between Protestant ministers had only led to institutional division in the 1590s, with magnates and nobles protecting rival Lutheran and Reformed churches.[24] In the royal free towns of Upper Hungary, Lutherans had tried to distance themselves from other illegal Protestant groups from the late 1540s. However, as in Germany, tensions emerged in the Lutheran camp between those who sought to defend orthodoxy and others in a Melanchthonian tradition, labelled as "crypto-Calvinists." Arguments focused on the use of images in churches and the doctrine of the real presence in communion. Typical of orthodox Lutheran opinion was a 1586 *Warning* by Georg Creutzer about the dangers of "sacramentarians," Zwinglians, and Calvinists.[25]

Protestant unionism and irenic projects were pursued by Calvinists in Royal Hungary in a number of ways during the early seventeenth century, but perhaps most significant were the initiatives undertaken by one leading Calvinist minister, Péter Alvinczi. Alvinczi was the son of a Reformed minister, born around 1575 at Nagyenyed (Aiud/Strassburg) in Transylvania. Alvinczi attended the local school, then went to the college at Nagyvárad (Oradea/Grosswardein) before going off to study at Wittenberg in 1598 and 1599. Alvinczi then studied at Heidelberg in 1600 and 1601 under David Pareus and completed a short tract which was included in a collection of former students' work published by Pareus in 1611.[26] David Pareus was a Silesian, who had himself studied at Heidelberg in the late 1560s, then returned to teach in the Palatinate from the mid-1580s and was appointed as professor of Old and New Testament theology at Heidelberg after 1598. Pareus was well-known to a generation of Hungarian students who travelled to Heidelberg in the 1600s and 1610s and corresponded with leading Reformed clergy including István Miskolczi Csulyak, Albert Szenczi Molnár, and János Keserüi Dajka.[27]

When Alvinczi returned to Hungary in 1601, he taught at the school in Debrecen before being ordained as a Reformed minister in 1604. Alvinczi was appointed minister at Nagyvárad and archdeacon of the Bihar district, before becoming caught up in István Bocskai's anti-Habsburg revolt. After Bocskai had taken the town of Kassa in Upper Hungary, Alvinczi moved there as his court preacher in March 1605.[28] Alvinczi was involved in the production of an *Apology* in 1606 which defended Bocskai's revolt and denied Catholic claims that Bocskai was an Arian.[29] On Bocskai's death in 1606, Alvinczi moved his family to Kassa, one of Hungary's largest towns. He was ennobled in 1612 and was made a citizen of Kassa in 1615. Alvinczi worked for the rest of his career based in this mostly German-speaking, Lutheran town until his death in 1634.[30] As a royal free town Kassa had defended its right to appoint Lutheran ministers in the 1540s, and the town council consistently supported Lutheran clergy throughout the sixteenth century. During Rudolf's attempt to establish Habsburg and Catholic control of the region, the Catholic bishop of Eger was sanctioned in 1603 to use imperial troops to occupy Kassa. The town's Lutheran ministers were expelled, and even the private practice of Lutheranism was forbidden during this occupation. This imposition of Catholicism was reversed thanks to Bocskai's army, and Lutheran clergy were able to return to Kassa in 1605. The council then defended the exclusive rights of Lutherans to worship in the town against any encroachment by either Catholics or Calvinists.[31]

From his station at Kassa in Upper Hungary, Alvinczi became the chief propagandist for the Reformed Church against the growing attacks of Catholic writers. He clashed in particular with Péter Pázmány, from 1616 archbishop of Esztergom. Pázmány, a child convert to Catholicism, published a number of polemic works attacking Protestant faiths as devilish heresies. In 1613 Pázmány produced *A Guide Leading to the Truth of God*, a major work on Catholic dogma that included the claim that Calvin had made God the author of sin.[32] Alvinczi responded with accusations that Catholics were idolaters in a work published in 1609 and in his 1614 *Mirror*.[33] A 1616 *Guide to Catholic Religion* also responded to Catholic attacks and attempted to prove the continuous existence throughout history of an unseen church of reformers leading up to Luther and Calvin.[34] The outbreak of the Thirty Years' War produced another outburst of polemic. In 1620 Pázmány completed *A Short Answer to Two Calvinist Books*, which specifically ridiculed the notion of a joint Protestant heritage. Pázmány argued that Lutherans and Calvinists could not agree among themselves, and that "perhaps Calvinist preachers, and those who row in Calvin's boat, often lie about what they believe for friendship's sake."[35]

This polemical literature was immediately related to the political situation in Hungary and Transylvania. Alvinczi became a close advisor to the Transylvanian prince Gábor Bethlen in the 1610s. In 1619 renewed defiance of Habsburg rule spread to Hungary, and the Hungarian estates offered widespread support to Bethlen's anti-Habsburg policies. As during Bocskai's revolt, this anti-Habsburg alliance included Lutheran as well as Reformed nobles. By August 1620 Bethlen controlled most of Royal Hungary, and the Hungarian diet offered the Transylvanian prince the holy crown of St. Stephen.[36] Alvinczi justified Bethlen's intervention against the Habsburgs on the grounds that it was his duty to defend Hungarian constitutional liberties and Protestant rights. Alvinczi accused Jesuits of being responsible for instigating attacks against Protestants in Royal Hungary, and three Jesuits were murdered in Kassa in 1619 when it was taken by Bethlen's forces.[37] In 1620 Bethlen sent troops to aid his ally Frederick V in Bohemia, but after Frederick's defeat Bethlen soon agreed to peace terms with Ferdinand II. In December 1621 under the treaty of Nikolsburg (Mikulov), Bethlen gained control for his lifetime of seven northeastern Hungarian counties including Kassa in Abaúj county.[38]

When Alvinczi, who had been ordained a Reformed minister, had first moved in 1605 to serve the Hungarian community of Kassa he was pressured by the town's authorities not to attend Abaúj Reformed district synods, nor accept Reformed discipline, and to subscribe to the Augsburg Confession. István Miskolczi Csulyak, Reformed archdeacon of neighboring Zemplén county, wrote to David Pareus in 1607 to inform his former Heidelberg teacher of how Kassa's "ubiquitarians" had forbidden Alvinczi from visiting his Reformed colleagues.[39] Alvinczi faced opposition in Kassa from the German minister, Andreas Musculus, and there was growing concern among the German community about the increasing number of Hungarians in the town. In 1611 Alvinczi was again requested by the council to sever all connections with the regional Reformed Church and to join meetings of clergy from Kassa and the other Lutheran royal free towns of Upper Hungary. The council suggested that his absence from these meetings raised the suspicion that he was a Calvinist and alerted Catholics to the potential existence of schism in Kassa. Alvinczi gave way on this issue, obeyed the council, and also subscribed to the *Confessio Pentapolitana*. The council's concerns proved wellfounded since Péter Pázmány called for an investigation into the state of religion in Kassa at the 1613 diet and pressed for Catholics to be allowed to gain entry to the town if Calvinists were already found to be present.[40]

The way in which Alvinczi organized the Hungarian church in Kassa gave the council continuing cause for anxiety. Reflecting the nature of earlier debates between Lutheran and Reformed writers in Hungary, the use of images and styles of worship proved particularly contentious. Alvinczi cleared many of the images and the organ out of his church and did not wear some of the liturgical vestments favored by Lutherans when he conducted the sacraments. However, Alvinczi was prepared to use wafers instead of bread and wine during communion, which was interpreted as signalling his acceptance of the real presence of Christ in the sacrament. Alvinczi later explained his actions in a work dedicated to Gábor Bethlen, *A Short Warning about the Lord's Holy Supper from the Teaching of the Holy Apostle Paul,* which was published at Kassa in Hungarian in 1622.[41] Alvinczi argued that the church ought to remain at peace over the whole question of how to receive the elements in communion. He noted that some congregations took communion seated while others stood, some received communion daily, others weekly, or thrice annually, some gathered around a table while others moved to an altar, some received the bread in their hands but others received the bread directly from the hands of the clergy into their mouths, some used leavened bread and others unleavened bread. For Alvinczi, all these different practices in the celebration of the sacrament were insignificant. He argued that where the sacrament was received in good conscience and without superstition, then its effect was to bring people to live in grace. Alvinczi then moved on to discuss how Christ's body and blood were represented in the sacrament. He argued that for believers the bread was more than "mere bread" and provided a sign and pledge of salvation through Christ. Alvinczi concluded that the substance and form of the elements remained unchanged but that the communicant received Christ's body and blood through them. In the second part of the book, Alvinczi took up the question of the validity of using wafers in communion. He suggested that this was permissible only where a community was not ready to accept the change to using bread and wine. According to Alvinczi, this variety of practice again did not affect the function of the communion service so long as the ceremony remained free from all superstition.[42]

Alvinczi was not the only Reformed writer to attempt to reconcile Calvinist and Lutheran positions on the key issue of communion theology, which above all others separated the two traditions. Another former Heidelberg student, János Samarjai, also advanced ideas about possible union between Protestants. Samarjai had studied at Heidelberg in 1609, then worked as a minister in western Hungary, and from 1622 was superintendent of the Upper Danubian Reformed Church province. In 1628 Samarjai published *Magyar Harmony*, which called for Protestant union against the Catholic Church. Samarjai also attempted to demonstrate that the Helvetic and Augsburg confessions could be unified, with his arguments supported by frequent use of Pareus's famous *Irenicum*. On the problematic issue of communion, Samarjai emphasized that the sacrament was not a mere memorial of Christ's death but a necessity for salvation in which Christ was spiritually present through the bread and wine. Samarjai stood by the need for communion in both kinds and claimed, as Pareus had done, that most Lutherans did not hold to the doctrine of the real presence as set out in the Augsburg Confession.[43]

Samarjai also produced a service order-book for his province, published in the Lutheran town of Lőcse in 1636, which made no mention of the Helvetic

Confession. He suggested that the details of sacramental liturgy were open to different interpretations under "Christian freedom." On the ceremony of communion services, Samarjai argued that it was of little importance whether a communicant should stand or kneel, or whether the elements should be received in the hands or in the mouth, at an altar or on a table. Samarjai did assume, however, that wafers would not be used in the sacrament but described the bread as more than mere bread which was secretly united for the believer with Christ's body in the sacrament.[44] Another writer who supported Protestant union was Imre Pécseli Király, who had studied at Heidelberg in 1609. Pécseli, from 1622 the minister at Érsekújvár (Nové Zámky/ Neuhäusel), argued against using the labels of Lutheran and Calvinist in a text produced on the instructions of prince Gábor Bethlen. He also produced a *Catechism* in 1624 which integrated the Heidelberg *Catechism* and Luther's *Shorter Catechism*.[45]

Alvinczi and other Reformed ministers in Royal Hungary tried to allow for variety in the conduct of communion services as a means of advancing Protestant union. Alvinczi's carefully argued position on communion theology certainly enabled him to outmaneuver suspicious German ministers in Kassa, who repeatedly tried and failed to have him barred from preaching on the grounds that he was a Calvinist. In July 1623 Alvinczi reported to the council in Kassa that Michael Bussaeus, the German minister in the town, was refusing to speak to him and had described those attending Alvinczi's communion services as having the reverence of pigs. Alvinczi commented that in all his years of service in Kassa he had always maintained good connections with the German community and had distanced himself from every controversy and source of discord. Alvinczi at first declared that he would no longer preach from the same pulpit as Bussaeus. However, negotiations between the two men were brokered in September 1623, when both Alvinczi and Bussaeus were given the opportunity to restate their positions, and some sort of reconciliation was effected.[46]

Further controversy soon flared up between the two communities' clergymen. In June 1625 Alvinczi told the council that he intended to leave Kassa, alleging that Bussaeus had continued to insult him. Alvinczi again insisted upon the essential unity of Protestants in Kassa and warned the council against claiming that there were two religions in the town, since Catholics would then demand also to be allowed to practice their religion. Alvinczi reiterated his view that "there is only one true biblical religion here." Alvinczi entirely discounted Bussaeus's claims that he taught that Christ's body and blood were not really present in the Eucharist and flatly rejected the label Calvinist as a term of abuse. Alvinczi told the council that "I am certainly not a Calvinist, neither am I a Lutheran, but a true Christian named after Jesus Christ."[47]

On the understanding that he would receive no more insults from his German colleague, Alvinczi was eventually persuaded to stay in Kassa in October 1625. Bussaeus, however, persisted with his attacks in 1626, describing the town's Hungarian congregation as Calvinist heretics. Alvinczi again appeared before the council to refute the charge of Calvinism, proclaiming that as "God is my witness, . . . I have held to every point of the Augsburg Confession." On the question of the real presence of Christ, Alvinczi stated that he accepted the omnipresence of God throughout the world, and that the Eucharist was no mere commemoration of the signs of salvation.[48] The council eventually lost patience with Bussaeus's behavior, and he was asked to leave Kassa in May 1626 to try to prevent any further scandals.[49] Despite Bussaeus's departure to Lőcse, controversy soon returned over the conduct of communion services in the Hungarian church. In April 1627 two assistant Hungarian ministers distributed bread and wine to their congregation. The council demanded that the ministers involved must promise to use only the wafer in future or leave the town. One of the ministers, Pál Tyrnavius Nagy, left Kassa before the end of the year for the village of Tarczal. Alvinczi again appealed to the council to support Protestant concord and warned them that further arguments would give the Catholic Church a clear excuse to press for entry into Kassa if they accepted that Calvinists were already present.[50]

After Gábor Bethlen's death in 1629, Abaúj county was returned to Habsburg control under the terms of the 1621 Nikolsburg treaty. Alvinczi remained in Kassa but was anxious to justify his position to György Rákóczi, the leading Reformed landowner in northeastern Hungary and soon to be the new Transylvanian prince. Alvinczi wrote to Rákóczi claiming support from Calvin for his stance on communion and stressing points of agreement between what Calvin and Luther had written on the role of the sacraments.[51] Alvinczi's balancing act at Kassa became increasingly difficult to sustain under Habsburg sovereignty in the early 1630s, especially after demands from the council for uniformity of ceremony in the town's churches. Some Hungarian residents in Kassa were called to appear before the council after they went to receive communion in Reformed churches in neighboring villages rather than receive the wafer from Alvinczi. This provides a rare glimpse of popular Reformed attitudes to Alvinczi's unionist project in Kassa and suggests that he faced difficulties in getting the Hungarian community to accept his vision of a united Protestant church. However, Alvinczi maintained his position at Kassa until his death in 1634, publishing volumes of his sermons in 1633 and 1634.[52]

The efforts of Péter Alvinczi to maintain Protestant unity between the German and Hungarian communities in Kassa did not long survive him. In 1644 Prince György I Rákóczi led Transylvania into battle against the Habsburgs after lengthy negotiations with western allies. Rákóczi's attack made good progress, and he gained control over Upper Hungary. When the prince moved to Kassa in March 1644, the Hungarian church became a clearly Reformed church, holding communion celebrations using bread and wine. By this time the Hungarian community in Kassa had outgrown the German population. In 1645 Rákóczi agreed to terms with Ferdinand III in the Peace of Linz, which gave the prince control over the seven counties of northeastern Hungary previously held by Bethlen, including Kassa. However, on Rákóczi's death in 1648, Abaúj was among five counties that reverted to Habsburg sovereignty once again. The consequences of the breakdown of the Lutheran monopoly in Kassa in 1644, which the council had worked so hard to prevent, were exactly those which they had long feared. In 1649 the Hungarian diet at Pozsony (Bratislava/Pressburg) offered equal rights for Lutherans, Calvinists, and Catholics to worship freely in Kassa, and in 1657 the Jesuits were able to open a college in the town.[53]

While Péter Alvinczi, János Samarjai, and Imre Pécseli Király were willing to blur issues over which Lutherans and Calvinists were divided, the vast majority of Reformed clergy in Transylvania and the *Partium* remained clear in their defense of Calvinist orthodoxy on communion theology. There was, however, some expression of support for Protestant unionism in the Transylvanian Reformed Church. In 1634 John Dury, a leading advocate of Protestant irenicism during the Thirty Years' War, addressed the Transylvanian Reformed synod on the need for a conference to resolve key problems between Lutheran and Reformed theologians. Dury's appeal also stressed how Catholics, and particularly the Jesuits, had worked to maintain divisions between Protestants. Dury reported that the Transylvanians took his appeal for Protestant unity "into serious consideration."[54] In February 1634 a decree was signed by superintendent István Geleji Katona and all Transylvania's Reformed archdeacons. It was also signed by three German Reformed teachers then working at the princely academy in Gyulafehérvár—Johann Heinrich Alsted, Johann Heinrich Bisterfeld, and Ludwig Piscator. Alsted had previously studied under David Pareus at Heidelberg in 1608.[55] The decree declared that the Transylvanian Reformed Church shared Dury's aim to find church unity in order to combat the Antichrist more effectively. It emphasized that the Reformed community in the principality were neighbors with barbarians and were compelled by the country's laws to live alongside the Orthodox Church, Arians, Anabaptists, Jews, and atheists, so that they had every reason to seek unity with Saxon Lutherans. The Reformed Church leadership apparently signed up readily in 1634 to Dury's call for Protestant unity. However, Transylvania's Reformed clergy seemed more willing to signify their acceptance of Protestant unionism in a wider continental context rather than make any specific plans for union with local Lutherans or to compromise on key points of theological difference. Consequently, the proposal made no perceptible impact on confessional relations in the principality.[56]

The emergence of Reformed irenicism in Hungary did not mark the revival of some native spirit of religious tolerance first expressed in the 1560s decisions of the Transylvanian diet. Transylvania's laws on religion reflected the need to provide some means of holding together a state under pressure from internal religious divisions and bounded by Ottomans and Habsburgs. The political compromise agreed by the diet in the 1560s to offer equal status to a range of received religions ensured the legal freedoms of the Lutheran and Reformed churches in the principality. These two churches continued to dispute points of theological difference, even if the stridency of their rivalry was muted to some extent because their support mostly came from different linguistic communities. In Royal Hungary, the legal freedoms of the Lutheran and Reformed churches were only secured in the 1600s but remained threatened by the determination of the Habsburg court to undermine and overturn Protestant privileges. In Habsburg Hungary the religious liberties of the Reformed Church remained insecure, and particularly in those areas where Calvinists were in a minority and felt especially vulnerable, the potential benefits of uniting with Lutherans were most obvious.

The emergence of Reformed irenicism in Hungary between the 1600s and 1630s was directly related to efforts to combine Reformed and Lutheran nobles in Royal Hungary in campaigns against the Habsburgs. Irenic sentiments were expressed by Reformed preachers during the period of István Bocskai's revolt, and irenicism received support from some Reformed clergy close to Gábor Bethlen's court. Both Bocskai and Bethlen partly justified their anti-Habsburg policies on religious grounds but were well aware of the need to appeal for support from beyond the Reformed community. The period up to the Thirty Years' War was also marked by close connections between the Reformed political and ecclesiastical elites of Hungary and Germany. These linkages with German Calvinists were certainly significant in shaping the irenic appeals made by some Hungarian ministers but were not decisive, as the careers of ministers such as István Geleji Katona and István Melotai Nyilas, who both studied at Heidelberg, demonstrate. Similarities between the position of the Reformed churches in Germany and Hungary were also important. Hungarian Reformed students who travelled to the Palatinate studied under German Calvinists whose religion lacked legal sanction. Some German Reformed leaders attempted to buttress their position by uniting with Lutherans against the Habsburgs and Catholic party in the Empire. Reformed appeals for Protestant union mostly assumed that after open debate Lutherans would soon see the error of some of their beliefs. However, Calvinist efforts to unite with Lutherans in Germany were rejected by a religious community which held legal status, which had seen some of its princes defect to the Reformed camp, and which had struggled to achieve unity over some of the issues which Reformed theologians wanted to re-examine.

Lutherans in Hungary also swiftly went into print to reject the appeals for Protestant unity made by János Samarjai and Imre Pécseli Király.[57] Despite his years of work in Kassa, Péter Alvinczi's Lutheran colleagues seemed constantly on guard to reveal "crypto-Calvinism" in his Hungarian congregation. They almost seem to have agreed with Péter Pázmány's charge that "those who row in Calvin's boat, often lie about what they believe for friendship's sake."[58] Although Lutherans reacted with deep suspicion to the appeals of their putative Protestant partners, and although there was a significant political context for Reformed irenic appeals, this should not be taken to indicate that Reformed irenicists were acting with duplicity. The idea of Protestant church unity was sincerely advanced by some Calvinists, even if they largely expected Lutherans to become more Reformed in the process. The limits of Reformed irenicism in Hungary were certainly partly set by the capacity of most Calvinists to contemplate compromise with Lutherans over key points of doctrine. The boundaries of irenicism were even more firmly established around those towns and regions where Calvinists felt most threatened by Catholic Reform. Hungarian Reformed clergy who advanced unionist ideas hoped above all to buttress the "Protestant cause" and prevent Catholic domination of Hungary.

NOTES

1. Kálmán Benda, "La réforme en Hongrie," *Bulletin de la Société de l'histoire du Protestantisme Français* 122 (1976): 30–53. Katalin Péter, *Papok és nemesek. Magyar művelődéstörténeti tanulmányok a reformációval kezdődő másfél évszázadból* (Budapest: Ráday Gyűjtemény, 1995), 10.

2. Robert Evans, *The Making of the Habsburg Monarchy, 1550–1700* (Oxford: Clarendon, 1979). Márta Fata, *Ungarn, das Reich, der Stephanskrone, im Zeitalter der Reformation und Konfessionalisierung. Multiethnizität, Land und Konfession 1500 bis 1700* (Münster: Aschendorff, 2000). Robert Kann and Zdeněk David, *The Peoples of the Eastern Habsburg Lands 1526–1918: A History of East Central Europe 6* (Seattle: University of Washington Press, 1984). Peter Sugar, *Southeastern Europe under Ottoman rule, 1354–1804: A History of East Central Europe* (Seattle: University of Washington Press, 1977).

3. David Daniel, "Calvinism in Hungary: The Theological and Ecclesiastical Transition to the Reformed Faith," in Andrew Pettegree, Alastair Duke, and Gillian Lewis, eds., *Calvinism in Europe, 1540–1620* (Cambridge: Cambridge University Press, 1994), 205–30. Katalin Péter, "Hungary," in Bob Scribner, Roy Porter, and Mikuláš Teich, eds., *The Reformation in National Context* (Cambridge: Cambridge University Press, 1994), 155–68.

4. Robert Evans, "Calvinism in East Central Europe: Hungary and her Neighbours," in Menna Prestwich, ed., *International Calvinism, 1541–1715* (Oxford: Clarendon, 1985), 167–96.

5. Mihály Bucsay, *Der Protestantismus in Ungarn, 1521–1978. Ungarns Reformationskirchen in Geschichte und Gegenwart. 1. Im Zeitalter der Reformation, Gegenreformation und katholischen Reform* (Vienna: Böhlau, 1977). Jenő Zoványi, *A reformáczió magyarországon 1565-ig* (Budapest: Genius, 1921). Jenő Zoványi, *A magyarországi protestántizmus 1565-től 1600-ig* (Budapest: Akadémiai kiadó, 1977). Imre Révész, ed., *A magyar református egyház története* (Budapest: Kossuth könyvkiadó, 1949).

6. Róbert Dán and Antal Pirnát, eds., *Antitrinitarianism in the Second Half of the Sixteenth Century* (Budapest: Akadémiai kiadó, 1982). Mihály Balázs and Gizella Keserű, eds., *György Enyedi and Central European Unitarianism in the Sixteenth and Seventeenth Centuries* (Budapest: Balassi kiadó, 2000). Earl Wilbur, *A History of Unitarianism in Transylvania, England and America* (Cambridge, Mass.: Harvard University Press, 1952). George Williams, *The Radical Reformation* (Philadelphia: Westminster Press, 1962), 708–32.

7. Sándor Szilagyi, ed., *Monumenta comitialia regni Transylvaniae. Erdélyi országgyűlési emlékek* (Budapest: MTA, 1875–1898), 2:374.

8. Ludwig Binder, *Grundlagen und Formen der Toleranz in Siebenbürgen bis zur Mitte des 17. Jahrhunderts* (Cologne-Vienna: Böhlau, 1976). Katalin Péter, "Tolerance and Intolerance in Sixteenth-century Hungary," in Ole Peter Grell and Bob Scribner,

eds., *Tolerance and Intolerance in the European Reformation* (Cambridge: Cambridge University Press, 1996), 249–61. Krista Zach, *Orthodoxe Kirche und rumänisches Volksbewusstsein im 15. bis 18. Jahrhundert* (Wiesbaden: Harrassowitz, 1977).

9. These laws on religion were codified in 1653 as *Approbatae Constitutiones,* i/ i/ 1–12, in Dezső Márkus, ed., *Magyar Törvénytár. 1540–1848 évi erdélyi törvények* (Budapest, 1900).

10. Mihály Balázs, *Az erdélyi antitrinitarizmus az 1560-as évek végén. Humanizmus és Reformáció 14* (Budapest: Balassi kiadó, 1988). Sámuel Kohn, *A szombatosok: történetük, dogmatikájuk es irodalmuk* (Budapest, 1890).

11. Szilagyi, *Erdélyi országgyűlési emlékek* (1882), 8:143–5. Elek Jakab, "Erdély és az anabaptisták a xvii–xviii. században," *Keresztény Magvető* 11 (1876): 1–14.

12. Graeme Murdock, "International Calvinism, Ethnic Allegiance, and the Reformed Church of Transylvania in the Early Seventeenth Century," in Maria Crăciun and Ovidiu Ghitta, eds., *Ethnicity and Religion in Central and Eastern Europe* (Cluj: University Press, 1995), 92–100.

13. Carmen Florea, "Shaping Transylvanian Anti-Trinitarian Identity in an Urban Context," in Maria Crăciun, Ovidiu Ghitta, and Graeme Murdock, eds., *Confessional Identity in East-Central Europe* (Aldershot: Ashgate, 2002).

14. Katalin Péter, "Kolozsvár a magyar műveltségben," in *Papok és nemesek* (1995), 115–28.

15. László Makkai, "István Bocskai's Insurrectionary Army," in János Bak and Béla Király, eds., *From Hunyadi to Rákóczi: War and Society in Late Medieval and Early Modern Hungary* (New York: Brooklyn College Press, 1982), 275–97. Kálmán Benda, "Le droit de résistance de la Bulle d'Or hongroise et le calvinisme," in Béla Köpeczi and Éva Balázs, eds., *Noblesse Française Noblesse Hongroise XVIe-XIXe Siècles* (Budapest: Akadémiai kiadó, 1981), 155–63. Kálmán Benda, "A kálvini tanok hatása a magyar rendi ellenállás ideológiájára," *Helikon* 17 (1971): 322–30. László Makkai, "Nemesi köztársaság és kálvinista teokrácia a 16. századi lengyelországban és magyarországon," *Ráday Gyűjtemény Évkönyve* 3 (1983): 17–29.

16. Graeme Murdock, *Calvinism on the Frontier, 1600–1660: International Calvinism and the Reformed Church in Hungary and Transylvania* (Oxford: Clarendon, 2000), 46–76.

17. Murdock, *Calvinism on the Frontier, 1600–1660,* 50. "A wittenbergi egyetem magyarországi hallgatóinak névsora 1601–1812," ed. Miklós Asztalos, *Magyar Protestáns Egyháztörténeti Adattár* 14 (1930): 111–74. "A heidelbergben tanult magyarok névsora," ed. József Szeremlei, *Sárospataki Füzetek* 5 (1861): 452–71; 6 (1862), 559–67. József Pongrácz, *Magyar diákok angliában* (Pápa, 1914).

18. For example, use of the Heidelberg Catechism increased in Hungary after 1600. Ferenc Szárászi, *Catechesis, azaz kerdesök es feleletök az kerestyeni tudomannak agairol. Az iambor istenfelö harmadik Friderik herczek birtokaban, Palatinatusban levö tudos bölcs doctorok altal irattatot, deakbol penig magyar nyelvre fordittatot, hogy mind az kisdedöknek az scholakben, mind penig az egyigyüeknek az ecclesiaban lelki éppületökre*

lenne (Debrecen, 1604). Albert Szenczi Molnár, *Kis katekizmus, avagy az keresztyén hütnec részeiröl rövid kérdesekben es feleletekben foglaltatot tudomány . . . szedetött az haidelbergai öreg Katekizmusból* (Herborn, 1607). Albert Szenczi Molnár, *Szent Biblia . . . az palatinatusi katekizmussal* (Oppenheim, 1612). Graeme Murdock, "Calvinist Catechising and Hungarian Reformed Identity," in Crăciun, Ghitta, and Murdock, eds., *Confessional Identity in East-Central Europe* (2002).

19. István Melotai Nyilas, *Az mennyei tudomány szerint valo irtovany, melyböl az veszedelmes tevelygeseknek es hamis velekedeseknek kárhozatos, tövisses bokrai az Istennek szent igeje altal ki irtogattatnak, es az igassagnak üdvösseg termö agazati erös be oltattatásokkal helyben hadgyattatnak* (Debrecen, 1617).

20. István Melotai Nyilas, *Agenda; az az, anyaszentegyhazbeli szolgálat szerént valo czelekedet* (Gyulafehérvár, 1621).

21. Melotai, *Agenda* (1621), 152–53, 191–92, 198–200.

22. István Geleji Katona, *Váltság-Titka, . . . és a' tévelygőnek, ugy- mint Sidoknak, Socinianusoknak, Blandristáknak, Pápistáknak, Lutheranus atyafiaknak, és egyebeknek ellenkező vélekedésik meg-czáfoltatnak* (3 vols.), (Nagyvárad, 1645–1649), intro. to vols. i–iii, 3:825–1586, see for example sermon 24.

23. Kálmán Benda, "Habsburg Absolutism and the Resistance of the Hungarian Estates of the Sixteenth and Seventeenth Centuries," in Robert Evans and Trevor Thomas, eds., *Crown, Church and Estates: Central European Politics in the Sixteenth and Seventeenth Centuries* (London: Macmillan, 1991), 123–28. Katalin Péter, "Az 1608 évi vallásügyi törvény és a jobbágyok vallásszabadsága," *Századok* 111 (1977): 93–113.

24. Evans, "Calvinism in East Central Europe," 175.

25. Georg Creutzer, *Warnung vor der Sacramentierer, Zinglianer und Calvinisten Lehre, auch gewisse Merckzeichen, wobey solche verfürische Geister zu erkennen* (Bártfa, 1586). György Ráth, "A felsőmagyarországi kryptokálvinisták hitvitázó irodalmáról," *Irodalomtörténeti Közlemények* 2 (1892): 310–24. Daniel, "Calvinism in Hungary," 224.

26. David Pareus, *Collegiorum theologicorum pars prima* (Heidelberg, 1611).

27. János Heltai, *Alvinczi Péter és a heidelbergi peregrinusok* (Budapest: Balassi kiadó, 1994), 65–95.

28. Heltai, *Alvinczi Péter és a heidelbergi peregrinusok*, 95–100. Sándor Imre, *Alvinczi Péter* (Marosvásárhely, 1898).

29. *Apologia et protestatio legatorum et ecclesiarum Hungaricarum, adversus iniquissimas monacho-Iesuitarum criminationes* (Bártfa, 1606). Kálmán Révész, "Bocskay István apologiája," *Protestáns Szemle* (1906): 304–12.

30. Heltai, *Alvinczi Péter és a heidelbergi peregrinusok*, 100–15.

31. Oszkár Paulinyi, "Iratok Kassa szabad király város 1603–1604-ben megkisérelt rekatolizálásának történetéhez," *Magyar Protestáns Egyháztörténti Adattár* 14 (1930): 57–61.

32. Péter Pázmány, *Egy kereztien predikatortul S. T.D.P.P. az cassai nevezetes tanitohoz, Alvinczi Peter uramhoz iratot eot szep level* (Graz, 1609). Pázmány, *Isteni igazsagra vezerleo kalauz, mellyet írt Pazmany Peter, iesuitak rendin valo tanito* (Pozsony, 1613).

Pázmány, *Az calvinista predikatorok igyenes erkeolcseu tekelletessegének teukeore* (Vienna, 1614). Pázmány, *Az igazsagnak gyeozedelme, mellyet az Alvinci Peter Teukeoreben meg mutatot Pazmany Peter* (Pozsony, 1614).

33. Péter Alvinczi, *Egy tetetes, neve vesztett pápista embertől S.T.D.P.P.től küldetett szines öt levelekre rend szerint való felelet Alvinczi Pétertől a kassai m. ekklesia lelki pásztorától* (Debrecen, 1609). Alvinczi, *Tükör* (Kassa?, 1614).

34. *Itinerarium catholicum, az az nevezetes vetelkedes az felöl: ha az evangelicusok tudományaje uy, vagy az mostani romai vallason valo papistake? Es: az papistak ecclesiajaje vagy az evangelicusoke igaz es vilagh vegeigh allando* (Debrecen, 1616).

35. "... talán az kálvinista prédikátorok, is az Calvinus hajójában eveznek, és gyakran barátságért azt is hazudjék, amit nem hisznek?" in Péter Pázmány, *Rövid felelet ket calvinista könyvecskere, mellyeknek eggyke okát adgya, miért nem felelnek az calvinista praedikátorok az Kalauzra, masika Itinerarium catholicumnak neveztetik* (Vienna, 1620), 436.

36. Katalin Péter, "Two Aspects of War and Society in the Age of Prince Gábor Bethlen of Transylvania," in Bak and Király, eds., *War and Society in Late Medieval and Early Modern Hungary,* 297–313. Joachim Bahlcke, "Calvinism and Estate Liberation Movements in Bohemia and Hungary (1570–1620)," in Karin Maag, ed., *The Reformation in Eastern and Central Europe* (Aldershot: Scolar, 1997), 72–91.

37. [Péter Alvinczi], *Querela Hungariae. Magyarorszag panasza* (Kassa, 1619). Péter Alvinczi, *Machiavellizatio qua unitorum animos Iesuaster quidam dissociare nititur. Detecta per quendam et in gratiam dni. archiepiscopi castissimae vitae, Petri Pazman succincte excepta* (Kassa, 1620). Péter Pázmány, *Falsae originis motuum Hungaricorum succincta refutatio. Az magyar orszagi tamadasoknak hamissan költött eredetinek rövid velös hamissitasa* (Vienna, 1620). Tamás Balásfi, *Castigatio libelli Calvinistici, cui titulus est Machiavellizatio* (1620). Péter Alvinczi, *Resultatio plagarum castigatoris autorem Machiavellizationis reverberata in Thomam Balasfia, ejectum episcopum Bosznensem, nec non depositum Posoniensem* (Kassa, 1620).

38. The seven counties were Szabolcs, Szatmár, Bereg, Ung, Zemplén, Borsod, and Abaúj. Imre Lukinich, *Erdély területi változásai a török hódítás korában, 1541–1711* (Budapest, 1918), 199–335.

39. Lajos Dézsi, ed., *Szenczi Molnár Albert naplója, levelezése és irományai* (Budapest, 1898), 213.

40. Lajos Kemény, "Alvinczy Péter életéhez," *Irodalomtörténeti Közlemények* (1910): 102–6. Heltai, *Alvinczi Péter és a heidelbergi peregrinusok,* 109–11.

41. Péter Alvinczi, *Az Urnak szent wacsoraiarol valo reovid intes az Szent Pal apostol tanitasa szerent egy néhány szükséges kerdésekel és feleletekel egyetemben* (Kassa, 1622).

42. Alvinczi, *Az Urnak szent wacsoraiarol* (1622), 27–28, 39–40, 48, 52, 68.

43. János Samarjai, *Magyar harmonia, az az Augustana és az Helvetica Confessio articulussinac eggyezö értelme, mellyet Samaraeus Janos superattendens illyen ockal rendölt öszve, hogy az articulusokban fundamentomos ellenközés nem lévén az két con-*

fessiot követö atyafiak is az szeretet által eggyessec legyenec. Ez mellé Paraeus David d. Irenicumjábol XVIII ragalmas articulusokra valo feleletek és az eggyesegre kétféle indito okok adattanac (Pápa, 1628). Samarjai used David Pareus, *Irenicum, sive de unione et synodo evangelicorum concilianda liber votivus* (Heidelberg, 1614).

44. János Samarjai, *Agenda. Az helvetiai vallason levő ecclesiaknak egyházi ceremoniajokrol es rend tartasokrol valo könyetske* (Lőcse, 1636). Géza Kathona, *Samarjai János gyakorlati theologiája* (Debrecen, 1939).

45. Imre Pécseli Király, *Catechismus; az az, a keresztyeni tudomannac fundamentomirol es agairol valo rövid tanitás* (Pápa, 1624; Lőcse, 1635). Pécseli Király, *Consilium ecclesiae catholicae doctorum super ista quaestione: An homo Christianus possit et debeat se cognominare Lutheranum vel Calvinistam ad religionem puram ab impura recte discernendam?* (Kassa, 1621). János Heltai, "Irénikus eszmék és vonások Pécseli Király Imre műveiben," in Béla Varjas, ed., *Irodalom és ideológia a 16–17. században. Memoria Saeculorum Hungariae 5* (Budapest: Akadémiai kiadó, 1987), 209–30.

46. Kassa council records were published by Kemény, "Alvinczy Péter életéhez" (1904), 112–19, 234–46, 364–67, 490–500; (1907), 243–48; (1910), 102–6; (1911), 366–69.

47. Kemény, "Alvinczy Péter életéhez" (1904), 234–40.

48. Kemény, "Alvinczy Péter életéhez" (1904), 241–46.

49. Kemény, "Alvinczy Péter életéhez" (1904), 364.

50. H. Kiss Kálmán, "Alvinczi Péter, a kassai magyar pap," *Protestáns Egyházi és Iskolai Lap* (1893/4).

51. Sándor Szilágyi, "Rákóczyak levéltárából, 1611–1630," *Történelmi Tár* (1895): 140–41.

52. Péter Alvinczi, *Postilla, azaz egymas utan következö praedikatiuk az urnapi szent evangeliumok szerént rövid magyarázatockal és világos tanúságockal* (Kassa, 1633). Alvinczi, *Következik az postillanak masodik resze, melyben foglaltatnak az nyari praedicatiuk Szentháromság vasárnaptúl fogva advent elsö vasárnapig* (Kassa, 1634).

53. Kálmán Révész, *Százéves küzdelem a kassai református egyház megalakulásáért, 1550–1650* (Budapest, 1894). Fata, *Ungarn* (2000), 209.

54. John Dury, *Motives to Induce the Protestant Princes to mind the Worke of Peace Ecclesiasticall amongst themselves* (London, 1641). Dury, *A Brief Relation of that which hath been Lately Attempted to Procure Ecclesiasticall Peace amongst Protestants* (London, 1641). Joseph M. Batten, *John Dury: Advocate of Christian Reunion* (Chicago: University of Chicago Press, 1944).

55. On Alsted see Howard Hotson, *Johann Heinrich Alsted, 1588–1638: Between Renaissance, Reformation, and Universal Reform* (Oxford: Clarendon, 2000).

56. House of Lords Record Office, MSS Braye 1, 102, 104–14, "István Geleji Katona to George Abbot, the Archbishop of Canterbury, referring to John Durie's mission for the pacification of Protestant churches," and a transcribed version of the reply to Dury, "Reply of István Geleji Katona with regard to the problem of obtaining ecclesiastical peace among Protestant churches."

57. Response to Imre Pécseli Király from György Zvonarics, *Rövid felelet, melyben Pécseli Imrének . . . tanácsa meghamisittatik . . . e kérdés felől: a keresztyén embernek kellessék-e lutheránusnak avagy kálvinistának neveztetni* (Csepreg, 1626). Response to János Samarjai from István Lethenyei, *Az Calvinistac magyar harmonianac. Azaz: az Augustana es Helvetica Confessioc Articulusinac . . . öszve-hasomlétásanac meghamisétása* (Csepreg, 1633).

58. Pázmány, *Rövid felelet ket calvinista könyvecskere* (1620), 436.

9

Confessional Accommodation in Early Modern Bohemia

Shifting Relations between Catholics and Utraquists

ZDENĚK V. DAVID

A REMARKABLE ERA OF RELIGIOUS TOLERATION IN BOHEMIA WAS reaching its peak in the second half of the sixteenth century. This period of confessional coexistence was in large part based on a resolution that had been passed a century earlier when Hus's successors had met with their Catholic rivals to settle their differences at the negotiation table. In 1485 at Kutná Hora, some seventy years before the Peace of Augsburg, these two parties jointly declared:

> With regard to the Catholic and the Utraquist churches, no party will in the future be allowed to suppress the other, neither in secular, nor in spiritual matters and both should have sympathy for each other. Priests of both parties . . . will freely preach the Gospel . . . none of them will call the other heretic, and dukes, lords and knights and royal towns will not oppress their subjects because

of their faith . . . nor oppose their achieving salvation according to their customs and creed.[1]

But though the latter years of the sixteenth century witnessed the climax of religious accommodation in this region, they also marked a critical turning point in relations between Utraquists and Catholics. This study will track the deteriorating relationship between the two groups before concluding with a general assessment of Utraquism as a broader reform movement of late medieval and early modern Christianity.

Before we begin this discussion, however, it may be useful to provide some background for those not familiar with Bohemia's complicated religious history. Utraquism, which emerged from the Bohemian Reformation of the late fourteenth and early fifteenth centuries, aimed at purging the medieval church of material wealth and political pretensions while preserving its sacramental character and historic episcopate. The formal name of the Utraquist (in Czech *pod obojí*) Church was derived from the Latin phrase *sub utraque specie* (under each of two kinds), which referred to its belief, contrary to the current rules of the Church of Rome, in the theological necessity of communion for the laity in both kinds. Moreover, this applied not only to adults and older children, but also to infants and young children.[2] The early prominent spokesman for the reform movement in Bohemia was Jan Hus, and his execution at the Council of Constance in 1415 led to an administrative separation of the Bohemian Church from the Church of Rome by 1420. The Four Articles of Prague were an early articulation of the reform program of the Utraquist movement. Freedom of preaching, an enforced poverty of the clergy, the public punishment of notorious sinners, and communion in both kinds was emphasized. Papal authority was questioned, monastic orders rejected, and the practice of indulgences abandoned. The indigenous church grew in strength much to the dismay of Rome, and defying the odds, the defenders of the Bohemian Reformation defeated five imperial and papal crusades between 1420 and 1431. Radical groups known as Taborites, Orebites, and Orphans emerged during the religious wars and questioned the dogma and the liturgy of the medieval church. In the end, however, the mainline Utraquists prevailed and consolidated their influence. While opposing their liberal ecclesiology to Rome's authoritarianism, the mainstream preserved medieval orthodoxy. The governance of the Utraquist Church was vested in the Consistory, headed by an administrator who was chosen and appointed from the canonically ordained priesthood either by the Diet of Bohemia or the Royal Chancery. In 1436 the legitimacy of Utraquism was recognized by the Roman Church through an agreement negotiated at the Council of Basel known as the *Compactata*. This recognition, in fact, established two Roman Catholic Churches in Bohemia—the Utraquists and those receiving communion under one species, henceforth referred to as *sub una*. The few remaining adherents of the Holy See, the *sub una*, were administered by a separate Consistory in Bohemia. Eventually, they would come under the archbishop of Prague when the office was filled once again in 1561 after a lapse of more than 130 years. Long before then, however, in 1462 Pope Pius II declared the *Compactata* invalid, leaving formal relations between Rome and the Utraquists in a perpetually unsettled state. Nevertheless, the *Compactata* remained a part of the Bohemian legal system (after 1567 in a modified form), and within Bohemia the Utraquists' validity could not be legally denied even by the diplomats of the Roman Curia. Their effect within Bohemia was fortified in 1485 by the Peace of Kutná Hora, which bound the Utraquists and the *sub una* to recognize each other as equally orthodox Christians. The Utraquist priests continued to be ordained (in a somewhat irregular way) by bishops in communion with the Roman See.

With the onset of the Lutheran Reformation in 1517, the Utraquist Consistory refused to embrace the principles of *sola fide* and *sola scriptura*, and the Utraquist Church came to occupy a middle position between Rome and Wittenberg. As the sixteenth century progressed, a religious cleavage developed in Bohemia along social lines. The numerically weak but politically powerful nobles (barons and knights) were increasingly attracted to the Augsburg Confession, while the Czech commoners (townspeople and peasantry) remained under the Consistory within the Utraquist fold.[3] Devoid of legal protection for their religious orientation, the Lutheran nobles pressed the king of Bohemia (and the Holy Roman Emperor), Maximilian II, at the Diet of 1575 to grant recognition to the Bohemian Confession, a Protestant statement of faith that though borrowing liberally from the Augsburg Confession compromised with the more Calvinist leanings of the Bohemian Brethren.[4] It was the resolution of this request that set the scene for Bohemia's remarkable and distinctive religious pluralism into the seventeenth century. In a paradoxical move, the Utraquist towns supported the nobles' demand for the legalization of the Protestant confession. There were, however, cogent reasons for their political stance. First, their main sense of threat came less from the Lutherans and more from the Catholic Reformation, which was gathering strength in the Habsburg realms after the Council of Trent. Second, they feared political isolation vis-à-vis the king and the Roman Church if they broke the united front of the anti-Roman dissidents by failing to support the nobles' request. Third, the nobles assured the towns that the Bohemian Confession would merely define the outer limits of religious acceptability without imposing a Protestant conformity on Utraquism.

In the final resolution, Maximilian II insisted on overtly preserving the legal status quo under which only Utraquism together with the few remaining *sub una* would be viewed as established.[5] Maximilian, however, offered to satisfy the nobles under a gentlemen's agreement, binding him as well as his son and heir apparent, Rudolf II, to protect the existing adherents to the Bohemian Confession, provided that there were no encroachments on the current status and position of Utraquism and the remnants of those *sub una*. In addition to the Lutherans, Maximilian's promised freedom of religion covered the hitherto unprotected Unity of Brethren. The latter was a relatively small but devout sect which had emerged in 1450s. Through its ecclesial organization and Biblicist orientation, it revived and perpetuated some of the radical tenets of the Taborites, a distinct strand associated with the early Bohemian Reformation.[6]

An Era of Good Feelings

Let us turn our attention now toward the relationship between Catholics and Utraquists in the sixteenth century as reflected in the theological literature of the day. The Roman Curia's attitude toward Utraquism executed a conspicuous zigzag in the aftermath of the German Reformation. The initial reaction was to discredit Luther by linking him with Hus. This was the line pursued by the polemicists on Rome's behalf, especially by Johann Eck at the Leipzig debate of 1519 and Nuncio Girolamo Aleandro at the Diet of Worms in 1521. This stratagem proved counterproductive; if anything it pushed Luther into greater radicalism and made his cause even more popular. The Roman policy makers, therefore, shifted gears. The new approach to damage-control called for weakening the dissidents by separating the Bohemians as much as possible from Luther's cause. The aim was to convince the Bohemians that Luther was a dangerous heretic who had departed from several traditional doctrines of Christianity which the Utraquists cherished.[7] This approach was adopted on behalf of Rome in the 1520s by Hieronymus Dungersheim, Hieronymus Emser, and Johannes Cochlaeus.[8] In 1525 even Bishop John Fisher in faraway England called attention to the fact that Luther was more radical than Hus, and that the two were not in mutual agreement.[9]

The high point of the Curia's friendly overtures to the Bohemians was a resumption of negotiations toward a reconciliation between Rome and the Utraquists in Buda in February 1525.[10] It was hoped that the Holy See might compensate for its losses in Germany by regaining Bohemia. Although the Buda *pourparlers* ended in failure, Rome's interest in courting the Utraquists continued. A new actor entering the scene was Johann Faber, the bishop of Vienna, who was brought to Bohemia by King Ferdinand I as his confidant and advisor on religious affairs. Faber published a pamphlet, *Confutatio gravissimi erroris* (1537), arguing that the Czechs, under influences from abroad, were embracing religious innovations and straying from the orthodox teachings of traditional Utraquism.[11] He praised the classical Utraquist theologians, such as Jan of Příbram, for upholding Christ's entire presence in each of the two species of the eucharist at the Synod of 1421 and for promulgating orthodox definitions of the sacrament of the altar at the Synods of 1429 and 1432.[12] Faber stressed the role of Jan Rokycana, the famous fifteenth-century Utraquist leader, in helping negotiate the *Compactata*.[13]

Cochlaeus, on the other hand, continued his efforts to separate Hus from Luther in his magnum opus, *Historiae Hussitarum libri duodecim*. Although not published until 1549, much of the book was composed in the 1530s. By 1534 he had reached the year 1457 in his account, and in 1537 he published an extract under the title *Wahrhaftige Historia von Magister Johannes Hus*.[14] Once more perpetuating the approach of earlier authors, like Hieronymus Emser, he sought to show the Bohemians how far Luther diverged from the beliefs of Utraquism. In a letter of July 1534, Cochlaeus confided to Nuncio Vergerio his intention to revise his manuscript further toward placating the Czechs. He would use against Luther his own assertion of 1520 that if Hus were heretical, he himself was an even greater heretic ("si ille [Hus] fuit haereticus, ego plus dicies haereticus sum").[15]

Inside Bohemia, in the early and mid-sixteenth century, the discourse of theologians *sub una* continued to be conciliatory toward their compatriots *sub utraque*, reflecting the spirit of the agreements following the settlement of the Bohemian religious wars. As noted earlier, the harmonious coexistence of the Utraquists and those under the Roman Curia was explicitly codified by the Peace of Kutná Hora of 1485, after having been informally observed since the adoption of the *Compactata* of Basel in 1436. These legal instruments prohibited accusations of heresy and mutual vilification between the two religious groups.[16]

This type of tolerant and cooperative attitude was displayed on the Roman side in an exemplary fashion by Tomáš Bavorovský (d. 1562). Serving as a priest *sub una* in Plzeň, 1546–1552, he was appointed a canon in the chapter at St. Vitus Cathedral of Prague, finally serving as the chapter's dean in 1559–1561. His principal work, the homiliary *Postila česká* (1557), reflected his conciliatory demeanor. The Utraquists were for him true Christians, unlike the Zwinglians, Lutherans, or the Brethren, who rejected the doctrine of real presence. Accordingly, referring to the Utraquists, Bavorovský admonished his flock to "Think well of them, . . . and love them like brothers." Even their insults should not be answered in kind but borne patiently.[17]

There were also notable cases of cooperation between the *sub una* and *sub utraque* both as individuals and on an institutional basis. Bavorovský was close personally to Jan Straněnský (fl. 1545–1584), an Utraquist scholar who wrote a preface to his *Postila*. In his own introduction to the homiliary, Bavorovský called Straněnský "a faithful colleague and at the same time a dear brother in Christ the Lord," who not only edited the book but also prepared a voluminous index.[18] In the preface to his friend's *Postila*, Straněnský addressed an admonition to properly ordained priests, including presumably those *sub una*. Aside from the predictable stress on the pursuit of learning and proper pastoral care, Straněnský introduced the characteristically Utraquist injunction against clergy's involvement with acquisitive affairs and particularly condemned the preoccupation with trade or commercial agriculture.[19] In an earlier work, *Kázání o svatém pokání* (Sermon on the Holy Penance) (1552), Bavorovský had also referred to Straněnský as "my dear friend," who had edited the book's manuscript. Straněnský had helped make arrangements for publication of Bavorovský's writings partly with the printer Gunther in Olomouc, partly with Melantrich in Prague.[20]

At the institutional level, the Utraquist Consistory appeared to cooperate with the Consistory *sub una* in assessing religious literature. Thus Bavorovský's book, *Kázání o svatém pokání*, was submitted for approval to both consistories. Its colophon stated that the publication took place "after an examination and with the approval of the Reverend Lord Administrators of the parties *sub una* and *sub utraque* of the Archbishopric of Prague."[21] That such a cooperative arrangement was not unusual is indicated by the grievance of the Utraquist Consistory that the *Kronika česká* (Bohemian Chronicle) (1543) of Václav Hájek of Libočany had not been submitted for its examination before publication.[22] According to Jiří Pešek, examination of theological books was entrusted jointly to the two consistories.[23] It is likely that the two religious groups shared certain of the pre-Tridentine liturgical books like the incunabula of the late fifteenth century, published apparently in Plzeň.[24] In a way, this guarded cooperation continued to reflect the fact that—in an apt phrase of Jarold K. Zeman—the *Compactata* of 1436 had in effect established two Catholic Churches in Bohemia.[25] Even though the Holy See disavowed the document in 1462, the *Compactata* continued to form a part of Bohemia's constitutional law until 1567 and, in an altered form, also thereafter.

The Onset of a Roman Ice Age

In many ways the completion of the Council of Trent in 1563 foreshadowed for Bohemia the end of the era of good feelings and the onset of a frostier relationship. The Roman Curia felt more self-confident as the religious situation stabilized. The need to hold onto Bohemia, even at the cost of concessions, did not seem so compelling as in the immediate post-Reformation era. There were now agencies in place in Bohemia to work toward the application of the Tridentine principles and hence toward greater rigidity, namely (1) the Jesuit order, introduced to Bohemia in 1556; (2) the archbishop of Prague, restored after a vacancy of more than a century in 1561; and (3) a permanent papal nuncio, established in Prague in 1583 after the transfer of the imperial court from Vienna to the Bohemian capital.[26] As a result, Rome was fully armed and ready to advance in the arena of confessionalization and began to undermine the established religious peace in Bohemia. There were two landmark events in the 1580s which signaled the Curia's stiffening attitude toward the Bohemian exceptionalism. Pope Gregory XIII on 15 March 1580 issued a bull indiscriminately condemning the "Hussites" together with the Wyclifites, Zwinglians, Calvinists, and other heretics.[27] Even more symbolic was the ironic placement of Cochlaeus's *Historiae Hussitarum libri duodecim* (1549), a left-handed attempt to conciliate the Utraquists, on the Index of Prohibited Books by Sixtus V (1585–1590).[28]

The marked shifts in the orientation of the Bohemian nobility had a significant bearing on the increase of religious tensions. As noted previously, the earlier trend involved a switch of allegiance by the nobles in the party *sub utraque* from Utraquism to Lutheranism and the Unity of Brethren, that is, a turn from the Bohemian brand of Roman Catholicism to Protestantism or near-Protestantism. These defections had relatively little direct effect on the strength of Utraquism because the number of nobles was small in comparison to the total population,[29] and the nobles, turning Protestant, continued even after 1575 to cooperate politically with the Utraquist commoners in the Bohemian Diet and elsewhere.[30] Of greater importance was the indirect effect of the nobility's secessions on the relationship between Utraquism and the party *sub una*. First, its plebeianization caused the Utraquist Church to lose some of its weight and prestige in the relationship with the Holy See, which deferred more to an aristocratic than to an urban leadership.[31] Second, the Utraquist townsmen's political alliance with the Lutheran and Unity nobles caused the political gap to widen between the Utraquists and the party *sub una*, even though in the religious respect the Utraquist Consistory maintained its traditional orthodoxy.

More critical, however, was the later trend—the shift of the nobility *sub una* from the Bohemian tradition of cooperation across religious lines to greater intransigence, often characteristic of the Catholic Reformation. As noted earlier, a spirit of cooperation had been inculcated under the *Compactata* and further affirmed by the Peace of Kutná Hora in 1485. Conscious of the weakness of the party *sub una*, these leaders tried to avoid any outright confrontation and showed considerable political and diplomatic skills in seeking compromises. They also tended to be less than enthusiastic about the nuncios' periodic suggestions for a more active policy against the religious dissidents, whether Utraquists, Lutherans, or Brethren.[32] In fact, they were willing to share with the Utraquists what would later become known as an anti-ultramontane position.[33] The nobles *sub una* had a reason of their own to exercise some caution in relation to Rome. Without resorting to crass economic determinism, it can be pointed out that their reluctance to submit fully to the Curia's will was also rooted in a material interest. Their earlier seizures of ecclesiastical estates were safeguarded by a political system that eliminated direct papal jurisdiction.[34]

The new generation of nobles *sub una*, who replaced their more conciliatory predecessors at the turn of the sixteenth century, were often influenced by the Jesuits or trained in their schools and tended to be particularly consistent and militant in their religious commitment. Moreover, in the latter part of the sixteenth century, the likelihood of Rome's insistence on the lost properties vanished, and the nobles *sub una* lost much of their inhibition against wholehearted support of the Curia.[35] The radicals replaced the moderate notables, who had led the party *sub una* in Bohemia into the last two decades of the sixteenth century.[36] The new chancellor, Zdeněk of Lobkovice, and his deputy, the new Vice-Chancellor Jindřich Domináček of Písnice, in particular exemplified the uncompromising spirit of the Catholic Reformation.[37] Although substantially weakened, the spirit of cooperation between the nobles *sub una* and the party *sub utraque*, however, did not entirely collapse even in the wake of the Letter of Majesty in 1609, which guaranteed religious freedom not only for the Utraquists but also for the Lutherans and Unity of Brethren.[38]

The unyielding and aggressive support of Tridentine conformity became evident in foreign theologians' assessment of the Bohemian Reformation. The distinction between Hus and Utraquism, on one hand, and Protestantism, on the other—once customary among irenic Roman theologians—was largely obliterated. The placing of Cochlaeus's *Historiae Hussitarum* on the Index was highly symptomatic of the trend away from regarding Utraquism as something more benign than outright Protestantism. There were many foreign theologians and writers of note who pronounced uncomplimentary verdicts on Hus and the Bohemian Reformation during the last third of the sixteenth century.[39] We will focus on the most distinguished one, Edmund Campion, the English Jesuit and martyr. Sent to Bohemia from Rome, where he entered the Jesuit order in 1573, Campion spent a year in Brno, then taught at the Jesuit College of St. Clement in Prague for six years, first rhetoric, then philosophy.[40] In the fall of 1576, he gave an opening address for the new school year at the Jesuit gymnasium in Prague in which he spoke in most uncomplimentary terms about the Bohemian Reformation, particularly Jan Hus. He exhorted the inhabitants of Prague to return to the spiritual traditions of their saints, Wenceslaus, Adalbert, and Procopius, or at least to those of Emperor Charles IV, instead of invoking, ". . . some reckless preachers, or an infamous military leader [presumably Jan Žižka], or a base apostate [presumably Jan Hus], who has brought into your venerable walls so many sects, so many schisms, so much mischief and so many vices, so much dark ignorance, and yes, an entire enormity of evil."[41]

Two legacies of Campion's stay in Prague merit particular mention. One was the training of future Archbishop of Prague Johann Lohelius (1612–1622), who became an important Catholic leader in the White Mountain era. He was responsible for the papal prohibition of the lay chalice and for the jailing and possible execution of the last Utraquist leader, the priest Jan Locika of Domažlice.[42] Having entered the Jesuit college in 1575, Lohelius studied rhetoric, then philosophy under Campion.[43] Campion was also the director of the first Marian sodality in Bohemia, established at the Jesuit Clementinum in 1575.[44] The brotherhood became one of the foci of militant Catholicism. By 1578 it consisted of three sections, one of which grouped the elite of the Roman Church's adherents: nobles, professors, lawyers, and physicians. Several of the sodality's members would subsequently star in the Bohemian Catholic Reformation, most notably Jaroslav Martinic, Vilém Slavata, Filip Fabricius, and Johann Lohelius.[45]

While in Prague, Campion was in touch with Archbishop Brus, who would occasionally consult him on the administration of the *sub una*, for like the Catholics in England, they were a distinct minority in Bohemia. Brus ordained Campion to the priesthood at the beginning of September 1578. After the ceremony, Brus is said to have declared, "All kinds of evil invaded Bohemia because of Wyclif, an Englishman; now the Lord has furnished us with another Englishman who would heal the wounds inflicted on the Bohemians by Wyclif."⁴⁶ During Campion's last Easter in Bohemia in 1579, Brus chose him as a preacher in St. Vitus Cathedral for Holy Thursday.⁴⁷ Less then a year later, in early March 1580, Campion left Prague via Rome for a mission to England, where he met his end on the gallows of Tyburn.

Within Bohemia the native clergy of the *sub una* assessed Utraquism in a slightly different fashion. In the last quarter of the sixteenth century Catholic theologians still made some allowances for Hus and Utraquism. The main thrust of their critical zeal was aimed at the Unity of Brethren and to a lesser extent at the Lutherans. Direct attacks on Utraquism were left to foreign theologians, like Campion or the Pole Wujek z Wągrowca. Translations of their works apparently evaded, rather than violated, the letter of the Bohemian law against the vilification of the *sub utraque* by the *sub una* as expressed in the *Compactata* and the Peace of Kutná Hora. The focus on the Brethren seemed to be conditioned by two considerations: (1) sowing discord among the opponents; and (2) the Brethren's relative vulnerability. In part, the aim was to alienate the Utraquists from their more radical allies, the Brethren and the Lutherans, and thus to weaken the cohesion of those who dissented from the Roman Curia. Such an approach represented an extension of the tactics pursued by Roman polemicists, like Faber and Cochlaeus, earlier in the century. From another angle, unfriendly critique of the Brethren was less hazardous than theological attacks against the Utraquists. In contrast to the Utraquists, whom Bohemia's constitutional law unequivocally protected against vituperation by the *sub una,* the legal protection of the Unity and of the Lutherans was more precarious, resting as it did, not on explicit edicts, but merely on the gentlemen's agreement of 1575 between Maximilian II and the Bohemian estates. The Brethren became still more vulnerable because of the mandates against the "Pikharts" which Rudolf II issued in 1584 and in 1602. These edicts made attacking the Brethren in print less risky, even though they did not directly endanger their institutional existence.⁴⁸

Stressing the relative orthodoxy of Hus and Utraquism in contrast to the teaching of the Unity of Brethren was characteristic of the writings of the Bohemian Jesuit Václav Šturm (1533–1601). Šturm, an expert on the theology of the Brethren, held the distinction of being one of the very first Czech-speaking Jesuits, having been sent to Rome in 1555 with eleven other Bohemian boys. He spent much time in Olomouc, which facilitated his research into the Brethren's theology inasmuch as the Unity was particularly well represented in Moravia. His main polemical works were *Srovnání víry a učení bratří starších* (The Arrangement of the Faith and Teaching of the Brethren's Elders) (1582), *Krátké ozvání . . . proti kratičkému ohlášení Jednoty* (A Brief Response . . . to the Short Declaration of the Unity) (1584), and *Rozsouzení a bedlivé uvážení Velikého kancionálu* (A Study and a Careful Assessment of the Great Hymnal) (1588). [49]

Šturm had established a point of agreement with the Utraquists in the spring of 1575. At that time he prepared with his Jesuit colleague Baltazar Hostovský a critical assessment of the Bohemian Confession, pointing out its heterodox inspiration by the Augsburg Confession. Their views were endorsed not only by the party *sub una,* but also by the Utraquist Consistory.[50] The partial agreement, of course, did not signify a coincidence of theological views between Šturm and the Utraquists. The Jesuit author viewed the seminal figures of the Bohemian Reformation, like Hus or Rokycana, as far from blameless. In his *Srovnání víry a učení bratří,* Šturm classified Hus among those who were not inspired by the Holy Ghost. While the Holy Spirit had only one voice, the spirit of error spoke with many, often contradictory, voices, "And thus Arius once spoke with one spirit, Macedonius with another, Wyclif with another, Master Jan Hus with another, the Taborites with another, the Lutherans with another, the Zwinglians with another, your Brethren with another, and so each and every one has a different novelty, a different sect, a different priesthood, a different congregation, and none agrees with another."[51]

Nevertheless, on the whole, Šturm's polemics were not directed against the Utraquists, but focused on the Brethren. In fact, he relied on comparisons with Hus and the Utraquists to underscore the unorthodoxy of the Unity. The Brethren, for him, were breakers of Christian community to the second degree, having themselves seceded from schismatics. Along these lines, Šturm inventoried several areas in which Hus's teaching was more orthodox than the Brethren's. In particular, he lauded Hus's insistence on canonical priesthood and the use of special vestments for the Lord's Supper, which the Brethren rejected. Šturm also noted that Hus, unlike the Brethren, supported the doctrine of transubstantiation. He contrasted the Brethren's secretiveness about their theology with Hus's openness. Hus's views could be documented by his own works, published both in Bohemia and elsewhere in Europe. Like the Utraquist theologians Bohuslav Bílejovský and Pavel Bydžovský before him, Šturm asserted that the Brethren wrongly claimed to be the heirs of either Hus or of the Bohemian Reformation. In the light of their disagreements with his teachings, the Brethren viewed Hus not as a precursor but as an opponent. In fact, for them, Hus was no less an Antichrist than were the followers of the Holy See.[52] Šturm claimed support for this extraordinary allegation in that the Brethren's Confession of 1574 condemned both the adherents of Rome and the Utraquists—the former for their alleged idolatry, the latter for their practice of infant communion.[53] Like Bydžovský, Šturm pointed out repeatedly that even Luther surpassed the Brethren in relative orthodoxy and cited the Unity's theological disagreements with the German reformer as well as with the prominent Matthias Flacius Illyricus, particularly on the issue of real presence.[54]

While earlier the Roman side seemed willing to grant certain latitude to the Utraquist position, their attitude shifted at the end of the sixteenth century. The possibility of a *modus vivendi* between Tridentine Rome and Utraquist Prague virtually vanished. While earlier expressions of a harsh Roman view toward Utraquism had been left by and large to foreigners, writers *sub una* began to manifest a sterner intransigence within Bohemia at the turn of the century. The tenor of their polemics reflected this deterioration: (1) the range of what was acceptable to Rome shrank to temporary toleration of the lay chalice; (2) the whole area of concession to liberal ecclesiology (in a way the most important aspect of the Utraquist position) became foreclosed and non-negotiable. As a bottom line, acceptable Utraquism became restricted to an "Old Utraquism" satisfied with nothing more than a highly qualified and circumscribed lay communion in both kinds. This definitional restriction, in turn, could pave the way to a complete proscription and annihilation of Utraquism, inasmuch as against this mythical standard the actually existing mainline Utraquism was guaranteed to appear deviant. The latter could then be condemned by the Roman Curia without obviously violating previous recognition of the legitimacy of Utraquism, such as in the *Compactata*, or without making the Habsburg monarchs guilty of contravening the oaths of their ancestors to uphold Utraquism.[55]

A particularly prominent Bohemian participant in the overtly anti-Utraquist campaign on the Roman side was Petr Linteo of Pilsenburgk, a priest in Litomyšl and an alumnus of the College of St. Clement in Prague. In 1593 he wrote *Jistá a patrná církve svaté znamení* (Certain and Distinct Signs of the Holy Church), a polemic aimed at demolishing the stature of Jan Hus. According to Linteo, Hus could not be a saint because he had not performed any miracles nor had the final fire spared him, unlike the true saints who experienced fire without burning as in the case of Sts. Agnes and

Juliana.[56] Similarly, Hus's followers and disciples were unable to perform true miracles. Linteo discredited the cures and other marvelous signs allegedly attached to a site near Nymburk where the Taborites had executed an Utraquist priest in 1425. According to Linteo, the priest betrayed the church by condoning communion in both kinds and could be responsible only for pseudo-miracles that would be unmasked as such at the Last Judgment.[57] Likewise Luther, Calvin, or their followers could not perform miracles although they tried or pretended to do so.[58] In one respect, Linteo did admit Hus's superiority over Luther and Calvin. The Bohemian respected the authority of patristic literature, which the others debunked.[59] Nevertheless, Hus—not the Council—was responsible for his death because of his own disobedience. The clinching argument of Hus's perversity for Linteo was his alleged statement that he wished for his soul to rest in the same place as Wyclif's.[60]

In the same book, Linteo aimed his second principal thrust at lay communion in both kinds. In effect, he asserted that the lay chalice was illegitimate, except in the most unusual circumstances and then only on the basis of a specific temporary papal dispensation.[61] Turning against the Utraquist view that communion *sub utraque* was mandated by Christ and necessary to salvation, Linteo resorted to a pragmatic argument that God was too merciful to let some be damned because of the manner of communion. He bolstered his position against the lay chalice by rather mundane arguments that (1) some communicants, in delicate health, might be injured by drinking or just scenting wine, and (2) that there were regions where importing wine was prohibitively expensive, or where climatic conditions caused wine to turn rapidly to vinegar. Linteo—perhaps with a touch of sarcasm—commended the view that had Christ intended obligatory communion in two kinds, he would have substituted water for wine in view of the precarious status of the latter.[62] Linteo also rejected the historical argument that from early Christianity to the reign of Charles IV communion *sub utraque* was common in Bohemia, as maintained by Utraquist theologians, in particular Bohuslav Bílejovský.[63] His stand was that in Bohemia communion *sub utraque* had never existed before 1414. Then it was not introduced as a restoration but an innovation.[64]

Catholicism with a Liberal Ecclesiology

Let us now review the entire complex of the continuing awkward and unresolved ties between Utraquism and the Roman Curia with a focus on the second half of the sixteenth century. Two principles helped define Utraquist identity in this period: (1) the ordination of clergy by bishops in communion with the Holy See; and (2) an insistence on belonging to the Roman Catholic Church. For both of these principles, the Utraquists have been sternly criticized, particularly by Czech historians. Standard historical literature has usually viewed the umbilical cord of canonical priesthood, which tied the Utraquists to the Roman Church, as an obstructing and even shameful liability.[65] Conventional historical literature also viewed the Utraquist insistence on maintaining their conceptual belonging to the Roman Catholic Church as a rather demeaning enterprise. Josef Pekař, for instance, depicted the Utraquists as standing at the Curia's door like humble petitioners asking to be tolerated or like beggars imploring the authorities for their indulgence.[66] From the viewpoint of the Roman Curia, the Utraquists could supply a mode of reform or renewal which was alternate to that adopted at the Council of Trent. This liberal, yet non-Protestant, model was in harmony with the ideals of other reformers, who upheld traditional orthodoxy. In addition, it had a special distinction in that it had existed as a functioning ecclesiastical community for almost two hundred years.

Contrary to conventional historiography, the Utraquists did not approach Rome as humble beggars. From their own point of view, the heirs of Hus adopted the self-confident stance of prophets of righteousness, whom God had commissioned to exhort the Roman Curia to recognize its failings and make amends. They did not plead with the Roman Church to admit them, rather they challenged the latter to listen and respond constructively to what they considered a divinely sanctioned critique.[67] In their witness the Utraquists saw themselves as a voice of conscience on behalf of Western Christendom, representing a constant reproach to Rome for its errant ways. The issue was not whether Rome was willing to readmit the Utraquists, but whether the Roman Church was willing to reform according to the Utraquist model. Looking at the relationship in another way, the Utraquists did not accept that they were in schism from the true Christian church but rather that the schism was on the part of the Roman Church, which had repudiated the *Compactata*, in 1462.[68] They did not feel the need to be authenticated by Rome but that Rome needed to be authenticated by them. Rome had not rehabilitated them by its approval of the *Compactata* but by adopting the latter the Church of Rome might start rehabilitating itself. As mentioned earlier, the Utraquists thought of themselves as exemplary Roman Catholics, and readily called themselves a part of the "Catholic Church" (Církev Katolická).[69]

Utraquism offered to the Church of Rome an alternate model of non-Protestant reform to that which the latter embraced at the Council of Trent. From the beginning the Utraquists drew support for their audacity from sacred history. They pointed to the precedent of the chosen people of Israel struggling for God against discouraging odds.[70] The Utraquist stand in the sixteenth and early seventeenth centuries required a considerable degree of moral courage, inasmuch as they resisted the leadership of the church, which they recognized as the necessary historic center of Western Christendom and of which they themselves were a part. It was in a sense a non-violent extension of the war which their ancestors had fought against the imperial and papal crusaders in the early years of the Bohemian Reformation. It was also a continuing and continuous reprise of the predicament which Jan Hus had experienced in a personal and more painful way at Constance, the dilemma between moral conviction and established authority. Historical literature by and large has neglected the inspirational side of the Utraquists' role as champions of renewal in the Roman Church. Instead, subsequent historiography seemed to be drawn to the seamy side of their relations with the Holy See, filled with a variety of deceptions and misleading moves.[71]

Contrary to conventional historiography, the Utraquists' stand was neither idiosyncratic nor quixotic. The Utraquists were not unique or alone in casting a jaundiced eye from the vantage point of traditional orthodoxy at the model of church renewal taking shape at the Council of Trent (1545–1563), and in this respect may be viewed as participants, albeit distinctive ones, in a more general phenomenon, sometimes called Humanist Catholicism. Unlike the proponents of anathemas and exclusions, who prevailed at Trent, these reformers were advocates of dialogue and liberal moderation as a path to renewal.[72] Let us now situate the Utraquists within the landscape of these anti-Tridentine reformist trends within Roman Catholicism of the sixteenth century.

To some extent, the Utraquist stance paralleled the reforms proposed by Georg Witzel and also endorsed by Ferdinand I.[73] Witzel, an ordained priest, married and served as Lutheran minister in Saxony in the 1520s. After the adoption of the Augsburg Confession in 1530, he rejoined the Roman Church as a married lay preacher and lived in Dresden, Berlin, and Mainz. His proposed remaking of the Roman Church resembled the goals of the Bohemian Reformation, including a liberal ecclesiology (based on patristics and eschewing scholastic formulae), lay communion *sub utraque,* a vernacular liturgy, and a de-emphasis on the veneration of saints. After visiting

Bohemia in the early 1540s, Witzel gained the favor of Ferdinand I, and subsequently of his son and successor, Maximilian II.[74]

More surprisingly, the Utraquist prescription was likewise akin to the liberal or populist ecclesiology of Thomas More, who—according to Brendan Bradshaw—also opposed "the institutionally oriented ecclesiology of late medieval clericalism," which would triumph at Trent.[75] Paradoxically—in view of subsequent developments—in his comments on Henry VIII's critique of Luther, *Assertio septem sacramentorum* (1521), More cautioned his sovereign to be less emphatic in stressing papal primacy.[76] The parallels of Utraquism, however, are perhaps best seen with Erasmus. Erasmus himself inveighed against "certain monks and theologians, who under the guise of religion established a tyrannical empire for themselves, and whose aim it was to prey upon men's souls and property alike."[77] His aversion to papal monarchism involved him in a qualified sympathy with Luther's views, and his clear break with the German Reformer was delayed until 1524. Even afterwards, Erasmus remained highly critical of the curial establishment.[78]

Utraquist authors for their part were familiar with their liberal counterparts abroad. Utraquist Bohemia showed an active interest in Christian humanism, specifically with Erasmus and his reformist ideas. Three of his important works were translated into Czech early in the sixteenth century: *Chvála bláznovství* (Praise of Folly) in 1513, *Enchiridion militis Christiani* in 1519, and *Výklad na Otčenáš* (Explanation of the Lord's Prayer) in 1526. In addition, eight more of Erasmus's works were published in Czech translations in Bohemia between 1519 and 1595, some in several editions.[79] Erasmus corresponded with a number of Bohemians including the humanist Jan Šlechta of Všehrdy, who invited him to visit Prague in 1519,[80] and the nobleman Arkleb of Boskovice, who supplied Erasmus with reliable information on the character of the Bohemian Reformation.[81] Witzel, too, was known in Utraquist circles and often cited in support of their *via media*.[82] In 1554, Pavel Bydžovský, the outstanding Utraquist theologian of his day, published a treatise in which he praised Witzel and exhorted the Evangelicals or Lutherans (*Euangelicastros, intelligo Luteranos*) of Bohemia to listen to the German's message.[83] In the same pamphlet, Bydžovský included eulogies of Thomas More and Bishop John Fisher as exemplary Christian martyrs. Šimon Ennius Klatovský, the Utraquist translator of Robert Barnes's *Vitae Romanorum Pontificum* (Basel, 1535), was likewise familiar with Witzel's irenic position. In addition, he expressed an admiration for More, who though recognizing the necessity of the papacy, sought to diminish its power.[84]

Aside from those proponents of Roman renewal whose ideas paralleled Utraquist ecclesiology, there were those for whom Utraquism provided a practical model for Rome's accommodation with the German Reformation, including Erasmus and his close Italian friend Cardinal Jacopo Sadoleto.[85] The latter, although more cautious, was willing like Erasmus to sidetrack the scholastics and appeal directly to biblical and patristic authority on issues of ecclesiology. The cardinal had "an inveterate contempt for the scholastics and a clear preference for the Greek fathers, Chrysostom in particular."[86] He would in turn participate after 1535 in the commission on church reform, headed by Cardinal Gasparo Contarini, another Erasmian, who endeavored to find a *modus vivendi* with the Lutheran challenge, particularly at Regensburg in 1541.[87] Erasmus believed that the *Compactata* could serve as a model for Rome's response to the issues raised by the Reformation in Germany and in Switzerland.[88] With much interest he followed the renewed Roman negotiations with the Utraquists at Buda in the spring of 1525, which were conducted by his acquaintance, Cardinal Lorenzo Campeggio (1472–1539), who hoped that a settlement with the Utraquists might offset Luther's defection in Germany by regaining Bohemia. Moreover, Campeggio and his entourage expected that Erasmus's non-confrontational approach might eventually succeed in quieting dissent in Germany. This might happen if religious passions were allowed to subside through benign neglect rather than being aggravated by Rome with "excessively violent and elaborate threats."[89] Erasmus spoke of a "Hussite" solution in his correspondence with Sadoleto in 1530 urging negotiation and compromise with the Protestants.[90]

It is important to note that Erasmus and his friends viewed Utraquism as more than a practical model for the church. They had a genuine respect for its history and traditions. Maarten van Dorp argued that Jerome of Prague, Hus's fellow martyr at Constance, was wiser than any of the Council fathers.[91] Erasmus himself maintained that the Council executed Hus and Jerome without refuting their ideas;[92] accordingly, he considered the Bohemians schismatics rather than heretics.[93] More seems to have come to the same conclusion by 1532.[94] If from no other source than his Bohemian correspondents, Erasmus was in a position to secure reliable information about the character of the mainline Utraquist Church, in particular to distinguish it from the more radical spin-offs of the Bohemian Reformation such as the Taborites and the Unity of Brethren.[95] His Roman opponents in turn accused Erasmus of siding with the Utraquists in scaling down papal authority.[96]

In addition to those who saw usefulness in Utraquism in the procedural sense, as an aid in finding a *modus vivendi* between confessional rivals, others proposed the use of Utraquism in an even more positive sense, leading to a lesser or a greater degree of "utraquistization" of the Roman Church. Peter Fraenkel suggests that the discussions preceding the Pacification of Nuremberg of 1531–1532 between the Lutherans and the Roman Church were inspired by hopes of reaching an "Utraquist settlement." In his opinion, it was particularly Charles V who with the advice of Bishop Christoph von Stadion aimed at such a solution, including lay communion *sub utraque,* vernacular mass, married clergy, and a de-emphasis, if not an outright abolition, of monasticism.[97] What was relevant in the Utraquists' experience was their objection to the medieval popes' tendency to impose on the faithful rules and regulations the Bohemian reformers called "human inventions" (*nálezky lidské*), and which actually may have contradicted biblical injunctions.[98] In Utraquism this discriminatory skepticism went back all the way to the precursors of Hus, like Matěj of Janov, who designated as "human inventions" all that was not in a straightforward harmony with the lives, practices, and examples of Christ, the apostles, and the church of the first millennium.[99]

After the Council of Trent, however, it became quite evident that Rome would not reform itself along Utraquist lines. Indeed, it seemed unlikely that reconciliation between these two groups was possible. By the latter part of the sixteenth century, neither papal pronouncements nor the polemicists for the Roman Church drew any qualitative distinction between the Utraquists (as a lesser evil), on the one hand, and the Lutherans, Calvinists, and various sectarians, on the other. It is hardly surprising, then, that the political leaders of Utraquism came to regard the Roman Curia as the main threat to the continued existence of their religious identity. It can be argued that Rome's intolerance was more menacing for the Utraquists than for their more radical fellow dissidents, the Unity of Brethren and the Lutherans of Bohemia. A Roman *Gleichschaltung* would deprive the latter two of their physical abode but the Utraquists of their distinctive essence. The Lutherans could continue to practice their religion in Brandenburg, Saxony, or Scandinavia, and the Brethren had their places of escape ready abroad, particularly in Poland. The Utraquists had nowhere to go, and no alternative to seeing their faith at risk in Bohemia. This sense of danger provided a background for a tightening of the paradoxical alliance between the Utraquists and other religious dissidents in Bohemia. By 1609 the largely urban leaders of the Utraquists would be ready to intensify their political cooperation with the largely aristocratic leaders of the Lutherans and the Brethren. As noted earlier, the negotiations for the Bohemian Confession had foreshadowed such an alliance in 1575. The Utraquists would be ready, without altering their own High Church tenets, to support full religious freedom for their Unity and Lutheran compatriots under the banner of the Bohemian Confession and the legal shield of the Letter of Majesty. Moreover, Utraquist leaders would consent to share the administrative services of the hitherto Utraquist Consistory with the Lutherans and the Brethren.[100]

To say that the Curia did not appreciate the Utraquists' concern for the well-being of the Roman Church would be, of course, a major understatement. In fact, the Utraquist Church came to represent a well-nigh intolerable nuisance from the viewpoint of Tridentine Rome. Utraquism could be neither written off as a heretical institution, nor sidetracked—in view of its universalist pretensions—with an autonomous Uniate-like status (as, for instance, the Ruthenians by the Union of Brest in 1596). The Roman Church would eventually resolve the dilemma by resorting to what, if performed in a Greek tragedy, might be called a filicide of its truculent Bohemian daughter. Such an opportunity would present itself in the biennium of 1621–1622 after the battle of the White Mountain.

NOTES

1. Cited in J. V. Polišenský, *History of Czechoslovakia in Outline*, 2d ed. (Prague: Bohemia International, 1991), 54.

2. On the significance of Utraquist eucharistic reforms see three articles by David R. Holeton, "Sacramental and Liturgical Reform in Late Medieval Bohemia," *Studia Liturgica* 28, no. 1 (1987): 94; idem, "The Communion of Infants and Hussitism," *Communio Viatorum* 27 (1984): 217–19, and idem, "The Communion of Infants: The Basel Years," *Communio Viatorum* 29 (1986): 35–36.

3. On the origins and character of Utraquism see Howard Kaminsky, *A History of the Hussite Revolution* (Berkeley: University of California Press, 1967); Zdeněk V. David, "The Strange Fate of Czech Utraquism: The Second Century, 1517–1621," *Journal of Ecclesiastical History* 46 (1995): 641–68; on the ecclesiastical administration of those under the Roman Church, see Veronika Macháčková, "Církevní správa v době jagellonské na základě administrátorských akt," *Folia Historica Bohemica* 9 (1985): 235–90.

4. On the Bohemian Confession see Howard Louthan, *Johannes Crato and the Austrian Habsburgs* (Studies in Reformed Theology and History), vol. 2, no. 3 (1994), 22, 23.

5. The proportion of the *sub una* (i.e., the adherents of the Roman Curia) within Bohemia's population has been estimated at 12 to 15 percent for the second half of the sixteenth century; see, for instance, Josef Pekař, *Dějiny československé* (Prague: Akropolis, 1991), 91–92.

6. On the Unity and its origins, see Rudolf Říčan, *The History of the Unity of Brethren: A Protestant Hussite Church in Bohemia and Moravia*, trans. C. Daniel Crews (Bethlehem, Pa.: Moravian Church in America, 1992); Peter Brock, *The Political and Social Doctrines of the Unity of Czech Brethren in the Fifteenth and Sixteenth Centuries* (The Hague: Mouton, 1957); and Murray L. Wagner, *Petr Chelčický: A Radical Separatist in Hussite Bohemia* (Scottsdale, Pa.: 1983).

7. Jaroslav Pelikan, "Luther's Attitude Toward John Hus," *Concordia Theological Monthly* 19 (1948): 757–61.

8. On Dungersheim see his *Dialogus ad Lutherum*, cited by Arnošt Kraus, *Husitství v literatuře, zejména německé*, 3 vols. (Prague: Česká akademie pro vědy, slovesnost a umění, 1917–1924), 1:154; Ernst Ludwig Enders, *Dr. Martin Luthers Briefwechsel* (Calv and Stuttgart: Verlag der Vereinsbuchhandlung, 1887), 2:176. For Hieronymus Emser consult his *De disputatione lipsicensi ad Boemos obiter deflexa est (1519). A venatione Luteriana Aegocerotis assertio (1519)*, ed. Franz Xaver Thurnhofer (Münster: Aschendorf, 1921), 14, 33. On Emser see also Gustav Kawerau, *Hieronymus Emser: Ein Lebensbild aus der Reformationsgeschichte* (Halle: Verein für Reformationsgeschichte, 1898), 18, but Emser still denounced Hus in 1523 as an old heretic from whom Luther drew his ideas, ibid., 46–47. Finally, on Cochlaeus turn to Pelikan, "Luther's Attitude Toward John Hus," 757–58. Cochlaeus knew about those trends in Bohemian theology, which were more radical than Utraquism. He published a book against an early Czech Lutheran, Ulrichus Velenus, who denied Peter's residence in Rome, *De Petro et Roma aduersus Velenum Lutheranum, libri quatuor* (Cologne: Quentell, 1525). In it, however, Cochlaeus still equated Hus with Wyclif as a heretic; Johannes Cochlaeus, *De Petro et Roma aduersus Velenum Lutheranum . . .* ([Cologne], 1525), B4v.

9. Edward Surtz, *The Works and Days of John Fisher: An Introduction to the Position of St. John Fischer (1469–1535), Bishop of Rochester, in the English Renaissance and Reformation* (Cambridge: Harvard University Press, 1967), 329.

10. On the Curia's expectations see the letter from Floriano Montini to Erasmus, February 22, 1525, from Buda, Desiderius Erasmus, *The Correspondence*, 11 vols. (Toronto: University of Toronto Press, 1974–1994), 11:49. On the background of the negotiations see also Anna Skýbová, "Česká šlechta a jednání o povolení kompaktát r. 1525," in *Proměny feudální třídy v Čechách v pozdním feudalismu*, ed. Josef Petráň, Acta Universitatis Carolinae, Philosophica et historica I, Studia historica XIV (Prague, 1976), 81–112; Václav V. Tomek, *Dějepis města Prahy*, 12 vols., (Prague: Řivnáč, 1855–1901), 10: 544–47, 575–82.

11. Johann Faber, *Confutatio gravissimi erroris asserentis in sacramento altaris post consecrationem nisi corpus tantum et sub specie vini non esse nisi sanguinem tantum* (Leipzig: Nicholas Wolrab, 1537). Czech trans. Johann Faber, *O potupení bludu* and *O zpovědi*, manuscript, arranged by Augustin Schwarzel of Třebenice in 1540, Olomouc University Library, sign. M44; see Eduard Petrů, *Z rukopisných sbírek Universitní knihovny v Olomouci* (Prague: Státní pedagogické nakladatelství, 1959), 57.

12. Ibid., 11–113. On the early Utraquist synods see Blanka Zilynská, *Husitské synody v Čechách, 1418–1440* (Prague: Univerzita Karlova, 1985), 16–17, 19–21.

13. Faber, *Confutatio gravissimi erroris*, 113–14.

14. Remigius Bäumer, *Johannes Cochlaeus (1479–1552): Leben und Werk im Dienst der katholischen Reform* (Muenster: Aschendorf, 1980), 84, 112–14.

15. Pelikan, "Luther's Attitude Toward John Hus," 760–61.

16. Václav Koranda, *Traktát o velebné a božské svátosti oltářní* (Prague: Tiskař Korandy, 1493), A3v–A4r; Ernest Denis, *Fin de l'indépendance bohême*, 2nd ed., 2 vols. (Paris: Librairie Leroux, 1930), 2:208–9.

17. Tomáš Bavorovský, *Postila česká* (Olomouc: Jan Gunther, 1557), 100r; 377v–378r.

18. "V kteréžto práci měl jsem věrného tovaryše a spolu Bratra v Pánu Kristu milého, slovutného Jana Straněnského . . ." Bavorovský, *Postila*, 4v–5r.

19. Ibid., *Postila*, xir–v (pp. 11–12).

20. Josef Jireček, *Rukověť k dějinám literatury české do konce XVIII. věku*, 2 vols. (Prague: Tempský, 1875–1876), 2:246.

21. ". . . s přehlédnutím a povolením Důstojných Pánů Administrátorů strany pod Jednou i pod Obojí Arcibiskupství Pražského"; Tomáš Bavorovský, *Kázání o svatém pokání* (Prague: Bartoloměj Netolický, 1552), Hh2v.

22. Jaroslav Kolár, "Hájkova kronika a česká literatura," in Václav Hájek z Libočan, *Kronika česká* (Prague: Odeon, 1981), 10.

23. Jiří Pešek, *Měšťanská vzdělanost a kultura v předbělohorských Čechách, 1547–1620* (Prague: Karolinum, 1993), 74. See also Antonín Škarka, "Ze zápasů nekatolického tisku s protireformací: Literární a tiskařská aféra z r. 1602," *Český časopis historický* 42 (1936): 2.

24. Emma Urbánková, "Nejstarší prvotisky českého původu," in *Knihtisk a kniha v českých zemích od husitství do Bílé hory: Sborník prací k 500. výročí českého knihtisku*, ed. František Šmahel (Prague: Academia, 1970), 24–30; for references to the traditional Utraquist liturgical books see, for instance, Koranda, *Traktát o velebné a božské svátosti*, S3r–S3v.

25. Jarold K. Zeman, "The Rise of Liberty in the Czech Reformation," *Central European History* 6 (1973): 136, citing Reginald R. Betts, *Essays in Czech History* (London: University of London, Athlone Press, 1969), 264.

26. Škarka, "Ze zápasů nekatolického tisku," 2.

27. Klement Borový, *Antonín Brus z Mohelnice, arcibiskup pražský; Historicko-kritický životopis* (Prague: Dědictví sv. Prokopa, 1873), 227.

28. Theodor Kolde, "Cochlaeus," *Realenzyklopaedie für protestantische Theologie und Kirche* (Leipzig: Hinrichs, 1896–1913?), 4:200, cited by Pelikan, "Luther's Attitude Toward John Hus," 759, n. 95.

29. The nobles constituted less than 1 percent of the population with the number of families estimated at 1,400 in 1600; see Jan Kapras, *Právní dějiny zemí koruny české*, 3 vols. (Prague: Unie, 1913–1920), 2:436.

30. On these denominational and political shifts see Zdeněk V. David, "The Plebeianization of Utraquism: The Controversy over the Bohemian Confession of 1575," in *The Bohemian Reformation and Religious Practice*, Vol. 2: Papers from the XVIIIth World Congress of the Czechoslovak Society of Arts and Sciences, Brno 1996, eds. Zdeněk V. David and David R. Holeton (Prague: Academy of Sciences of the Czech Republic, Main Library, 1998), 127–58.

31. These relations are analyzed by Zdeněk V. David, "The Utraquists and the Roman Curia, 1575–1609: Institutional Aspects," in *The Bohemian Reformation and Religious Practice*, Vol. 4: Papers from the IVth International Symposium on Bohemian Reformation and Religious Practice, under the auspices of the Philosophical Institute of the Academy of Sciences of the Czech Republic, Vila Lanna, Prague, 27 June 2000 (Prague: Academy of Sciences, Main Library, 2002), 225–260.

32. Václav Novotný, "Náboženské dějiny české ve století 16.," in *Česká politika*, ed. Zdeněk V. Tobolka, 5 vols. (Prague: Jan Laichter, 1906), 1:634.

33. Bruno Bernard, *Patrice-François de Neny, 1716–1784: portrait d'un homme d'état* (Brussels: Editions de l'Université de Bruxelles, 1993), 150.

34. These (mis)appropriations happened during the wars of the Bohemian Reformation, allegedly to protect the church lands from the religious dissidents; see Skýbová, "Česká šlechta a jednání o povolení kompaktát," 81–82.

35. On the radicalization of the nobles *sub una* see, for instance, Jaroslav Pánek, "Stavovství v předbělohorské době," *Folia Historica Bohemica* 6 (1984): 176, 190.

36. Representative of this generation was Chancellor Vratislav of Pernštejn (d. 1582), Count Palatine Vilém of Rožmberk (d. 1592), and Chancellor Adam of Hradec (d. 1596).

37. Karel Stloukal, *Papežská politika a císařský dvůr pražský na předělu XVI. a XVII. věku*, Facultas philosophica Universitatis Carolinae Pragensis. Práce z vědeckých ústavů, 9 (Prague: Řivnáč, 1925), 188–91.

38. Only the exceptional hard-liners among the nobles *sub una* refused to endorse the document in 1609.

39. Examples include the German Jesuit Alexander Höller, and the Poles Jakób Wujek z Wągrowca and Bartołomiej Paprocki z Glogoł.

40. Antonín Rejzek, *Blahoslavený Edmund Kampián, kněz Tovaryšstva Ježíšova, pro sv. víru mučeník ve vlasti své* (Brno: K. Winiker, 1889), 92–93, 98, 103.

41. Ibid., 110–11. Campion seemed to esteem Wenceslaus highly, classing him later with such exemplary Christian sovereigns as Edward of England, Louis

of France, Hermenegilda of Spain, Henry of Saxony, and Leopold of Austria. Ibid., 126.

42. Ibid., 118–19. On Locika see also Jaroslav Kadlec, *Přehled českých církevních dějin*, 2 vols. (Prague: Zvon, 1991), 2:74; Václav Líva, "Studie o Praze pobělohorské," *Sborník příspěvků k dějinám hl. města Prahy* 7 (1933): 22–23.

43. Bohumír J. Dlabač, *Leben des frommen Prager Erzbischofs Johann Lohelius, ehemaligen Strahower Abtes* (Prague: Christen, 1794), 11–12.

44. Rejzek, *Blahoslavený Edmund Kampián*, 155.

45. Ibid., 160–62. Martinic, Slavata, and Fabricius were the three Catholic victims of the famous 1618 defenestration.

46. Thomas M. McCoog, ed., *The Reckoned Expense: Edmund Campion and the Early English Jesuits* (Woodbridge, Suffolk: Boydell Press, 1996), 112. See also Rejzek, *Blahoslavený Edmund Kampián*, 150; Edmund Campion, *Spis krátký Edmunda Kampiána Societatis Jesu, Theologa a Mučedlníka Božího, který ne tak dávno pro víru S. Katolickau smrt ukrutnau podstaupil: Vznešeným Doktorům a Mistrům učení Oxonienského a Kantabrigienského podaný* (Prague: Jiřík Nygrin, 1601), C10r.

47. See Rejzek, *Blahoslavený Edmund Kampián*, 169.

48. The edicts' force was blunted in two ways. First, they contradicted Maximilian II's grant of tolerance, mentioned above. Second, the Brethren rejected the designation as "Pikharts," although almost everybody else in Bohemia called them that. See *Sněmy české od léta 1526 až po naši dobu*, 15 vols. (Prague: Zemský výbor, 1877–1941), 11:54–56.

49. Václav Šturm, *Srovnání víry a učení bratří starších* (Litomyšl: Andreas Graudenc, 1582); idem, *Krátké ozvání . . . proti kratičkému ohlášení Jednoty Valdenské neb Boleslavské* (Prague: Jiřík Dačický, 1584); and idem, *Rozsouzení a bedlivé uvážení Velikého kancionálu od Bratří Valdenských, jinak Boleslavských, sepsaného . . .* (Prague: Burián Valda, 1588).

50. Ferdinand Hrejsa, *Česká konfesse: Její vznik, podstata a dějiny* (Prague: Česká akademie pro vědy, slovesnost a umění, 1912), 205.

51. "A protož jiným Duchem někdy mluvil Arius, jiným Macedonius, jiným Donatus, jiným Wyclif, jiným Mistr Jan Hus, jiným Táboři, jiným Luteránové, jiným Cvinglianové, jiným Bratři vaši, a tak jeden každý jinou má novotu, jinou Sektu, jinou Víru, jiné Kněžstvo, jiný zbor, a tak jiný že žádný s jiným se nesrovnává." Šturm, *Srovnání víry a učení bratří*, 103.

52. Ibid., 375–78, 419.

53. Šturm, *Krátké ozvání . . . proti kratičkému ohlášení*, 3.

54. Šturm, *Srovnání víry a učení bratří*, 340, 420–22.

55. See, for instance, the views of Nuncio Caetani in 1592 cited in Alena Pazderová, "Instrukce pražského nuncia Caetaniho pro jeho nástupce Speciana," in Ivan Hlaváček and Jan Hrdina, eds., *Facta probant homines: Sborník příspěvků k životnímu jubileu prof. dr. Zdeňky Hledíkové* (Prague: Scriptorium, 1998), 359. An almost necessary corollary was the fabrication of another mythical entity, later to be known as

"Neo-Utraquism," in which the Utraquism of the *Compactata* became infiltrated by—from Rome's viewpoint—corrupting Protestant elements.

56. Petr Linteo z Pilzenburgku, *Jistá a patrná církve svaté znamení* (Litomyšl, 1593), 220–21. A second edition of Linteo's book appeared in 1725 (Prague: Wolffkang Wickhart, 1725).

57. Ibid., 223–25.

58. Ibid., 227–31.

59. Ibid., 100.

60. Ibid., 286–87, 291.

61. Ibid., 163–64.

62. Ibid., 164–65.

63. Bohuslav Bílejovský, *Kronika církevní*, ed. Josef Skalický (pseudonym for Josef Dittrich) (Prague: Fetterl z Vilden, 1816). 2, 28.

64. Linteo z Pilzenburgku, *Jistá a patrná církve svaté znamení*, 167–68.

65. For a reference to this issue see, for instance, Noemi Rejchrtová, "Role utrakvizmu v českých dějinách," in *Traditio et Cultus: Miscellanea historica bohemica Miloslao Vlk, archiepiscopo Pragensi, ab eius collegis amicisque ad annum sexagesimum dedicata*, ed. Zdeňka Hledíková (Prague: Univerzita Karlova, 1993), 75.

66. Josef Pekař, *Žižka a jeho doba*, 4 vols. (Prague: Vesmír, 1927–1933), 3:327.

67. Bílejovský, *Kronika církevní*, 13–14; Vavřinec z Březové, *Husitská kronika*, ed. Marie Bláhová (Prague: Svoboda, 1979), 88–89. See also Božena Kopičková, *Jan Želivský* (Prague: Melantrich, 1990), 94.

68. Amedeo Molnár, "Martin Lupáč: Modus disputandi pro fide," *Folia Historica Bohemica* 4 (1982): 161–77.

69. Valentin Polon, *Pomni na mne: Knižka obahující v sobě kratičká spasidedlná Naučení a sebrání*... (Staré Město Pražské: Buryan Valda, 1589), f. Club 5–1b, A6–2b, A6–3a, A6–3b. Bílejovský states literally: "... we Czechs *sub utraque* are the true Romans" (... my Čechové pod obojí jsme praví Římané), *Kronika církevní*, 27. In the ecclesiastical area, their resistance was comparable—in its tenor, if not in its results—to the political opposition of the North American colonies to the British monarch claiming to defend the rights of Englishmen.

70. Bílejovský, *Kronika církevní*, 14.

71. See for example the maneuvers around Administrator Rezek's apostasy in 1592–1593. Denis, *Fin de l'indépendance bohême*, 2:298–301; David, "The Strange Fate of Czech Utraquism," 648–51.

72. Peter Matheson, *Rhetoric of the Reformation* (Edinburgh: T&T Clark, 1998), 215–37.

73. On Witzel see Winfried Trusen, *Um die Reform und Einheit der Kirche: Zum Leben und Werk Georg Witzels*, Vereinsschriften der Gesellschaft zur Herausgabe des Corpus Catholicorum, 14 (Münster: Aschendorffsche Verlagsbuchhandlung, 1957), 48–83; Barbara Henze, *Aus Liebe zur Kirche Reform: die Bemühungen Georg Witzels um die Kircheneinheit* (Münster: Aschendorff, 1995), 91–151.

74. Trusen, *Um die Reform und Einheit der Kirche*, 22–26; Henze, *Aus Liebe zur Kirche Reform*, 23. For irenic activity at Maximilian's court see Howard Louthan, *The Quest for Compromise: Peacemakers in Counter-Reformation Vienna* (Cambridge: Cambridge University Press, 1997).

75. Brendan Bradshaw, "The Controversial Sir Thomas More," *Journal of Ecclesiastical History* 36 (1985): 564.

76. Thomas More, *Complete Works*, 21 vols. (New Haven: Yale University Press, 1963–1997), 5, pt. 2:721.

77. Erasmus, *The Correspondence*, 11:193.

78. Erasmus, *The Correspondence*, 11:xii.

79. Jaroslav Kolár, *Návraty bez konce: Studie k starší české literatuře*, ed. Lenka Jiroušková (Brno: Atlantis, 1999), 120, 141, 175–77; *Knihopis českých a slovenských tisků*, 2 vols., vol. 2 in 9 parts (Prague: Nakladatelství Československé akademie věd, 1925–1967), nos. 2348–2369. See also Mirjam Bohatcová, "Erasmus Roterdamský v českých tištěných překladech 16. - 17. století," *Časopis národního muzea*, Řada historická 155 (1986): 37–58.

80. Erasmus, *The Correspondence*, 6:321–23. See also ibid., 7:89–95, 119–28.

81. "For pray take it as certain that, whatever opinion you come to, people in my country will easily and gladly agree with you, and will value what you say far more than if one were to confront them with decrees of the supreme pontiff or any thunderbolt of opposition launched by men." Erasmus, *The Correspondence*, 8:75–76.

82. Kolár, *Návraty bez konce*, 179.

83. Pavel Bydžovský, *Historiae aliquot Anglorum martyrum, quibus Deus suam ecclesiam exornare sicut syderibus coelum dignatus est* (Prague: J. Cantor, 1554), Br.

84. Robert Barnes, *Kronyky. A životů sepsání nejvrchnějších Biskupů Římských jináč Papežů*, trans. Ennius Glatouinus (Nuremberg: Woldřich Nejber and Jan Montán, 1565), 195v, 198r–198v.

85. Richard M. Douglas, *Jacopo Sadoleto, 1477–1547: Humanist and Reformer* (Cambridge, Mass.: Harvard University Press, 1959), 74.

86. Ibid., 80–81, 116.

87. Contarini showed his spirit of accommodation in negotiations at the Diet of Regensburg in 1541 when he tried to find a common ground with the Lutherans on justification; see Elisabeth G. Gleason, *Gasparo Contarini: Venice, Rome, and Reform* (Berkeley: University of California Press, 1993), x, 241–45; James Atkinson, "Die römisch-katholische Kirche und die Reformation in anglikanischer Sicht," in Franz Lau, ed. *Vierhundertfünfzig Jahre lutherische Reformation* (Göttingen: Vandenhoeck und Ruprecht, 1967), 14–15.

88. Josef Macek, "Osudy basilejských kompaktát v jagellonském věku," *Jihlava a Basilejská Kompaktáta: Sborník příspěvků z mezinárodního sympozia k 555. výročí přijetí Basilejských kompaktát, 26–28. červen 1991* (Jihlava: Muzeum Vysočiny, 1992), 199–200. See also Alain Dufour, "Humanisme et Reformation," in his *Histoire politique et psychologie historique* (Geneva: Librairie Droz, 1966), 54.

89. Letter from Floriano Montini (secretary to Cardinal Campeggio) to Erasmus, February 22, 1525, from Buda, in Erasmus, *The Correspondence*, 11:48–49; on Erasmus's friendship with Campeggio see ibid., 11:84, 323.

90. Erasmus's letter to Sadoleto is cited in Douglas, *Jacopo Sadoleto, 1477–1547*, 115.

91. ". . . indeed it is the opinion of that great man Jerome the Hussite that universities do no more good to the church of God than the Evil One himself. Nor does it move the schoolmasters in the slightest that his opinion was condemned at the Council of Constance, for it is notorious that the council did not contain a single educated man or one who knew Greek." Letter from Maarten van Dorp, August 27, 1515, in Erasmus, *The Correspondence*, 3:160.

92. Ibid., 6:15.

93. Letter to Ricardo Bartolini, March 10, 1517, in ibid., 4:279.

94. See in particular *The Letter against Frith*, in More, *Complete Works*, 7:257, 391; compared with his view of the Bohemians as heretics in *Dialogue Concerning Heresies* (1529?), see ibid., 6, pt. 1:315, 379, pt. 2:473–74.

95. See, for instance, the disquisition of Jan Šlechta of Všehrdy in his letter of October 10, 1519, to Erasmus, in Erasmus, *The Correspondence*, 7:91–94. For Erasmus's awareness of the Taborite violence see ibid., 8:25.

96. Letter of Diego Lópes Zuñiga to Juan de Vergara of May 4, 1522, in ibid., 8:345, 460 n. 8.

97. Peter Fraenkel, "Utraquism or Co-Existence: Some Notes on the Earliest Negotiations Before the Pacification of Nürnberg, 1531–1532," *Studia theologica* 18, 2 (1964): 130, 132–34.

98. Barnes, *Kronyky. A životů sepsání*, 3v–4r.

99. Jana Nechutová, "Matěj of Janov and His Work *Regulae Veteris et Novi Testamenti:* The Significance of Volume VI and Its Relation to the Previously Published Volumes," in Zdeněk V. David and David R. Holeton, eds., *The Bohemian Reformation and Religious Practice*, vol. 2: Papers from the XVIIIth World Congress of the Czechoslovak Society of Arts and Sciences, Brno 1996 (Prague: Academy of Sciences of the Czech Republic, Main Library, 1998), 16; see also František Bartoš, *Husitská revoluce*, 2 vols., *České dějiny*, vols. 7–8 (Prague: Nakladatelství Československé akademie věd, 1965–1966), 1:21, 37; and Augustin Neumann, *K dějinám věku poděbradského* (Brno: Nákladem vlastním, 1933), 7.

100. Zdeněk V. David, "A Cohabitation of Convenience: The Utraquists and the Lutherans under the Letter of Majesty, 1609–1620," in Zdeněk V. David and David R. Holeton, eds., *The Bohemian Reformation and Religious Practice*, vol. 3: Papers from the XIXth World Congress of the Czechoslovak Society of Arts and Sciences, Bratislava 1998 (Prague: Academy of Sciences of the Czech Republic, Main Library, 2000), 173–214.

10

From Rudolfine Prague to Vasa Poland

Valerian Magni and the Twilight of
Irenicism in Central Europe

HOWARD P. LOUTHAN

THERE ARE TWO COMMON ASSUMPTIONS THAT TEND TO INFORM most discussion on irenicism in seventeenth-century central Europe. The first concerns its confessional character. The primary focus of research has been Protestant.[1] In Heidelberg David Pareus put forth a plan of Protestant re-union to Gustav Adolf while in Helmstedt Georg Calixt worked on his own scheme of reconciliation between Calvinists and Lutherans. Slightly farther to the west, Hugo Grotius articulated his solution to confessional conflict, and the wandering Czech emigré John Amos Comenius made ports-of-call across the continent bringing with him his pansophic proposals for peace and harmony within the Christian community. The thought and work of these individuals have been well studied.[2] On the other side of the confessional ledger, however, one often encounters the view that central Europe's Catholic leaders had little sympathy for or interest in religious compromise. This region after all was the target of Rome's most aggressive campaign to restore the old faith. Here we find the zealous imperial confessor Guillaume Lamormaini inexorably driving Ferdinand II towards the Edict of Restitution and the fiery Jesuit preacher Piotr Skarga railing against Poland's Protestant nobility.

Apart from these confessional stereotypes, there are also problems of chronology. It is generally assumed that the Thirty Years' War marks the outer end of irenic activity in central Europe. It certainly cannot be denied that religious differences between combatants were resolved at some level by 1648. In retrospect, Comenius seems somewhat myopic with his vague hopes that a place would be restored for Protestants in Habsburg Bohemia after the peace negotiations. It is also significant that Calixt's efforts during this period were directed towards an intra-Protestant union. Though Leibniz and others would later elaborate and expand on the ideas of an earlier generation of irenicists, realistic prospects for meaningful Protestant-Catholic dialogue in this region seemed to have literally gone out the window with Slavata and Martinic in 1618.[3]

The Capuchin friar Valerian Magni (1586–1661) is an important figure to consider, as he challenges both of these presuppositions and helps broaden our understanding of late irenicism in central Europe.[4] At first glance, Magni may seem like an unlikely character to single out as a proponent of theological compromise. Born in Milan, he first fell under the sway of the vigorous Lawrence of Brindisi, who helped persuade the young man to join the Capuchins. He became an energetic member of the order, worked diligently to revise its constitution, and accepted a commission to serve as a missionary in central Europe. He would later enjoy the reputation of a controversialist, even provoking the ire of the normally mild Comenius. Despite these credentials, Valerian Magni was arguably the most effective advocate of confessional reunion in seventeenth-century central Europe. Advising popes and princes for nearly fifty years, he worked tirelessly as a mediator across the continent. His career as diplomat and missionary took him from Rome to Danzig, from the Ukraine to France. His work as a scholar ranged almost as widely. Scientist, philosopher, and theologian, he produced a staggering amount of written material.[5] In spite of this activity, Magni has attracted relatively little attention. Though he was well connected with the literati of his day, receiving a brief mention in Pascal's *Provincial Letters,* a pall of silence descended after his death in part as a result of a bitter feud with the Jesuits and an embarrassing public arrest in Vienna.[6]

Although born in Milan, Magni was intellectually a product of Rudolfine Prague. His father had found employment at the emperor's court and moved his family north in 1589. The precocious Magni took full advantage of the cosmopolitan environment in which he was raised. Not surprisingly, his scientific interests were nurtured in this period. Here he met the imperial astronomer Tycho Brahe. It also seems likely that he interacted with Kepler both in Prague and shortly thereafter in Linz. He would later become an ardent defender of Galileo and use his findings in his own work. Magni made important contributions in the field of optics and also conducted a series of vacuum experiments that may well have predated Pascal's better-known investigations.[7] Magni's formal education, however, began in theology. In 1602 he started his studies as a new member of the Capuchin order in Prague. Once more, it is clear that he was influenced by the various currents of late humanist thought circulating at the imperial court. His ideas were a compelling mixture of neoplatonic philosophy and Augustinian theology and in many ways represented a Catholic equivalent of the more famous pansophic ideas of John Comenius.[8] Magni's world remained remarkably broad and open even after the death of Rudolf and the slow but gradual intellectual stagnation that accompanied the recatholicization of Bohemia. Despite the difficulties of war, he nurtured his contacts abroad. Most significant in this respect was his relationship with Marin Mersenne. He had first met Mersenne in Paris in the 1620s and remained an important part of that learned circle throughout his life. In the Bohemian setting he maintained contact with many of the Protestants who had been exiled from the Czech lands after the Habsburg victory at White Mountain.[9]

To understand Magni's importance in the central European context, his career must be examined at a number of levels. Magni rose to prominence as an astute and effective agent for the Habsburg family during the Thirty Years' War. During the war years he endeavored to maintain good working relations between the major Catholic states. In 1622 he was in Paris in an effort to ease tensions between the Habsburgs and Bourbons in response to the Valtelline controversy. The emperor dispatched him to Regensburg in 1630 to help resolve the War of the Mantuan Succession. The Capuchin's most delicate mission during this period was to Poland. Here, he gently dissuaded King Władysław IV from marrying the Protestant Elizabeth of Bohemia and afterwards promoted a match with Cecilia Renata of Austria, the sister of Emperor Ferdinand III.[10]

Within the imperial lands Magni also played an instrumental role as mediator. He was involved in the sensitive negotiations surrounding the elevation of the Bavarian duke to electoral status, a decision that troubled both Protestant and Catholic princes.[11] Magni would develop a particularly close relationship with Bavaria's Duke Maximilian. The archives are full of their correspondence that details the Capuchin's various peace proposals during the stormy decades of the Thirty Years' War.[12] Magni's sympathies as diplomat are perhaps most clearly seen during the deliberations surrounding the 1635 Peace of Prague. Before accepting the agreement, Ferdinand had invited a panel of theologians to discuss the moral and theological dimensions of the peace accord. The papal representatives and the Jesuits vigorously protested any rapprochement with the heretics. Lamormaini interpreted the recent Swedish defeat at Nördlingen as a sign of divine favor. Another member of the Jesuit party, Ludwig Crasius, argued that Ferdinand would be guilty of sin if he agreed to the peace. Magni, on the other hand, urged the emperor to accept the compromise as a platform to establish a lasting confessional settlement in the empire. He even encouraged Ferdinand to move forward without seeking formal permission from the pope.[13]

Though Magni assumed a variety of diplomatic roles throughout his career, his contributions as theologian and missionary were even more significant in his quest to reunite the fractured Christian community of central Europe. His first real opportunity in this regard came in the early 1620s. After the defeat of the Czech estates at the Battle of White Mountain, the Bohemian kingdom was subjected to a very energetic and often forceful campaign of recatholicization. Admittedly, at first glance, post–White Mountain Bohemia seems an unlikely setting to find any attempts of conciliation with the region's non-Catholic populace. The Habsburgs frequently employed blunt methods to reunite the renegade kingdom with Rome. The Czech lands lost their elective status, a new constitution redistributed power and privilege, and one-fifth of the nobility was forced to emigrate. It is from this period that we have stories of individuals like the Jesuit priest Father Firmus. Wearing heavy clogs with sharp spikes, Firmus would allegedly stomp on the feet of peasants until they divulged the whereabouts of Protestant books they had hidden away.[14] Though Magni's role is either conveniently forgotten or merely overshadowed by these strong-arm tactics employed by many of the Jesuits and other Habsburg allies, he offered an alternative approach to resolving Bohemia's confessional problems.

Magni was sent back to Prague in 1623 as the provincial superior of the Capuchin order. There he worked as a type of mentor to the young and inexperienced archbishop of Prague, Ernst von Harrach.[15] At the age of twenty-five, Harrach had been entrusted with the Herculean task of overseeing an archdiocese that comprised all of Bohemia. Apart from the inherent administrative challenges of this position, Harrach also sparred with the Jesuits concerning the nature and manner of Catholic reform in the Czech lands. Harrach and Magni maintained that the restoration of Catholicism should not be effected through imperial diktat but instead be gradually implemented through more moderate policies. Harsh punitive measures such as forced exile or other forms of public discipline should be eschewed in favor of a milder program of education, preaching, and open debate. In 1628 Magni clearly expressed many of these ideas in his treatise *De acatholicorum credendi regula iudicium*. Magni's *Iudicium*, which provoked a minor firestorm with both Protestant and Catholic reformers, is his most important piece of controversialist literature and the best introduction to his philosophical and theological convictions.

The most obvious feature of this text is its surprising lack of attention to doctrinal detail. Magni in fact began the *Iudicium* by observing, "All Christians in this age believe in God, Christ, and sacred Scripture."[16] For Magni the debate between Catholic and Protestant was actually more philosophical than dogmatic in nature. Though both believe that "the written word of God is certain and infallible," they differ on how it should be interpreted.[17] While Catholics aver that "the church as a whole propounds the true sense of sacred Scripture to the Christian world," the "Biblicists," as he named them, doubt this authority and instead "separately consult the Holy Spirit from the sacred text and so decide what conforms and conflicts with the word of God."[18] He continued by arguing that Protestants have put themselves in a difficult position logically by admitting that both individual Christians and councils can err. The consequences are obvious. On the specific level, the Biblicists cannot be sure what actually constitutes Scripture as they cannot be confident that the early councils correctly judged issues of canonicity. More generally, they admit a sense of doctrinal uncertainty they can never adequately resolve.[19] Like the foxes of Samson whose tails were tied together, the Biblicists mercilessly tug and pull at each other theologically.[20] They have no hope of finding common ground. In the end they become "a confused company of fanatics in which there is no order and where horror is eternally present."[21]

Though the arguments Magni developed in the *Iudicium* were not particularly original, there are three important points that should be noted with regard to this text. First, the tone is remarkably free of polemical rhetoric. Although Magni was clear and direct in his critique of Protestantism, he did not trade insults with his confessional opponents, nor did he debate his points in the *ad hominem* manner that is so typical of this type of literature. Rather, he engaged his opponents on their own terms, considering what he understood as the implications of a theology constructed around the Protestant premise of *sola Scriptura*. This approach of open dialogue and discussion was characteristic of Magni's missionary activity as a whole. When the Saxons captured Prague in 1631, Magni was one of the few Catholics who remained in the city. During this brief interval of Lutheran rule, he organized a number of public disputations with leading members of the Protestant community.[22] He insisted that only through reason and gentleness could central Europe's fractured religious community be reunited. Secondly, there is a sense of urgency to this text. Magni was clearly troubled by the philosophical implications of Protestant hermeneutics, which he believed would inevitably lead to the disintegration of the church. What he outlined in the *Iudicium* is almost a Cartesian search for certainty in an age of growing theological doubt. Magni contended that if his opponents were correct, "I would be forced to affirm that the Bible is not sacred but profane, Scripture not holy but false, Christ not a Savior but a seducer."[23] The *Iudicium* was a last-ditch attempt by a man desperate to heal the breaches in the Christian community before any hope of unity was lost forever. The third and final point goes to the heart of Magni's critique of Protestantism. Where does one find binding and conclusive authority in the church? Is it located in the individual or in a broader body of believers as represented by church councils? Magni highlighted this distinction between the one and the many in the fourth chapter of the *Iudicium*:

> The *Biblicist* is a single man, but the fathers of the council are many. The *Biblicist* prays alone, but all who are attending the council, indeed the entire Christian world prays for the council. . . . The *Biblicist* may be an idiot or a clown, but those at the council are the most learned theologians of the Christian world.[24]

Throughout his career Magni was insistent that ecclesiastical power should be invested in the many as opposed to the few. His own revision of the Capuchin constitution in 1625 reflected this sentiment.[25] Though not denying the special position and prerogatives of the pope, Magni certainly downplayed their significance. His attempts to reunite both Protestant and Orthodox Christians with Rome were based on an almost conciliar understanding of church authority. These convictions informed his missionary activity in Bohemia as he advised Archbishop Harrach in the years following the imperial victory at White Mountain.

One of the most difficult problems Harrach faced after 1620 concerned the Carolinum, central Europe's oldest university. It was not without reason that the imperial administration viewed this institution as a "hotbed of heresy."[26] It had become a locus of Protestant discontent, and one of its most recent rectors, Jan Jessenius, was a key figure in the Bohemian uprising. In response, Emperor Ferdinand II authorized the Jesuits to reorganize the renegade university in 1622. The Society of Jesus already had its own school in Prague, the Clementinum. With imperial support the Jesuits would expand their theological and philosophical faculties and unite them with the older law and medical divisions of the Charles University to form a new institution. The school's rector and chancellor, elective positions in the old Carolinum, would now be appointed by Jesuit superiors. Only members of the order would be permitted to teach in the theology faculty, and control of censorship would be entrusted to the new Jesuit rector. This arrangement deeply troubled Harrach and Magni. With the Society's control of the university along with its smaller colleges in the Czech countryside, the Jesuits held a virtual monopoly over education in the Bohemian kingdom. Concerned by the stern Jesuit methods of conversion and in an effort to defend the traditional rights of the Bohemian church, the archbishop and his advisor waged a vigorous campaign to regain control of the Carolinum.[27]

To assist Harrach, Magni journeyed to Rome in 1626 and conferred with Urban VIII. He came back from his trip with a cardinal's hat for Harrach and a stern word from the pope warning the Jesuits that they "should in no way rebel against the archbishop."[28] The Jesuits, however, had a firm ally in the emperor, who continued to support their leadership of the university. As tensions mounted between Magni and his opponents, the Capuchin returned to Rome in 1629 advocating his cause before the newly established Congregation for the Propagation of the Faith, also known as the Propaganda. Magni specifically argued that the power of university appointment should be returned to the archbishop and that exclusive Jesuit control of theological training be terminated.[29] The fight for the university would become even more contentious in the next decade. In 1637 Magni wrote an impassioned petition to the new emperor, Ferdinand III. The tone of the text was urgent and bold. He raised a series of issues that he hoped would sway the young ruler. Why, he queried, had the theological orientation of the institution been entrusted not to the pope and the broader body of the church but to a specific religious order?[30] Why had the archbishop been impeded in his rightful responsibilities? Why had he been excluded for fourteen years from the administration of the university?[31] Though this feud continued and would not be definitively resolved for almost twenty years, the old division between the Clementinum and the Carolinum would be reinstituted the following year.[32]

While at first glance it may seem that this long-running dispute over the fate of the university was merely a "turf war" between rival ecclesiastical establishments, there were far deeper theological and philosophical issues at stake. Magni vigorously opposed the neo-scholastic curriculum and philosophy imported by the Jesuits into the Czech lands. This tradition was best represented in Bohemia by Rodrigo Arriaga. A Spanish Jesuit and imperial tutor, Arriaga came to Prague in the 1620s and played a significant role in the reorganization of the university. His massive *Cursus philosophicus* (1632) was a landmark of neo-scholastic thought. In the text's dedication he called on the future Ferdinand III to tend the "garden of philosophy" in an effort to ensure that "the true logic, physics, and metaphysics of Aristotle can flourish anew."[33] Though Magni did not engage Arriaga directly, he was a fierce opponent of what he bluntly described as the "atheism of Aristotle."[34] His opposition to Aristotle formed not only the foundation of his theology but also the basis of his natural philosophy. While in Poland, he would wage his fight against the Aristotelians in the laboratory. In 1647 he conducted a famous experiment before the king in which he illustrated that light could traverse a vacuum, thus disproving Aristotle by demonstrating that motion was possible in void.[35]

Deeply influenced by Cusanus, Magni offered a theological and philosophical alternative that drew heavily from the Platonic and Augustinian traditions. As he stated in the dedication of his *Principia et specimen philosophiae* (1652), "It is of critical importance for humanity that a new philosophy is taught that is better than the Aristotelian model."[36] The Capuchin believed that his system offered a way for Catholics and Protestants to bridge their differences in the fractured religious world of seventeenth-century central Europe. Practically, he was concerned that Jesuit control of theological education and their neo-scholastic orientation would doom any hope of confessional rapprochement in the Bohemian context. For this reason he worked creatively with Harrach to break the Society's pedagogical monopoly. Most important in this regard were their efforts to establish an archiepiscopal seminary that would train clergy in a different spiritual tradition.[37] At this new institution Magni taught Marcus Marci, a quiet irenic sympathizer who would become Bohemia's most acclaimed scholar in the century after White Mountain. After Magni passed from the scene, Marci would continue the campaign to separate the Jesuit college from the Charles University.[38] Magni also supported the work of the new Piarist order that was slowly expanding its scope beyond its Italian base. The order, which had been originally founded to provide schooling for poor boys, established its first school in the

Czech kingdom on the Moravian estate owned by Valerian's brother Francesco.[39] One of the only alternatives to the Jesuit schools, Piarist institutions spread quickly throughout central Europe but not without resistance from their rivals. As Piarist schools began to appeal to the higher strata of society, the Jesuits felt threatened and responded defensively. These schools also posed a distinct ideological challenge. Galileo and Campanella had close connections with the order, and the ideas of both the problematic astronomer and the wayward Dominican found a favorable reception with the Piarists.[40] Magni realized the Piarists could serve as an important counterweight to the Society of Jesus and did all in his power to promote their cause, especially during those difficult years when they faced possible suppression. The Piarists, in turn, promoted and popularized the Capuchin's theology and philosophy by incorporating it into their own educational program.[41]

Though Magni had a significant impact in Bohemia in the years following White Mountain, he played an even more influential role in the Polish-Lithuanian Commonwealth, but before we examine his contributions in this context, a few words should be said concerning the historiography of this area and period. English-language historiography of the Polish Reformation is remarkably thin. Paul Fox's 1924 overview, *The Reformation in Poland*, remains the last general survey of the movement.[42] Most scholars working in this field have tended to emphasize the material factors that led to the Reformation in Poland. Fox's study, for example, argues that social and economic forces were the basic impulse of reform. Scholarship within Poland has been much the same. As a result, theological concerns have often been marginalized. Janusz Tazbir has contended that the Polish Reformation is better characterized as a grand intellectual adventure than a deeper and more profound theological movement.[43] While Tazbir's argument has its merits, serious theologians and philosophers such as Valerian Magni have all too frequently been excluded from a broader assessment of Poland's confessional struggles.

The growth and development of toleration is one issue with theological implications that has been examined with some regularity in the Polish context. It is important to note, however, that at least in the English-speaking world the group that has received the most attention in this regard lies outside the traditional boundaries of orthodox trinitarian Christianity. Scholars of religion such as E. M. Wilbur and G. H. Williams popularized the thought and theology of the Socinians or Polish Brethren. These antitrinitarians, who were staunch supporters of religious toleration, have often been viewed as forerunners of eighteenth-century *philosophes*.[44] Historians have also argued that the story of toleration in Poland follows a different chronological pattern when compared to the rest of the continent. The highpoint of religious freedom came in the sixteenth century, while the seventeenth was marked by heightened intolerance among the confessions. Janusz Tazbir has noted, "Just as in the sixteenth century even the most fanatically Catholic king could not have halted the spread of the Reformation without risking civil war, so in the next century even the most tolerant king could hardly hold back anti-Protestant repression."[45] Most scholars contend that voices for restraint and compromise, especially on the Catholic side, were heard far less frequently once the Vasas had established themselves on the Polish throne in 1587.[46]

Valerian Magni is a significant figure, as he offers a very different perspective on this standard narrative. He is a reminder that the Polish Brethren were not the only representatives of a milder confessional spirit in the seventeenth century. The Erasmian tradition of conciliation, though certainly weaker, was not yet extinct in Catholic circles of this period. Scholars have not appreciated the extent to which Magni continued and expanded upon the efforts of the royal secretary A. F. Modrzewski, the primate of Poland, Jacob Uchański, and other sixteenth-century Polish irenicists. Indeed, I would argue that the court of Magni's powerful patron, King Władysław IV (1632–1648), was the last major venue of serious interconfessional dialogue in the Age of Reform. While the ideals of irenicism and ecumenism would continue to find expression in a variety of forms in subsequent generations, these later schemes and plans would be markedly different in tone and nature.[47]

Władysław's reign is rarely seen as a highpoint of irenic activity. In broader surveys tracking the evolution of religious toleration in early modern Europe, nearly all discussion of the Polish situation is limited to the sixteenth century.[48] In more specialized studies focusing specifically on Poland, the king's contributions have seldom received the attention they merit.[49] Despite the cosmopolitan nature of his court, the Vasa prince and his circle have been virtually ignored outside Poland. But like the Prague of Rudolf II, the Poland of Władysław IV attracted a remarkable array of painters and sculptors, poets and scientists. The comparison with Rudolf is instructive, as there are a series of interesting parallels between the two princes. Both showered lavish support on an imported cohort of Flemish and Italian painters. Both were avid collectors with similar proclivities. Władysław's *Kunstkammer* was eerily reminiscent of its imperial counterpart down to a Giambologna sculpture and an Abondio medal.[50] Perhaps most importantly, however, the two rulers presided over a court that resisted both Protestant and Catholic extremes. The cast of irenic characters who were active in Rudolfine Prague has long been a focus of scholarly research.[51] Less well known, but arguably even more significant, are the confessional activities of Władysław and his circle. The conciliatory Silesian Martin Opitz served as his personal secretary, while the king himself was one of the most outspoken supporters of Galileo. But undoubtedly, the most significant testimony to the irenic spirit of the Polish court were the activities of Valerian Magni.

Magni's initial contact with Poland had actually begun during the reign of Władysław's father, Sigismund III (1587–1632). The first of Poland's Vasa kings, the orthodox Sigismund invited the Capuchins to Poland in 1617. He planned to establish a monastery for them in Cracow with Magni as its superior. Shuttling between Rome and central Europe, Magni was closely involved with these negotiations, but the 1618 Bohemian rebellion delayed the order's arrival in the Polish kingdom.[52] During the various trips he took to Poland in these early years Magni formed a close attachment to Sigismund's son. When Władysław finally acceded to the throne, the Capuchin was well positioned to serve as one of the king's principal advisers on religious affairs. His impact was felt immediately. After the coronation, Władysław sent a delegation to Rome headed by Chancellor Ossoliński with three requests: the release of Galileo from house arrest, the immediate closure of Jesuit schools in Poland, and a cardinal's hat for Magni.[53] As we have already seen, Magni would play a significant role three years later nudging the king away from what many Catholics saw as a potentially disastrous match with the Protestant Elizabeth of Bohemia. His influence would later extend to the queen's household through his brother's spouse, who served as the chief attendant of Władysław's second wife, Louise Marie Gonzaga.[54]

The first serious attempt during Władysław's reign to reunite Poland's Protestants and Catholics began in 1643. While in Rome, Magni petitioned the Propaganda for permission to hold an interconfessional dialogue in Royal Prussia. His initial request was denied. The Propaganda argued that such disputations had long been forbidden, served only as a source of quarrels, and were injurious to the honor and dignity of the church.[55] Back in Poland, however, momentum for such a conference was slowly growing. With the king's assistance Magni worked diligently to build support for this endeavor. The primate of Poland, the archbishop of Gniezno, and the bishop of Samogitia were some of the early Catholic supporters of Magni's plan.[56] These leaders proposed a meeting with delegations from the kingdom's Calvinist and

Lutheran communities in the Royal Prussian city of Toruń. Magni continued to press church leadership for official permission to proceed with the meeting. He was back in Rome in 1645. In the year that the Chinese Rites Controversy was at the center of papal attention, Magni negotiated this matter in an adept and adroit fashion. Though Innocent X had certain misgivings concerning Toruń, he allowed the colloquy to proceed, fearing that the church might lose Poland altogether if he refused.[57]

The 1645 *Colloquium charitativum* of Toruń was the last great interconfessional conference of the Reformation era. Across Europe moderates on both sides of the confessional divide enthusiastically hailed the event. Hugo Grotius greeted the news with acclamation. In a letter to the Swedish chancellor, Axel Oxenstierna, Grotius optimistically opined that with good will on all sides, the proceedings could yield a positive result within Poland and more generally promote closer relations between Catholics and Protestants.[58] Though Grotius was unable to attend due to declining health, the *Colloquium charitativum* brought together many of central Europe's most important irenicists. Zbigniew Gorayski, the castellan of Chełm, headed the official Calvinist delegation, which included both John Comenius and the influential court preacher of Brandenburg, Johann Bergius.[59] Georg Wilhelm, elector of Brandenburg and duke of Prussia, actually sent two groups of envoys to the conference. The elector was a Calvinist prince who ruled a predominately Lutheran territory and was thus keenly interested in the outcome of the discussions. He selected the moderate Georg Calixt to lead his Lutheran contingent. In preparation for the event Calixt wrote his *Consideratio et epicrisis,* a tract that argued for a "practical" theology that would mediate many of the differences between Lutherans, Calvinists, and Catholics.[60] Many of the Catholics, too, were predisposed toward negotiation. Chancellor Ossoliński and Bishop Tyskiewicz recognized that there was a real possibility of civil war if confessional compromise was not achieved. Joining them were other like-minded individuals including Władysław's secretary, Bartholomäus Nigrin. Quietly pushing the proceedings forward, Magni worked behind the scenes in Rome as he endeavored to maintain the pope's reluctant sanction of the colloquy.

The king's representative, Jerzy Ossoliński, officially opened the conference on 28 August 1645. As the delegates gathered in Toruń's stately gothic city hall that morning, the chancellor addressed the conferees with a stern warning, "Up to this present moment Poland has escaped the barbarism [of religious war] thanks to the wise moderation of our ancestors. Nonetheless, it is still necessary to fear this plague that has infected all of Europe."[61] Despite royal encouragement, negotiations quickly bogged down. Three days alone were devoted to a tedious discussion of procedure, and when theological issues were finally brought to the fore, confessional leaders who were less inclined to compromise seized the initiative. Calixt was sidelined almost immediately. He was excluded from the official Lutheran delegation, which was directed instead by the more orthodox envoy from Wittenberg, Johann Hülsemann. Hülsemann was ably assisted by two theologians from Danzig, the inflexible Abraham von Calov and Johann Botsack, an old opponent of Magni. They argued forcefully against what they perceived as the great dangers of syncretism.[62] The conference was to close officially at the end of November, and by this date nerves had become so frayed that Calixt remarked what had begun so promisingly as the *Colloquium charitativum* had concluded disappointingly as a *colloquium irritativum*.[63] Despite the outcome of the colloquy, Władysław sought to build on this conference and continue negotiations with his kingdom's Protestant subjects. In May of the following year Gorayski was invited to Warsaw for a royal audience and enthusiastically reported that "the king wants to continue this holy undertaking."[64] The official acts of the colloquy that were handsomely published by Petrus Elert in Warsaw and then later reprinted were themselves testimony to Władysław's commitment to interconfessional dialogue.

The Protestants, though, were not the only religious minority with whom Magni worked during Władysław's reign. He also devoted substantial attention to the problems of Poland's Orthodox population. The Orthodox had a long and troubled history in the Polish lands. Pressured from without by Moscow, Constantinople, and Rome, they sought to preserve an independent identity, but there was also considerable division within their own ranks in large part precipitated by the contentious 1596 Union of Brest. After this date the hierarchy of the Orthodox Church was officially dissolved, and in the early years of the seventeenth century there were actual pitched battles between members of the new "Greek-Catholic Confession of the Slavonic Rite" and those who refused to recognize papal supremacy. Both Catholic and Orthodox moderates saw the accession of Władysław IV as an opportunity to redress grievances and heal confessional wounds. On November 1, 1632, a week before his election, Władysław signed the so-called *Articles of Pacification*. This document was in many respects an Orthodox equivalent of the famous 1573 Confederation of Warsaw, which guaranteed religious freedom to *dissidentes de religione*. The rights of the Orthodox Church were restored. Its hierarchy was reinstituted with the metropolitan of Kiev recognized as its head.[65]

The two most influential individuals behind this policy shift were Adam Kysil and Valerian Magni. Kysil was an Orthodox noble committed to irenic ideals. A product of the humanist school of Zamość, the voivode of Kiev was an important intermediary between Władysław's court and the restless Cossacks of his region. He saw the *Articles of Pacification* as a necessary step to preserve the unity of the commonwealth.[66] Magni, for his part, believed that the document could serve as the basis for a broader and more comprehensive effort to restore unity between Catholic and Orthodox. Notwithstanding the moderate inclinations of the king and his close advisors, this understanding with the Orthodox provoked a strong Catholic backlash. On instructions from Rome the papal nuncio, Onorato Visconti, raised serious objections to this arrangement. In response to the public outcry Władysław summoned a group of theologians to discuss the *Articles of Pacification* in February 1633. The papal curia adamantly opposed the return of benefices, buildings, or other types of privileges and property that had belonged to the Orthodox Church before 1596. Their voice was the dominant one at the king's conference. Of the thirteen theologians attending the discussions, only two supported the articles. Magni was one of them.[67]

The Capuchin was energetic in his defense of Władysław's policies vis-à-vis the Orthodox. He would travel to Rome and plead his case before the Propaganda. As Magni stated before this body, the pope could act either as a judge or a pastor in this affair. If he chose to function as the former, he would certainly be well within his rights to condemn the *Articles of Pacification*. He hoped, however, that Urban would approach this delicate matter as a wise pastor willing to tolerate a minor evil for a greater good.[68] To persuade his skeptical audience Magni made three basic arguments that highlight his broader irenic convictions. He first appealed to the political difficulties besetting the new king. Taking advantage of the confusion that came in the wake of Sigismund's death in 1632, a Muscovite army quickly crossed Poland's eastern frontier and laid siege to the strategic city of Smolensk. Young King Władysław needed the military assistance of his Orthodox Cossacks to repel the invaders. In a letter to Cardinal Barberini, Magni outlined this desperate situation. Years later, the king himself would remark that had he not granted the *Articles of Pacification* he would have surely lost Smolensk and quite probably have plunged the country into civil war.[69]

In a more militant tone Magni also contended that Rome had systematically squandered opportunities for confessional reunion. He insisted that an aggressive approach toward heterodoxy and heresy was counterproductive if not genuinely destructive. The burning of Hus and even the initial crises that triggered the Thirty Years' War could have been avoided if the church had responded to these problems with greater sensitivity and circumspection. The reckless abandon of many Catholic leaders had discredited their own faith and would ultimately destroy what possibilities still existed for reconciliation. By supporting the *Articles of Pacification,* Rome could undo the damage of the past, win the goodwill of Poland's Orthodox community, and lay the foundation for a full and complete reunion.[70] Magni's final argument in favor of this agreement reflected his broader strategy concerning Catholic reform in central Europe. In his mind the Polish king stood at the center of a grand scheme that could return a sizable portion of this region to the church. Władysław had a strong claim to the Swedish crown and might actually accede to this throne with military assistance. Magni also noted that Poland could exert its influence as a Catholic champion in the war-weary states of the Holy Roman Empire. Finally, in the east, a successful campaign against Muscovy could result with Władysław or his brother Jan Kazimierz as the new overlord of Russia. In all these instances, a Vasa ruler would have a far better opportunity of being accepted in these non-Catholic regions if he were known as a just and tolerant prince. From this conciliatory platform he could then initiate earnest and honest religious dialogue.[71] In the end, Magni was not able to persuade either the Propaganda or the pope to sanction the *Articles of Pacification.* His efforts, however, were not entirely fruitless. Though Urban VIII would not approve Władysław's agreement, he did assure the king of his continued friendship and general support of his efforts to reunite Orthodox and Catholic.

Despite this disappointing beginning, Magni continued to search for a more definitive settlement with the Orthodox. In the final years of Władysław's reign there were promising signs that his hard work would finally yield positive results, for the Capuchin had at long last found a partner in the Orthodox community. The metropolitan of Kiev, Peter Mohyla, came from a princely family in Moldavia. After service in the Polish military, he entered the Monastery of the Caves in Kiev and in 1632 would establish his celebrated theological academy that helped spark a significant revival in the Orthodox world.[72] But like Magni, Mohyla was very interested in the possibility of confessional reunion. From his perspective the Union of Brest was a disappointing failure. This unpopular settlement had been imposed on the Ruthenian people unilaterally by the church without sufficient debate or discussion.[73] Nonetheless, he believed that Catholics and Orthodox could still find a way to resolve their differences, and in 1645 he wrote an important memorandum outlining his ideas. Magni assisted him by serving as a mediator between Kiev and Rome. Delivering his proposal to the Propaganda, Magni described Mohyla as a man "whose good zeal, valor, and authority rests on the hope of the desired union [between Catholic and Orthodox]."[74]

Mohyla began his statement by summarizing what he considered as the weakness of Brest:

> Union and unity are very different. Unity excludes duality. Union, in contrast, seeks to combine two elements without the destruction of either. Such has been done in the past, the last time at Florence between the Greeks and Latins. The union of the Ruthenians with the Latins realized in this kingdom, however, seems to have gone beyond the true nature of union as it was not intended to save the Greek religion but to transform it into the Roman faith. Therefore, it did not succeed.[75]

Mohyla's solution, as he hinted in his opening remarks, was to revisit the Council of Florence. Theological differences, such as the sacraments, purgatory, and even the procession of the Holy Spirit, could be resolved by returning to this council as a doctrinal model.[76] The most difficult issue in Mohyla's mind, what he described as "the root of all these evils between Greeks and Romans," was the matter of papal supremacy.[77] On this point he recommended a novel course of action. He argued that if the patriarch of Constantinople were not under "the yoke of the pagans," he would in all probability recognize the leadership of the pope. Until that time, however, the Ruthenian Orthodox Church should continue to exist and function in an autonomous state with its metropolitan elected by its own bishops.[78]

Unlike the response to the *Articles of Pacification,* the work of Mohyla and Magni was greeted enthusiastically by Catholic leaders in Rome. The Propaganda believed that the memorandum could serve as a basis of serious discussions and instructed its nuncio in Warsaw to begin secret negotiations with Chancellor Ossoliński, the Orthodox bishops, and the primate of Poland. It even took the unprecedented step of confirming Mohyla's election as metropolitan. Though this project suffered a significant setback with the death of Mohyla in January 1647, Magni, Kysil, and others continued the work.[79] In May of that year Orthodox and Catholic leaders met in Vilnius to discuss their differences, and though their meeting was far from conclusive, they were able to draft a modest statement of accord. Władysław was hopeful that Mohyla's successor, Sylvester Kossów, would in time join the Catholic Church and a permanent union could be instituted.[80] This work came to an abrupt end in 1648. In April the Chmielnicki rebellion broke out in Poland's Orthodox territory, and a month later the king died, leaving the commonwealth in a dangerous interregnum.

Though Magni was the driving force behind Władysław's determined efforts to reconcile the commonwealth's rival confessional factions, the clearest expression of his irenic thought and theology was not with these high-profile campaigns. We must turn instead to a single relationship he developed with a Protestant clergyman, Bartholomäus Nigrin. The long and extended correspondence between the two offers critical insights into the mind of the Capuchin friar. Nigrin was the son of a Lutheran pastor from Silesia.[81] He, however, converted to the Reformed faith and in 1631 became the first Calvinist minister of the St. Peter's church in Danzig. Danzig in this period was the most dynamic city in Poland economically, culturally, and intellectually. The home of Hevelius and Opitz was easily the largest metropolis in the commonwealth. At 50,000 inhabitants in 1600, it was five times bigger than Warsaw and three times the size of Cracow.[82] At the beginning of Władysław's reign this cosmopolitan city of German, Polish, Dutch, and even Scottish inhabitants was the site of important interconfessional discussions. After the withdrawal of Russian troops from Smolensk, the king turned his attention to the Baltic, where he sought to preserve and even expand Poland's power. A stable Danzig, both religiously and politically, was critical for his designs. For that reason he devoted substantial attention to the thriving port as he turned toward Magni for assistance. It was in this context that Magni first met Nigrin. In 1636 a disputation between the city's Protesant and Catholic communities was staged in the home of Gerhard Dönhoff, the king's Pomeranian advisor.[83] Nigrin, who had a reputation as a brilliant debater, was selected to face the experienced Magni. The king was present at these lively proceedings and offered Nigrin a position as his private secretary after the meeting. But even more significantly, this initial interaction between the Capuchin friar and the Calvinist pastor led to a long relationship that would would eventually culminate with Nigrin's public conversion to Catholicism on Easter Day 1643.

Of the many letters exchanged between the two, a lengthy fourteen-page missive sent to Nigrin in April 1640 is arguably the best encapsulation of Magni's irenic theological convictions.[84] Responding to his friend's doubts and questions regarding conversion, Magni began his defense of Catholicism by restating a series of arguments he had first made in the *Iudicium*. Once more, he appealed less to specific doctrines than to reason as he queried, "Do not our *Biblicists* inquire whether Augustine, Luther, the Pope or even a council can err? Men are liable to faulty judgement."[85] By raising the issue of authority and illustrating what he saw as the inherent uncertainty of Protestant theology, he encouraged Nigrin to consider the Catholic alternative. Indeed, the heart of Magni's polemic centered on the problem of authority. As opposed to Lutherans and Calvinists, who judged doctrinal matters individually, Catholics stood on much firmer ground. He confidently stated, "Moreover, you will acknowledge that the visible church, the official convocation of Catholics drawn from the bishops and the people, is not able to err in recognized matters of faith that are of absolute necessity."[86] Elaborating on this point, he referred to Pope Liberius, who in the fourth century nearly capitulated to the demands of Emperor Constantius to sanction Arianism. Though Liberius may have faltered for a moment, the church universal stood firm and in the end condemned this heresy.[87] Magni insisted that the corporate nature of the church was its greatest strength as he adamantly declared, "The private authority of single bishops can never resolve [doctrinal] disputes." Such matters had to be laid before general councils.[88]

Magni's views on the power and authority of the pope were highly controversial within Catholic circles. The Jesuits attacked him mercilessly on this front. From their perspective the Capuchin in his zeal to accommodate the heretics was guilty of denying papal supremacy. Magni in his defense appealed to the Council of Florence.[89] Here, he argued, was an ideal solution to this thorny problem. The theological accord generated in 1439 affirmed that Peter "was given full power to feed, to rule, and to govern the universal Church" while acknowledging that the pontiff's authority must be exercised "in accordance with the acts of the ecumenical councils and holy canons."[90] This neo-conciliarist position reflected Magni's broader understanding of the church. Awkwardly mixing his metaphors, he wrote Nigrin, "We are sheep or wanderers who are led by the Lord. We set sail in the boat of Peter to the harbor of eternal life, but we are buffeted by waves. . . . This ship, however, is not blown about by all winds as it is controlled by the Holy Spirit through the church's doctors and pastors."[91] In tempestuous seas those who wish to be saved do not rashly throw themselves overboard. The ship is their only means of salvation. In times of crisis they turn to God for deliverance. So it is with the church. As Augustine observed, despite the abuses, despite the scandals, despite even the heresies, the church remains the church.[92] This issue was essential for Magni. He argued that Protestant and Orthodox Christians were not heretics in the strict sense of the word. Rather, they were schismatic members of the church. As such, they needed to be reconciled with Rome, not converted to Catholicism.[93]

The distinction Magni drew between conversion and reunion was not merely a matter of semantics. It was reflected most profoundly in his missionary activity. As schismatics, central Europe's Orthodox and Protestant communities should be treated gently and with great respect. He would later argue that if his methods of open debate and dialogue had been followed in this region, many wayward Christians would have been brought back to Rome.[94] The harsher Jesuit tactics of coercion had proved counterproductive as they drove a deep wedge between Catholic and non-Catholic. In contrast, he pointed to Nigrin as his model.[95] Magni believed that the discussions with the Calvinist pastor, which eventually led to his public profession of Catholicism, were an illustration of what could happen on a larger scale. Magni saw Nigrin as a key individual in Władysław's campaign to reunite his confessionally divided kingdom, and there were indications in the months after Nigrin's announcement that many more prominent Protestants would follow his example. Magni clearly believed that the momentum of Nigrin's decision would carry through the *Colloquium charitativum* and ultimately lead to a general reunion of all Christians in the Polish-Lithuanian Commonwealth.[96]

In hindsight Magni's optimism certainly seems naive. Nonetheless, few could have anticipated the speed at which his power and influence disappeared. There was a dramatic change in the religious climate after Władysław's death in 1648, and the once favored advisor shortly found himself an outcast. Increasing tensions with Sweden and the strains of the Chmielnicki rebellion made compromise with the Protestants and Orthodox impossible politically. Magni, who was living in Danzig at the time, became a target of conservative Catholics who distrusted his conciliatory temperament. In summer 1648, Bishop Mikołaj Gniewosz led an offensive to drive him from the city. Critical of the Capuchin's theology and fraternization with Protestants, Gniewosz ordered Magni to leave his diocese immediately or be prosecuted as an unwanted vagabond.[97] Pushed out of Poland, Magni was greeted with a chilly reception in Bohemia. His mild policies toward the region's Protestants had been explicitly repudiated, and in the early 1650s he was roundly attacked by his Czech opponents, who accused him of spreading Jansenism in Prague.[98] Even his greatest triumph in this period, the conversion of Landgrave Ernst von Hessen-Rheinfels, the great-grandson of Martin Luther's famous ally, was surrounded by acrimony and controversy in Catholic circles.[99] During these late years Magni would also become embroiled in a long and bitter polemical feud with the Jesuits. This quarrel ultimately led to a final disgrace in February 1661. In Vienna, under the cover of darkness, an imperial official arrested the friar on charges of heresy and led him away to prison. Six months later Magni was dead.

The life and work of Valerian Magni is certainly important on its own terms. The remarkably broad scope of his career offers the best overview of irenic activity in the German, Czech, and Polish lands of the first half of the seventeenth century. His story, however, is significant in another respect, for it illustrates the twilight of irenicism in central Europe. Though individuals like Leibniz, Zinzendorf, and Francke would be inspired by this ecumenical tradition, the tone and nature of their work would be very different and would lack serious political support. Realistic possibilities for meaningful and broad-based dialogue between Catholics and non-Catholics would be gone by the time of Magni's death in 1661. His career, in fact, serves as an accurate barometer of central Europe's changing confessional atmosphere. He began as a reformer in his own order. After quickly distinguishing himself in this capacity, he became one of Europe's most important Catholic diplomats. At the height of his power he was an advisor to popes, kings, and archbishops. His irenic schemes became the centerpiece of religious policy in Vasa Poland. His reversal of fortune after 1648 was equally dramatic. Driven from Poland, forced out of Bohemia, and imprisoned in Austria, he ended his life a lonely and isolated figure. His ideas concerning confessional reunion were seen as suspect if not dangerous. He was vilified by Catholics and Protestants alike. Comenius wrote a bitter tract against him in connection with the Nigrin affair, while the Jesuits described him as a "toad bloated with poison" and a "wolf in the sheepfold of the church."[100] Evidence even suggests that his Capuchin colleagues, fearful of inquisitorial proceedings, destroyed a number of his manuscripts.[101] His last letters clearly reflect his deep-seated frustrations and express a genuine sense of despair concerning the church's future.[102] After his death Magni was quickly forgotten. In contrast to other moderates who have received significant attention in recent decades, for both nationalistic and confessional reasons the Capuchin remains virtually unknown today despite his contributions that made him one of the most important churchmen of the early seventeenth century.[103]

If on the one hand, Valerian Magni represents the end of an era of interconfessional dialogue, his writings are also an early indication of important changes that would be occurring theologically and philosophically. His apologetic points to a new and significant way of resolving confessional differences. As we have already noted, one of the most distinctive features of his work was its lack of attention to theological detail. In his debates before Ernst von Hessen-Rheinfels, Magni was very reluctant to discuss the finer points of

Catholic doctrine with his Protestant interlocutors. He followed instead the spirit of the *Iudicium* as he appealed to reason and logic in his attempt to win over the Lutheran prince.[104] A seventeenth-century biography of the Capuchin explicitly stated that his defense of Catholicism was based primarily on reason.[105] Echoing this assessment, the Dutch Calvinist Gijsbertus Voetius in his treatise *De ratione humana in rebus fidei* (1636) referred to "the books of the papist Valerius (sic) Magnus on the rule of believing for non-catholics: in which the view of the Papists and our own view about the arbiter in matters of dispute are rejected and *natural human reason is set up as the judge and norm of faith.*"[106] With Magni, then, an older model of conciliation based upon a theological search for Christian unity was slowly transformed into a less dogmatic, more rational, and broader philosophical quest for religious harmony. It was Magni's ironic fate that though marginalized by both the Protestant and Catholic communities while theology itself was losing its preeminent status among the academic disciplines, his ideas found new life in the rationalism of Christian Wolff and Gottfried Wilhelm Leibniz.[107]

NOTES

1. Typical in this regard is G. H. M. Posthumus Meyjes, "Protestant Irenicism in the Sixteenth and Seventeenth Centuries," in D. Loades, ed., *The End of Strife* (Edinburgh: Clark, 1984), 77–93.

2. On Pareus see Howard Hotson, "Irenicism and Dogmatics in the Confessional Age: Pareus and Comenius in Heidelberg, 1614," *Journal of Ecclesiastical History* 46 (1995): 432–56. For Calixt see Christoph Böttigheimer, *Zwischen Polemik und Irenik: Die Theologie der einen Kirche bei Georg Calixt* (Studien zur systematischen Theologie und Ethik, 7; Münster: LIT, 1996); Johannes Wallmann, "Zwischen Reformation und Humanismus: Eigenart und Wirkungen Helmstedter Theologie unter besonderer Berücksichtung Georg Calixts," *Zeitschrift für Theologie und Kirche* 74 (1977): 344–70. The literature on Grotius and Comenius is of course extensive. Useful in this context is H. J. M. Nellen and E. Rabbie, eds., *Hugo Grotius Theologian* (Leiden: Brill, 1994). For Comenius one should begin with Milada Blekastad's magisterial biography, *Comenius* (Oslo: Universitetsforlaget, 1969).

3. For a general overview of the defenestration of Prague and the beginning of the Thirty Years' War see Geoffrey Parker, ed., *The Thirty Years' War*, 2d ed. (New York: Routledge, 1997).

4. The standard study of Magni is the biography by G. Abgottspon, *P. Valerianus Magni, Kapuziner* (Olten: Otto Walter, 1939). More recent is Stanislav Sousedík's monograph on Magni's philosophy, *Valerianus Magni 1586–1661: Versuch einer*

Erneuerung der christlichen Philosophie im 17. Jahrhundert (Sankt Augustin: Verlag Hans Richarz, 1982). The most useful tool on Magni is the bibliography by the Polish Capuchin Jerzy Cygan, *Valerianus Magni (1586–1661): 'Vita prima', operum recensio et bibliographia* (Rome: Institutum Historicum Capuccinum, 1989), 287–438. The first part of this text is the earliest biography of Magni, the *Vita prima*, which was compiled in 1662–1664 by two of Magni's Capuchin colleagues, Nicolaus Barsotti de Luca and Ludovicus de Salice.

5. For Magni's voluminous bibliography see Cygan, *Valerianus Magni (1586–1661): 'Vita prima', operum recensio et bibliographia,* 287–339.

6. Pascal, *The Provincial Letters*, trans. A. J. Krailsheimer (Baltimore: Penguin Books, 1967), Letter 15 (25 November 1656), 233–36. P. Ubald d'Alençon, "Les relations franciscaines de Blaise Pascal," *Études Franciscaines* 47 (1935): 72–85, esp. 73–79. Concerning the impact of his problems with the Jesuits and the papacy on his literary legacy see Hugo Bloth, "Der Kapuziner Valerian Magni und sein Kampf gegen den Jesuitenorden," *Materialdienst des Konfessionskundlichen Instituts* 7 (1956): 86.

7. The best synopsis of Magni's astronomical interests is Jerzy Cygan, "Das Verhältnis Valerian Magnis zu Galileo Galilei und seinen wissenschaftlichen Ansichten," *Collectanea Franciscana* 38 (1968): 135–66. On Magni's efforts to create a vacuum see Miecysław Subotowicz, "Najwcześniejsza drukiem wydana rozprawa o dowodzie istniena próżni [The earliest printed report concerning the demonstration of the existence of a vacuum]," *Kwartalnik Historii Nauki i Techniki* 4 (1959): 35–76.

8. A. Boehm, "L'Augustinisme de Valerien Magni," *Revue des sciences religieuses* 39 (1965): 230–65. Blekastad's *Comenius* devotes considerable attention to the interaction of Comenius and Magni. See especially 340–46 and 363. Also useful is Pavel Floss, "Komparace gnoseologických nazorů Valeriána Magniho a Komenského [A 'gnoseological' comparison of the views of Valerian Magni and Comenius]," *Studia Comeniana et Historica* 4 (1979): 39–45.

9. Blekastad, *Comenius*, 164–67, 471.

10. *Vita prima*, 71–72. More generally see Zofia Trawicja, "Projekt kalwińskiego małżeństwa Władysława IV [The Calvinist Marriage Project of Władysław]," *Odrodzenie i Reformacja w Polsce* 11 (1966): 93–100.

11. Ambroise Jobert, *De Luther à Mohila: La Pologne dans la crise de la Chrétienté 1517–1648* (Paris: Institut d'Études Slaves, 1974), 377.

12. See both Magni's letter to Maximilian and his broader proposal, *Ripiego per la pace dell'Imperio* (October 1629), Munich, Bavarian State Archives, Kasten schwarz 13 495, 160r–v, 162r–v. My thanks to James Mixson for providing a copy of this text.

13. For a summary of the theologians' conference see Robert Bireley, *Religion and Politics in the Age of the Counterreformation* (Chapel Hill: University of North Carolina Press, 1981), 215–19.

14. L. F. Miskovsky, "The Catholic Counter-Reformation in Bohemia," *Bibliotheca sacra* 57 (1900): 550.

15. See Magni's letter to Harrach dated 14 March 1626. Vienna, Allgemeines Verwaltungsarchiv, Gräflich von Harrach'sches Familienarchiv, fasc. 145, 33r–v. Magni's early biographers observed that "Magni's teaching, prudence and virtue were well known" by young Harrach; *Vita prima*, 50. In 1628 Magni was released from his administrative obligations as Capuchin superior to assist Harrach more closely. See the decree of the Propaganda in *Bullarium Ordinis FF. Minorum S.P. Francisci Capuccinorum* (Rome: Johannes Zempel, 1746), 4:182.

16. Valerian Magni, *De acatholicorum credendi regula iudicium* (Prague: Paulus Sessius, 1628), 1.

17. Ibid., 3.

18. Ibid., 4.

19. Ibid., 13–15.

20. Ibid., 27.

21. Ibid., 44.

22. Blekastad, *Comenius*, 191.

23. Magni, *Iudicium*, 55.

24. Ibid., 35.

25. See Magni's 1625 *Tractatus de recta ratione administrandae regularis reipublicae fratrum minorum nuncupatorum capuccinorum*, in Costanzo Cargnoni, ed., *I frati cappuccini: Documenti e testimonianze del primo secolo*, (Perugia: Edizioni Frate Indovino, 1988), 1983–2025. Also useful is the commentary of Jerzy Cygan, "Valeriani Magni propositum ad ordinem capuccinum reformandum (1625)," *Collectanea Franciscana* 58 (1988): 45–59.

26. Josef Hemmerle, "Die Prager Universität in der neueren Zeit," in Ferdinand Seibt, ed., *Sacra Bohemia* (Düsseldorf: Pädagogischer Verlag Schwann, 1974), 416.

27. For an overview of these complicated developments see I. Rakova, "Cesta k vzniku Karlo-Ferdinandovy Univerzity—Spory o pražské vysoké učení v l. 1622–54 [The road to the origin of *Universitas Carolo-Ferdinandea*—The fight over the university in Prague 1622–54]," *Acta Universitatis Carolinae—Historia Universitas Carolinae Pragensis* 24 (1984): 7–39. Also useful is the older article of Käthe Spiegel, "Die Prager Universitätsunion (1618–54)," *Mitteilungen des Vereins für Geschichte der Deutschen in Böhmen* 62 (1924): 5–94. Robert Bireley offers a brief summary in *Religion and Politics*, 33–36.

28. Blekastad, *Comenius*, 116.

29. Spiegel, "Die Prager Universitätsunion," 29.

30. *Libellus supplex apologeticus F. Valeriani Magni Capuccini ad Caesarem . . .*, Státní Ústřední Archiv (Central State Archives of the Czech Republic), IS IId. 422, Clem. 20/4, 17v. Related to this memorandum is an important letter Magni wrote to Mikołaj Łęczycki outlining many similar concerns he had in this affair. See letter dated 24 May 1637, IS IId. 422, Clem. 20/4, 14r–15v.

31. *Libellus supplex apologeticus F. Valeriani Magni Capuccini ad Caesarem . . .*, 19r.

32. Hemmerle, "Die Prager Universität," 416.

33. R. J. W. Evans, *The Making of the Habsburg Monarchy 1550–1700* (Oxford: Clarendon Press, 1979), 319.

34. See in particular Magni's tract *De atheismo Aristotelis* in his broader compendium *Principia et specimen philosophiae*, (Cologne: Apud Jodocum Kalcovium, 1652), 121–29. Best on Magni's relation to Arriaga is Sousedík, *Valerianus Magni*, 84–85. Magni's critique of Aristotle had arguably an even greater impact in Poland. On this matter see Jerzy Ochman, *Polemiki Waleriana Magniego (1586–1661)* [The Polemic of Valerian Magni (1586–1661)] (Cracow: Nakładem Uniwersytetu Jagiellońskiego, 1978) and Franciszek Gabryl, "O Waleryan Magni Kapucyn (1586–1661). Anti-Arystotelik w XVII wieku [The Capuchin Valerian Magni (1586–1661). Anti-Aristotelianism in the seventeenth century]," *Archiwum Komisji do Badania Historii Filozofii w Polsce* 1 (1915): 133–68.

35. Valerian Magni, *Admiranda de vacuo et Aristotelis philosophia, Valeriani Magni Demonstratio ocularis de possibilitate vacui* (Warsaw: Petrus Elert, 1647). Though there is some controversy surrounding Magni's work in this area, his text was the first printed account of a barometric experiment.

36. Cited in Paul Richard Blum, *Philosophenphilosophie und Schulphilosophie* (Stuttgart: Franz Steiner, 1998), 113. Blum offers the most recent synopsis of Magni's philosophy. See 102–16.

37. Hemmerle, "Die Prager Universität," 417.

38. On Marci see the recent collection of articles, Ivana Čornejová ed., *Jan Marek Marci 1595–1667: Život, dílo, doba* [Jan Marek Marci 1595–1667: Life, work and times] (Lanškroun: Nakl. Rosa), 1995.

39. The best overview of Magni's involvement with the Piarists is Jerzy Cygan, "Der Anteil Valerian Magnis an der Verteidigung des Piaristenordens," *Collectanae Franciscana* 38 (1968): 364–72. Ironically, this Piarist school on Francesco Magni's estate in Strážnice was built on the ruins of an older school of the Bohemian Brethren attended by John Comenius.

40. Paul Grendler, "The Piarists of the Pious Schools," in Richard DeMolen, ed., *Religious Orders of the Catholic Reformation* (New York: Fordham University Press, 1994), 266.

41. Cygan, "Der Anteil Valerian Magnis," 371.

42. There have been more recent surveys in other western European languages. The most accessible study is Ambroise Jobert, *De Luther à Mohila: La Pologne dans la crise de la chrétienté 1517–1648*. See fn. 11. For a useful overview of this literature see Paul Knoll's entry on "Poland" in Hans Hillerbrand, ed., *The Oxford Encyclopedia of the Reformation* (New York: Oxford University Press, 1996), 3:283–88. For a recent English overview of this period see Daniel Stone, *The Polish-Lithuanian State, 1386–1795* (Seattle: University of Washington Press, 2001).

43. See Janusz Tazbir, *Reformacja w Polsce* [Reformation in Poland] (Warsaw: Książka i Wiedza, 1993), and more recently Tazbir's *Reformacja, kontrreformacja, tol-*

erancja [Reformation, Counter-Reformation and Tolerance] (Wrocław: Wydawnictwo Dolnośląskie, 1997).

44. See Zbigniew Ogonowski's comments in "Faustus Socinus," in Jill Raitt, ed., *Shapers of Religious Traditions in Germany, Switzerland, and Poland, 1560–1600* (New Haven: Yale University Press, 1981), 208, 209. Also relevant is E. M. Wilbur, *A History of Unitarianism* (Cambridge: Harvard University Press, 1945). On Williams turn first to his mammoth *The Radical Reformation* (Philadelphia: Westminster Press, 1962), esp. 639–69, 685–707, 733–63. Also see the two-volume series he edited of primary material, *The Polish Brethren* (Harvard Theological Studies 20, Missoula, Mont., 1980).

45. Janusz Tazbir, *A State without Stakes: Polish Religious Toleration in the Sixteenth and Seventeenth Centuries*, trans. A. T. Jordan (New York: Twayne, 1973), 193.

46. Especially relevant here is Tazbir's "Katoliccy zwolennicy tolerancji [Catholic supporters of toleration]," in his *Dzieje polskiej tolerancji* [History of Polish Toleration] (Warsaw: Wydawnictwo Interpress, 1973), esp. 97, 98.

47. On this point see the comments of Howard Hotson, 257–67.

48. See the classic but very dated treatment of Joseph Lecler in his *Toleration and the Reformation* (New York: Association Press, 1955), 1:385–423. Lecler actually concludes his discussion with Sigismund III, whom he sees standing at the end of Poland's golden age of religious toleration. More recent is Michael Müller's article, "Protestant Confessionalisation in the Towns of Royal Prussia and the Practice of Religious Toleration in Poland-Lithuania," in Ole Peter Grell and Bob Scribner, eds., *Tolerance and Intolerance in the European Reformation* (Cambridge: Cambridge University Press, 1996), 262–81.

49. Władysław's court is essentially ignored in Tazbir's *A State without Stakes*. The standard study on Władysław is Władysław Czapliński, *Władysław IV i jego czasy* [Władysław IV and his times] (Warsaw: Wiedza Powszechna, 1976). Czapliński devotes relatively little attention to religion in this standard biographical account. More promising is the very brief mention of Władysław's circle in the recent overview of Jerzy Kloczowski, *A History of Polish Christianity* (Cambridge: Cambridge University Press, 2000), 123. Unfortunately, Kloczowski devotes little more than a few sentences to the king and his court. For a more specialized examination of confessional issues see Jan Dzięgielewski, *O tolerancję dla zdominowanych* [Toleration for the Governed] (Warsaw: Państwowe wydawnictwo naukowe, 1986).

50. For a description of Władysław's *Kunstkammer* see the catalog *Land of the Winged Horsemen: Art in Poland 1572–1764* (Alexandria, Va.: Art Services International, 1999), 108, 109. Also useful on the connection between the two princes is Howard Louthan, "Coming to Terms with the Habsburg Legacy: A Recent Overview of Rudolfine Literature," *Acta Comeniana* 13 (1999): 172–73.

51. R. J. W. Evans offers the best overview here in *Rudolf II and His World*, 2d ed. (London: Thames and Hudson, 1997).

52. Jerzy Cygan, "I tentativi di Sigismondo III Wasa per l'introduzione dell'ordine dei Cappuccini in Polonia (1617–1627)," *Collectanea Franciscana* 56 (1986): 304–5.

53. Blekastad, *Comenius*, 209. Władysław would repeatedly petition the pope to appoint Magni a cardinal. See in particular his 1636 letter to Urban VIII, a clear testament to the close relationship that had developed between the two. *Bullarium*, 4:193–94.

54. Władysław Czapliński, *Na dworze króla Władysława IV* [At the Court of Władysław IV] (Warsaw: Książka i Wiedza, 1959), 456.

55. Jobert, *De Luther à Mohila*, 386. For background and a general overview of this period see Kai Eduard Jordt Jørgensen, *Ökumenische Bestrebungen unter den polnischen Protestanten bis zum Jahre 1645* (Copenhagen: Arnold Busck, 1942).

56. The most recent and most thorough treatment of the preparations for this conference at Toruń is Edmund Piszcz, *Colloquium Charitativum w Toruniu A.D. 1645: Geneza i przebieg* [The Colloquium Charitativum in Toruń: Its Origins and Course] (Toruń: Wydawnictwo Konserwatora Diecezjalnego, 1995), 78–110.

57. Blekastad, *Comenius*, 399.

58. Jobert, *De Luther à Mohila*, 390.

59. There is a complete list of official participants in Piszcz, *Colloquium Charitativum w Toruniu A.D. 1645*, 210–213. On Bergius see Bodo Nischan, "John Bergius: Irenicism and the Beginning of Official Religious Toleration in Brandenburg-Prussia," *Church History* 51 (1982): 389–404. The Toruń colloquy was the inspiration of one of Comenius's most important irenic texts, *Christianismus reconciliabilis reconcilatore Christo*. This manuscript, which was dedicated to Władysław, disappeared in the late seventeenth century.

60. Böttigheimer, *Zwischen Polemik und Irenik*, 53–57.

61. *Acta Conventus Thoruniensis* (Warsaw: Petrus Elert, 1646), A2.

62. Piszcz, *Colloquium Charitativum w Toruniu A.D. 1645*, 121–23. For Botsack's polemic against Magni see his *Antivalerianus* (Leipzig: Johannes-Albertus Minzelius, 1631).

63. Blekastad, *Comenius*, 406.

64. Cited in Jobert, *De Luther à Mohila*, 393.

65. On attempts to bring Orthodox and Uniates together in the 1630s see Serhii Plokhii, *Papstvo i Ukraina* (Kiev: Golovnoe izd-vo izdatel'skogo ob'edineniia "Vyshcha shkola," 1989), 139–58; Mykola Andrusiak, "Sprawa patriarchatu kijowskiego," *Prace historyczne w 30–lecie działalności profesorskiej Stanisława Zakrewskiego* (L'viv, 1934), 269–85; A. Wojtyła, "De tentaminibus novae Unionis Universalis in Polonia-Lithuani anno 1636 factis," *Orientalia Christiana Periodica* 18 (1952): 158–97.

66. For Kysil see Frank Sysyn, *Between Poland and the Ukraine: The Dilemma of Adam Kysil, 1600–1653* (Cambridge, Mass.: Harvard University Press, 1985).

67. Dzięgielewski, *O tolerancję*, 67–69.

68. Jobert, *De Luther à Mohila*, 381.

69. Magni to Cardinal Barberini, 26 February 1633. Reprinted in E. Šmurlo, *Le Saint-Siège et l'Orient orthodoxe russe 1609–1654* (Prague: Orbis, 1928), 2:99.

70. Cygan, "Valerian Magni und die Frage der Verständigung mit der orthodoxen Kirche unter Ladislas IV. Wasa in den Jahren 1633/34," *Collectanea Franciscana* 51 (1984): 364, 365.

71. Magni to Cardinal Barberini, 26 February 1633. Reprinted in Šmurlo, *Le Saint-Siège*, 2:99.

72. Most recently in English on Mohyla is the 1984 edition of *Harvard Ukrainian Studies* (VIII, nos. 1–2), celebrating the 350th anniversary of his academy in Kiev. See in particular Ihor Ševčenko, "The Many Worlds of Peter Mohyla," 9–40; Frank Sysyn, "Peter Mohyla and the Kiev Academy in Recent Western Works: Divergent Views on Seventeenth-Century Ukrainian Culture," 155–87.

73. *Sententia cuiusdam nobilis Poloni Graecae religionis*, reprinted in Atanasio Gregorio Welykyj, "Un progetto anonimo di Pietro Mohyla sull'unione delle chiese nell'anno 1645," in *Studi e Testi*, vol. 233, *Mélanges Eugène Tisserant* (Vatican City: Biblioteca apostolica vaticana, 1964), 3:467.

74. Valerian Magni to the Cardinal Prefect of the Congregation for the Propagation of the Faith, 28 January 1645, reprinted in Šmurlo, *Le Saint-Siège*, 2:156. On the unification project of 1645 see Arkadii Zhukovs'kyi, *Petro Mohyla i pytannia iednosty tserkov* (Kiev: Mystetstvo, 1997), 131–52.

75. *Sententia cuiusdam nobilis Poloni Graecae religionis*, 467.

76. Ibid., 471.

77. Ibid., 470.

78. Ibid., 472.

79. See in particular Magni's 1647 letter to Francesco Ingoli, secretary of the Propaganda. Magni to Ingoli, 8 June 1647, reprinted in Šmurlo, *Le Saint-Siège*, 2:171–72.

80. Jobert, *De Luther à Mohila*, 397, 398.

81. For a short biographical sketch of Nigrin see Jerzy Cygan, "Bartołomiej Nigrin (ok. 1595–1646): działalność ekumeniczna [Bartholomäus Nigrin (ca. 1595–1646): ecumenical activity]," *Archiwum Historii Filozofii i Myśli Społecznej* 38 (1993): 79–88.

82. For a brief introduction to the importance of Danzig economically and culturally in this period see Maria Bogucka, "Gdańsk—Polski czy międzynarodowy ośrodek gospodarczy? [Danzig—Polish or international economic center?]," in Andrzej Wyczański, ed., *Polska w epoce odrodzenia* [Poland in the Renaissance Era] (Warsaw: Wiedza Powszechna, 1986), 199–222. Peter Bietenholz offers an English overview of the theological and intellectual currents of the city during this period through the lens of Daniel Zwicker. See his *Daniel Zwicker 1612–1678: Peace, Tolerance and God the One and Only* (Florence: Olschki, 1997), 1–28.

83. Blekastad, *Comenius*, 238, 239.

84. Magni to Nigrin, 26 April 1640, Prague, Státní Ústřední Archiv, APA D151 Kart. 2734, 26r–32v.

85. Ibid., 28r.

86. Ibid., 26r.

87. Ibid., 26r.

88. Ibid., 29v. Magni continued his argument by briefly describing the seven ecumenical councils of the church and the doctrinal matters they resolved.

89. Bloth, "Der Kapuziner Valerian Magni," 84, 85. Magni frequently pointed to the Council of Florence as a model interconfessional settlement. See for example his *Apologia Valeriani Magni contra imposturas Jesuitarum* (Vienna, 1658), 95, 96. Also note Magni's reference to Florence in Peter Haberkorn's *Wahrhaffte und auffrichtige Erzehlung der jenigen Handlungen* . . . (Giessen: Joseph Dietrich Hampeln, 1652), 65, 66.

90. John Meyendorff, *Byzantine Theology* (New York: Fordham University Press, 1974), 111.

91. Magni to Nigrin, 26 April 1640, 311−v.

92. Ibid., 32r.

93. Magni later wrote to Nigrin, "Before the pope and his court I will defend my belief that Protestants are not heretics in the strict sense of the word, for they derive their view from Scripture, from the councils, and from the fathers." Cited in Amedeo Molnár and Noemi Rejchrtová, eds., *Jan Amos Komensky: O sobě* [John Amos Comenius: On Himself] (Prague: Odeon, 1987), 175, 176. This is an argument that Zdeněk David has observed was made also with regards to the Utraquist church.

94. Magni, *Apologia*, 116, 117.

95. See Magni's 1641 letter to Francesco Ingoli; reprinted in Jerzy Cygan, "Zum Übertritt des Kalviner Pastors Bartholomäus Nigrin zur Katholischen Kirche (1636−1643). Ein Beitrag zur Geschichte des Ökumenismus in Polen," *Collectanea Franciscana* 40 (1970): 112−14. Also see Magni's comments in his *Apologia*, 116.

96. Magni, *Apologia*, 116−20.

97. Sousedík, *Valerianus Magni*, 54, 55. For Gniewosz's scathing indictment of Magni see his June 1648 letter to Poland's papal nuncio, Giovanni de Torres. Reprinted in Cygan, "Das Verhältnis Valerian Magnis zu Galileo Galilei," 149.

98. A. Rezek, "Tak zvaná 'Idea gubernationis ecclesiasticae' z času kardinála Harracha [The so-called 'Idea gubernationis ecclesiasticae' from the time of Cardinal Harrach]," *Věstník Královské České Společnosti Nauk* 22 (1893): 1−7.

99. For Magni's own account of Ernst's conversion see *Bullarium* 4:196−98. For the broader context see Manfred Finke, "Toleranz und 'Discrete' Frömmigkeit nach 1650: Pfalzgraf Christian August von Sulzbach und Ernst von Hessen-Rheinfels," in Dieter Breuer, ed., *Frömmigkeit in der frühen Neuzeit. Studien zur religiösen Literatur des 17. Jahrhunderts in Deutschland* (Amsterdam: Rodopi, 1984), 193−212.

100. Bloth, "Der Kapuziner Valerian Magni," 85. For Comenius's critique of Magni see *Judicium de Judicio Valeriani Magni* (Amsterdam, 1644). One of the most severe Protestant attacks on Magni was the anonymous tract *Vertrauliches Gespräch zwischen vier päpstischen Scribenten* (Leipzig: Johannes Bauer, 1653). For a critique from the

Catholic side see the pamphlet of the Jesuit Johannes Rosenthal, *Außführliche Wider-hol und Vermehrung der kürtzen Bedencken vom beständigen Baw auff den Felsen und nicht auff den Sand* (Cologne: Hermann Mylius, 1653).

    101. Eduard Winter, "Die Macht des Geistes gegen die Macht der Gewalt," in Winter, *Ketzerschicksale* (Berlin: Union Verlag, 1983), 141.

    102. See Magni's two letters dated June 28, 1660, and April 15, 1661. Vienna, Allgemeines Verwaltungsarchiv, Gräflich von Harrach'sches Familienarchiv, fasc. 145r–v, 182r, 184r.

    103. See our comments in the introduction to this volume, 8–9.

    104. Illustrative here is Magni's obvious hesitancy to enter into a debate with the Lutheran theologian Peter Haberkorn concerning Eucharistic theology. See Haberkorn, *Wahrhaffte und auffrichtige Erzehlung,* 157, 158.

    105. *Vita prima,* 117.

    106. Cited in Klaus Scholder, *The Birth of Modern Critical Theology* (Philadelphia: Trinity Press International, 1990), 22. Italics are my own.

    107. On Wolff's debt to Magni see for example his *Psychologia Empirica* (Frankfurt: Renger, 1738), 42. Among the many references Leibniz made to Magni see his *Philosophische Schriften* (Berlin: Akademie-Verlag, 1971), 1:494, 547. For a broader assessment of Magni's philosophical contributions, including his relation to Leibniz, see Sousedík, *Valerianus Magni,* 57, 132–40.

II

Irenicism in the Confessional Age

The Holy Roman Empire, 1563–1648

HOWARD HOTSON

Irenicism from Trent to Westphalia: Historiographical Overview

As German history moves through the middle of the sixteenth century, it passes over two closely related watersheds, one historical, the other historiographical. At the death of Luther in 1546, the greatest individual protagonist of the Reformation era leaves the stage and the interest of historians of Protestant theology, already on the wane, typically dwindles rapidly. With the dramatic reversals of the emperor Charles V and the conclusion of peace in Augsburg in 1555, Luther's heirs win a legal right to exist in the empire which will prove permanent; the greatest drama of the Reformation era comes to an end, and the interest of secular historians traditionally also wastes away. Finally, with the long-delayed conclusion of the Council of Trent in 1563, the greatest institutional protagonist of the struggle has redefined itself with such unshakable authority that it can never substantially alter its position without surrendering its claim to infallibility, and the possibility of any complete reconciliation of the great schism between Catholics and Protestants seems eternally foreclosed. History, of course, is endless, and we know that Germany gradually descends into a seemingly endless and endlessly complicated war. But scholars' time and patience are finite, and with the great struggle of the Reformation basically resolved, the attention of theologians and historians traditionally leaps to other themes, eras, or areas to find equally compelling material for study. Such has been the consequent neglect of the post-Reformation period in Germany that we have, until relatively recently, not even known what to call it, although we all know its dates: 1555 to 1648.

Interest in this period has recently revived, and considerable progress has been made in characterizing it and charting its course. This interest was initially stimulated by the most important confessional innovation introduced in the years after the Peace of Augsburg: the introduction of Calvinism into the empire, signalled by the conversion of the elector Palatine, Frederick III, in December 1559 and the publication of the Heidelberg Catechism in 1563, only a few months before the conclusion of the Council of Trent. From there a second wave of research has spread to the other two main confessions in Germany and is now appearing outside Germany as well. At the center of this new perspective is the concept of "confessionalization," which sees the division of Germany into three distinct and often mutually hostile confessions as the central process of the period, which brings many of the other political, social, cultural, and intellectual processes in its train.[1]

Viewed from the perspective of the history of ecclesiastical reconciliation, this periodization might seem at first sight problematic, for one of the few things widely known about the intellectual history of central Europe in the seventeenth century is its long and distinguished tradition of ecclesiastical irenicism. Though overshadowed by the canonical figures of the Reformation era, the leaders of this tradition include some of the central intellectuals of the age, whose importance often transcends the ecclesiastical history of Germany and relates them to the intellectual history of northern, Protestant Europe more generally. They include the leading theologian at the Reformed citadel of Heidelberg before the war, David Pareus (1548–1622), his student, the great Moravian pedagogue and pansophist Jan Amos Comenius (1592–1670), Comenius's close collaborator, the indefatigable Scottish irenicist John Dury (1596–1680), and perhaps the most remarkable Lutheran theologian of the period, Georg Calixt (1586–1656) of Helmstedt.

The presence of these leading irenicists in the midst of a landscape supposedly dominated by confessionalization raises three related sets of important questions. What, in the first place, is the relationship of these figures to the previous tradition of ecclesiastical reconciliation of the Reformation era itself? Are they merely a continuation of earlier efforts or a new phenomenon characteristic of a different period? How, secondly, do they relate to their own age? Are they rare and isolated individuals, however distinguished, or the figureheads of larger and well-established groups? Are they anomalies within this so-called confessional age or are they characteristic of it? Do they undermine the paradigm of confessionalization or somehow reinforce it? And how, finally (and more tangentially for present purposes), do they relate to the postwar efforts at ecclesiastical reconciliation, such as those which so absorbed the greatest German philosophical mind of the latter seventeenth century, Gottfried Wilhelm Leibniz (1646–1716)? Do their most characteristic efforts gradually dissipate with the Peace of Westphalia, or do they flow seamlessly into those of the younger generation and thence to the age of Pietism and Enlightenment?

The existing synoptic literature, and particularly that in English, is of little use in answering these questions precisely because it tends to assume a substantial degree of continuity with the past or with the future. This tendency is an inevitable by-product of the general historiographical neglect of the period: figures encountered in the unfamiliar context of late sixteenth to mid-seventeenth-century Germany are naturally defined in terms of the more familiar intellectual landscape of earlier or later periods or neighboring areas.[2] The result is a plethora of conflicting interpretations. Read through the familiar terminological matrix of the sixteenth century, the irenicists of the following period are inevitably characterized by reference to an amorphous Erasmianism, a moderate, undogmatic, learned humanism still operating between the growing monoliths of Protestantism and Catholicism. Observed from the more exotic prospect of turn-of-the-century Prague, it is tempting to see them as mannerist figures, even hermeticists, struggling to preserve intellectual, spiritual, and political unities in the face of growing confessional divisions. Viewed from an insular standpoint, it is common to mistake John Dury—a Scottish Presbyterian raised in Holland, converted to irenicism by Swedes in Poland, and devoting his life to the solution of a peculiarly German problem—for a transplanted advocate of the Anglican *via media*. Judged from the age of Leibniz, the irenicists are transformed into antecedents of the early Enlightenment, forerunners of the precursors of the *philosophes*. Still more difficult to resist is the temptation to introduce them into general surveys of that favorite liberal narrative: the rise of toleration. Most common of all is the urge to salute them as ancestors of the ecumenical movements of the nineteenth and twentieth centuries: in general surveys they are often treated as minor examples of an age-old ecumenical tradition;[3] in more specialised literature they are often celebrated as heroic exemplars of the struggle for ecclesiastical reunion.[4] What all these perspectives have in common is a tendency to take the irenicists' writings at face value, to view them in the most sympathetic light, to lump them into a small number of pre-established categories, to judge them primarily with reference to analogous movements at one or more removes from them, and to position them on a thin but important line of liberal thought linking the Renaissance with the Enlightenment. What all of these approaches lack is an analysis based firmly in the times and places in which these individuals wrote and acted. Even without contesting these characterizations in detail, the very multitude of imported and anachronistic categories competing to describe these individuals establishes the acute need for a fresh reassessment. No less unsatisfying is the juxtaposition in the tiny body of English historical literature on German Calvinism of this broadminded, Erasmian tradition of religious irenicism with a characterization of Calvinist religious policy in the empire as reckless, aggressive, and radical.[5]

In order to approach the topic afresh, with limited reliance on existing surveys, the first task is bibliographical, namely, to assemble as large as possible a sample of irenical literature from this period. Even in the course of doing so, a first conclusion becomes unmistakably obvious: irenicism is not a dead issue in the later sixteenth century, in the early, mid-, or late seventeenth century. On the contrary, it is the subject of great debates, enormous efforts, and a substantial body of literature; and the handful of figures celebrated in more general literature are just the tip of an iceberg. The first main attempt to compile a bibliography of irenical literature—published by Johann Christoph Koecher in 1764—provides a wealth of references, including several to still-earlier histories of the tradition.[6] Further searching under a variety of headings in the great seventeenth-century topical bibliographies of Draudius and Lipenius doubles this number again.[7] Research in the paradigmatic contemporary library in Germany, the Herzog August Bibliothek in Wolfenbüttel, rounds out the collection, since debates of the kind characteristic of this literature are often found bound together in *Sammelbände*. Very little of the literature encountered in this way has been studied in any depth, with the appropriate balance of sympathy and critical detachment, or with an awareness of both content and context. Very little of it, indeed, is even listed in more recently published bibliographies of irenical literature in the period.[8] Nowhere has anything like a full conspectus of the irenical literature of the confessional period been assembled in one place. A first attempt to do so can obviously make no claim to completeness, still less can it hope to study this huge collection of literature in any detail. But it can demonstrate the sheer volume of this literature, establish some of its main categories, and begin to explain the general shape of the irenical traditions of this neglected period. The task is made more manageable by the fact that three of the most fundamental characteristics of the tradition are readily apparent once a critical mass of data is in hand.

Pre-war Irenicism: An Asymmetrical Debate

The first of these observations is that the nature of the irenical discussions has shifted. The emphasis in the first half of the sixteenth century had been on the search for a means of *preserving* a unity inherited from the past that was in increasingly radical danger of being lost. The provisional recognition of the two main confessions in the empire in 1555 and their definitive doctrinal self-definitions in the 1560s and 1570s undermined these hopes. What replaced them was rather the search for means of *restoring* a unity that the church had once enjoyed, which it clearly should enjoy, but which it was manifestly not presently enjoying. The latter sixteenth century therefore sees a shift in the process from conciliation to reconciliation. At the same time, the goal of this process very often retreats from full reunion to mere ecclesiastical pacification, from a harmonization of liturgy and doctrine to a mere cessation of theological hostilities. The most appropriate term to describe the conciliatory activity of this period is therefore "irenicism": a term which acknowledges the state of ongoing theological warfare and the basic goal of achieving a confessional cease-fire, whether as a first step toward full reconciliation, as a precondition of enduring political alliance, or even as an end in itself.

More fundamental still is a second change: of the great mass of irenical pamphlets, disputations, and massive treatises published in the empire in the late sixteenth and early seventeenth century, very little is dedicated to the reunion of Catholics and Protestants. Existing literature is virtually silent on Catholic efforts at reconciliation within the empire after Cassander. Draudius and Lipenius produce a mere handful of promising titles, and further inquiry suggests that most of these are misleading.[9] While conciliatory tendencies continued in some court circles, theological literature devoted to negotiating an end to the schism is extremely rare by the last decades of the sixteenth century. With the successful conclusion of Trent after so many delays and the success of the Catholic Reformation in central Europe, it would appear, the Roman church had finally seized the initiative and was in no mood to pursue compromise. Nor, for that matter, is there any more literature of this sort from mainstream Protestants in the late sixteenth and early seventeenth centuries.[10]

The overwhelming emphasis of German irenical literature in the confessional period, therefore, is on inter-Protestant reconciliation, that is, on the reconciliation (or, failing that, pacification) of Lutherans with Calvinists, Evangelicals with Reformed. And here a third striking feature of the confessional situation is immediately apparent: the irenical debates of the period are radically asymmetrical. Irenical initiatives stem almost entirely from the Reformed side. In the last three decades of the sixteenth century and the first three of the seventeenth, irenical treatises were published in every major Reformed academic center within the empire, culminating in a flood of literature between 1614 and 1626. Lutheran responses to these advances were equally voluminous and widespread, but virtually unanimous in rejecting the irenical advances of the Reformed.[11] A brief review of this asymmetrical debate will establish both the extent of the irenical literature of the period and its almost exclusively Reformed origin.

The three greatest contributions to this literature were made by the three largest states to convert to the Reformed cause in this period: the Palatinate, Hesse-Kassel, and Brandenburg. The Palatinate launched the tradition immediately after the publication of the Heidelberg Catechism and led it for half a century thereafter.[12] In 1564 an attempt was made to unite the churches of the Palatinate and Württemberg at the colloquy of Maulbron; a few years later a general Protestant synod was proposed by Zacharius Ursinus as a means of achieving reunion;[13] in the late 1570s Johann Casimir strenuously promoted pan-European Protestant unity as an alternative to the process of Lutheran confessionalization leading to the Formula of Concord;[14] and a final wave of still more urgent efforts culminated in 1614 in the *Irenicum* of the leading Heidelberg theologian David Pareus, the single most important work of this whole tradition.[15] The conversion of most of Hesse to the Reformed camp after 1604 initiated a further wave of irenical treatises from Kassel and Marburg, which continued to appear at an almost annual rate until Hesse-Marburg was reclaimed by the Lutherans in 1623.[16] When Brandenburg underwent a second, Calvinizing reformation ten years later, this process was repeated. Here too the lead was taken by the senior churchman in the territory: the court preacher Johann Bergius.[17] Similar patterns were replicated on a smaller scale in the lesser Reformed states and cities in Germany. Irenical literature began to issue from the Reformed academy in Herborn shortly after its foundation in 1584 and from the counties of Hanau-Münzenberg and Anhalt shortly after their conversions to Calvinism in the 1590s.[18] The Reformed academy in Steinfurt produced irenical writings in response to Pareus's landmark work, while the tradition of particularly moderate Reformed theology taught in the academy in Bremen produced an important irenical tradition which endured through the entire confessional age.[19]

Virtually every one of these Reformed writings provoked a response from the Lutherans. In fact many of them triggered an exchange of writings which exceeded the original in length many times over. But in every case in this period that I am aware of the Reformed overtures of reconciliation were flatly rejected by the Lutherans.[20] Pareus's *Irenicum* is a prominent case in point. The work of 349 quarto pages appeared from Heidelberg at the book fair in Frankfurt in the spring of 1614 and was reissued in Latin, German, and Dutch translations the following year.[21] An onslaught from Saxony began immediately. In July of 1614 the Wittenberg theologian Friedrich Balduin directed an academic oration against the work.[22] By November his colleague, Leonhart Hutter, had conducted eight disputations against the *Irenicum*,[23] and the court preacher in Dresden, Matthias Höe von Höenegg, had argued that Calvinist teaching was so full of errors that it could be safely condemned without the need for a synod.[24] A further disputation followed in 1615, together with an 829-page diatribe from Höe; and three more Saxon refutations appeared in 1616.[25] Other leading Lutheran universities were no slower off the mark. Pareus's old sparring partner in Tübingen, Johann Georg Sigwart, rushed off a refutation of the *Irenicum* in 1614 which grew to over 750 pages in its second edition of 1616 and was abridged in German translation in 1618 along with yet another series of disputations.[26] Another old enemy, the Jesuit Adam Contzen in Mainz, contributed to the fray the most imaginative work, which prophesied that a Protestant synod, far from reconciling their differences charitably, would gradually kindle such a pitch of fury on both sides that the Lutherans and Calvinists would disperse with their mutual hatred further inflamed.[27] Pareus clearly saw that the debate roused by the *Irenicum* was heading in precisely the direction that Contzen foresaw. So after issuing a single oration and a few notes by way of rejoinder,[28] he preferred to withdraw into silence, "For the fire-brand which will ignite the whole of Europe in the end will surely be this irreligious quarrelling about religion."[29]

Pareus's experience was not atypical. Several predecessors and successors in the Reformed irenical tradition were more persistent, but none more successful. Two examples must stand for many. In 1606 an anonymous pamphlet appeared in Heidelberg, commissioned by the church council in Heidelberg and written in the name of the entire Palatine church by the court preacher, Bartholomäus Pitiscius.[30] Its message was simple: in light of the great danger which the Catholic resurgence poses to both Protestant confessions in Germany and the inessential nature of the theological differences separating them, the unnecessary and damaging condemnation of one side by the other should be set aside in a manner befitting Christians and brethren. Its tone was conciliatory, its proposals modest, and its length a mere thirty-one pages. No sooner had this pamphlet appeared, however, than it was assaulted from all sides. The very next year, three works totalling over six hundred pages were directed against the inoffensive little pamphlet; and in the following five years, ten more would follow, the smallest of these several times the pamphlet's length, and the largest running to over four hundred pages. After the *Irenicum* and outside Heidelberg, the fate of Reformed irenicists was no better. A single irenical sermon preached by the Marburg theologian and superintendent Paul Stein in June 1618 at the marriage uniting a noble couple of the two main Evangelical confessions provoked an exchange of some eight further publications pro and con, including eighteen disputations under the Giessen theologian Balthasar Mentzer and a three-volume, 1,172-page treatise by Stein on Evangelical church brotherhood.[31]

A bibliographical sounding in the irenical literature of the confessional age therefore reveals a striking distribution. Virtually every Calvinizing "second reformation" in Germany was immediately accompanied by a wave of irenical literature. And virtually all of the main writings of this Reformed irenical tradition were immediately assaulted from the Lutheran camp. The confessional distribution of irenical writings in Germany in the decades around 1600, therefore, could hardly be clearer. Irenical overtures came overwhelmingly from the Reformed, and the Lutheran response to them was overwhelmingly negative.

The contrast of the two theoretical positions developed within these parallel literatures was equally extreme. Reformed irenicists applied all their learning and acumen to the demonstration that the two Evangelical confessions were fundamentally in agreement; Lutherans employed no less industry and ingenuity in demonstrating that they were fundamentally irreconcilable. A common basic strategy for demonstrating Evangelical unity, pioneered by Ursinus and finding its classic expression in Pareus, was reflected in whole or in part by most of the lesser works of the Reformed irenical tradition as well. The obvious first step was to show how many articles united the two confessions. The fourth-longest chapter of the *Irenicum* accordingly lists some 165 theses on thirty-four articles of faith on which both main Evangelical churches agreed.[32] The corollary was to stress how few articles separated the two confessions. Building directly on the precedent established at the colloquy of Marburg in 1529, Pareus reduced the disputed points between Evangelicals and Reformed to a single article: the Lord's Supper. Even within this article, he itemized six important points on which the two confessions agreed, which left only two points dividing them: the Real Presence and the oral eating of the body of Christ in the Lord's Supper.[33] More important still was argumentation designed to minimize their theological significance. The typical strategy was to distinguish between essential and inessential doctrines, between those which are necessary for salvation and those which are not, and correspondingly between fundamental and non-fundamental differences.[34] Pareus, for example, distinguished between "articuli catholici," which form the foundation of faith and salvation and must therefore be taught to all Christians, and "articuli theologici," which pertain to theological knowledge proper to the profession of theologians but are not part of saving faith. The few questions separating the Evangelical churches belong to the category of inessential, non-fundamental, "theological" articles, which are not legitimate grounds for dividing the churches.[35]

Many of the numerous articles separating Evangelicals from Catholics, however, were deemed fundamental. The second-longest chapter of the *Irenicum* itemizes 239 theses on thirty-nine articles of faith on which Catholics and Evangelicals fundamentally disagree, or on which the Catholics disagree amongst themselves.[36] Since Evangelicals agree with one another on all the fundamentals of faith and disagree with Catholics on many of them, a union of Evangelicals was therefore deemed proper; and since both Protestant confessions inside and outside Germany were threatened by papal tyranny, it was also necessary. Finally, if union was proper and necessary, then the obvious means to achieve it were those sanctioned by biblical precedent and ancient usage: a general Evangelical synod. German Protestants, Pareus pointed out, had long campaigned for a free, fair, and open council on German soil to resolve their differences with Rome. Why should not the rules proposed by the Protestant princes for the conduct of such a council but rejected in Trent be employed in resolving the relatively minor differences between the two Evangelical confessions in Germany?[37] Pareus developed a detailed plan for the convocation and conduct of a pan-Evangelical synod and called upon his readers to suggest better arrangements if his seemed defective. Reformed theologians throughout Germany immediately expressed their approval of these proposals.

Lutheran theologians opposed this basic line of Reformed reasoning at every step. Rather than attempting to minimize the number of articles separating the two confessions, they sought to maximize it. Matthias Höe von Höenegg's gigantic *Triumphus Calvinisticus* of 1615 argued in detail that Calvinists erred on sixty-six different points scattered through fifteen of the twenty-eight articles of the Augsburg Confession.[38] Six years later, he published a lengthy *Proof, that the Calvinists Agree in Ninety-Nine Points with the Arians and the Turks.*[39] Some were content to establish that the two confessions disagreed on *many* fundamental articles of faith; others enumerated more than two hundred Calvinist "errors and lies."[40] The logical extension of this assertion, evident in a title from Hamburg in 1612, was that Calvinists err in "virtually *all* articles of faith."[41] Conversely, one could seek to demonstrate—as the Stralsund superintendent Konrad Schlüsselburg did in a series of lengthy treatises assembled from over two hundred Calvinist writings—"that the sacramentarians understand virtually *no* article of Christian doctrine properly."[42] After the Reformed theologian Christoph Pelargus published a Latin disputation refuting the assertion that "Lutherans and Calvinists disagree on almost all articles of faith," Schlüsselburg responded with an almost pathologically furious denunciation.[43]

Equal intransigence was displayed at every other step of the argument. The issues dividing the two camps were unanimously declared fundamental. On an almost annual basis in the decade after 1615, Lutheran disputations appeared providing—to quote a particularly confident title—an "apodictic demonstration that Lutherans and Calvinists disagree on many fundamental articles of faith."[44] Rather than embracing the term "Evangelicals," Lutheran polemicists delighted in designating their enemies as every species of heretics that ingenuity could plausibly associate with some aspect of Reformed religion, including Neoterics, Schwenckfeldians, Anabaptists, Photinians, Nestorians, Arians, Pelagians, Papists, Turks, and Jews.[45] A syncretism of such fundamentally opposed religions was abhorrent: Christ commanded that we love our neighbor, not that we love his enemy.[46] A Protestant synod was futile and unnecessary: if Calvinists really want unity, they must merely renounce their novelties and return to the uncorrupted doctrine of Martin Luther, as expressed in the original Augsburg Confession and expounded in the Formula of Concord.[47] Confessional union of

Lutherans with Calvinists against Catholics was therefore impossible. Pareus devoted the last and longest chapter of the *Irenicum* to a detailed refutation of an anonymous German pamphlet listing nineteen reasons why the Lutherans "neither can nor should stand with the Calvinists in religious matters as one man against the Papists."[48] The most successful Lutheran work in this vein went through at least four editions during the course of the Thirty Years' War.[49]

This deep-seated Lutheran determination to distinguish their doctrine as clearly as possible from the Reformed sometimes overturns entirely the basic confessional typology implicit in the generic term "Protestantism." Polycarp Leyser, for instance, argued in 1596 "that the doctrine of the Lutherans has more affinity with that of the Romanists than with the doctrine of the Calvinists."[50] Others turned the tables further still and argued that it was the Calvinists who were little more than Papists. One year after Pareus advocated his Evangelical syncretism against popery, a Giessen disputation by Johann Himmel proposed an alternative *syncretismus calvino-papisticus.*[51] After Hermann Fabronius's irenical work on the *Concordia Lutherano-Calvinistica* appeared in Hesse later that year, Himmel not only refuted it in a *Concordia discors Luterano Calviniana* but added a *Harmonia calvino-papistica,* designed to demonstrate "that Calvinists and Papists come together in many headings of life and teaching."[52] Stung by this ingenious association, the Mainz Jesuit Johann Andreas Coppenstein responded, denying the unanimity of Catholics with Calvinists, reasserting the essential consensus of Calvinists with Lutherans, and thereby touching off a furious exchange with Himmel and his colleagues, so determined were they to deny any family resemblance between the two Evangelical churches.[53] More typically, Catholic polemicists were delighted to cooperate with the Lutherans in pointing out the disagreements dividing Protestant schismatics from each other, the political advantages of which were obvious. In 1608, for instance, the Lithuanian Andrzej Jurgiewicz juxtaposed the anathematizations of each main Protestant group by the others in an attempt to disrupt the concord established between Lutherans, Calvinists, and the Bohemian Brethren in Poland a few years earlier. Reformed strategists saw perfectly clearly that dividing Protestants in this way was the necessary precondition to reconquering Poland completely for the Roman church. "The strength of the Evangelical rulers and estates," Pitiscius warned, "is a nothing against the Papacy, if they are divided into two or three parts and one part wants to help annihilate the other."[54] But prudential arguments of this kind evidently had no weight with the Lutheran theologians of the period.

Reformed Irenicism in Context

The persistence with which the Reformed in Germany proposed making peace with the Lutherans appears self-contradictory. No sooner had they purged their churches of Lutheran "defects" than they turned around and sought reunion with the very confession from which they had just emerged. These persistent irenical proposals also appear to contradict the defining characteristic of confessionalization. At the height of the confessional age, in the very years in which Germany was supposedly dividing into three mutually hostile camps, one of these three was doggedly, tenaciously courting union with another, despite the most violent rebuffs.

The ferocity with which the Lutherans rejected these persistent Reformed advances is more paradoxical still. The modern discipline of history came of age in Germany in the early nineteenth century, during the period in which Evangelical and Reformed churches in Germany were finally reconciled and institutionally united. Theologians and church historians have long had a vested interest in reinforcing the sense of essential concord of these two sister churches, and their textbooks have traditionally emphasized more or less explicitly the fundamental unanimity underlying these two main species of "Protestantism" while neglecting almost completely this protracted period of violent antagonism. Some senior church historians even insist that it is wrong to describe the second, Calvinizing wave of reformation experienced in some German states as a "second reformation" because this term "calls into question the essential unity of the Reformation."[55] But no terms which modern historians apply could remotely match the rich vocabulary of invective with which orthodox Lutherans in this period called that unity into question.

Lutherans and Calvinists in central Europe around 1600 were clearly living in a world very different from that which their descendants have occupied since the nineteenth century. Given that theological concord has now been established, theology alone cannot explain this lengthy period of violent discord. In order to understand this paradoxical pattern of behavior, it is necessary to return to the late sixteenth and early seventeenth centuries and examine the concrete conditions which shaped the wholly asymmetrical nature of this exchange. More specifically, we must descend from the abstract world of academic theological polemics into the concrete domain of politics and consider the political conditions underlying this relationship on at least three levels: international, imperial, and territorial.

The most obvious and important level of conditions structuring this complex debate was the imperial one. The crucial political fact underlying this polarized debate was the very different legal status of the two main Protestant confessions in the Holy Roman Empire. Only the churches subscribing to the Confession of Augsburg had obtained a degree of provisional legal toleration within the empire in 1555. Having enshrined the Augsburg Confession at the heart of the Book of Concord, the Lutherans thought their legal position secure. The Reformed, however, with their well-known dissent from the doctrine of the Real Presence, were in a far more vulnerable legal position, and it was uncertain from the beginning whether they would be granted enduring *de facto* toleration or repressed at the earliest convenient opportunity.[56] Confronted by this fundamental political fact, the Reformed in the empire, led by the Palatinate, needed to persuade the Lutherans of at least one of two things. The first was legal: they needed to convince the Lutherans that they too had a right to legal protection under the terms of the Peace of Augsburg. The second was political: they needed to persuade Lutheran princes and cities to join with them in resisting any attempt to repress either of the two Reformation churches by force. The first of these strategies was played out essentially on the imperial level of the debate; the second expanded to include the international level as well.

The Reformed claim to shelter under the Confession of Augsburg was not as hopeless as one might suppose. Given the various versions of the confession in circulation, the origins of so many architects of the German Reformed in the tradition of its author, Philipp Melanchthon, the defense of it by Bucer, Calvin, and even Beza, there was plenty of material at hand for elaborating this claim.[57] If challenged on their conception of predestination, they pointed to the strong statement of similar views in Luther's *De servo arbitrio.* When confronted with their departures from the crucial tenth article on the Lord's Supper, they responded that they had departed less from the words of the confession than the Ubiquitarians, who could find no support for their doctrine either in the confession itself, or in the whole corpus of Luther's writings, or in the clear testimony of Scripture. A large genre of irenical debate developed in which Reformed theologians pressed their claims for inclusion in the Peace of Augsburg and the concordial Lutherans responded by insisting that the Formula of Concord was the only authentic interpretation of that confession. The most abstruse and convoluted points of eucharistic theology therefore took on direct legal and political significance. The religious provisions of the Peace of Augsburg, while suspending the military conflict between the Protestant princes and the Catholic emperor, had also inaugurated a period of incessant trench warfare between Evangelical and Reformed theologians.

Above and beyond merely legal defenses, the second response was to build a political and military defense: that is, to persuade the Lutherans to join the Reformed in a Protestant Union designed to oppose any attempt to rescind the (still officially provisional) concessions of the Peace of Augsburg and to overcome the (unacceptable) limitations placed on the advancement of Protestantism by the Peace. Here too, as is well known, the Reformed incentives for pursuing such a union were far stronger that the Lutheran ones. Given their potential exclusion from the provisions of the Peace of Augsburg, the Reformed were far more vulnerable to imperial retribution than the Lutherans. Confessionally, dynastically, and even militarily engaged with Calvinist communities across Europe, they were also far more acutely aware of the attempts of Catholic parties to suppress Protestantism militarily in France and the Netherlands.[58] Their sense of legal vulnerability at the imperial level was thus reinforced by an awareness of military vulnerability at the international one. A further species of irenical literature therefore developed which sought theological peace between Lutherans and Calvinists as the precondition of a sound political and military alliance of Protestants against Catholics.

The international origins of this dimension of the German Reformed irenical tradition are perhaps most evident in the series of warnings of the threat of papal tyranny circulating in Germany after the St. Bartholomew's Day Massacre and the assassination of William the Silent.[59] Within a few years, the urgent need for Protestant reconciliation to counter this threat became fully explicit in pamphlets like the disputation, repeatedly published in Heidelberg and Zerbst, *On the question whether in this time of growing papal tyranny, a syncretism or coalition against the common enemy ought to be established among the evangelical churches.*[60] The most famous example of this literature is Pitiscius's *Trewhertzige Vermahnung,* the reaction to which was mentioned previously. Here too the title alone links the threat of papal tyranny with the need for Protestant reconciliation: it was entitled *A Sincere Warning from the Palatine Church to all other Evangelical Churches in Germany, that they finally take note of the great danger which the papacy poses to them as well as us and that they at last break off and set aside the wholly unnecessary quarrel with us in a Christian and brotherly fashion.*[61] Nor were such emphases confined to pamphlet propaganda for the Protestant Union. They were equally evident in the most learned and distinguished Latin treatises on ecclesiastical irenicism. The central section of Pareus's *Irenicum,* for instance, was devoted to establishing the necessity of a "syncretism or friendly association [of the main Protestant churches] against the Papacy," a "syncretism against the common enemy, Antichrist."[62] Other irenical works expressed similar sentiments.[63] This question was equally prominent in the furor raised by the *Irenicum*. It is explicit both in the title of Leonhard Hutter's first response to Pareus in 1615 and in Pareus's rebuttal of Hutter the following year.[64] And the belligerent intentions underlying Palatine irenicism were even more obvious to the party against which this "syncretism" was directed. In the main Catholic attack on the *Irenicum*, the Jesuit polemicist Adam Contzen skillfully misconstrued Palatine calls for a defensive alliance against Habsburg aggression into a monstrous conspiracy against pope, emperor, and princes, which aimed ultimately to unleash a gigantic war in Germany in which Lutherans and Catholics would be exterminated.[65] Here too he was strangely prescient, although in the war that followed it was the Reformed party which was most nearly destroyed.

Clearly, one did not need to be a theological moderate in order to advocate religious reconciliation in these conditions; nor did one need a peace-loving temperament in general to write this species of irenical literature. A degree of irenicism vis-à-vis Lutheranism could and often did go hand in hand with the utmost belligerence vis-à-vis Catholicism. The two seemingly contradictory aspects of the Palatinate in the prewar period—its ecclesiastical irenicism and its political belligerence—are in fact two perfectly consistent faces of the same coin. Here too the immediate diplomatic and political significance of ecclesiastical irenicism is overwhelmingly apparent. Heidelberg's ecclesiastical diplomacy was explicitly designed to buttress the cornerstone of Palatine military diplomacy within the empire: the Protestant Union.

A third and final important level of the motivations generating this huge Reformed irenical tradition was not imperial or international but territorial. This level of the tradition is perhaps most clearly illustrated by the case of Brandenburg. The elector of Brandenburg first received the Lord's Supper in the Reformed manner in December of 1613, almost a century after the outbreak of the German Reformation. Like his predecessors in taking this step, he then sought to impose a second wave of Reformation from above, with the active assistance of only a small corps of officers, ministers, and academics. In Brandenburg, however—in a particularly striking example of a problem encountered in similar reformations in other German territories—this further reformation was rejected by a populace which had already embraced a very conservative form of Lutheranism for generations. The result was a stalemate, and the unavoidable coexistence of two confessions within an individual state. As well as constituting a further anomaly within the Peace of

Augsburg, this situation provided a strong additional political incentive for ecclesiastical pacification, reconciliation, and eventual reunion at the territorial level. In this case, however, the prospect of enduring coexistence and the ability of the ruler to reward cooperative leaders on both sides of the confessional divide seems to have inspired more genuine theological moderation on the Reformed side and more active cooperation on the Lutheran one, despite strident protests from university theologians in Saxony and Königsberg. In this domestically oriented species of Reformed irenicism, moreover, the need for a hostile posture over against Rome was less directly implicit. The presence of the standard anti-papal epithets in the writings of even the most genuine theological moderate among German Reformed irenicists is therefore particularly striking. Johannes Bergius, court preacher in Berlin-Cölln and tutor of the Great Elector, called the Catholics "Roman-Spanish birds of prey" who sought to reduce Protestant Germany to "Egyptian slavery." "Their sole aim," he wrote, "is to ruin all Evangelical lands and to exterminate our churches."[66] As in the case of England and Scotland, the specter of an Antichristian enemy provided the strongest available means of fashioning a common sense of identity within a religiously divided state.[67]

International, imperial, and territorial conditions all combined, therefore, to encourage the Reformed party in the empire to seek reconciliation with their Lutheran "brethren." In addition to these political motives, the theology, liturgy, and church polity of the German Reformed provided an advantageous basis for irenical efforts. All of the churches which underwent a second reformation in Germany had previously been Philippist as opposed to concordial Lutheran. Most of the first generation of theologians in these churches were Philippists excluded from Wittenberg, Leipzig, Silesia, Strasbourg, and elsewhere as a consequence of Lutheran confessionalization. This theological heritage, coupled with the political constraints imposed by the Peace of Augsburg and the desire of the rulers to retain control of the church in their territories, placed the German Reformed in a position genuinely intermediary in several respects between the concordial Lutherans on the one hand and the genuine Calvinists on the other.[68] The Heidelberg Catechism—the document which, more than any other, united these churches doctrinally—was characterized less by a zeal for absolute clarity than by a desire to express the controversial doctrines in a conciliatory form. The catechism was an integral part of the Palatine church order of 1563, in which specifically Calvinist influences were subsumed in a general structure derived from Lutheran Württemberg. Church polity was also not a bone of contention. The conflict between Lutheran episcopacy and truly Calvinist presbyterianism which so plagued the British kingdoms was avoided by the hybrid nature of German Reformed ecclesiastical polity, which introduced Calvinist mechanisms of church discipline into structures of ecclesiastical government retained from the earlier, Lutheran phase of reform.[69] While the special political circumstances of the Reformed party in Germany motivated their uniquely active search for inter-Protestant reconciliation, their peculiar theological and ecclesiastical ancestry provided a more promising starting point for reconciliation at this level than those possessed by their Calvinist contemporaries in the Swiss cities, France, the Dutch provinces, or the British Isles.[70]

An even more crucial theological element was the great debt of the movement to Luther himself. In the Reformed camp, in all but its most polemical moments, Luther's central role in the early Reformation in Germany could be readily acknowledged. He had not, of course, gone far enough: the imperfections in his theology, particularly in his conception of the sacraments, needed to be removed. His pioneering attempt to translate the Bible into German required periodic emendation. His contribution as a reformer was sometimes relativized. In response to the Lutheran tendency to proclaim the Reformation the personal achievement of one prophetic figure, deviation from whom represented the work of the Devil, the German Reformed developed a more pluralistic tradition of ecclesiastical historiography more representative of their own needs, which stressed the earlier breakthroughs of Wyclif, Hus, the Bohemians, the Waldensians, and the Albigensians as well as the contributions of Luther's contemporaries—Zwingli, Melanchthon, Bucer, Bullinger, and Calvin—and their own role in bringing the process of reformation to completion.[71] But the imperfections of Luther's theology could easily be excused by stressing his role as a pioneer, raised in popish idolatry from which he had not quite completely escaped; and their harshest comments were reserved for Luther's misguided followers, who had retreated from the unflinching assertion of predestination in Luther's *De servo arbitrio* and had advanced beyond both Luther and the Augsburg Confession in buttressing the main flaw in Luther's sacramental theology with their unscriptural and illogical doctrine of ubiquity. Hostility to certain aspects of Lutheran "orthodoxy" could thus coexist with a genuine appreciation of Luther which provided an important theological and historiographical foundation upon which the Reformed irenical tradition was built.

In short, the Reformed sincerely believed two things. The first was that they agreed with Lutherans on fundamentals. The second was that on less fundamental matters the Lutheran formulae were flawed and their own formulations were better. They therefore felt justified *both* in further reforming previously Lutheran churches when opportunities arose *and* in seeking fraternal relations with those Lutheran churches which resisted further reformation. Their position was sincere and internally consistent. But it was not one well calculated to inspire love from their Evangelical brethren.

Lutheran Anti-irenicism in Context

In the theological as well as the political sphere the Lutheran situation was radically different. At one level, the Lutheran response was also rooted in recent historical experience. In the 1570s Lutherans concluded a generation of theological infighting after Luther's death by hammering out an irenical program of their own—the Formula of Concord—which although narrow in its theological remit had proved very effective in limiting internecine theological warfare. They had been quite willing to exclude the followers of Melanchthon—the "Philippists," whom they regarded as "crypto-Calvinist"—as the price for such internal theological harmony. And after watching many of the leading Philippists gravitate from Wittenberg, Leipzig, Strasbourg, and elsewhere to Heidelberg, Bremen, and Herborn, they were in no mood to reunite with the very people and principles which they had just so laboriously excluded.[72]

This recent experience, however, was rooted in a deeper antipathy. The esteem in which Zwingli and Calvin held Luther was not reciprocated; and a similar asymmetry became a structural condition skewing the relations between the traditions which derived from them. Upon leaving the colloquy with Zwingli in Marburg, Luther had vowed to "give the sacramentarians no peace" and his followers made this vow their own. Pareus might well ask why the personal feelings and authority of one man should remain a permanent bar to reconciliation;[73] but there was far more structuring this unequal exchange than personal feelings or loyalties. Luther and Melanchthon, the German Reformed could not but admit, had helped lay the foundations upon which their own church rested. It was a historical fact that their second phase of reformation built upon the foundations laid by the first, Lutheran phase. But Zwingli, Bullinger, Calvin, and the rest had made no fundamental contribution to the Lutheran reformation. On the contrary, they were setting out to corrupt and destroy it. To Luther and the gnesio-Lutherans, the Swiss were schismatics, who had threatened the integrity of Luther's reformation with their sacramentarian theology while making no positive contribution to it.[74] And if Calvinism outside Germany was viewed as a regrettable corruption of Lutheranism, inside Germany this corruption was being imposed on Lutheran churches—with the enthusiastic support of the Reformed "irenicists"—through naked political force.[75]

Here the example of Hesse is particularly instructive.[76] When the crypto-Calvinist Landgrave Moritz of Hesse-Kassel inherited the neighboring territory of Hesse-Marburg from his childless Lutheran uncle in 1605, he immediately set about imposing a further, Calvinizing reformation directly contrary to the provisions of his uncle's will and the loudly expressed preference of the overwhelmingly Lutheran populace. Among his first measures was to purge the theological faculty at Marburg of its unyielding Lutherans. A new university was immediately established to accommodate these academic refugees in Giessen, on the lands of the staunchly Lutheran Landgrave of Hesse-Darmstadt; and it is scarcely surprising that the theologians exiled to Giessen should not have responded graciously to the irenical overtures which began to issue from Marburg and Kassel the moment the Reformed party had consolidated its position there. Balthasar Mentzer, who led the relentless campaign against Paul Stein's irenical sermon of 1618, had been Stein's teacher and supervisor in Marburg before 1605; and in a passage still seething with fury fifteen years later, he recalled how Stein, ever the irenicist, had expected him to extend the hand of friendship to his Calvinist ruler in the very meeting in which he was evicted from his chair.[77] If unity is of paramount importance, Mentzer and his colleagues asked, then why are we all in exile in Giessen? If concord is so desirable, then why have these divisive reforms been forcefully imposed in the first place? If the Calvinists are the Lutherans' brethren in Christ, why are they forcefully repressing Lutheran worship whenever they gain the upper hand?

These questions were the more pressing since these further reformations in Marburg and Brandenburg were rapidly followed by the participation of theologians from all these centers in the Synod of Dort in 1618–1619. Differences on the Lord's Supper had dogged proponents of Protestant reconciliation since the confrontation of Luther and Zwingli at Marburg in 1529; issues of Christology had compounded the problem since the Formula of Concord; and as the century came to a close predestination emerged as a third main point of doctrine separating the two confessions at the Mömpelgard colloquy in 1586.[78] The invitation to attend a synod called to pass judgment on Arminian conceptions of election, atonement, and grace more similar to the Lutheran than to the strict Calvinist position therefore put many German Reformed advocates of Protestant reconciliation in an acutely uncomfortable position. Johannes Bergius held views on the atonement similar to the Arminians: namely, that Christ died not only for the elect but for all mankind, although the fruits of his death and resurrection would be enjoyed only by believers. Warned in advance by a colleague already at Dort that the synod was dominated by hard-line Calvinists determined to crush the Arminians and defend a limited atonement, Bergius declined repeated requests from the elector that he represent Brandenburg at Dort. Matthias Martinius, the leader of the equally moderate school of Reformed theology in Bremen, was less circumspect. He encountered such hostility to his universalist conception of atonement that he nearly withdrew from the synod, and he returned home after its conclusion bemoaning the "disaster and division" he had witnessed there and vowing never to set foot in a similar assembly again.[79] The delegation from the Palatinate, on the other hand, showed no qualms about roundly condemning the pernicious errors of the Remonstrants and submitted some of the most rigorous formal defenses of predestinarianism contained in the synod's proceedings.[80] The leader of the delegation, Abraham Scultetus, preached a sermon to the synod, ostensibly in praise of ecclesiastical concord, which ended with a prayer that God might help the synod destroy the "hateful lies" which have infected the Dutch church.[81] Even the great irenicist David Pareus, though detained at home by frail old age, supported the synod's severity without qualification in an oration delivered in Heidelberg in February and read *in absentia* before the synod in March.[82] His testament four years later records how he detested the abhorrent delusions of the Pelagians with all his heart.[83] Given the obvious implications of this stance for the prospects of ecclesiastical reconciliation, one can only suppose that the Palatine court, having exhausted all hopes of reconciliation with Lutheranism within Germany, had decided to throw in its lot with international Calvinism outside it.

The effect of the synod's four articles in further undermining the prospects of reconciliation back in Germany quickly became clear. Academic disputations and vernacular tracts immediately flooded from Giessen, Wittenberg, Leipzig, and Tübingen displaying the slipperiness and hypocrisy of the German Calvinists assembled at Dort.[84] Dort not only increased Lutherans' suspicion of the Reformed proposals for a synod; it also solidified the place of predestination and related issues on the list of doctrines separating the two confessions. It was fairly plausible in 1614 for Pareus to argue that Evangelicals were separated only by a few points of academic sacramental theology which were not fundamental articles of faith; but this became increasingly difficult after 1618. Fundamental doctrines, Lutheran theologians argued, are those basic to saving faith. The doctrine of the person and work of Christ is the "corner stone" of this foundation. Differing conceptions of election, atonement, predestination, and all the other doctrines which derive from them therefore pertain not to extra-fundamentals but to the very foundation of saving faith. By anchoring predestination at the center of the most international, authoritative, and contemporary statement of Reformed theology, Dort greatly increased the difficulty of reconciliation with Lutheranism and offered an obvious standard in terms of which Lutherans could reject the advances of genuinely moderate Reformed theologians as unrepresentative of their confession as a whole.[85] When Bergius—although now the leading religious advisor of the most powerful Reformed ruler in Germany and therefore arguably the most senior Reformed churchman in the empire—employed his universalistic doctrine of the atonement as a means to bridge the gap between Evangelicals and Reformed in the Mark, it got him nowhere. Not only did he incur the wrath of his colleague, the Reformed professor of theology at Frankfurt an der Oder, Wolfgang Crell; he could make no headway with the Lutherans either, who argued with complete conviction that Bergius was merely stating his own private opinion, which on this point was directly contrary to the most authoritative doctrine of the confession he purported to represent.[86] Nor was it difficult to portray his, in this case perfectly sincere, dissent from Dort as just another example of the Machiavellian hypocrisy typical of the *Hof-Calvinisten*—the "court Calvinists" who, the Lutherans complained, flocked around powerful magnates like the elector.[87] In short, just as the general church council so long sought by the Lutherans, when it finally finished in Trent, was of no use in mending the divisions between Protestants and Catholics within the empire, so the general synod so long sought by the German Reformed, when it finally finished in Dort, dashed rather than fulfilled their earlier hopes for mending divisions with the Lutherans.

Lutherans therefore regarded the Reformed not as true brothers but as false brethren, not as precursors who had helped paved the way for full reformation but as traitors who had departed from it and who were spreading their corruption further with every passing generation. This theological perspective was powerfully reinforced by a perhaps even more crucial point which seems to have been generally overlooked in the limited literature on this subject. The Reformed confession was steadily expanding in the empire throughout the period between the reconversion of the Palatinate to Calvinism in 1583 and the Bohemian revolt, and almost all of this expansion was at the expense, not of Catholics, but of Lutherans.[88] Johann Casimir and the Wetterau counts had attempted to secularize the archbishopric of Cologne, but this had proved a disastrous failure.[89] All the territories which converted more or less permanently to the Reformed religion had previously been Lutheran—albeit Philippist rather than gnesio-Lutheran—and several other Lutheran states in Germany, including Saxony itself, had almost fallen as well. Given the prohibition in the Peace of Augsburg of further secularization of ecclesiastical territories and the success of post-Tridentine efforts to shore up allegiance to the Roman church among Catholic rulers and aristocracy, Lutherans and Calvinists within Germany were locked in a zero-sum game. The Calvinists could only expand at the expense of the Lutherans. Every Reformed gain was therefore a Lutheran loss. Outside the states ruled by Protestants, Evangelicals of all varieties were coming under increasing pressure from a resurgent Catholicism. But within the states in which all these anti-irenical professors, pastors, and court preachers were employed, Lutheranism was proving far more vulnerable to Calvinist advances than to Catholic ones. When Reformed irenicists urged the necessity of joining forces to resist the Roman Antichrist, Lutherans refused to cooperate, not simply because they were unconcerned about the progress of the Catholic counter-reformation, but because they were still more worried about the progress of the Calvinist second reformation.

This balance of concern is directly reflected in the literature at only one remove from the anti-irenical tradition. In the last two decades of the sixteenth century and the first two of the seventeenth, as Calvinist presses issued a series of pamphlets by Dutch, French, and German writers warning of the gathering forces of Catholic reconquest outside the empire, Lutheran divines broadcast regular *Trewhertzige Erinnerungen, Vermahnungen,* and *Warnungen* of their own to mark every stage of the consolidation and expansion of Calvinism within the empire. The reconversion of the Palatinate in 1584, the conversion of Anhalt to Calvinism in 1596, the invasion by "Calvinist and sacramentarian errors" of Silesia after 1600, of Brandenburg in 1614, and of Bohemia and Moravia in 1620—each of these stimulated a published pamphlet warning of this kind.[90] Innumerable lesser events received the same treatment: the very offer of evangelical brotherhood in Pitiscus's *Trewhertzige Vermahnug,* seconded in the sermons of the Dillenburg court preacher in 1606, prompted a *Trewhetzige Warnung* from Wittenberg in 1608.[91]

Moreover, this steady advance of Calvinism in the years around 1600 seems to have convinced both parties that its momentum was becoming inexorable. Lutherans clearly believed that the Calvinists were determined to impose their sacramentarianism on the whole of Lutheranism. Any concessions or cooperation from the Lutheran side, any relaxation of the political pressures endured by the Reformed, would only accelerate this process. This worry is present even in one of the earliest pamphlets warning against the spread of Calvinism in Germany. The more time passes, Lucas Osiander the Elder wrote as early as 1577, the wider the Zwinglian error spreads, though often by disguising itself initially as a less malign doctrine.[92] Osiander's colleagues in Württemberg expressed similar fears in their response to Pitiscius's *Trewhetzige Warnung* in 1608. The real danger comes not from the Catholics, who abide by the provisions of the Peace of Augsburg, but from the Calvinists, whose ultimate aim is to extend their hegemony over all Germany.[93] In 1615 Matthias Höe von Höenegg greeted the second reformation in Brandenburg with his 829-page tome warning of a looming *Triumphus Calvinisticus* which explicitly related this fear of Calvinist dominance to the rejection of Pareus's irenical overtures published the year before.

The pessimism of the Lutherans was matched by the optimism of the Reformed, who clearly believed that they had revelation, reason, political prudence, and international solidarity on their side. A characteristic expression of this optimism is the sermon celebrating the centenary of the Reformation which the Palatine court preacher, Abraham Scultetus, preached in Heidelberg on 2 November 1617. In 1580, he recalled, when the Book of Concord established the error of the Real Presence as the doctrine of so many churches, the only Reformed states in the empire were Bremen in the far north and Neustadt in the Palatinate. But the past thirty-seven years have seen a flood of conversions: Nassau-Dillenburg, Wittgenstein, Solms, the Upper and Lower Palatinate, Basel, Zweibrücken, Anhalt, Hanau, Isenburg, Liegnitz, Brieg, Lippe, Hesse-Kassel, Hesse-Marburg, Brandenburg, Jülich, Cleves, and Berg, not to mention the princes which had attempted to follow them, the electors of Cologne and Saxony, the duke of Holstein, even King Charles of Sweden. Who can review such a rapid spread of illumination to so many illustrious princes and regions in so brief a space of time and not see the hand of God at work? And who can doubt that there are many more such conversions to come in the future? In the coming generation this steady unfolding of true reformation will spread still further, not through the efforts of Luther, Zwingli, Oecolampadius, or anyone else, but through a dawning divine illumination until at last the truth is revealed to the whole world.[94] Höe von Höenegg responded immediately with a *Trewhertzige Warnung für der JubelfestsPredigt*. Here, he exclaimed, are the true intentions lurking behind the smokescreen of Calvinist "irenicism"! In this declaration of war against Lutheran churches everywhere, the Calvinists' will to dominate the whole of Germany is finally made explicit.[95]

The climax of the Lutheran anti-irenical tradition came in a series of pamphlets from Höe von Höenegg, published in 1620 on the eve of the decisive battle of White Mountain.[96] Saxony found itself in an intolerable situation: with Brandenburg to the north, the Bohemian lands to the east, the Upper Palatinate to the south, and Anhalt to the west all converting to Calvinism, Saxony would be virtually surrounded. Polycarp Leyser's notorious argument that the Lutherans had more in common with Papists than with Calvinists now took on heightened political relevance, and Höe reissued it as another pamphlet demonstrating *Why one should Prefer to make Common Cause with the Papists . . . than with the Calvinists.*[97] Höe himself went a crucial step further, abandoned theology, and entered directly into the key political questions underlying the anti-irenical tradition. He argued that the true duty of an Evangelical prince was *not* to support the Bohemian rebels *nor* to remain neutral but to join the emperor in crushing the Calvinists who had imperilled the imperial constitution and were attempting to destroy the true Lutheran religion wherever they gained control.[98] As if to drive home one more time the ultimate stake underlying the Reformed irenical tradition, the Calvinists responded by republishing in Heidelberg, Amberg, and Silesia the chapter refuting Leyser's argument from Pareus's *Irenicum.*[99] But the time for irenical arguments was over. The fate of the Palatinate, Bohemia, and with them of the historical core of the Reformed tradition within the empire, was sealed.

Wartime Irenicism: Variations on an Established Theme

The temptation to conclude an analysis of irenicism in the confessional age at this point is almost irresistible. Never was the triumph of confessionalism over irenicism more complete than in the military onslaught by the secular leader of one confession on the secular leader of another who had so often signalled his willingness to discuss the few points of academic theology that separated them. The military campaigns of 1620 and the propaganda which accompanied them mark the unprecedented and unsurpassed nadir of Protestant Christian ecumenism. But within the narrower story of irenicism within the empire in the confessional age, they changed nothing. Indeed, they merely aggravated the previous situation. The chief cause of the strikingly asymmetrical relationship of the two main Protestant confessions in

Germany, as we have sought to describe it, was their very different legal status within the empire: the security of the Lutherans versus the vulnerability, real and perceived, of the Reformed. In the years after 1620, however, the Reformed in central Europe were not merely vulnerable but mortally wounded.

The importance of this inequality in creating these unbridgeable divisions becomes still clearer if the situation in Germany is compared briefly with that in the neighboring areas. In Poland and Bohemia, where none of the Protestant churches were legally protected and where a display of unity was necessary in order to achieve legal protection, evangelical concord proved far less elusive. In 1570 the three main Protestant churches of Poland—the Bohemian Brethren, the Lutheran, and the Reformed—signed the Consensus of Sandomierz, attesting their agreement on fundamentals and their resolution to refrain from damaging controversies, though without achieving complete unity in doctrine and worship.[100] Inspired by the Polish example, a similar concord was reached in Bohemia, this time also including the Utraquists, in the *Confessio Bohemica* of 1575.[101] Polish Protestants immediately appealed to their German neighbors to imitate this concord as well, and the literature thus generated fed directly into the German Reformed irenical tradition.[102] In France likewise—three years after the last great Huguenot stronghold, La Rochelle, was taken by the armies of Louis XIII—the national synod of the French Reformed church unanimously agreed to admit Lutherans to communion in 1631.[103] In subsequent years the irenical project received valuable support from several Huguenot writers, most notably the controversial leader of the academy at Saumur, Moyse Amyraud.[104] In the Netherlands, however, the rousing calls for unity against the common enemy so necessary at the height of the Dutch revolt fell silent once the United Provinces had consolidated its military and economic position and the Dutch Reformed church had repressed the Arminians. John Dury complained that endorsement of his irenical program was blocked in the Dutch synods by "Dr. [Jan] Bogermannus, who presided at the Synod of Dort and still exercises (though in secret) the authority of a perpetual dictator."[105] The only valuable support which his irenical campaign received from the republic came from outside the Dutch Reformed church: from Arminians like Grotius, exiles like Comenius, and from Gottfried Hotton, a refugee from the Palatinate and pastor of the Walloon church in Amsterdam.[106] The Swiss likewise—unaffected by the restrictions imposed on Calvinism within the empire—showed little desire to compromise their theological clarity by becoming entangled in the Protestant synods sponsored by the Palatinate.[107]

Vulnerability to Catholic repression, then, and the need for protection from it were the most powerful motives for seeking inter-Protestant reconciliation during the confessional age. The Lutherans in Germany, having achieved protection for themselves in 1555 and internal concord by 1580, stood apart from these irenical efforts; and feeling themselves more vulnerable on their Calvinist than on their Catholic flank, they did everything in their power to undermine them. But the Saxons had famously overestimated the security which the Peace of Augsburg afforded them and had grossly underestimated the emperor's desire to gain confessional and political absolutism within the Reich. The clearest manifestation of the link between vulnerability and irenicism would eventually come from the most anti-Calvinist quarter of Protestant Germany: from the Saxon elector and his court preacher, Matthias Höe von Höenegg.

As the repression of Protestantism in Bohemia became unmistakable and the main theater of operations shifted to Lutheran Germany in 1626, the anti-Calvinist diatribes from Dresden rapidly died away, finally to be replaced by anti-papal tirades as the worst of Calvinist fears was realized in the Edict of Restitution of 1629. In that year the Habsburg emperor, at the apogee of his power, having militarily subjected north and south Germany, Reformed and Evangelical alike, unilaterally demanded the restitution of all church rights and property secularized since 1552. The enforcement of this edict would have crippled most Protestant states and churches, and the situation was made more dangerous still by the simultaneous appearance of a Jesuit pamphlet, the *Pacis Compositio*, arguing that the Concordial Lutherans no longer adhered to the letter of the Augsburg Confession, that they therefore violated the terms of the Peace of Augsburg, and clearly implying that they too had forfeited the right to legal protection in the empire.[108] The inclusion of Lutheranism and the putative exclusion of Calvinism from the provisions of Augsburg had set the fundamental conditions within which both the Reformed irenical and the Lutheran anti-irenical traditions had developed over the past seventy-five years. Now that the Religious Peace of 1555 was called into question, even the most intransigent Saxon opponents of the Calvinists and their proposals for concord were converted to the irenical position within a matter of months. In January of 1631, after persistent coaxing from the elector of Brandenburg, the elector of Saxony invited all the major Protestant princes and cities to a convention in Leipzig.[109] Between mid-February and mid-April the assembled rulers negotiated the creation of the *Leipziger Bund*—a defensive association designed to resist the imposition of the Edict of Restitution while avoiding an offensive alliance with the Swedes against the emperor. With them these princes brought their leading theologians, and acting again on Brandenburg's initiative the opportunity was taken to complement the formal political negotiations with private, informal discussions exploring the possibility of theological reconciliation.

For the first time since the colloquy of Maulbron sixty-seven years earlier, six senior German Reformed and Lutheran theologians met face to face for three weeks in Leipzig during the spring of 1631 in an attempt to broker theological concord.[110] The Reformed delegation included two of the most senior irenicists—Johann Bergius of Berlin and Johannes Crocius of Kassel—as well as the Kassel theologian Theophil Neuberger. The Saxons, by contrast, were represented by the previously implacable foe of all things Calvinist, Matthias Höe von Höenegg, Polycarp Leyser the Younger, and Heinrich Höpfner. A few years earlier, such a meeting would have been utterly unthinkable, but in these transformed circumstances it was astonishingly successful. In a mere six sessions, typically lasting no more than three hours, the six theologians reached basic agreement on twenty-six of the twenty-eight articles of the unaltered Augsburg Confession. Six more sessions were then devoted to the three outstanding points of contention, and here too wide though incomplete agreement was reached. In the Lord's Supper, they concluded, "not merely a symbol of the body and blood of Christ, but his true real body . . . and true real blood . . . were truly and physically offered, distributed and taken by virtue of the sacramental union," though they were unable to agree on the *manducatio oralis* and *manducatio indignorum*. Regarding the nature and office of Christ, they agreed on twelve important points and disagreed only on the *communicatio idiomatum*. Finally, moving outside the Augsburg Confession itself to the further disputed issue of predestination, they failed to square the Calvinist insistence on God's absolute decree with the Lutheran *fidem praevisam*, though Bergius held out the hope that these differences were essentially semantic. As in Poland and Bohemia in the 1570s, complete unanimity proved unreachable; but the immediate goals of the entire Reformed irenical tradition—a cessation of theological hostilities, an expression of concord on the fundamentals of faith, and a political union against the common enemy—seemed suddenly within reach. Pending a future meeting, the participants dispersed with the promise to show one another Christian love in the future and, in the words of Höe himself, "to stand as one man against the papacy"[111]—precisely the resolution which had been deemed impossible in the radically different circumstances eleven years before.

If 1620 witnessed the lowest point in the entire history of Lutheran-Calvinist relations, 1631 represented the apex of Evangelical concord in the confessional era. At this moment of greatest hope, moreover, two new figures appeared on the scene working in tandem for Evangelical reunion: the savior of Protestantism, the Lutheran king of Sweden, Gustavus Adolphus, and the greatest Reformed irenicist of the wartime period, the itinerant Scotsman John Dury.[112] Yet these uniquely favorable auspices were misleading, for the very arrival of these two outsiders transformed the conditions of irenical debate once again, and within a few years the achievements of the Leipzig Colloquy were irredeemably compromised.

In part this was due to the naivete of the Reformed irenicists, in part to the intransigence of their Lutheran brethren, but ultimately it was the ironic result of the stunning victories of the Swedish king. The sensational success of the Swedish campaign rapidly removed the threat of immediate enforcement of the Edict of Restitution which had made Evangelical cooperation necessary. Moreover the Swedish king, though strongly in favor of Evangelicals joining forces against the Papists, wanted an alliance under his leadership, not an independent third party interposed between himself and the enemy. As he skillfully dismembered the *Leipziger Bund* in the summer of 1631, the religious concord superimposed upon it came to pieces as well.[113] With the option of armed neutrality foreclosed, the Saxon elector gravitated back to the imperial camp along with his chief religious adviser. By 1634 Höe was again arguing that to give military aid to the Calvinists "was tantamount to rendering feudal service to the devil, the originator of Calvinism."[114] The following year Saxony made a separate peace with the emperor in Prague which, had it held, would have been highly detrimental to Protestants throughout central Europe.

With the general political situation thus returned to roughly the position before the Edict, polemics flared up once again in a form virtually indistinguishable from the period before Leipzig. The Reformed, to be sure, now restated their old case with enhanced conviction. The wide-ranging agreements demonstrated a century earlier in Marburg and renewed in Leipzig demonstrate beyond all doubt, they claimed, that the Lutherans and the Reformed are united in essentials. The Reformed have never been formally excluded from the Augsburg Confession and therefore deserve protection under the provisions of the Peace of Augsburg.[115] Lutheran hard-liners were no less hesitant to deny that any agreement had been reached at Leipzig or was reachable thereafter. The differences between Calvinist error and Lutheran truth, they asserted once again, are indeed fundamental. The two confessions are therefore irreconcilable. Far from being Evangelicals, the Calvinists were soon once again being classed with Schwenckfeldians, Judaizers, and Nestorians.[116]

This is not the place to rehearse the vicissitudes of the Reformed irenical tradition in the final years of the war, as uniquely personified in the career of John Dury.[117] It need only be said that Dury's program essentially replicated the pattern of the Reformed irenicists of the previous generation while magnifying it on a European scale. His basic objective was the same: to unite Lutherans and Calvinists in Germany into a force capable of resisting Roman repression. "If Protestants be not be reconciled together," he wrote in a pamphlet of 1641, "it will be impossible to prevent the utter ruine of their Churches, and overthrow of their States in Germanie."[118] The basic argumentative strategies with which he sought to achieve this were initially those of the longstanding central Europe Reformed tradition, updated at the Leipzig Colloquy. His support came, as always, from the party most vulnerable to this repression: the Reformed, or rather what was left of the Reformed: originally the shattered communities on the middle Rhine, later the moderate theologians of Bremen and Berlin, still relatively unscathed by the war. The Lutherans in Germany responded by rehearsing the arguments they had developed to block earlier generations of Reformed irenicists.[119] Dury's attempt to circumvent the intransigent German Lutherans by involving the prestigious kingdoms of Sweden and Denmark in the negotiations was a novel gambit, but one predestined to fail. His irenical vocation had been promoted by a Swedish statesman, had reached its apogee in a verbal offer of official support from the Swedish king, and was backed again in Swedish diplomatic circles; but the national synod of Swedish clergy, like their Lutheran counterparts to the south, denounced any proposals for concord not based on complete acceptance of the unvaried Augsburg Confession in 1637. Dury's visit to Denmark the following year produced another variation on this old theme already familiar to Ursinus, Pitiscius, and Pareus. Though old links with the house of Stuart facilitated high-level political backing, the Danish clergy ultimately refused to consider even opening negotiations until the Calvinists had formally renounced their errors.[120] Dury's efforts to gain backing from the most powerful and prestigious sources in the Reformed world proved equally frustrating. In Holland, as already mentioned, the dead hand of Dort weighed heavily on his attempt to win the endorsement of the Dutch synods. England, rent between Presbyterians, moderate Puritans, and Laudians in the 1630s, descended into outright warfare in the 1640s, and Dury was forced to make so many changes of confessional and political allegiance in order to retain any meaningful support there that he ultimately destroyed his credibility as a principled and impartial broker of religious discord.[121]

The Peace of Westphalia: A New Beginning

If we seek a turning point, an event that fundamentally altered the course and nature of inter-confessional discussion, it is to be found neither in 1618 nor in 1631 but in 1648. If the years after 1555 established the local, imperial, and international conditions which would structure irenical activities for nearly a century, the settlement hammered out in Westphalia and the still broader changes associated with it fundamentally altered those conditions and with them the ecumenical activities of the subsequent period.

As in the previous era, the implications of the Peace of Westphalia were most immediate at the imperial level. With the official inclusion of the Reformed confession in the Peace of Westphalia, the specifically Reformed motivation for seeking mutual understanding with the Lutherans was laid to rest. The final surge of stout volumes justifying or challenging Reformed claims to the Confession of Augsburg which accompanied the protracted peace negotiations dwindled away to nothing after 1648.[122] The desperate calls for a pan-Evangelical synod which had been heard so often became a thing of the past. Utopian projects continued to be pursued by a few isolated figures like Comenius, whose Bohemian and Moravian co-believers found no consolation in the provisions of the peace.[123] But Comenius's friend John Dury found markedly less enthusiasm for his global irenical schemes even among his Reformed brethren upon returning to the upper Rhine for a second extended visit in the latter 1650s.[124]

The most important efforts at inter-Protestant reconciliation now shifted from the imperial level to the more manageable level of the individual territories. This too was a direct effect of the peace, as the case of Hesse illustrates particularly well. In 1648 the Reformed Landgrave of Hesse-Kassel regained half of the territory around Marburg that his grandfather had lost twenty-five years before, but only on the condition that the Lutheran confession there remain unchanged. He also received part of the Lutheran county of Schaumburg with its university at Rinteln, and therefore found himself ruling over universities as well as subjects of both confessions. In this case, however, a degree of reconciliation was facilitated by the presence in Rinteln's theological faculty of students of the uniquely conciliatory Georg Calixt. A colloquium was eventually held in Kassel in 1661 between two Reformed theologians from Marburg and two Helmstedt-trained Lutheran theologians from Rinteln. Although full unity again proved beyond reach, Lutheran as well as Reformed theologians agreed that they were united in the fundamentals of faith and therefore would maintain "fraternal peace, unity, and mutual tolerance" in the future. The kind of concord which had proved impossible to achieve under the conditions of the Peace of Augsburg was effected in Hesse within thirteen years of the Peace of Westphalia, though after the war it still remained difficult to isolate such local achievements from the disruptive tactics of hard-line theologians elsewhere.[125] Similar attempts were pursued in the now somewhat diminished Rhine Palatinate, where the son of the Winter-King of Bohemia, Karl-Ludwig, attempted to reach formal Evangelical concord with neighboring Württemberg and to establish an ecumenical church in Mannheim. Indeed Karl-Ludwig went further still. Himself religiously indifferent, he attempted to repopulate his devastated inheritance by attracting immigrants from Holland, France, England, and the Swiss cantons with little consideration of their religious affiliation. Even Mennonites and numerous Jews were settled in the refounded city of Mannheim; and with an open-mindedness which would have horrified Pareus, he even sought to attract to the re-established university in Heidelberg, once the citadel of Reformed orthodoxy in the empire, the most heterodox philosopher of the age, Baruch Spinoza.[126]

At the national and territorial dimension of the problem, therefore, the search for inter-Protestant reconciliation retreated from grand, pan-European schemes to modest regional efforts. At the international level, finally, the mutual fear of the three confessions of one another momentarily lessened and an even more significant change emerged. Throughout the final phases of that conflict, the greatest miseries had been inflicted on Germans of all confessions not by their religious antagonists within the empire but by their political enemies outside it: the upstart Protestant monarchy to the north and the increasingly over-mighty Catholic kingdom to the west; and the decades immediately after the war saw a dramatic revival of the ancient threat posed by the Islamic empire to the east. Thirty years of civil war had weakened all three confessional parties within the empire, leaving them all vulnerable to arbitrary actions of monarchs who had spent those decades consolidating their power. Nowhere was this more apparent than on the banks of the Rhine, where the Catholic elector in Mainz, the Reformed elector in the Palatinate, and the Lutheran duke of Württemberg found themselves equally vulnerable to the inexorable expansion of France. In order to defend itself, the empire needed to be united. In order to be united, it had to lay its religious divisions to rest at least in some degree. And the greatest of these divisions was not that separating Lutherans and Calvinists, upon which so much energy had been expended in the previous three generations, but the far deeper divide which had so long been neglected separating Protestants of both varieties from the Roman Catholic Church.

If the beginning of the confessional age in Germany was marked by the disappearance of attempts to broker a reconciliation of Protestants and Catholics, its end was therefore signalled by the gradual resurrection of efforts to resolve this greatest of all ecumenical problems. The pioneer of this revival is perhaps the most exceptional figure in the history of ecumenism in confessional Germany: Georg Calixt (1586–1656).[127] In other contexts, Calixt might be portrayed above all as the last representative of the previous tradition of humanist conciliation. The son of a student of Melanchthon and ardent admirer of Erasmus, he was educated amongst the final flourishing of humanism in Germany at the Philippist University of Helmstedt. It would be no less accurate to portray him as a unique figure, silenced by confessional pressures during the middle phase of his career, emerging into dominance in Helmstedt only after the war itself had killed off the strictly orthodox older generation of theologians, and afterward assaulted unanimously by the academic Lutheran theologians of his day.[128] In the present context, however, it is most useful to see him as a pioneer of the ecumenical efforts that began to revive as that era came to a close. His importance for the future is evident above all in his concentration on mending the divide between Lutheranism and Catholicism: Protestant reconciliation was consistently pursued by Calixt only as a first step toward a broader union, not as the union of two parties against a third. Calixt thus represents a thin but perfectly genuine line of late humanist thought, long submerged by the dominance of Lutheran orthodoxy and the vicissitudes of war, but eventually re-emerging to pioneer a new era of efforts at Catholic-Protestant reconciliation.

Calixt's most sympathetic readers outside Helmstedt were Reformed irenicists like Dury and Bergius; and several of these register a transition from narrow irenical to broader ecumenical conceptions in this period. Given the complete intolerance and merciless persecution which he and his confession had suffered at Catholic hands, Comenius long harbored an eschatological antipathy toward the Roman church; but in the final years of his life his viewpoint too seems to have softened.[129] In 1646 Comenius dedicated a work entitled *Christianismus reconciliabilis* to Władysław IV—the Catholic king of Poland who had sponsored the colloquy in Toruń one year before;[130] and his crowning pansophic proposal for universal reform—the unfinished *Consultatio catholica*—also invited the Catholics to participate and claimed that they have a special contribution to make.[131] Dury was slower to follow this path. As late as 1658 he pressured Comenius into suppressing from a collection of his irenical writings proposals to include Catholics in plans for truly universal ecclesiastical reconciliation.[132] But Dury too eventually announced a similar conversion. The preface to his late treatise *Touchant l'intellegence de l'Apocalypse* of 1674 expressed both his deep disappointment over the failure of his lifelong campaign to reconcile Lutherans and Calvinists and his vow to devote the rest of his life to the still grander enterprise of reconciling Protestants and Catholics.[133]

Particularly for the Reformed, this move from an irenical tradition motivated by the need to withstand the resurgent Antichrist to an ecumenical program devoted to seeking reunion with Rome represented a remarkable conversion. To the great distress of Hartlib, Dury, and Comenius, however, several members of their circle—prompted not least by the proven incapacity of the main Protestant churches to lay their quarrels to rest—moved farther still in these years and actually converted to Catholicism.[134] The Reformed pastor in Danzig, Bartholomäus Nigrin, stunned his colleagues in Danzig by announcing his conversion to Catholicism in 1643, leaving Comenius, who had recently confided his own ecumenical plans to him, in a dangerously compromised position.[135] One of Hartlib's oldest friends, the Nuremberg patrician and diplomat Johann Abraham Pöhmer, converted to Catholicism in 1655 and transferred his services to the elector-archbishop of Mainz.[136] One of the central figures of Hartlib's circle in England, Joachim Hübner, was dismissed from his position as librarian to the elector of Brandenburg for refusal to attend church and transferred his services in 1662 to a recent convert to Catholicism, Pfalzgraf Christian August von Sulzbach, who raised him to privy councilor within two years.[137] More distressing and surprising still must have been the conversion of the sons and daughters of the greatest secular patrons of the previous generation's irenical efforts. The offspring of Frederick V, the elector Palatine and king of Bohemia, converted in droves. Louise Hollandine, Eduard, Liselotte, even the unforgettably named Gustavus Adolphus all became Catholic, while three remaining children—Karl Ludwig, Elizabeth, and Sophie—remained Reformed or Lutheran in little more than name.[138] The original Gustavus Adolphus's daughter, Queen Christina of Sweden, followed suit in 1654, and the agony of her conversion must have been increased by the knowledge that she had been tutored as a child by Johan Matthiae, the one patron among the Swedish bishops of Dury's irenical efforts. More important than any of these in the ecumenical efforts of the new era was Ernst von Hessen-Rheinfels—the grandson of Johann the Elder of Nassau-Dillenburg, who had introduced Calvinism into the Wetterau counties, the son of Moritz the Learned of Hesse-Kassel, who had Calvinized both upper and lower Hesse, and the half-brother of Wilhelm V of Hesse-Kassel, one of the most belligerent Calvinists in the latter stages of the war.[139] He too converted to Catholicism in the Cologne cathedral in 1652.

The subsequent career of this remarkable figure leads immediately into the center of a highly placed group of Catholics, converts, and loyal Protestants working towards a comprehensive ecclesiastical reunion with an energy and imagination which Germany had not seen for a century. In the years surrounding his conversion, Ernst von Hessen-Rheinfels organized a series of colloquia in Rheinfels (1651), Kassel (1652), and Giessen (1653) which brought several of the leading figures of the previous debates together, including Johannes Crocius, Balthasar Mentzer, and the remarkable Capuchin friar Valerian Magni. More important still, it was Ernst in all likelihood who originated the "Mainz plan" for ecclesiastical reunification adopted and strenuously pursued by the elector-archbishop of Mainz, Johann Philipp von Schönborn, his suffragan, Peter van Walenburgh, and his minister of state, Johann Christian von Boineburg.[140] It was through this circle at Mainz that the young Gottfried Wilhelm Leibniz (1646–1716) was converted to his lifelong pursuit of ecclesiastical reunion.[141] Due partly to the mediation of Ernst von Hessen-Rheinfels, Leibniz eventually transferred to the court of Johann Friedrich of Hannover, who had also converted to Catholicism in 1650. After the death of Schönborn, Hannover and the other courts of Braunschweig-Lüneburg became the main centers of reunionist activity in the final third of the century.[142] There Leibniz and Gerhard Walter Molanus (1633–1722), abbot of Loccum and student of Calixt,[143] engaged in intensive discussions with the bishop of Tina, Christoph de Rojas y Spinola (1626–1695), on a plan for reunion backed by the emperor Leopold and popes Clement X and Innocent XI.[144] No less important was the extensive correspondence—mediated in part by two daughters of the king and queen of Bohemia, Duchess Sophie of Hannover and Louise Hollandine, abbess of Maubuisson—between Leibniz and Jacques Bénigne de Bossuet (1627–1704), bishop of Meaux and confessor of Louis XIV, Paul Pellisson-Fontanier (1624–1693), another convert who acted as court historian to the French king, and the great Jansenist Antoine Arnauld.[145] Although initially aloof from these efforts, Brandenburg was also eventually drawn into the discussion, most notably in the case of Daniel Ernst Jablonski (1660–1741), the grandson of Comenius and court preacher to Frederick I, king of Prussia.[146]

As even this roll-call of major participants suggests, the motivations underlying these ecumenical discussions had also changed. In the seventy-five years before Westphalia, appeals for inter-Protestant unity had been advanced almost exclusively by vulnerable groups seeking to protect themselves against larger, more powerful political opponents: Dutch and French rebels, waging war against their powerful rulers; the Reformed party in Germany, excluded from the Peace of Augsburg; Protestants of all kinds in Poland and Bohemia, joining forces to defend their liberties against Catholic rulers; Remonstrants ejected from their livings in Holland; exiles of all kinds driven from their homelands by thirty years of war; Socinians evicted from their churches in Poland; and briefly, in Leipzig, even orthodox Lutherans, confronted at long last by the prospect of complete domination by their Catholic emperor. The cast of characters involved in the postwar ecumenical discussions is strikingly different. Here the initiative comes from senior figures on *both* sides of the confessional divide who are in no obvious relations of vulnerability to or dependence on one another. The direct participants range from the senior elector and primate in Germany, the archbishop of Mainz, through an impressive hierarchy of princes and princesses, abbots and abbesses, bishops, court preachers, theologians, philosophers, and senior court advisors and intellectuals. It would be rash to oversimplify the motivations at work in this company. As more than one leading expert has emphasized, "Indifferentism, rationalism, and materialism on the one hand, religiosity (deepened by the dire straits of the Thirty Years' War), eschatological and pietistic currents, religioecclesiastical and political motives on the other are all in league with one another in the irenical efforts and those aimed at reunion."[147] Amidst the plethora of conflicting motivations, it is nevertheless possible to detect one overriding concern: a new source of vulnerability shared by Protestants and Catholics alike. The war in Germany had been so miserably protracted not merely by religious divisions themselves but because these internal divisions had so weakened Germany that she could no longer defend herself against her more powerful neighbors such as Sweden and France. While indifferentism, rationalism, and the consolidation of authority in secular hands all helped to ease confessional antagonism, the fact that the greatest threats for Germany now so clearly came from outside her borders also encouraged the search for religious reunion from both sides of the main confessional divide. In the latter half of the century, in other words, vulnerability remained a motive for seeking reunion, but it was a vulnerability based not on unequal legal standing or political power within the empire but on unequal political centralization and military force between Germany as a whole and her immediate neighbors.[148]

As the focus and purpose of ecumenical collaboration changed, its mode shifted accordingly. With so many scholars and churchmen involved, this change of atmosphere and orientation also unleashed a flood of books.[149] Consideration of them and their authors would widen the cast of characters and their geographical distribution still further to include figures like Thomas Henricus in Freiburg im Breisgau, the Jesuit Jacob Masenius in Cologne, the convert from Württemberg, Timotheus Laubenberger in Mainz, Michael Praetorius, the Lutheran convert to Catholicism from Königsberg, Dionysius von Werl in Hildesheim, and Joan Dez in Cologne. But the most important evidence of this change of direction is not to be found in these books. Print had been the preferred medium in the previous era, in which irenicism had been intimately allied with official ecclesiastical diplomacy and political propaganda. But the stakes in the new efforts at reconciliation went well beyond the attempt to construct a religious platform for stable political alliances in a confessional age; and in the radically changed new context publication was a liability rather than an asset. Publication fixed positions in print. Correspondence, on the other hand, left room for gradual shifts and accommodations in the course of long and scrupulous discussion. Publication exposed discussions to the enemies of reunion, to the orthodox academics in all camps who wanted neither compromise nor reconciliation. Correspondence was relatively private and allowed for frank, open discussion and courageous exploration of all avenues of reconciliation which would have been impossible in public. The main sources for understanding the ecumenical efforts of this period are therefore not massive polemical publications but huge collections of posthumously published letters.[150] Leibniz's ecumenical efforts in particular have to be reconstructed from the thousands of tiny fragments in his enormous *Nachlaß*. Of the not inconsiderable number of books published by other advocates of reunion, perhaps the most important and characteristic is the *Discrete Catholische* of Ernst von Hessen-Rheinfels.[151]

Finally, if public statements did not provide the most hopeful means of repairing the schism, then neither did public meetings, synods, or councils. A general church council had once been the means favored in Germany for repairing the schism within the empire. It remained so until 1545, when the long-awaited council was called in Trent, on the Italian side of the Alps, and likewise tailored to a Roman rather than a German agenda. Even after that point, a general Evangelical synod remained the obvious way to reunite

Protestants in Germany; but after the modification of the religious peace in 1648 made that reunion unnecessary, efforts dropped to the more realistic level of territorial and even local reconciliation, and calls for such synods fell silent. The epoch-making resumption of efforts to repair the greater rift between Catholics and Protestants, however, did not lead to a resumption of similar demands. Roman authorities were bound to maintain that such a council had already been held and that the conclusions of Trent established the context within which any future reunion might take place. Protestant authorities inevitably regarded this solution as no solution at all. The differences separating these two parties could never be worked out in a public forum, and even in private ecumenical discussions the topic of a general council was more likely to feature as a problem in its own right than as an immediate solution. Rather than resolving the problem of disunity, a general, public, ecumenical council could be called only after Trent had been suspended, public reform had removed abuses, and unity in essentials had already been prepared by private discussion. Given the length of this agenda, even those, like Leibniz, who saw a general council as necessary for the final step towards unity did not expect to see it in his lifetime.[152] Intimate discussions abounded in the postwar period, private colloquies multiplied, but conciliarism, for the foreseeable future at least, had run its course. Ironically perhaps, the end of the confessional age in the mid-seventeenth century therefore also saw the end of the far lengthier conciliar epoch.

It is of course important not to be too sanguine about these postwar ecumenical efforts either. Religious conversion could be prompted by base as well as lofty motives, and willingness to participate in ecumenical discussions does not necessarily indicate willingness to compromise. In some respects, the *Colloquium charitativum* in Toruń, for instance—which perhaps more than any other event marks the watershed between these two periods—does not so much break new ground as rehearse all the reasons why previous colloquia of this kind had also failed. As usual, a moment of vulnerability stimulated the whole project. The secular patron of the colloquium, King Władysław IV of Poland, called the meeting not least because his regime and religion were endangered by a possible alliance between Sweden and Brandenburg-Prussia. Pope Innocent X permitted it for fear "that the church might lose Poland altogether if he refused." One of its chief organizers, Bartholomäus Nigrin, intended that the meeting should provoke on a mass scale the kind of conversion to Catholicism which he himself had just experienced. Archbishop Matthias Lubienski, who issued the formal invitations to attend, had similar hopes. Perhaps the most genuinely ecumenical Protestant at the gathering, the pansophical Comenius, convinced anxious colleagues in the Bohemian Brethren that attendance could hold no danger precisely because "We are certain that the truth is on our side." The Brethren and their Reformed colleagues attempted to unite with the Lutherans beforehand on the basis of their consensus on the fundamentals of the faith and their "common hatred of the opponent." The Lutherans, as always, refused to contemplate any "Religionsmischerei oder Synkretismus," excluded the one genuine moderate, Georg Calixt, from their delegation before the colloquium began, and absented themselves from the opening prayers because they were presided over by a Catholic.[153] Yet however far short Toruń may have fallen of a fully ecumenical ideal, an ecumenical meeting did take place; and that mere fact is certainly consequential. For the first time in nearly a century, official representatives of the three main confessions in central Europe—supplemented in this case by those of the oldest Protestant churches, those of Bohemia—came together in one place to consider the prospects of ecclesiastical reconciliation. If, as Howard Louthan has argued elsewhere in this volume, that meeting represented the last act of the long and honorable tradition of ecclesiastical conciliation in east-central Europe,[154] it simultaneously opened a new chapter in the ecumenical history of the lands to the west, and the next forty years would see a flurry of activity aimed at reconciling Catholics and Protestants not seen in Germany for a century.

Viewed in broad chronological perspective, the irenical traditions within the empire fall into a distinct pattern in the confessional age. The conclusion of the Council of Trent on 6 December 1563 seems to have spelled the end of attempts at Protestant-Catholic reconciliation in Germany for several generations. The entry of Calvinism into the empire at almost precisely the same moment entailed that efforts at reconciliation would focus instead on a grotesquely distorted debate on the reconciliation of Evangelicals in Germany which political necessities of one kind compelled the Reformed to promote while political necessities of another compelled the Lutherans almost as firmly to reject. The resulting pattern was essentially maintained until the conclusion of the Thirty Years' War disrupted it, partly by extending a degree of religious toleration to Calvinism, partly by redrawing territorial boundaries and consolidating the authority of their rulers, but also by demonstrating that the main dangers to Germans of all three confessions now came from more powerful and unified political enemies outside their borders. Periodizations are difficult to come by in history, and no one would propose that a new era suddenly began on 25 September 1555, Christmas Day 1559, or 6 December 1563 and ended suddenly on 24 October 1648. But if the irenical forces ostensibly working against the process of confessionalization are any indication, the confessional age is a distinct period which needs to be examined on its own terms and no longer simply conceived as an extension of the Reformation era or a precursor of Pietism, absolutism, or Enlightenment, or simply banished to obscurity under the deadening rubric of "orthodoxy" and ignored altogether.

On the contrary, the history of the irenical efforts of the confessional age is highly instructive from a number of different perspectives. For the general historian, it helps to reinforce the identity of the confessional age as a distinctive period. The rigidifying divisions between the confessions are now commonly advanced as a central characteristic of the period. The persistence of an irenical tradition explicitly dedicated to overcoming confessional divisions might seem at first glance an important qualification of confessionalization as the defining characteristic of the period. But on closer inspections, both the persistent Reformed irenical tradition and the equally persistent Lutheran rejection of it can be seen to arise directly from the fundamental confessional exigencies of the period. Far from qualifying the confessional age, this distinctive tradition of Reformed irenicism actually reinforces the definition of the period between 1563 and 1648 as a distinct period in the confessional history of Europe, for this strangely unilateral tradition in which Calvinists propose and Lutherans reject concord is strikingly different from the bipartisan efforts at achieving the reunion of all of Christendom both before and after this period.

It is no less instructive to view the irenicism of the confessional era in a still wider geographical and chronological perspective. Within the broader history of irenicism, this reveals the necessity of viewing the irenical traditions of the confessional era in an international and comparative context which sets German activities in the midst of the Bohemian, Polish, Swedish, Dutch, French, and indeed English and Scottish efforts and puts the Scottish irenicist John Dury back in the middle of central Europe where he belongs. Within the longer history of ecumenism, this Reformed tradition reaching from Ursinus, Pareus, and Bythner to Dury and Comenius represents the long death throes of the conciliar age, the period in which the conciliar ideal, foreclosed by Trent as the solution to the general problem of the reunification of Christendom, remained the obvious solution to the particular problem of uniting the Protestant churches.

If historians still have much to learn about and from the irenicism of the confessional age, ecumenists today can also learn most from this painful period not by continuing to ignore it or by subtly taking sides in the polemical campaigns of the period, but by contextualizing and therefore under-standing it more thoroughly. For this long story of division and distrust is not without its consolations. Reformed ecumenists can take pride in the only persistent irenical tradition in central Europe reaching unbroken from the beginning to the end of the confessional era, though they must recog-nize both the political ambitions that fostered it and the serious limitations which undermined it. Lutheran ecumenists can take solace not only in the dormant strand of irenicism eventually reawakened in Georg Calixt, but also in the fact that it was concrete political circumstances which so greatly mag-nified in the mind of Lutheran orthodoxy the genuine theological differ-ences separating the Evangelical churches. And Catholic ecumenists, though confronted by the virtual absence of predecessors in the empire for almost a century after Trent, can take comfort in the fact that, when the confessional era was finally over, it was Catholic kings, princes, bishops, and archbishops who, in partnership with Calixt and his school, took the first concrete ini-tiatives towards really catholic reconciliation in Toruń in 1645, in Mainz in 1660, and in the quarter century which followed.

NOTES

This essay is dedicated to the memory of the leading American scholar of German irenicism, Bodo Nischan, whose sudden and unexpected death occurred while it was in preparation. Special thanks are due to the Herzog August Bibliothek, Wolfen-büttel, the Max-Planck-Institut für Geschichte, and the Staats- und Universitäts-bibliothek in Göttingen, in the collections of which most of the research for this paper was conducted.

    1. Cf. the proceedings of three coordinated symposia: Heinz Schilling, ed., *Die reformierte Konfessionalisierung in Deutschland* (Gütersloh, 1986); Hans-Christian Rublack, *Die lutherische Konfessionalisierung in Deutschland* (Gütersloh, 1992); and Wolfgang Reinhard and Heinz Schilling, eds., *Die katholische Konfessionalisie-rung* (Gütersloh, 1995). Important syntheses and reviews include Heinrich Rich-ard Schmidt, *Konfessionalisierung im 16. Jahrhundert* (Munich, 1992); and Thomas Kaufmann, "Die Konfessionalisierung von Kirche und Gesellschaft. Sammelbericht über eine Forschungsdebatte," *Theologische Literaturzeitung* 121 (1996): 1008–25, 1112–21.

    2. For the following, cf. for instance Hugh Trevor-Roper, "The Religious Ori-gins of the Enlightenment," in *Religion, the Reformation, and Social Change* 3rd. ed. (London, 1984), 193–236; Friedrich Heer, *Die dritte Kraft. Der europäische Humanismus*

zwischen den Fronten des konfessionellen Zeitalters (Frankfurt am Main, 1959); Francis A. Yates, *The Rosicrucian Enlightenment* (London, 1972); R. J. W. Evans, *Rudolf II and his World: A Study in Intellectual History, 1576–1612* (Oxford, 1973).

3. Carl Wilhelm Hering, *Geschichte der kirchlichen Unionsversuche seit der Reformation bis auf unsere Zeit* (2 vols., Leipzig, 1836–1838); Martin Schmidt, "Ecumenical Activity on the Continent of Europe in the Seventeenth and Eighteenth Centuries," in Ruth Rouse and Stephen Neill, eds., *A History of the Ecumenical Movement, 1517–1948* (Philadelphia, 1954), 73–120; Friedrich Wilhelm Kantzenbach, *Das Ringen um die Einheit der Kirche im Jahrhundert der Reformation. Vertreter, Quellen und Motive des "ökumenischen" Gedankens von Erasmus von Rotterdam bis Georg Calixt* (Stuttgart, 1957); Peter Kawerau, *Die ökumenische Idee seit der Reformation* (Stuttgart, 1968).

4. The only monographic study of Pareus, the standard biography of Dury, and an infinite number of articles on Comenius all fall into this pattern: see Günter Brinkmann, *Die Irenik des David Pareus* (Hildesheim, 1972); J. Minton Batten, *John Dury: Advocate of Christian Reunion* (Chicago, 1944); and J. M. Lochman, "Jan Amos Comenius: Bahnbrecher ökumenischer Hoffnung," in P. van Vliet and A. J. Vanderjagt, eds., *Johannes Amos Comenius (1592–1670): Exponent of European Culture?* (Amsterdam, 1994), 47–51.

5. I refer here particularly to the only synoptic book on the subject in English: C.-P. Clasen, *The Palatinate in European History* (Oxford, 1966, rev. ed. 1969). Cf. for instance Simon Adams in Geoffrey Parker, *The Thirty Years' War* (London, 1984), 25–38.

6. Koecher, *Abbildung einer Friedenstheologie oder der Gottesgelahrtheit . . . . Nebst einer Bibliotheca Theologiae Irenicae* (Jena, 1764), 161–306.

7. Draudius, *Bibliotheca classica: sive catalogus officinalis in quo singuli singularum facultatum ac professionum libri, qui in quavis fere lingua extant, . . . ordine alphabetico recensentur* (Frankfurt am Main, 1625). Idem, *Bibliotheca librorum germanicorum classica, Das ist: Verzeichnuß aller und jeder Bücher, so fast bey dencklichen Jahren biß auffs Jahr nach Christi Geburt 1625 in Teutscher Spraach . . . in Truck außgangen etc.* (Frankfurt am Main, 1625). Martin Lipenius, *Bibliotheca realis theologica* (2 vols., Frankfurt am Main, 1685; repr. Hildesheim, 1973).

8. Axel Hilmar Swinne, *Bibliographia irenica, 1500–1970* [Studia irenica, 10] (Hildesheim, 1977); Jan van der Haar, *Internationale ökumenische Beziehungen im 17. und 18. Jahrhundert: Bibliographie von den aus dem Englischen, Niederländischen und Französischen ins Deutsche übersetzten theologischen Büchern von 1600–1800* (Erveen, 1997).

9. See for example Adam Contzen's *De pace germaniae libri II: Prior de falsa pace alter de vera pace* (Mainz, 1616). The depth of Contzen's irenicism is open to question: the entire work builds toward the conclusion articulated in liber II, cap. 32: "Concilium Tridentinum suscipiendum esse, vt pax Germaniae reddatur," 744–69.

On Contzen, see Robert Bireley, *Maximilian von Bayern, Adam Contzen S.J. und die Gegenreformation in Deutschland 1624–1635* (Göttingen, 1975), here 27–30.

10. The only exception I have seen discussed before the Peace of Prague is a single work by Conrad Berg published anonymously in 1628 — a year of particularly grave political difficulty, as Wallenstein consolidated imperial control over northern Germany. See Hans Leube, *Kalvinismus und Luthertum im Zeitalter der Orthodoxie* (Leipzig, 1928; repr. Aalen, 1966), 56–58. Additional evidence may, of course, lie in private correspondence. See for instance G. H. M. Posthumus Meyjes, "Protestant Irenicism in the Sixteenth and Seventeenth Centuries," in D. Loades, ed., *The End of Strife* (Edinburgh, 1984), 77–93, here 88–93, which mainly discusses humanist figures in Holland and England.

11. The most extensive treatment of both sides of this debate remains the often very partisan study of Hans Leube, cited in the previous note. Brief but admirably balanced accounts of the Reformed initiatives are two articles by Gustav Adolf Benrath, "Irenik und Zweite Reformation," in Schilling, ed., *Die reformierte Konfessionalisierung*, 349–58; and "Konfessionelle Irenik und Konkordienversuche im 16. und 17. Jahrhundert. Eine Skizze," in Helmut Baier, ed., *Konfessionalisierung vom 16.-19. Jahrhundert* (Neustadt an der Aisch, 1989), 155–66.

12. The most comprehensive survey is the valuable but unpublished disseration by Wilhelm Holtmann, "Die pfälzische Irenik im Zeitalter der Gegenreformation" (Inaugural-Dissertation, Göttingen, 1960). Here Leube's Lutheran bias provokes a countervailing sympathy for the Reformed position.

13. Wilhelm Holtmann, "Vorschlag für ein allgemeines Konzil von Zacharias Ursinus," *Reformierte Kirchenzeitung* 105 (1964): 63 ff; and idem, "Die pfälzische Irenik,"122–97.

14. Th. Gümbel, "Die Berührungen zwischen evangelischen Engländern und Pfälzern im Zeitalter der Reformation," *Neues Archiv für die Geschichte der Stadt Heidelberg* 6 (1905): 229 ff; Leube, *Kalvinismus und Luthertum*, 22–28. Jill Raitt, "The Elector John Casimir, Queen Elizabeth and the Protestant League," in Derk Visser, ed., *Controversy and Conciliation: The Reformation and the Palatinate 1559–1583* (Allison Park, Pa., 1986), 117–45.

15. The most extensive study of any single work of this tradition is the absurdly pious work of Günter Brinkmann, *Die Irenik des David Pareus* (Hildesheim, 1972). Cf. the more balanced and perceptive sketch of Gustav Adolf Benrath, "David Pareus," in Helmut Neubach and Ludwig Petry, eds., *Schlesier des 15. bis 20. Jahrhunderts* (Schlesische Lebensbilder, 5. Band) (Würzburg, 1968), 13–23. The literature from Heidelberg was complemented by a smaller but important increment from Amberg, the main ecclesiastical center of the Upper Palatinate.

16. Early irenical works from Hesse include the following: "Erasmus Sabinus Hofnerus" [i.e., Hermann Fabronius], *Der Evangelischen Kirchen Einigkeit zum uralten Glauben: Christlicher Raht unnd Vorschlag zu Wahrheit und Frieden* (Kassel, 1607).

H. Ewald, *Irene Sacra, ein Christliche Predigt von Fried und Einigkeit in der Kirchen Christi* (Marburg, 1608). Hermann Fabronius, *Concordia Lutherano-Calvinistica* ([n.pl., 1615]; Schmalkalden, 1616, 1618). Later contributions include Johannes Crocius, *Conversatio Prutenica* (Marburg, 1620) and idem, *Paci et concordiae evangelicorum sacra defensio* (Marburg, 1623).

   17. For a brief biography of Bergius and full bibliography including half a dozen irenical works, see Lothar Noack and Jürgen Splett, *Bio-Bibliographien. Brandenburgische Gelehrte der frühen Neuzeit. Berlin-Cölln 1640–1688* (Berlin, 1997), 14–23. A specialized treatment is Bodo Nischan, "John Bergius: Irenicism and the Beginning of Official Religious Toleration in Brandenburg-Prussia," *Church History* 51 (1982): 389–404.

   18. For Herborn, see Georg Spindler, *Klarer und wahrer Bericht von vrsach alles Irrthumbs vnd Streits in Religionsachen* (Herborn, 1592); Wilhelm Zepper, *Bericht von den dreyen Hauptpuncten, welche zwischen den Evangelischen Kirchen . . . fürnemlich im streit stehen* (Herborn, 1592, 1616); idem., *Christliches Bedencken, Vorschlag und Raht, Durch waserley mittel vnd wege dem hochbetrübten zustand der Kirchen Gottes . . . absuhelffen seyn möge* (Herborn, 1594); Lyle D. Bierma, "Lutheran-Reformed Polemics in the Late Reformation: Olevian's Proposal," in Visser, ed., *Controversy and Conciliation,* 51–62; and Holtmann, "Die pfälzische Irenik," 229–34. For Hanau, see [Heinrich Büllinger the Elder, et al.] *Von Fried vnd Einigkeit, Drei Christliche Predigen* (Hanau, 1599); and Josef Benzing, "Die Hanauer Erstdrucker Wilhelm und Peter Antonius (1593–1625)," *Archiv für Geschichte des Buchwesens,* 21 (1980), 1005–1126, nos. 56, 94, 111, 161, 202. For Anhalt, see note 60 below and Irenaeus Palaeus [i.e., Caspar Ulrich, Superintendent in Zerbst], *Rathsam Bedenken Der Mängel und Ursachen, umb welcher willen . . . nun fast uber 64. Jahr, hochärgerlicher Zweispalt in den Evangelischen Kirchen . . . geblieben, und wie . . . solchem in etwas abzuhelffen* (Hanau, 1610).

   19. Hermann Ravensperger (professor of theology in Steinfurt), *Via Veritatis & Pacis, quibus modis . . . firmam concordiam pertingere possit* (Hanau, 1614). On the Bremen theologians, see J. Fr. Iken, "Bremen und die Synode von Dordrecht," *Bremisches Jahrbuch,* 10 (1878), 11–105. Irenical works include Johannes Lampadius, *Disputatio de Conciliis ad oblatam à Palatinis Concordiam stabiliendam* (Bremen, 1615); Franciscus Junius, *Consilium de pace et concordia in ecclesia Dei colenda,* ed. Ludwig Crocius (Bremen, 1615); Crocius, *De vera religione* (Bremen, 1619); idem, *Apologeticus pro Augustana Confessione* (Bremen, 1621). For later works see note 115 below.

   20. Cf. Benrath's statement to the same effect in "Irenik und Zweite Reformation," 357.

   21. Pareus, *Irenicum sive de unione et synodo evangelicorum concilianda liber votivus paci ecclesiae . . . dicatus* (Heidelberg, 1614, 1615); German trans. by Gwinandus Zosius, *Irenicum oder Friedemacher* (Frankfurt am Main, 1615). A Dutch translation is mentioned by Benrath. On the date of the first edition, see *Catalogus universalis pro nundinis Francofurtensibus vernalibus, de anno M.DC.XIV.* (Frankfurt am Main [1614]), fol. B3r.

22. Balduinus, *Oratio panegyrica de synodo evangelicorum generali: Quam in componendis controversiis sacramentariis frustra urget D. Pareus in suo Irenico* (Wittenberg, 1614).

23. Hutter (praes.), Michael Siricius (resp.), *Quaestionum octo controversarum, De pace et unione Lutheranorum [et] Calvinianorum: Irenico D. Davidis Parei . . . opposita, publicae vero disputationi subjecta* (Wittenberg, 1614).

24. Höe von Höenegg, *Kurtzer und deutlicher Discurs, Ob die Calvinische Lehr, ohne Erkenntnüß eines allgemeinen Concilii oder Synodi nicht könne noch solle für unrecht erkläret oder verdammet . . .* (Leipzig, 1614).

25. For the disputation see note 64 below. Höe von Höenegg, *Triumphus Calvinisticus . . . Darinnen . . . für die Augen gestellet wird, welch ein Wust, welch eine, sonst fast ungläubliche menge der grösten abschewlichsten Irrthumbe vnd Grewel in der Calvinistischen Lehrer Schrifften zu finden . . seyen* (Leipzig, 1615). The relation to Pareus is spelled out in the preface, esp. fol. aiiiv. Balduin, *Rettung/seiner Lateinischen Oration de Synodo generali Evangelicorum* (Wittenberg, 1616); Hutter, *Irenicum vere Christianum: sive De synodo et unione Evangelicorum non-fucata concilianda, tractatus theologicus* (Wittenberg, 1616; repr. 1618, 1619, 1661); Polycarp Leyser, *Vindiciae Lyserianae An syncretismus in rebus fidei cum Calvinianis coli possit, et in Politica conversatione Pontificij illis praeferendi sint? Oppositae calumniis Irenici Pareani* (Leipzig, 1616).

26. Sigwart, *Admonitio christiana de Irenico sive libro votivo: Quem David Pareus . . . de unione, synodo et syncretismo inter Evangelicos, hoc est, Lutheranos & Calvinianos, constituendo* (Tübingen, 1614, 1616), 744 pp. Idem, *Kurtzer Extract Oder Summarischer Außzug Deren Admonition-Schrifft, so im 1616. Jahr zu Tübingen auff David Parei . . . Irenicum, in Truck verfertiget worden: In welchem . . . gründtlich angezeigt würdt: Warumb zwischen den genanten Lutherischen und Calvinischen noch der Zeit kein Vereinigung in Religions-Puncten gemacht werden könne* ([Tübingen], 1618), 408 pp. See also his *Responsionis ad orationem Dav. Parei de pace et unione ecclesiar. evang. partes duae* (Tübingen, 1617).

27. Adam Contzen S.J., *De unione et synodo generali evangelicorum theologis et politicis necessaria consultatio* (Mainz, 1615). Cf. Bireley, *Maximilian von Bayern, Adam Contzen S.J. und die Gegenreformation in Deutschland*, 27–30.

28. Pareus, *De pace et unione ecclesiarum evangel. oratio inauguralis habita in solenni universitatis Heidelbergensis . . . 11. April. 1616. . . . Cum brevi protestatione D. Parei, cur adversarios pacis & synodi &c. responso nullo digultur* (Heidelberg, 1616), here quoting the epilogue, 23–24: "Et cui bono? Pro pace ego centifoliis scriptis centifoium opponam? Adversarii duplicabunt? Triplicabunt? Pacis consilium ibit in immensae contentionis finem? Minime!" Pareus, *Notae In Problema Theologicum: An Syncretismvs Fidei & religionis inter Lutheranos & Caluinianos ideo iniri vel poßit, vel debeat, ut Antichristi Tyrannis coniunctis viribus & studiis facilius & felicius reprimi poßit?* (Heidelberg, 1616). For an analysis of the oration, see Holtmann, "Die pfälzische Irenik," 253–55.

29. Pareus, *Irenicum*, 345.

30. For this work and the debate provoked by it, see Leube, *Kalvinismus und Luthertum,* 50–53; and esp. Holtmann, "Die pfälzische Irenik," 205–25.

31. (1) Paul Stein, *Concio Irenica oder FriedensPredigt* (Kassel, 1618). (2) Baltha-sar Mentzer, *Wolgemeinter Erinnerung von der Concione Irenica oder Friedens-Predigt* (Giessen, 1619). (3) Stein, *Rettung der zu Cassel am 22. Junii Anno 1618 gehaltenen FriedensPredigt* (Kassel, 1619). Answered by (4) Peter Tuckermann, *Antwort auff Ehrn Pauli Steinii, Hoffpredigers zu Cassel, Rettung* (Wolfenbüttel, 1619); (5) Mentzer, *Exa-men oder Prob der Rettung/Ehrn Pauli Steinii* (Giessen, 1620); and (6) Mentzer (praes.), *Disputationes novem Anti-Steinianae* (Giessen, 1620). (7) Stein, *Evangelischer Kirchen Brüderschafft,* (3 vols., Kassel, 1622–1623). (8) Mentzer, *Concordiae Fons Veritas. Brevis consideratio libri, quem hoc anno edidit Paulus Steinius . . . sub titulo: Evangelischer Kir-chen Brüderschaft* (Giessen, 1623). (9) Mentzer, *Wolbegründete Antwort auff Ehrn Pauli Steinii . . . Evangelischer Kirchen Brüderschafft* (Giessen, 1624). For discussion, cf. Leube, *Kalvinismus und Luthertum,* 53–55; Winfried Zeller, "Die niederhessische Irenik," *Jahrbuch der Hessischen Kirchengeschichtlichen Vereinigung* 18 (1967): 137–65; Benrath, "Die hessische Kirche und die Synode von Dordrecht," ibid. 20 (1969): 64–65, 83–86.

32. Pareus, *Irenicum,* 3v and 149–90.

33. Pareus, *Irenicum,* 67, 68–74.

34. Prominent examples include Hermann Fabronius, *Concordia Lutherano-Calvinistica . . . : Darinnen begrieffen wird: . . . Daß die Lutheraner und Calvinisten . . . im Fundament des Glaubens einig seyn* ([n.pl., 1615]; Schmalkalden, 1616, 1618). Johann Bergius (praes.), *De Quaestione theologica, an Evangelicae per Germaniam ecclesiae dis-sentiant in fundamento fidei?* ([Frankfurt an der Oder], 1617). See also G. H. Turn-bull, *Hartlib, Dury and Comenius: Gleanings from Hartlib's Papers* (London, 1947), 175; Nischan, "Bergius," 395–96.

35. Pareus, *Irenicum,* 149–50; cf. also 67–68, 340–42.

36. Ibid., 197–241.

37. Ibid., 23–28.

38. Cf. the references to the earlier pamphlet in *Triumphus Calvinisticus,* "Vorrede," aijr–v, eivr.

39. Höe von Höenegg, *Augenscheinliche Prob, Wie die Calvinisten in Neun und Neuntzig Punkten mit den Arrianern und Türcken vbereinstimmen* (Leipzig, 1621). Cf. also his *Xenium Calvino Turcicum pro Rebellibus Bohemis* (n.pl., 1621).

40. Johann Klein, *Demostratio apodictica, Lutheranos & Calvinianos in funda-mentalibus fidei articulis plerisque non consentire* (Rostock, 1623); Johann Olearius, *Verzeichniß mehr denn 200 Calvinischen Irrthumb, Lügen . . . wider alle Artikel der Augsburg'schen Confession* (Halle, 1597).

41. Peter Hinckelmann, *Calvinismi errores praecipui vere ortodoxi, in omnibus fere articulis fidei, . . . cum succincta eorum refutatione ad disputandum propositi* (Ros-tock, 1611).

42. Schlüsselburg, *Theologiae Caluinistarvm libri tres, in qvibvs . . . plvsqvam ex CCXXIII. sacramentariorum publicis scriptis . . . demonstratur, eos de nullo ferè doctrinae*

Christianae articulo, recte sentire . . . (Frankfurt am Main, 1592–94): *Verzeichnis der im deutschen Sprachbereich erschienenen Druckschriften des XVI. Jahrhunderts* (22 vols., Stuttgart, 1982–95), 16, S 3041–46 (hereafter *VD 16*); *Theologiae Calvinistarum liber qvartvs* (Frankfurt am Main, 1610).

43. Pelargus (Storch), *Quaestionis, an inter Lutheranos et Calvinianos, dissidentes cùm in alijs ferè omnibus, tum in articulis maximè de persona Christi et de S. Coena, medium dari possit? Apophasis, confirmata brevibus, et in disputationem proposita* (Frankfurt am Main, 1591): *VD 16*, S 9324. Schlüsselburg, *Endliche, bestendige, christliche, nothwendige Antwort vnd Erklärung auff die Schmehekarten vnd Lesterschrifft des Grossen Heuchlers vnd unbestendigen, wetterwendischen Ecebolisten und nunmehr Calvinisten D. Christophori Pelargi* . . . (Rostock, 1616).

44. Cf. note 40 above with the following examples: Eilhard Lubin (praes.), Johann Quistorp (resp.), *Quaestio de fidei ac salutis fundamento, an illud Calviniani sartum tectumq[ue] retineant, ita ut inter Lutheranos et Calvinianos super illo sit consensus* ([Rostock], 1616). Balthasar Meisner (praes.), Andraes Groshenning (resp.), *Disputatio theologica de nobili quaestione: an Luterani et Calviniani in fundamento fidei consentient* (Wittenberg, 1617). Andreas Schlüsselburg, *Facula quaedam sacra* . . . *an Lutherani et Calviniani in fundamento notoriè* (Rostock, 1618). Balthasar Meisner (praes.), Abrahamus Carius (resp.), *De dissensu Lutheranorum et Calvinianorum in fundamento fidei* (1620), in Meisner, *Collegii adiaphoristici Calvinianis oppositi* (Wittenberg, 1620; 2nd. ed. 1628). Johann Klein, *Demostratio apodictica, Lutheranos & Calvinianos in fundamentalibus fidei articulis plerisque non consentire* (Rostock, 1623). Balthasar Mentzer (praes.), Johannes Vitus (resp.), *De consensu Lutheranorum et Calvinianorum in fundamento christianae religionis, disputatio* (Giessen, 1623). Joh. Falco and Theodorus Thummius, *Synopsis praecipuorum articulorum fidei, nostro seculo maximè controversorum : in qua fundamenta fidei contra Judaeos, Photinianos, Papanos, Calvinianos* . . . *diluuntur* (Tübingen, 1625). Jacobus Durfeldius, *Nova consideratio considerationis Joh. Crocii* . . . *de dissensu Calvinistarum in fundamento fidei* (Rostock, 1625, 1626). Nicolaus Hunnius, *Diaskepsis theologica de fundamentali dissensu doctrinae Evangelicae-Lutheranae, et Calvinianae, seu reformatae* (Wittenberg, 1626). More examples could certainly be found in specialized catalogs of disputations. Cf. also Holtmann, "Die pfälzische Irenik," 216 n. 3. For a general discussion, see Otto Ritschl, *Dogmengeschichte des Protestantismus* (Göttingen, 1927) 4: 231–68.

45. See esp. Draudius, *Bibliotheca classica*, 72, 109–11. Examples include Johann Modest (pseud.), *Beweis aus H. Schrifft, das die Sacramentirer, Zwinglianer und Calvinisten nicht Christen sind, sondern getauffte Jüden und Mahometisten* (Jena, 1591); Aegidius Hunnius, *Calvinus Judiazans* (Wittenberg, 1593; Frankfurt am Main, 1595); Jakob Heilbrunner, *Schvvenckfeldiocalvinismvs* (Lauingen, 1597; Frankfurt am Main, 1598); Albertus Grawerus, *Harmonia praecipuorum Calvinianorum et Photinianorum* (Jena, 1613, 1617); Fridericus Petri, *Calvinianorum Nestorianismus* (Frankfurt am Main, 1613); Johannes Schreiter, *Theses Theologicae de christomachia calvino-ariana* (Leipzig,

1613); Johann Himmel, *Calvino-Papismus* (Jena, 1623); Zachaeus Faber, *Calvinischer und Türckischer Alcoran* (Halle, 1623).

46. Georgius Mylius (praes.), Polycarpus Lyserus (resp.), *De pace ecclesiae evangelicae positiones*... (Wittenberg, 1607); as reported in Holtmann, "Die pfälzische Irenik," 216 n. 2.

47. Cf. Holtmann, "Die pfälzische Irenik," 214–15, 220, 221, 223, 224; Höe von Höenegg, *Kurtzer und deutlicher Discurs.*

48. Pareus, *Irenicum,* 282–349. The pamphlet, *Motiven und ursachen / Warumb man mit den Calvinisten in Religions sachen nicht kan oder soll wieder die Papisten für einen mann stehen,* has not been identified.

49. Johannes Tarnovius, *Quaestionum et quae foedera cum diversae religionis hominibus, et praecipuè à Lutheranis cum Calvinianis salvâ iniri possint,*... (Rostock, 1618; 2nd ed. 1624; repr. 1631, 1646).

50. Leyser, *Erklerung deß Christlichen Catechismi Herrn doctoris Martini Lutheri, in acht Predigten gefasset. Darinnen einfeltig geweiset wird, in welchen Stücken desselben die Caluinisten mit vns streitig sein* (Wittenberg, 1595); repr. as *Calvinismus, das ist: Ein Erklerung des christlichen Catechismi*... (Wittenberg, 1596; Leipzig, 1596): *VD 16,* L1452–52. Pareus responded in *Irenicum,* 137–49.

51. Caspar Finck (praes.), Johann Himmel (resp.), *Disputatio theologica, de natura ecclesiae, Item syncretismo calvino-papistico* (Giessen, 1615).

52. Johann Himmel (praes.), Antonius Mylius (resp.), *Concordia discors Luterano Calviniana* (Jena, 1618); idem, *Calvino-Papismus seu harmonia calvino-papistica theoretico-practica* (Jena, 1622).

53. Coppenstein, *Controversiarum omnium hujus aevi Lutherocalvinisticarum libri tres* (Mainz, 1625–1627); idem, *Genealogia luthero-calvinisticae: I. Theomachiae. II. Ecclesiomachiae. III. Mysteriomachiae. IV. Charitomachiae* (Mainz, 1625). Himmel responded with *Concordia Concors papae-calvinistica opposita concordiae luthero-calvinisticae Johan-Andreae Coppensteinii* (Jena, 1625). Coppenstein answered with a *Spongia concordiae Papae-Calvinisticae: sive Detersio infamiae Papae-Calvinismi inauditi, Romano-Cath. esse Papae-Calvinistas; contra D. Ioannem Himmelium* (Mainz, 1626). Nicolaus Hugo, the court preacher in Colburg, then took up the Lutheran cause with *Luthero-Calvinistae Elenchus, Sive refutatio consensus Lutheranorum et Calvinianorum* (Frankfurt am Main, 1627). To this Coppenstein responded with *Christus defensus contra theomachiae antichristianismos Luthero-calvinianos:*... *adversus Nicolaum Hugonem* (Heidelberg, 1629).

54. Jurgiewicz, *Bellum quinti evangelii: in quo contra Larvatam harmoniam Genevensium, et fucatum consensum Sendomiriensem clarissime ostenditur, nullam esse apud Evangelicos nostri temporis, fidei unitatem vel certitudinem* (Cologne, 1595); trans. as *Krieg deß fünfften Evangelii* (Münster in Westphalia, 1602). [Pitiscius], *Trewhertzige Vermahnung,* 26. Cf. Pareus's response to Jurgiewicz: *Irenicum,* 3v and 191–96.

55. Wilhelm Heinrich Neuser, "Die Erforschung der 'Zweiten Reformation'— eine wissenschaftliche Fehlentwicklung," in Schilling, ed., *Die reformierte Konfessionalisierung,* 379–86; cited sympathetically in Kaufmann, "Konfessionalisierung," 1011.

56. Martin Henckel, "Reichsrecht und 'Zweite Reformation': Theologisch-juristische Probleme der reformierten Konfessionalisierung," in Schilling, ed., *Die reformierte Konfessionalisierung*, 11–43.

57. See here esp. Leube, *Kalvinismus und Luthertum*, 39–50.

58. Useful recent studies include Georg Schmidt, *Der Wetterauer Grafenverein. Organisation und Politik einer Reichskorporation zwischen Reformation und Westfälischem Frieden* (Marburg, 1989); Holger Th. Gräf, *Konfession und internationales System. Die Aussenpolitik Hessen-Kassels im konfessionalen Zeitalter* (Darmstadt and Marburg, 1993); Bodo Nischan, *Prince, People and Confession: The Second Reformation in Brandenberg* (Philadelphia, 1994), ch. 3; and Eike Wolgast, *Reformierte Konfession und Politik im 16. Jahrhundert. Studien zur Geschichte der Kurpfalz im Reformationszeitalter* (Heidelberg, 1998).

59. An important example is the anonymous pamphlet commonly ascribed to Philips van Marnix, the close confidant of William of Orange and one of the leaders of the Dutch Revolt, first published in Latin in 1584 and frequently reprinted in German as *Ein sehr Nothwendige, Trewhertzige vnd wolgemeinte warnung vnd Vermanungs Schrifft. Darinne der Spanier Tyranney, List, Ansschlege, und Practicken wider die Christen entdecket, vnnd bey zeite jhre Gewalt zu brechen sey . . . Ahn alle Chur vnd Fuesten Stende vnnd Staedte des Heiligen Reichs Deutscher Nation . . . Vmb Den gemeinen Nutz, Freyheit vnd Wolfart . . . der gantzen Christenheit zuerhalten. . . .* (n.pl., 1585, 1587, 1599): *VD 16*, M 1039–44. For still earlier French campaigns, see Robert K. Kingdon, *Myths about the St. Bartholomew's Day Massacres 1572–1576* (Cambridge, Mass., 1988), 107–24.

60. *De quaestione illa, an hoc tempore gliscentis vel potius grassantis tyrannidis pontificiae syncretismus & coitio fieri inter ecclesias evangelicas de coena Domini dissidentes adversus communem hostem debeat disputatio* (Heidelberg, 1588): *VD 16*, Q 19. Reprinted with (1) *Confessio cuiusdam I. C. clarissimi, de sacra domini coena* (Zerbst, 1593) and (2) *Hubert Sturm, De aeterna & immutabili Praedestinatione Dei; Electione atque Reprobatione Diatribe* (Editio secunda, Zerbst, 1597): *VD 16*, S 9887.

61. *Trewhertzige Vermahnung der Pfältzischen Kirchen, An alle andere Evangelische Kirchen in Deutschland: Daß sie doch die grosse Gefahr, die jhnen so wol als vns vom Bapsthumb fürstehet, in acht nemmen: . . . . So im Jahr 1585. zu Tübingen in Druck gegeben worden, Durch Lucas Osiander D. . . .* ([n.pl.], 1606). Nischan, following Goldast (1614), gives the publication date as 1585, but the furor after 1606 makes this unlikely. Accompanying Pitiscius's text was a second *Warning about the Jesuit's Bloodthirsty Schemes*, a rare Lutheran contribution to this admonitory literature which had first been published in 1580 by Lukas Osiander sen. of Tübingen as *A Christian and Sincere Admonition to the Evangelical Churches in France and the Netherlands*.

62. Pareus, *Irenicum*, "Ad Lectorem," 3v, 66.

63. E.g. Zepper, *Christlich Bedencken*, 3, 4–5, 42–45, 146; Holtmann, "Die pfälzische Irenik," 231, 232.

64. Cf. Hutter, *Problema theologicum, an syncretismus fidei et religionis inter Lutheranos et Calvinianos ideo iniri vel possit, vel debeat, ut Antichristi tyrannis, conjunctis*

viribus & studijs, facilius et felicius reprimi possit (Wittenberg, 1615); and Pareus, *Notae in problema theologicum:* . . . (Heidelberg, 1616).

65. Contzen, *De Pace Germaniae Libri II* . . . (Mainz, 1616), ch. 5.

66. Nischan, "Bergius," 395, citing treatises from 1624, 1632, and 1640.

67. Cf. Bodo Nischan, "Confessionalism and Absolutism: The Case of Brandenburg," in Andrew Pettegree, Alastair Duke, and Gillian Lewis, eds., *Calvinism in Europe, 1540–1620* (Cambridge, 1994), 181–204; Arthur H. Williamson, "Scotland, Antichrist and the Invention of Great Britain," in John Dwyer, et al., eds., *New Perspectives on the Politics and Culture of Early Modern Scotland* (Edinburgh, 1982).

68. For the following, cf. Holtmann, "Die pfälzische Irenik," 38–44; Gustav Adolf Benrath, "Die Eigenart der pfälzischen Reformation und die Vorgeschichte des Heidelberger Katechismus," *Heidelberger Jahrbücher* 7 (1963): 13–32; Walter Henß, "Zwischen Orthodoxie und Irenik. Zur Eigenart der Reformation in der rheinischen Kurpfalz unter den Kurfürsten Ottheinrich und Friedrich III," *Zeitschrift für die Geschichte des Oberrheins* 132/N. F. 93 (1984): 152–212.

69. Paul Münch, *Zucht und Ordnung. Reformierte Kirchenverfassungen im 16. und 17. Jahrhundert (Nassau-Dillenburg, Kurpfalz, Hessen-Kassel)* (Stuttgart, 1978).

70. If mannerist strivings to preserve harmony redolent of Rudolphine Prague contributed to this irenical tradition, these are the consequence of further layers of philosophical influence reaching Marburg and Herborn through the mediation of the courts, most evident in the alchemical patronage network of Moritz of Hesse-Kassel. See for instance the influences described in Bruce T. Moran, *The Alchemical World of the German Court: Occult Philosophy and Chemical Medicine in the Circle of Moritz of Hessen (1572–1632)* (Stuttgart, 1991); Howard Hotson, *Johann Heinrich Alsted* (Oxford, 2000), ch. 1.iv and 3.i; Heiner Borggrefe, Vera Lüpkes, and Hans Ottomeyer, eds., *Moritz der Gelehrte: ein Renaissancefürst in Europa* (Eruasburg, 1997). For a suggestive point of overlap between philosophical eclecticism and theological irenicism, see Zeller, "Die niederhessische Irenik," 164; citing Mentzer, *Examen oder Prob der Rettung* (1620), 12–13.

71. Leube, *Kalvinismus und Luthertum*, 34–37; Gustav Adolf Benrath, *Reformierte Kirchengeschichtsschreibung an der Universität Heidelberg im 16. und 17. Jahrhundert* (Speyer am Rhein, 1963); Hans-Jürgen Schönstadt, *Antichrist, Weltheilsgeschehen und Gottes Werkzeug. Römische Kirche, Reformation und Luther im Spiegel des Reformationsjubilaeums 1617* (Wiesbaden, 1978).

72. A convenient synopsis of this process is lacking. For recent guidance, cf. Heinz Scheible, ed., *Melanchthon in seinen Schulern* (Wiesbaden, 1997); Carl Andresen, ed., *Handbuch der Dogmen- und Theologiegeschichte* 2nd. ed. (3 vols., Göttingen, 1998–1999), vol. 2; and Karin Maag, ed., *Melanchthon in Europe: His Work and Influence beyond Wittenberg* (Carlisle, 1999).

73. Pareus, *Irenicum*, 281: "An vera unius hominis affectu vel authoritate stare aut perire oportebit Ecclesiam?"

74. Leube, *Kalvinimus und Luthertum*, 34.

75. On this point in general, cf. for instance Schilling, ed., *Die reformierte Konfessionalisierung;* Henry J. Cohn, "The Territorial Princes in Germany's Second Reformation," in Menna Prestwich, ed., *International Calvinism 1541–1715* (Oxford, 1985), 135–65; R. Po-Chia Hsia, *Social Discipline in the Reformation: Central Europe 1550–1750* (London, 1989), ch. 2; Meinrad Schaab, ed., *Territorialstaat und Calvinismus* (Stuttgart, 1993).

76. On this second reformation in Hesse, see Gerhard Menk, "Die 'Zweite Reformation' in Hessen-Kassel," in Schilling, ed., *Die reformierte Konfessionalisierung*, 154–83; and idem, "Absolutistisches Wollen und verfremdete Wirklichleit - der calvinistische Sonderweg Hessen-Kassels," in Schraab, ed., *Territorialstaat und Calvinismus*, 164–238. On the founding of Giessen, see M. Rudersdorf, "Der Weg zur Universitätsgründung in Gießen," in P. Moraw and V. Press, eds., *Academia Gissensis* (Marburg, 1982), 45–82.

77. Zeller, "Die niederhessische Irenik," 148, 164; citing Mentzer, *Examen oder Prob* (1620), IIv and 12–13.

78. Cf. Ritschl, *Dogmengeschichte des Protestantismus*, 4:106–56; Leube, *Kalvinismus und Luthertum*, 107–10; and Hans E. Weber, *Reformation, Orthodoxie und Rationalismus*, (Gütersloh, 1951), 2:98–175.

79. Nischan, "Bergius," 398; J. Fr. Iken, "Bremen und die Synode von Dordrecht," *Bremisches Jahrbuch* 10 (1878): 11–105; Hotson, *Alsted*, 117–19.

80. *Acta synodi nationalis . . . Dordrechti habitae,*(Leiden, 1620), 2:15–23, 83–88, 136–42, 205–11; W. R. Godfrey, "Tensions within International Calvinism: The Debate on the Atonement at the Synod of Dort, 1618–1619" (unpublished Ph.D. dissertation, Stanford University, 1974), 188–91, 221–23.

81. *Acta synodi nationalis*, 1:352–60; Scultetus, *De curriculo vitae* (Emden, 1625), 119–35; Holtmann, "Die pfälzische Irenik," 265–68.

82. Pareus, *Oratio de synodo nationali Dordracena Calendis Februar. Ann. 1619. . . .* (Heidelberg, 1619); *Acta synodi nationalis*, 1:202–31.

83. Philipp Pareus, "Narratio Historica de curriculo vitae . . . Patris D. Davidis Parei," in David Pareus, *Operum theologicorvm exegeticorvm pars prima* (Geneva, 1642), c5r.

84. Johann Donner, *Christliche Betrachtung, etlicher zwischen den Lutherischen und Calvinischen streittigen Religionsfragen; gezogen auß dem zu Dordrecht gehaltenem Synodo* (Frankfurt am Main, 1620); Lucas Osiander, *Scultetus Atheus* (Tübingen, 1620), 13–14; Balthasar Mentzer (praes.), *Trias disputationum theologicarum De Aeterna Filiorum Dei ad vitam aeternam Electione: . . .* (Giessen, [1621]); Thomas Weinreich, *Examen sententiae Synodi Dordrechtanae de absoluto Praedestinationis ac Reprobationis decreto* (Leipzig, 1624); Nicolaus Hunnius, *Diaskepsis theologica . . . Cum praemissa consideratione hypokriseos Calvinianae, Dordrechtana synodo prodita* (Wittenberg, 1626).

85. Cf. Leube, *Kalvinismus und Luthertum*, 250–56 (on Meisner and Hülsemann); Schmidt, "Ecumenical Activity," 79, 87 (on Meisner and Hunnius).

86. Nischan, "Bergius," 398.

87. Cf. Leonhard Hutter, *Calvinista Aulico-Politicus* (Wittenberg, 1609, 1610, 1613, 1615); idem, *Caluinista Aulico-politicus alter* (Wittenberg, 1614); Hermann Fabronius, *Vom Politischen Hoff-Calvinisten Leonhard Hutters* (Eisenstad, 1614, 1615).

88. The best chronicle is J. F. Gerhard Goeters, "Genesis, Formen und Hauptthemen des reformierten Bekentnisses in Deutschland. Eine Übersicht," in Schilling, *Die reformierte Konfessionalisierung*, 44–59.

89. M. Lossen, *Der Kölnische Krieg* (2 vols., Gotha, 1882; Munich and Leipzig, 1897); Georg Schmidt, *Der Wetterauer Graftenverein* (Marburg, 1989), 339–47.

90. Lukas Osiander sen., *Warnung an die Christliche Prediger vnd Zuhörer in der Churfürstlichen Pfaltz* (Tübingen, 1584); Johannes Olearius, *Wider den Calvinischen Grewel der Verwüstung, in des Fürstenthumb Anhalts Kirchen newlich mit gewalt eingesetzet: Trewhertzige Warnung und Bericht* (Magdeburg, 1597); Salomon Gesnerus, *Christliche, trewhertzige Warnung an die löblichen Stände, Stedte, unnd Gemeinen in Schlesien, das sie sich für einreissenden Calvinischen unnd Sacramentirischen Irrthumben . . . hütten und vorsehen wollen* (Wittemberg, 1601, 1602); Johannes Behm, *Gantz trewhertzige Warnung, an alle und jede des Hertzogthumbs Preussen Untersassen, sich für der verdamlichen Zwinglianischen oder Calvinischen Sect zu hütten* (Königsberg, 1614); *Trewhertzige Warnung, An alle Lutherische Christen, In Böhmen, Mähren, Schlesien vnd andern Ländern, Daß sie für Annehmung der irrigen vnd hochschädlichen Calvinischen Religion bestes fleisses sich hüten sollen/Gestellet Durch die Theologische Facultet zu Wittenberg* (Wittenberg, 1620).

91. Christophorus Iordanus, *Trewhertzige Warnung Für Calvinischer Brüderschafft, welche zu diesen Zeiten nechst Bernhardo Textore, in seinen Tillenburgischen Pandectis, die Pfältzer in einer vermeinten Trewhertzigen vermanung, den Lutherischen Kirchen angefordert haben* (Wittemberg, 1608). The work referred to here is Bernhard Textor, *Pandectae sacrarum concionum* (2nd. ed., 2 vols., Herborn, 1606). For further examples from 1563, 1606, and 1614, see Visser, ed., *Controversy and Conciliation*, 153 n. 7, 168 n. 15, 169 n. 23.

92. Lukas Osiander sen., *Warnung vor dem Zwinglischen Irrthumb, wölcher sich je lenger je weiter außbreitet, vnd durch newe Schrifften, vnter anderm schein, in die Kirche Gottes will eingeführet werden. . . . Auffs new vbersehen, vnd nachgetrukt.* (Tübingen, 1575): *VD 16*, O 1271. For the work of 1572 from which it comes, see *VD 16*, 1270.

93. Holtmann, "Die pfälzische Irenik," 221.

94. Scultetus, *De curriculo vitae*, 178–212, here esp. 210. Cf. Holtmann, "Die pfälzische Irenik," 264; Leube, *Kalvinismus und Luthertum*, 64–65.

95. Höe von Höenegg, *Trewhertzige Warnung, für der JubelfestsPredigt . . . von Abraham Sculteto* (Leipzig, 1618); cf. Helga Robinson-Hammerstein, "Sächsische Jubelfreude," in Hans-Christoph Rublack, ed., *Die lutherische Konfessionalisierung in Deutschland* (Gütersloh, 1992), 476.

96. On this remarkable figure, see Hans Knapp, *Matthias Hoe von Hoenegg und sein Eingreifen in die Politik und Publizistik des dreissigjährigen Krieges* (Halle,

1902); Hans-Dieter Hertrampf, "Höe von Höenegg—sächsischer Oberhofprediger 1613–1645," *Herbergen der Christenheit. Jahrbuch für deutschen Kirchengeschichte* [Beiträge zur Kirchengeschichte Deutschlands, vol. 7] (Berlin, 1969), 129–48. For background on the diplomatic situtation, see Axel Gotthard, "'Politice seint wir bäpstisch': Kursachsen und der deutschen Protestantismus im frühen 17 Jahrhundert," *Zeitschrift für Historische Forschung*, 20 (1993): 275–319.

97. *Eine wichtige, und in diesen gefährlichen Zeiten sehr nützliche Frag: Ob, wie, und warumb man lieber mit den Papisten gemeinschafft haben, und gleichsam mehr vertrawen zu ihnen tragen solle, den mit, und zu den Calvinisten. Erörtert durch Herrn Polycarpum Leysern den Eltern. . . . Sampt einer Missio Herrn Matthiae Hoen . . . wegen obgemeldter Frag* (Leipzig, 1620; repr. Erfurt, 1620).

98. [Höe von Höenegg], *Deutliche vnd gründliche Außfühung dreyer jetzo hochnötiger vnd gantz wichtiger Fragen: I. Ob einiger Evangelischer Chur= oder Fürst, Gewissenshalben verbunden gewesen, denen Herren Böhmen beyzustehen? II. Ob einiger recht Evangelischer Chur= oder Furst, mit gutem gewissen, dem Römischen Kayser in jetzigem Krieg, assistentz leisten können vnd sollen? III. Ob ein Christlicher Evangelischer Chur oder Fürst . . . mit gutem Gewissen, Fug, Recht, vnd Nutz, lieber Neutral bleiben, vnd keinem Theil beystehen solle, oder nicht?* ([Leipzig], 1620).

99. *Erwegung deren Theologen meynung, die sich nicht schewen, Evangelische Herrschafften zu bereden, daß sie lieber mit den Papisten, und dem Römischen Antichrist, als mit den Reformirten Evangelischen, die sie aus haß Calvinisch nennen, Gemeinschafft haben sollen. Aus dem . . . 1614. gedruckten Irenico Herrn Doctoris Parei gezogen, und . . . gegen dem Leyserischen widergedruckten Bedencken, aufs newe in Druck verfertigt* (Heidelberg, 1620; repr. Amberg, 1620; repr. Brieg, 1620, cited here). Cf. Pareus, *Irenicum*, 135–49. See also the similar *Gegenbericht, Auff Doctor Polycarpi Leisers Praefation, und Doctor Hoen Anhang : Darinnen sie fürgeben, daß man sicherer mit den Papisten, dann den Reformirten welche sie Calvinisten zunamen, zum wenigsten Politische Freundschafft halten solle . . . / Durch einen friedliebenden Patriotten an tag geben* (Amberg, 1621).

100. Kai Eduard Jordt Jørgensen, *Ökumenische Bestrebungen unter den polnischen Protestanten bis zum Jahre 1645* (Copenhagen, 1942), 252–79; Jaroslav Pelikan, "The Consensus of Sandomierz: A Chapter from the Reformation," *Concordia Theological Monthly* 18 (1947): 825–37; J. Tazbir, "Die Religionsgespräche in Polen," and P. Wrzecionko, "Die Religionsgespräche in Polen unter dem Aspekt ihrer Unionsbestrebungen," in G. Müller, ed., *Die Religionsgespräche der Reformationszeit* (Gütersloh, 1980), 127–44, 145–61.

101. Jarold K. Zeman, "Responses to Calvin and Calvinism among the Czech Brethren (1540–1605)," *American Society for Reformation Research: Occasional Papers* 1 (1977): 41–52; R. J. W. Evans, "Calvinism in East Central Europe," in Menna Prestwich, *International Calvinism 1541–1715* (Oxford, 1985), 167–96, here 171; Christine van Eickels, *Schlesien im böhmischen Ständestaat* (Cologne, 1994), 53–99.

102. This literature is too extensive to survey here, but cf. Pareus, *Irenicum*, 83–88, 120–35; A. Starke, *Fraterna Exhortatio (1607/1614). Eine Denkschrift der*

reformierten Kirchen in Polen zur Einigung der evangelischen Kirchen Europas [*Jahrbuch des Theologischen Seminars der Unierten Evangelischen Kirchen in Polen,* III] (Poznañ, 1937); Jørgensen, *Ökumenische Bestrebungen,* 12–13, 286–88, 330–38; Holtmann, "Die pfälische Irenik," 235–37; Tazbir, "Religionsgespräche," 131–32.

103. [Jean Aymon, ed.], *Tous les synodes nationaux des églises réformées de France* (2 vols., The Hague, 1710), ii. 500–504. On the background situation see A.D. Lublinskaya's *French Absolutism: The Crucial Phase, 1620–1629,* trans. Brian Pearce (Cambridge, 1968), ch. 4.

104. Amyraud, *De secessione ab ecclesia Romana, deque ratione pacis inter Evangelicos in religionis negotio constituendæ disputatio* (Saumur, 1647); German trans. (Kassel, 1649). For Amyraud and his context, cf. Richard Stauffer, *Moïse Amyraut. Un précurseur français de l'œcuménisme* (Paris, 1962); Yves Congar, "Turenne et la réunion des chrétiens," *Revue d'Histoire de l'Eglise de France* 62 (1976): 309–28; François Laplanche, *L'Écriture, le sacré et l'histoire. Erudits et politiques protestants devant la Bible en France au XVIIème siècle* (Amsterdam: APA-Holland Univeristy Press, 1986); R.J.M. van de Schoor, "The Irenical Theology of Théophile Brachet de La Milletière (1588–1665)," *Studies in the History of Christian Thought* 59 (1995).

105. Dury to Sir Thomas Roe, 17 Aug. 1635; as quoted in Batten, *Dury,* 62. Cf. Turnbull, *Hartlib, Dury and Comenius,* 172.

106. Hotton, *De Christiana concordia, sive tolerantia Evangelicorum stabilienda* (Amsterdam, 1649). The work received immediate translations into Dutch, French, and German. On Hotton's origins, see Georg Biundo, *Die evangelischen Geistlichen der Pfalz seit der Reformation* (Neustadt an der Aisch, 1968), no. 2345; *Nieuw nederlandsch biografisch woordenboek,* ed. P.C. Molhuysen and P.J. Blok, 10 vols. (Leiden, 1911–1937), viii. 855–56. On his relations with Dury, see Turnbull, *Hartlib, Dury and Comenius, ad indicem.*

107. Leube, *Kalvinismus und Luthertum,* i. 26–28.

108. Martin Heckel, "Autonomia und Pacis Compositio. Der Augsburger Religionsfriede in der Deutung der Gegenreformation," *Zeitschrift der Savigny-Stiftung für Rechtsgeschichte, Kanonistische Abteilung* 76 (1959): 140–249. Robert Bireley, S.J., "The Origins of the 'Pacis Compositio' (1629): A Text of Paul Laymann, S.J.," *Archivum Historicum Societatis Jesu* 42 (1972): 106–27.

109. Bodo Nischan, "Brandenburg's Reformed *Räte* and the Leipzig Manifesto of 1631," *Journal of Religious History* 10 (1979): 365–80.

110. A valuable introduction to this event and the tradition leading up to it can be found in Bodo Nischan, "Reformed Irenicism and the Leipzig Colloquy of 1631," *Central European History* 9 (1976): 3–26, here esp. 19–25. In the following discussion, material is also added from Knapp, *Hoe von Hoenegg,* 30–41, and Hertrampf, "Höe von Höenegg," 141–45.

111. Höe, *Vnvermeidentliche Rettung* (Leipzig, 1635), 409; as quoted in Hertrampf, "Höe von Höenegg," 143.

112. On the Swedish king's support for Protestant reconciliation, cf. Gunnar Westin, *Negotiations about Church Unity, 1628–1634: John Durie, Gustavus Adolphus, Axel Oxenstierna* (Uppsala, 1932), 42–59, 79–80.

113. Michael Roberts, *Gustavus Adolphus: A History of Sweden 1611–1632* (London, 1953–1958) 2:483–90.

114. Höe, "Oraculum Dodonaeum" (1634), as cited and translated in Nischan, "Leipzig Colloquy," 25–26.

115. Among the most prominent of many treatises were Conrad Berg, *Fundamentum et summa veri christianismi* (Frankfurt an der Oder, 1633); idem, *Epistola de concordia et discordia Protestantium* (Bremen, 1635; German trans. 1635); Johann Bergius, *Vnterscheidt vnd Vergleichung der Evangelischen, in Lehr vnd Ceremonien* (Berlin, 1635, 1644, 1653; Bremen, 1640; Frankfurt an der Oder, 1666; Regensburg, 1723; English trans. London, 1655); Johannes Crocius, *Summarische Nachricht vnd beweißliche Anzeige, daß die Evangelischen reformierter Religion . . . niemahl . . . von Gemeinshafft der augspurgischen Confession außgeschlossen, vnd deß ReligionsFriedens . . . vnfähig . . . erklärt . . . worden* (Grebenstein, 1636; enlarged ed. Hofgeismar, 1645); Georg Pauli, *Augustanus Reformatus* (Bremen, 1637); Johannes Spitowedus, *De pace religionis evangelicos procuranda* (Bremen, 1639); Johannes Crocius, *De Ecclesiae unitate et schismate* (Kassel, 1650).

116. On the Lutheran reaction see Johann Flotwell, *Consideratio praeliminaris scripti D. Johannis Bergii, cui titulus: Unterschied und Vergleichung der Evangelischen ihr Lehr und Ceremonien & c. Qua demonstratur: . . . 2. Calvinianos a Lutheranis in fundamenti fidei maxime dissentire* (Königsberg, 1641); Johann Hülsemann (praes.), Peter Rhebinder (resp.), *Calvinismus irreconciliabilis . . . exercitii scholastici gratia propositus in Academia Wittebergensi 1641* (Wittenberg, 1644); Jacob Weller, *Massonius skeletodes . . . : Aut Anatomiae Christophori Massonii universalis partis . . . refutatio* (Wittenberg, 1636), which includes I.x: *De Calvino-Swenckfeldianismo,* resp. Johannes Olearius; I.xi: *De Calvino Judaizante,* resp. Joachimus Brockwedelius; II.i-ii: *De Extra Nestorio-Calvin* [*sic*], resp. Casparus Remer and Andreas Müllerus; II.iv: *De Nestorianismo Calviniano,* resp. Albertus Günzelius.

117. The most complete survey of Dury's career remains J. Minton Batten's rather hagiographic account, *John Dury: Advocate of Christian Reunion.* See also George Henry Turnbull, *Hartlib, Dury and Comenius: Gleanings from Hartlib's Papers.* For a recent but brief overview see Scott Mandelbrote, "John Dury and the Practice of Irenicism," in Nigel Aston, ed., *Religious Change in Europe 1650–1914: Essays for John McManners* (Oxford, 1997), 41–58.

118. Dury, *Motives to induce the Protestant Princes to mind the worke of peace Ecclesiasticall amongst themselves* (London, 1641); as quoted in Westin, *Negotiations on Church Unity,* 15.

119. Leube, *Kalvinismus und Luthertum,* 245–56.

120. Batten, *Dury,* 65–79.

121. Anthony Milton, "'The Unchanged Peacemaker'? John Dury and the Politics of Irenicism in England, 1628–1643," in Mark Greengrass, Michael Leslie, and Timothy Raylor, eds., *Samuel Hartlib and Universal Reformation: Studies in Intellectual Communication* (Cambridge, 1994), 95–117.

122. Leube, *Kalvinismus und Luthertum*, 41–49, esp. 42.

123. Cf. for instance two articles by M. E. H. N. Mout: "Calvinoturcismus und Chiliasmus im 17. Jahrhundert," in Martin Brecht, Frederich de Boor, and Klaus Deppermann, eds., *Chiliasmus in Deutschland und England im 17. Jahrhundert* [Pietismus & Neuzeit, 14] (Göttingen, 1988), 72–84; and "Chiliastic Prophecy and Revolt in the Habsburg Monarchy during the Seventeenth Century," in Michael Wilks, ed., *Prophecy and Eschatology* (Oxford, 1994), 93–109.

124. Karl Brauer, *Die Unionstätigkeit John Duries unter dem Protektorat Cromwells* (Marburg, 1907), 103–71; Zeller, "Die niederhessische Irenik," 161; Benrath, "Die hessische Kirche," 88.

125. Zeller, "Die niederhessische Irenik," 161–65; Benrath, "Die hessische Kirche," 88–89.

126. Gustav Adolf Benrath, "Die konfessionellen Unionsbestrebungen des Kurfürsten Karl Ludwig von der Pfalz (d. 1680)," *Zeitschrift für die Geschichte des Oberrheins* 116/N. F. 77 (1968): 187–250; Albrecht Ernst, *Die reformierte Kirche der Kurpfalz nach dem Dreissigjährigen Krieg (1649–1685)* (Stuttgart, 1996); Steven Nadler, *Spinoza: A Life* (Cambridge, 1999), 311–14.

127. For an introduction see the excellent overviews of Johannes Wallmann: "Zwischen Reformation und Humanismus: Eigenart und Wirkungen Helmstedter Theologie unter besondere Berücksichtung Georg Calixts," *Zeitschrift für Theologie und Kirche* 74 (1977): 344–70; and "Georg Calixt," *Theologische Realenzyklopädie* 7:552–59. These can be supplemented with Hermann Schüssler, *Georg Calixt. Theologie und Kirchenpolitik* (Wiesbaden, 1961); Peter Engel, *Die eine Wahrheit in der gespaltenen Christenheit. Untersuchung zur Theologie Georg Calixts* (Göttingen, 1976).

128. Cf. Hermann Hofmeister, "Die Universität Helmstedt zur Zeit des 30jährigen Krieges," *Zeitschrift des Historischen Vereins für Niedersachsen* (1907): 241–77, esp. 246–50, 266; Lipenius, *Bibliotheca realis theologica*, 1:191–93.

129. Though the polyglot bibliography on Comenius positively overflows with articles on his irenicism in the vaguest sense of a general striving towards peace, scholarly treatments of the precise chronology and content of his efforts towards ecclesiastical reconciliation are rare. An important exception is Hans-Joachim Müller, "Die irenischen Bemühungen des Johann Amos Comenius in Polen 1642–1645 und die Entstehung der *Consultatio Catholica*," *Comenius-Jahrbuch* 4 (1996): 59–81.

130. On this see Milada Blekastad, *Comenius* (Oslo, 1969), 417, 729.

131. I follow here J. M. Lochman, "Jan Amos Comenius: Bahnbrecher ökumenischer Hoffnung," in P. van Vliet and A. J. Vanderjagt, eds., *Johannes Amos Comenius (1592–1670): Exponent of European Culture?* 47–51; though further documentation is needed.

132. Comenius, *Irenica quædam scripta pro pace ecclesiae* (n.pl. [1658]). The only known copy (in Göttingen SUB) ends abruptly on page 562. See Blekastad, *Comenius*, 590–91, 731. Cf. also Dury's reaction to Grotius's annotations on Cassander in 1642: Turnbull, *Hartlib, Dury and Comenius*, 226.

133. ([Kassel?], 1674). Unique copy in the Herzog August Bibliothek. On the work, see Richard H. Popkin, "The End of the Career of a Great 17th-Century Millenarian: John Dury," in Martin Brecht, Frederick de Boor, and Klaus Deppermann, eds., *Chiliasmus in Deutschland und England im 17. Jahrhundert*, 203–20.

134. See Ute Mennecke-Haustein, "Konversionen," in Wolfgang Reinhard and Heinz Schilling, eds., *Die katholische Konfessionalisierung*, 242–57, here esp. 253–57 on an earlier generation.

135. Jerzy Cygan, O. F. M. Cap., "Zum Übertritt des Kalviner Pastors Bartholomäus Nigrin zur katholischen Kirche (1636–1643). Ein Beitrag zur Geschichte des Ökumenizimus," *Collectanea Franciscana* 39 (1969): 282–303; 40 (1970): 97–152; Müller, "Die irenischen Bemühungen des Comenius 1642–1645," 62–75.

136. On this obscure figure, see Georg Andreas Will, *Nürnbergisches Gelehrten-Lexikon* (Nuremberg and Altdorf, 1755–1758), 3:210–11; Jan Kvačala, ed., *Die pädagogische Reform des Comenius in Deutschland bis zum Ausgange des XVII Jahrhunderts* [Monumenta Germaniae Paedagogica, vols. 26 and 32] (Berlin, 1903–1904), xxvi. no. 49; Blekastad, *Comenius*, esp. 591.

137. On the latter stages of Hübner's career, cf. Kurt Tautz, *Die Bibliothekare der Churfürstlichen Bibliothek zu Cölln an der Spree* (Leipzig, 1925; repr. Wiesbaden, 1968), 4–16; and Peter Bahl, *Der Hof des Großen Kurfürsten* (Cologne, Weimar, and Vienna, 2001), esp. 506. On his last patron see Manfred Finke, "Toleranz und 'Discrete' Frömmigkeit nach 1650: Pfalzgraf Christian August von Sulzbach und Ernst von Hessen-Rheinfels," in Dieter Breuer, ed., *Frömmigkeit in der frühen Neuzeit* (Amsterdam, 1984), 193–212.

138. Heribert Raab, "Attempts at Church Reform," in Wolfgang Muller, ed., *The Church in the Age of Absolutism and Enlightenment* [History of the Church 6] (London, 1981), 509–28, here 510 n. 4. This chapter also provides one of the best available introductions to this concluding topic.

139. The fullest account is Heribert Raab, *Landgraf Ernst von Hessen-Rheinfels (1623–1693)* (St. Goar, 1964). See also below, notes 144, 151.

140. On this plan, see A. Ph. Brück, "Der Mainzer 'Unionsplan' aus dem Jahre 1660," *Jahrbuch für das Bistum Mainz* 8 (1958–1960): 148–62. On the circle, Andreas Ludwig Veit, "Konvertiten und kirchliche Reunionsbestrebungen am Mainzer Hof unter Erzbischof Johann Philipp von Schönborn (1647–1673)," *Der Katholik. Zeitschrift für katholische Wissenschaft und kirchliches Leben* 97 (1917): 170–96. On the figure at its center, F. Jürgensmeier, "Johann Philipp von Schönborn," in *Fränkische Lebensbilder* (Würzburg, 1975), 6:161–84; and G. Mentz, *Johann Philipp von Schönborn, Kurfürst von Mainz, Bischof von Würzburg und Worms 1605–1673* (2 vols., Jena, 1896–1899).

141. Among innumerable discussions of Leibniz's contribution, two of the more important are F. X. Kiefl, *Leibniz und die religiöse Wiedervereinigung Deutschlands* (Regensburg, 1925); and Paul Eisenkopf, *Leibniz und die Einigung der Christenheit. Überlegungen zur Reunion der evangelischen und katholischen Kirche* (Munich, 1975).

142. Philipp Hiltebrandt, *Die kirchlichen Reunionsverhandlungen in der 2. Hälfte des 17. Jahrhundert. Ernst August von Hannover und die katholische Kirche* [Bibliothek des Preußischen Historischen Instituts in Rom, vol. 14] (Rome, 1922).

143. H. Weidemann, *Gerhard Wolter Molanus, Abt zu Loccum. Eine Biographie* [Studien zur Kirchengeschichte Niedersachsens 5] (2 vols., Göttingen, 1929); S. J. T. Miller, "Molanus, Lutheran Irenicist (1633–1722)," *Church History* 22 (1953): 197–218; H. W. Krumwiede, "Molans Wirken für die Wiedervereinigung der Kirche," *Jahrbuch für niedersächische Kirchengeschichte* 61 (1963): 72–114.

144. Important recent studies include Karin Masser, *Christóbal de Gentil de Rojas y Spinola O.F.M. und der lutherische Abt Gerardus Wolterius Molanus* (Münster, 2002); S. J. T. Miller and J. P. Spielman, *Cristobal Rojas y Spinola, Cameralist and Irenicist 1626–1695* [Transactions of the American Philosophical Society, new series, vol. 52/5] (Philadelphia, 1962); and Heribert Raab, "'De Negotio Hannoveriano Religionis'. Die Reunionsbemühungen des Bischofs Christoph de Royas y Spinola im Urteil des Landgrafen Ernst von Hessen-Rheinfels," in R. Bäumer, ed., *Volk Gottes. Festschrift für Josef Höfer* (Freiburg, 1967), 395–417.

145. Hans Friedrich Werling, *Die weltanschaulichen Grundlagen der Reunionsbemühungen von Leibniz im Briefwechsel mit Bossuet und Pellison* (Frankfurt am Main, 1977).

146. Regina Catsch, "Die Bedeutung von Leibniz, Molanus und Jablonski bei den kirchlichen Unionsbestrebungen im 17. und 18. Jahrhundert," in Gerhard Besier and Christof Gestrich, eds., *450 Jahre evangelische Theologie in Berlin* (Göttingen, 1989), 105–23.

147. Raab, "Attempts at Church Reform," 509, 510. Another valuable overview rejecting "eine monokausalen Deutung" of noble conversions in this period in favor of a "Komplex von Disposition und Motivation" is Günter Christ, "Fürst, Dynastie, Territorium und Konfession. Beobachtungen zu Fürstenkonversionen des ausgehenden 17. und beginnenden 18. Jahrhunderts," *Saeculum* 24 (1973): 367–87.

148. Ironically, the French threat that helped stimulate this phase of eccumenical discussion in Germany also ultimately undermined it. If fear of the growing power of France was one of the overarching motivations for pursuing ecclesiastical reunion in Germany at the highest levels, the brutal exercise of French power in the revocation of the Edict of Nantes, the annexation of Alsace, and the destruction of the Palatinate revived Protestant fears of popish tyranny across northern Europe and ended the most active and fertile phase of the postwar ecumenical discussions. Cf. on this point Raab, "Attempts at Church Reform," 514, 516–17; Miller and Spielman, *Cristobal Rojas y Spinola*, 79; Benrath, "Konfessionelle Irenik," 165.

149. See for instance the leads offered in Koecher, *Abbildung einer Friedenstheologie*, 236–41, and Lipenius, *Bibliotheca realis theologica*, 393–94.

150. Here Dury's enormous correspondence and incessant wanderings can be seen as a bridge between the thunderous published polemics of the period before Leipzig and the discrete discussions of the period after Westphalia. For other precursors, see Posthumus Meyjes, "Protestant Irenicism," 88–93.

151. Heribert Raab, "Der 'Discrete Catholische' des Landgrafen Ernst von Hessen-Rheinfels (1623–1693). Ein Beitrag zur Geschichte der Reunionsbemühungen und der Toleranzbestrebungen im 17. Jahrhundert," *Archiv für mittelrheinische Kirchengeschichte* 12 (1960): 175–98; and idem, "'Sincere et ingenue etsi cum Discretione.' Landgraf Ernst von Hessen-Rheinfels (1623–1693) über eine Reform von Papsttum, Römischer Kurie und Reichskirche," in R. Bäumer, ed., *Reformatio Ecclesiae. . . . Festgabe für Erwin Iserloh* (Paderborn, 1980).

152. Eisenkopf, *Leibniz und die Einigung der Christenheit*, 111–90, here esp. 171.

153. Cygan, "Übertritt des Nigrin," 109 ff, 124–25; Nischan, "Bergius," 401–3; Blekastad, *Comenius*, 399; Müller, "Die irenischen Bemühungen des Comenius," 62–63, 76–77; Inge Mager, "Brüderlichkeit und Einheit. Georg Calixt und das Thorner Religionsgespräch 1645," in Bernhart Jähnig and Peter Letkemann, eds., *Thorn. Königin der Weichsel 1231–1981* (Göttingen, 1981), 209–38; Jørgensen, *Ökumenische Bestrebungen*, 377–87.

154. See Louthan's essay in this collection. Jørgensen's assessment is similar: cf. for instance *Ökumenische Bestrebungen*, 9, 14, 388.

CONTRIBUTORS

Irena Backus is Professor at the Institut d'histoire de la Réformation, University of Geneva. Her main areas of research are the reception of the church fathers in the late Middle Ages and in the Reformation era, the history of biblical exegesis, and the role of philosophy in sixteenth-century theology. She is the author of many major monographs, including *The Reformed Roots of the English New Testament* (1980), *The Disputations of Baden (1526) and Berne (1528): Neutralizing the Early Church* (1993), *The Reception of the Church Fathers in the West: From the Carolingians to the Maurists* (ed.) (1997), *Reformation Readings of the Apocalypse: Geneva, Zurich, Wittenberg* (2000), and *Historical Method and Confessional Identity in the Era of the Reformation (1378–1615)* (2003).

Euan Cameron is the author of *The Reformation of the Heretics: The Waldenses of the Alps 1480–1580* (1984), *The European Reformation* (1991), and of *Waldenses: Rejections of Holy Church in Medieval Europe* (2000). He both edited and contributed to *Early Modern Europe: An Oxford History* (1999), and has contributed articles and papers to *The Oxford Dictionary of the Christian Church, The Oxford Companion to Christian Thought, Theologische Realenzyklopaedie,* and *Religion in Geschichte und Gegenwart 4,* as well as scholarly journals and conferences.

Nicholas Constas teaches courses in Patristics and Byzantine theology at Harvard Divinity School. Among his areas of interest are Christology, scriptural exegesis, and the theological study of icons and iconography. He is the author of *Proclus of Constantinople and the Cult of the Virgin in Late Antiquity* (2003), as well as a detailed study of the fifteenth-century Byzantine theologian St. Mark of Ephesus for the multivolume work *La théologie Byzantine* (2002). He is currently preparing a translation of four hundred scholia on Proverbs and Ecclesiastes by Evagrius Ponticus. His next major research project will combine his interests in theological aesthetics, allegory, and the patristic philosophy of language.

Zdeněk V. David is a Senior Scholar at the Woodrow Wilson International Center for Scholars, Washington, D.C., where he previously served as librarian. Educated as a historian (Ph.D. Harvard 1960) he taught Russian and East European history at the University of Michigan (Ann Arbor) and Princeton. He has published numerous articles on the history of Utraquism and on Jews in Czech historiography, and he is coauthor of *The Peoples of the Eastern Habsburg Lands, 1526–1918* (1984).

Karlfried Froehlich is B. B. Warfield Professor of Ecclesiastical History, emeritus, at Princeton Theological Seminary. His major interest is the history of biblical interpretation, especially in the early and medieval church. With Margaret Gibson, he edited a facsimile of the 1490 *Glossa ordinaria*, the standard Bible commentary of the Middle Ages. He was an official member of the Lutheran–Roman Catholic national dialogue team in the United States for twenty years and of the Lutheran-Reformed Conversations, which led to the declaration of full communion between the participating churches for their duration. For the past three years he has been organizing of the archival materials left by the late Oscar Cullmann, one of the leading Protestant ecumenists of the twentieth century.

Howard Hotson is Professor of Early Modern History and director of the Centre for Early Modern Studies at the University of Aberdeen. His main area of research interest is the intellectual history of Reformed central Europe in the sixteenth and seventeenth centuries and its relationship with broader European developments. He is currently completing a monograph for the Oxford-Warburg Studies entitled *Between Ramus and Comenius: Commonplace Learning in Reformed Central Europe, c. 1570–1630*.

Howard Louthan is an associate professor of history at the University of Florida. A cultural historian of early modern central Europe, he is the author of *The Quest for Compromise* (1997). With his wife, Andrea Sterk, he has translated one of the great classics of Czech literature and spirituality, John Comenius's *The Labyrinth of the World* (1998). He is currently finishing a study on the Catholic Reformation in the Bohemian kingdom.

Karin Maag obtained her Ph.D. from the University of St. Andrews in Scotland in 1994. She is currently the director of the H. Henry Meeter Center for Calvin Studies at Calvin College and Calvin Theological Seminary in Grand Rapids, Michigan. She is also associate professor of history at Calvin College.

Graeme Murdock is Senior Lecturer in modern history at the University of Birmingham. His published work includes *Calvinism on the Frontier: International Calvinism and the Reformed Church of Hungary and Transylvania, c. 1600–1660* (2000), *Confessional Identity in East-Central Europe,* (ed., with Maria Craciun and Ovidiu Ghitta) (2002), and *Beyond Calvin: The Intellectual, Political and Cultural World of Europe's Reformed Churches, c. 1540–1620* (2004).

Erika Rummel, professor of history emerita (Wilfrid Laurier University), is the author of several books on Erasmus. Among her recent publications are *The Humanist Scholastic Debate in the Renaissance and Reformation* (1995, repr. 1997), *The Confessionalization of Humanism in Reformation Germany* (2000), and *The Case Against Johann Reuchlin* (2002). She is presently adjunct professor at the University of Toronto and directing the edition of the correspondence of Wolfgang Capito.

Randall Zachman is associate professor of Reformation Studies at the University of Notre Dame. He is primarily interested in the history of Protestant theology, with an emphasis on the Reformation. He is the author of *The Assurance of Faith: Conscience in the Theology of Martin Luther and John Calvin* (1993), and is currently at work on a study of the theology of John Calvin entitled *The Living Icons of God: Manifestation and Proclamation in the Theology of John Calvin.*

INDEX